Green Home Improvement

65 projects that will:
- *Cut Utility Bills*
- *Protect Your Health*
- *Help the Environment*

Daniel D. Chiras, PhD

RSMeans

Green Home Improvement

65 projects that will:
- *Cut Utility Bills*
- *Protect Your Health*
- *Help the Environment*

Daniel D. Chiras, PhD

RSMeans

Copyright © 2008
Reed Construction Data, Inc.
Construction Publishers & Consultants
63 Smiths Lane
Kingston, MA 02364-3008
781-422-5000
www.rsmeans.com
RS**Means** is a product line of Reed Construction Data.

Managing Editor: Mary Greene. Editor: Andrea Sillah. Editorial Assistant: Jessica deMartin. Production Manager: Michael Kokernak. Production Coordinator: Jill Goodman. Composition: Paula Reale-Camelio. Proofreaders: Jill Goodman/Mary Lou Geary. Book and cover design: Norman R. Forgit. Contributing Photographer: Kimberly Potvin. Illustrations: Anil Rao. Cover Photography: Main photograph courtesy of Armstrong World Industries, Inc., top inset courtesy of Monte Carlo Fan Company, middle inset courtesy of TimberTech, bottom inset courtesy of Gardener's Supply, back cover left photograph by Norman R. Forgit, back cover right photograph courtesy of Neil Kelly Cabinet Co., taken by Photo Design, Portland, OR.

Printed in the United States of America

10 9 8 7 6 5 4 3 2 1

Library of Congress Cataloging in Publication Data

ISBN 978-0-87629-093-4

Table of Contents

Acknowledgments ix

About the Author xi

About the Reviewers xiii

Introduction xv

Part One: Green Home Improvement Projects 1

Green Flooring, Walls, Countertops & Cabinets

1. Cork Flooring..3
2. Bamboo Flooring 7
3. Reclaimed Wood Flooring.....................................11
4. All-Natural Linoleum Flooring 14
5. Laminate Flooring...17
6. Recycled-Content Tile 20
7. Recycled-Content Carpet 24
8. All-Natural Wool Carpet 27
9. Healthy Paints, Stains & Finishes........................30
10. Green Cabinetry 36

Heating & Cooling Your Home Efficiently

11. Home Energy Audit 40
12. Caulking & Weather Stripping 46
13. Insulating Your Home 53

14. Insulate While You Paint...60

15. Programmable Thermostat...63

16. Insulated Shades & Curtains 66

17. Solar Hot-Air Collector 71

18. Energy-Efficient Furnace 76

19. Energy-Efficient Boiler 81

20. Heat Pump & Solar Hot Water 85

21. Wood Stove..89

22. Pellet Stove 94

23. Fireplace Insert 98

24. Radiant Barrier 101

25. High-Efficiency Cooling Systems 106

26. Ceiling & Solar Attic Fans.. 112

27. Whole-House Fan..119

28. Radon Test & Mitigation...122

29. Energy-Recovery Ventilator 127

Conserving Water

30. Flushing Your Water Heater 131

31. Water Heater Blanket & Pipe Insulation...................................135

32. Adjusting Water Heater Temperature 139

33. Water Heater Anode Rod Replacement 142

34. Tankless Water Heater 146

35. Solar Hot-Water System 151

36. Faucet Aerators 156

37. Water-Efficient Showerheads 159

38. Water-Efficient Toilets..162

Cutting Electrical Usage

39. Eliminating Phantom Loads 167

40. Energy-Efficient Lighting..171

41. Energy-Efficient Appliances & Electronics 176

42. Solar Electricity 180

43. Purchasing Green Power..185

44. Timers & Motion Sensor Light Switches 189

Green Roofs, Siding, Doors & Windows

45. Tubular Skylights 194

46. Environmentally Friendly Roofing....................................198

47. Fiber-Cement Siding...202

48. Repairing Broken Windows 206

49. Storm Windows 209

50. Energy-Efficient Windows 213

51. Storm Doors 218

52. Door Sweeps 221

53. Gutters & Downspouts..223

54. Grading & Drainage 227

Green Paving, Landscaping & Pools

55. Green Patios, Walkways & Driveways..............................232

56. Composite Decks & Porches..236

57. Recycled Plastic/Composite Fencing...............................240

58. Outdoor Solar Lighting 244

59. Composting 248

60. Infiltration Basins for Trees & Shrubs 253

61. Rainwater Collection Barrels 256

62. Energy-Efficient Landscaping..261

63. Drip Irrigation System...266

64. Rain & Soil Moisture Sensors 271

65. Solar Pool Heater & Cover 275

Part Two: Building a New Green Home..279

Part Three: Appendix..285

Safety Tips...287

Glossary 289

Resource Guide 294

Index..299

Acknowledgments

I'd like to thank all those who helped me on this book. First and foremost, I'd like to express my deepest appreciation to the folks at RSMeans, who proposed this book to me, for their excellent assistance.

My editor, Mary Greene, worked closely with me at all stages, from the development of the table of contents to the final manuscript. She provided numerous, invaluable suggestions that made this book a much better and more useful resource for the reader. Mary also edited the manuscript on a very tight schedule.

I'd like to thank RSMeans' Andrea Sillah, editorial supervisor, who copyedited the book, and cheerfully coordinated this project, from manuscript through production.

Appreciation also goes to editorial assistant, Jessica deMartin, who helped secure photos, took a few of them herself, prepared a few of the illustrations, and helped coordinate the project. Many thanks to RSMeans' Norman Forgit for his excellent design and assistance with the art and photos and Paula Reale-Camelio, production supervisor, for her patient and creative composition on a tight schedule.

Kimberly Potvin, my photo researcher, did a remarkable job of rounding up photographs and was always a pleasure to work with. I'd like to thank Anil Rao as well, for his superb art, and author Charlie Wing for contributing fantastic drawings from his book, *How Your House Works*.

I'd like to gratefully acknowledge the contributions of Michael Berry and Clayton Schuller, Co-Chairs of the Sustainable Building Committee for the Builders Association of Greater Boston, for their review of the manuscript and helpful input.

Many thanks go to my family—Linda, Forrest, and Skyler—for their love and support throughout this project.

About the Author

Dan Chiras, PhD, is a nationally known green building expert. He consults with homeowners, architects, builders, and developers on sustainable home design, including energy-efficient passive solar strategies. He has been involved in the design of numerous homes in Maryland, New York, Wisconsin, Nebraska, Colorado, Utah, Wyoming, Montana, Washington, California, Oregon, and British Columbia, Canada.

Dan has published 23 books and hundreds of articles on sustainable design and related topics. He has presented lectures and workshops to university audiences, the general public, and many organizations including the U.S. Green Building Council; the American Institute of Architects; and Architects, Designers, and Planners for Social Responsibility. He teaches courses on green building, renewable energy, and environmental science at Colorado College and has presented workshops to K. Hovnanian Homes, the sixth largest homebuilder in the United States, SALA Architects, and others through the Colorado Renewable Energy Society and American Solar Energy Society.

Dan is currently being filmed for the Discovery Channel for an environment-focused series executive-produced by actor Leonardo DiCaprio. The series, called "Greensburg," will help launch Discovery Channel's Planet Green Network. It follows the rebuilding of the town of Greensburg, Kansas, after devastation by a tornado. The town will be rebuilt as a "sustainable model of eco-living" with built-in protections against future tornadoes.

Dan designed and lives in his own green home. He has carried out many of the book's projects himself, enabling him to offer valuable tips and specific resources for the do-it-yourselfer. His home has been featured on NBC Nightly News and in the magazines *Solar Today* and *Home Power*.

Dan is committed to sharing his knowledge of practical, economically viable solutions for sustainable living, and helping to bring green building into the mainstream.

About the Reviewers

Michael Berry is the co-chair of the Sustainable Building Committee (SBC) for the Builders Association of Greater Boston, coordinating training and networking events that introduce sustainable building practices to the greater Boston building community.

As an associate for ICF International, Michael facilitates the Massachusetts New Homes with the ENERGY STAR Program for the Joint Management Committee (JMC). He trains, educates, and also recruits new ENERGY STAR partners, including developers and builders, into the program.

Michael has worked in the energy conservation field for nine years, holding a Massachusetts construction supervisor's license and managing programs for the DOE, the DHCD in Boston, HUD, and several utility programs. He is currently earning his Certificate in Sustainability Management at the Harvard Extension School.

Michael resides in West Dennis, Massachusetts, is an avid surfer, and enjoys remodeling his antique home in his spare time.

Clayton Schuller is the founder and current co-chair of the Sustainable Building Committee of the Builders Association of Greater Boston (BAGB). He is on BAGB's Board of Directors and received the organization's 2008 President's Award for his efforts within the building community. Clayton is also a member of the Green Building Committee for the Associated Builders and Contractors (ABC) and is the chairman of their Green Strategic Alliance Sub-Committee.

As the business development manager at F.D. Sterritt Lumber in Watertown, Massachusetts, Clayton led the company to be the first FSC-certified retail lumberyard in Massachusetts—now one of the largest stocking dealers of certified lumber on the East Coast. He is a co-author of a new series of residential green building guidelines for the state of Massachusetts, serves as an expert panelist at green building conferences, and regularly gives presentations on this topic to construction groups.

Introduction

Green Home Improvement describes 65 projects that will help you "green" your home—and your life. These projects will help make your home healthier, safer, and more resource-efficient. They can also save you potentially huge amounts on your fuel bills and could even add to your home's sales appeal—and boost the selling price—when you're ready to put it on the market

This book describes how much skill and work it will take to carry out each of these improvements, and also what you'll gain by doing them. Although some of the projects in this book are best performed by professionals, many others can be carried out by homeowners with a little time and basic tools.

How the Book Is Organized

The bulk of the book consists of 65 green home improvement projects.

The green improvement projects in Part One are grouped by category, starting with healthy, environmentally friendly flooring, walls, countertops, cabinetry, and paint, then moving on to numerous projects that will save energy and water and make your home healthier in other ways.

These projects are followed by green roofing and siding, windows and doors, and a variety of outdoor and landscape projects—including lighting, paving, pools, fences and decks, and much more.

Each project begins with an environmental, comfort and health, savings, and level-of-difficulty rating—on a scale of 1 to 3 (shown in leaf icons in a box at the start of each project). These ratings indicate how each project ranks with respect to the benefits you'll receive, as well as the skill it takes.

The project discussions include:

- Rationale—ways in which the project may be worthwhile for you, your family, and the Earth.
- Materials and technologies—how a green product or material is made, advantages it offers, options you'll want to consider, and places to purchase it.
- Pros and cons of materials and techniques—taking into account costs, health, comfort, and environmental impacts.
- Installation—where pertinent, a step-by-step description of what is involved in carrying out the project—how difficult the work is, and whether it should be performed by a professional.
- Shopping tips and what to watch out for—advice to help you when purchasing or installing green products—or hiring someone to do the job for you.
- What Will It Cost? and What Will You Save?—an overview of project costs and resulting savings. This section includes considerations that affect the price, potential savings (for example, how much you could save on utility bills and replacement costs), and also national average cost estimates for projects that are typically done by professionals.

- Go Green! tips—quick, easy things you can do right away without special tools or skills—to save money, create a healthier, more comfortable home, and help the environment.

Part Two offers guidelines on building a new green home—from selecting and protecting the site for your home, to green design and materials, to construction methods.

The last part of the book contains some basic safety tips and helpful resources, including books, magazines, websites, and green building materials retailers to help you locate products that may not be available at local home improvement centers, lumberyards, or hardware stores. This section also includes a glossary of green building terms, from aerators to whole-house fans.

Why Is Green Home Improvement Important?

Although many people think that green building and green home improvement primarily benefit the environment, there's really much more to them. Green builders are fond of saying that their efforts are designed to create shelter that is good for people, good for the planet, and good for the economy.

Green home building and remodeling are good for people because they result in healthier and more comfortable homes. They are also good for us because they produce less pollution, protecting the air we breathe and the water we drink. As a result, green improvements help reduce the chance of contracting diseases caused by pollution, such as lung cancer and asthma.

Green home improvement can result in a much less resource-intensive lifestyle. Easing our demand for critical resources ensures future generations a chance to meet their needs and live a good life, too. Green home improvement is also good for workers in factories that produce building products, as well as those who install them, because it relies on materials that are made without toxic chemicals.

Green building is good for the economy, too. On a personal level, green improvements can help

homeowners and renters lower their gas and electric bills, saving substantial amounts of money, often immediately. Energy conservation and renewable energy measures provide a hedge against inflation caused by rising fuel prices. Some improvements, like water-efficient showerheads and toilets, help us reduce our water and sewer bills as well. All these economic benefits help make our lives more affordable. As energy and water costs rise, green home improvements also increase the value and appeal of our homes.

Green home projects provide community-wide benefits. They create jobs and new business opportunities for builders and subcontractors, and investment opportunities that help promote a strong and healthy economy, which helps all of us.

While the importance of protecting our health and controlling living expenses cannot be overstated, a primary reason for green home improvements is, of course, that they are good for the environment. By promoting the efficient use of natural resources and the use of renewable resources, these measures help prevent the destruction of the habitats of wildlife. Green home improvement also contributes to a higher level of environmental stewardship, helping create a healthier world, not just for people, but for the millions of species that share this planet with us.

Environmental protection efforts help preserve the most essential resources we depend on—the air we breathe and the water we drink. Truly, then, green home improvement is the ultimate form of self-protection. It helps to ensure a good life—now and into the future.

Return on Your Green Home Improvement Investment

Defining "Value"

While most remodeling projects are motivated by the desire to create more comfortable, functional, and pleasant spaces to live in, economic considerations also come into play. The dollar value of a green home improvement project can be measured in several ways.

One is to compare the money you spend on a project to the amount it could add to the sale price of your residence. Another is to determine how an improvement could attract buyers and speed up the sale of a home, if and when you put it on the market. For instance, durable siding or additional insulation could add significantly to your home's market value—and attract more buyers. Be sure to list all green features when marketing your home. They are becoming extremely important to home buyers. You may even want to find a realtor who specializes in green homes. They are increasing in number and prominence.

Another way to assess the dollar value of a green home improvement project is to determine how much money the project will save you on your utility bills while you are living in your home. For instance, replacing water-wasting toilets or showerheads with efficient fixtures and replacing old appliances with energy-efficient models can save substantial amounts of money. Some improvements, for example, installing an energy-efficient heating and air conditioning system, may also qualify you for rebates from your utility company or state or federal government—resulting in yet another way to save money.

Some green improvements, such as sealing leaks around windows and doors, not only save money, but make us more comfortable. Although comfort may not be quantifiable in dollars and cents, it is definitely a benefit that must be considered when calculating the value of a project.

Some green home improvements also make our homes healthier, for example, by reducing or eliminating toxic chemicals and mold buildup. Creating healthier living spaces reduces doctor's visits, trips to the emergency room to treat breathing disorders such as asthma, and the need for medication—and associated expenses. Although you may not be able to project actual savings in health care costs, they are definitely worth considering—along with a priceless, better quality of life!

Another factor to consider is replacement costs. Some green building materials, such as recycled-content roofing products and fiber-cement siding, are more durable and fire- and weather-resistant than conventional materials. Durability results in longer service, lower maintenance costs, and less frequent replacement compared to conventional building materials. You save money and time as a result. Some of these products may even qualify you for lower home insurance rates.

Do It Yourself, or Hire a Contractor?

Each of the projects in this book includes a ranking, not only of the potential savings, health, comfort, and environmental benefits, but also how challenging the work is for a do-it-yourselfer. One leaf indicates a job that can be accomplished by a novice who has the tools and equipment for small repairs and projects, but limited knowledge of remodeling. Two leaves indicate a project that can be performed by homeowners with moderate building skills and experience and a more extensive collection of tools. Projects with three leaves require extensive remodeling experience and tools.

While many of the projects are simple and straightforward, others require accurate layout and precise measuring, cutting, and assembly. Complex preparations and work involving structural elements of your home, such as framing, should be handled by qualified professionals. When in doubt, call a reputable contractor.

Electrical, plumbing, structural, and foundation work must comply with local building codes and may require a permit and submission of plans approved or certified by a licensed engineer or architect. These jobs are best performed by licensed professionals. In fact, your building department may require it.

You'll very likely find that most of the projects that require professionals are being performed by contractors or subcontractors (heating and air conditioning, tiling, etc.) in your area. You won't have to look hard, for example, to find a professional to install a green product such as wool carpeting or fiber-cement siding as these materials are installed in generally the same way as conventional materials. If you plan to purchase the materials directly from a retailer (versus the installer), ask them for guidance on finding a qualified installer. Home improvement centers contract directly with installers for many items and can line up installation for you.

For large or very specialized projects, such as a solar electric or geothermal installation, start by consulting remodelers who specialize in green building. They may know qualified installers in your area. Manufacturers often list distributors and installers on their websites. For projects you decide to take on, be sure to follow all instructions for tools, materials, appliances, and fixtures that come with products you purchase. Don't eliminate steps to save time.

Recycling

Many materials, including old appliances, electronics, doors, windows, and lumber can be recycled or reused. Check local recycling or reuse facilities. For non-recyclable items, check the trash pickup or dump rules and schedule. Find out in advance what materials are accepted, and when, and any special instructions for potentially hazardous materials, such as paint.

Plan Ahead

Plan carefully to reduce the number of trips to the local hardware store, home improvement center, or lumberyard. This saves time and gas. Be sure to store materials property. Some products may require airing or acclimation to your home's temperature and humidity before installation. Others may need to stay dry to prevent mold.

In summary, green home improvement creates a win-win-win situation. It's good for people, it's good for the economy at large and your own personal finances, and it's good for the environment. Your efforts, even modest ones, when combined with others, can have a huge impact. Let's say we get started . . .

Part

1 Green Home Improvement Projects

Green Flooring, Walls, Countertops
& Cabinets 3

Heating & Cooling Your Home Efficiently 40

Conserving Water 131

Cutting Electrical Usage.. 167

Green Roofs, Siding, Doors & Windows 194

Green Paving, Landscaping & Pools 232

Project 1

Cork Flooring

Cork flooring is an environmentally friendly product that's also comfortable to stand on and similar in price to hardwood flooring.

Invented by an American, John Smith, in 1891, cork flooring has since been used in homes, schools, hospitals, and libraries. It can be found in such prominent buildings as the Library of Congress, the Mayo Clinic, Frank Lloyd Wright's "Fallingwater" home, and the offices of several Fortune 500 companies. Aveda is installing it in their new environmentally friendly salons, too.

Cork is harvested from the bark of live cork oak trees in the Mediterranean and is used to make hundreds of products—from stoppers for wine bottles, to gaskets for engines, to fishing rod handles, in addition to flooring.

While removing bark would prove lethal to most trees, the cork oak tree regenerates its bark over and over, provided workers leave a thin layer of inner bark intact each time they harvest the outer layer. Bark can first be harvested when a tree is 20 years old, and, because it regenerates, bark can be harvested again in 9 to 14 years. Cork oak trees can live for 150 years.

Not only is cork a rapidly renewable resource, but it's also recyclable. Most of the cork used to make flooring is made from the waste from manufacturing other products, primarily wine bottle stoppers. For these reasons, cork is one of the greenest flooring options you can find.

Cork flooring is beautiful, comfortable, and durable.
Courtesy of WE Cork, Inc.

Harvested cork

Cork oak trees after the cork has been stripped

Courtesy of Amorim Flooring, Inc.

What Are Your Choices?

Cork flooring comes in planks and tiles. Planks typically consist of four layers. The top layer is an acrylic coating that is applied in multiple coats to increase the life of the product. Beneath this is a thick layer of cork veneer. Next is a layer made of an exterior-grade fiberboard. On the bottom is another layer of cork for additional cushion.

No formaldehyde is used in the production of cork flooring, but some types (those that don't click in place) require glue. Ask the supplier or installer for the healthiest glue that's compatible with the product you are using.

Cork tiles are typically square (6", 9", 12", 18", and 24"), although some manufacturers, such as Globus Cork, offer rectangular ones in a variety of widths (6", 9", 12", and 18") and lengths (ranging from 9" to 36"). The company also custom-manufactures odd-shaped tiles.

Go Green!

If you're not ready to invest in a resilient cork floor, try softening up your existing hard flooring with washable cotton or natural wool area rugs.

Layers in cork floor plank
Courtesy of Amorim Flooring, Inc.

Benefits of Cork

☑ Cork flooring is soft and resilient—with the warmth and appeal of a natural material and comfort for those who stand and walk on it, especially barefoot. "Cork is firm, but not bouncy," according to the folks at Green Building Supply. Furthermore, if you drop a coffee mug or plate, there is a good chance it won't break when it strikes a cork floor, as it would if it fell onto a tile or hardwood floor. Cork flooring will dent if struck by a hard object, or if something heavy is placed on it, but in a couple of hours the dent should vanish as the cork bounces back. This makes cork a great option for kitchens and play rooms.

☑ Cork dampens sound, which means it is also ideally suited for second-story rooms and hallways.

☑ Cork is durable and can last for many years with proper care. It is typically coated with multiple layers of acrylic and cured with ultraviolet light. The joints between cork tiles or boards are sealed to increase durability. Cork floors typically come with a 15-year warranty and can be refinished with a new acrylic surface to look like new when they age.

☑ Cork is hypo-allergenic and naturally resistant to fire, insects, and moisture. High-quality cork flooring is often mounted on high-density fiberboard that resists moisture penetration from below—for example, from a concrete floor.

Installation

Like laminate flooring, cork is relatively easy to install. That's because many of these products consist of glue-less interlocking tiles. They can be installed by do-it-yourselfers so long as the floor plan is not too complex or broken up by columns and other features that require lots of trimming of planks or tiles. Manufacturers and retailers typically offer detailed instructions on their websites, and these should be followed carefully. If, after studying the instructions, you question whether you're up to the task, hire a professional.

If the installation requires some trimming, be sure you have the proper tools. For best results, use a table saw. (Circular saws can be used, but it is often difficult to cut straight lines with them.)

When installing a cork floor, bear in mind that baseboard molding will need to be installed along the perimeter to cover the gap between the flooring and the wall.

Tiles and planks may need time to adjust to the temperature and humidity of your home prior to installation to reduce expansion or contraction after installation. WE Cork, for instance, recommends that installers of their glue-down tiles and planks allow the tiles to acclimate in the room in which they are going to be installed for at least three days prior to installation. Be sure to remove the flooring from the box and remove plastic wrap, if any.

Check to make sure your material actually requires acclimation. Some, like the Avant-Garde Collection of floating floors from WE Cork, do not. The manufacturer says that this product should be installed directly out of the box.

Cork floors can generally be installed in homes with in-floor heating—either radiant or electric—but check the manufacturer's specifications to be certain. When installing cork floor in such instances, the manufacturer may suggest running the in-floor heat for five to six days prior to installation, regardless of the season. Be sure that the adhesive you use is compatible with both cork and radiant heat. If possible, use a low- or no-VOC adhesive.

Cork flooring can be installed directly on any level concrete floor or level wood subflooring. It can also be installed over most finished flooring, except carpeting and some types of ceramic tile. Cork flooring can be used in bathrooms, but glue-down (rather than floating, click-in-place) is recommended for these areas. Be sure to caulk carefully around the tub, shower, and toilet to prevent moisture from seeping under the flooring. You may also want to apply an additional coat of urethane (or wax if you've installed a wax-finished cork product) to seal the seams between tiles or planks.

If you're using cork flooring in a new kitchen, it's best to install floating (click-in-place, glue-less) flooring after the cabinets are in place. Glue-down tiles and planks can be installed before or after the cabinets. In basements, floating (non-glued-down) floor products are recommended.

Cork will fade in direct sunlight, so you may want to avoid installation in such areas. Cork flooring also tends to yellow with age and may expand and contract a bit (leading to buckling and gaps) with changes in relative humidity and heat. If you do the installation, be sure to leave a small gap between the tiles and the wall to accommodate expansion.

Shopping Tips

When shopping for cork flooring, look for moisture-resistant products. Not all cork products are designed to prevent moisture from entering from below. Compare warranties. Green home building materials outlets can also advise you. (They tend to carry the products that perform the best.)

Maintenance Tips

As mentioned before, indentations in cork flooring, such as those caused by heavy furniture, should

disappear once the pressure is removed, because cork flooring slowly springs back. Furniture coasters can help prevent dents.

Cork, like any flooring product, requires periodic cleaning. Wet mopping is not recommended and may cause the seams to swell. Instead, wipe down the flooring with a damp cloth. Wax-finished cork floors are cleaned and maintained entirely differently from cork flooring that is coated with varnish or polyurethane. Be sure to follow the specific manufacturer's maintenance recommendations, often posted on their websites.

Consumer Reports notes that while cork is soft and quiet, it can be stained by spilled liquids if they are not wiped up promptly. In its rating of green floor products, *Consumer Reports* also notes that cork is susceptible to scratching and fading.

What Will It Cost?

Cost Estimate: Installation of cork flooring for a 12' x 16' room

Cost for materials only: $1,350

Contractor's total, including materials, labor, and markup: $1,900

Flooring options, cost per square foot installed:

Cork: $10

Oak strip: $9

Pre-finished oak strip: $11

Laminate: $9

Recycled-content tile (from basic-tile-only installation to higher quality tile including new wood underlayment): $10 to $33

Conventional ceramic tile: $13

Linoleum: $7

Costs are national averages and do not include sales tax.

Project 2 Bamboo Flooring

Project Rating:

Savings
🍁 🍁 🍁

Environmental Benefit
🍁 🍁 🍁

Health/Comfort
🍁 🍁 🍁

Level of Difficulty
🍁 🍁 🍁

Bamboo flooring, somewhat of a curiosity just a few years ago, has gained in popularity and is now often installed in place of conventional wood flooring. Although bamboo is substituted for wood, it is not wood. It is a member of the grass family. Bamboo used for flooring comes from an extremely fast-growing species harvested in Southeast Asia, principally China and Vietnam.

The plant consists of hollow, round stalks, called culms, which are cut into strips, boiled, and dried. The strips are then glued together to produce laminated strip flooring. The adhesive that holds the strips together is either urea-formaldehyde resin, which releases small amounts of either formaldehyde or isocyanate (a glue that, once dry, produces no toxic pollutants). In some cases, bamboo flooring is treated with a preservative, including the relatively nontoxic boric acid.

Material Options

Bamboo flooring comes in two basic varieties: solid and engineered. The solid type consists of tongue-and-groove planks, with the bamboo strip oriented either vertically or horizontally. (See photos on next page.) The horizontal product is harder and provides a more traditional, wood-floor type of look.

Solid bamboo flooring can also be made from stalks that are crushed rather than sliced. This process produces long strands, glued together lengthwise to form strand tongue-and-groove strip flooring. Denser and harder than other bamboo flooring products,

stranded bamboo flooring has a totally different appearance, as you can see in the photos on the next page.

Engineered flooring, the second option, consists of a top layer of horizontally or vertically oriented strips. They are glued to a backing to form veneered tiles or planks.

Bamboo forest
Courtesy of BAMBOOADVANTAGE

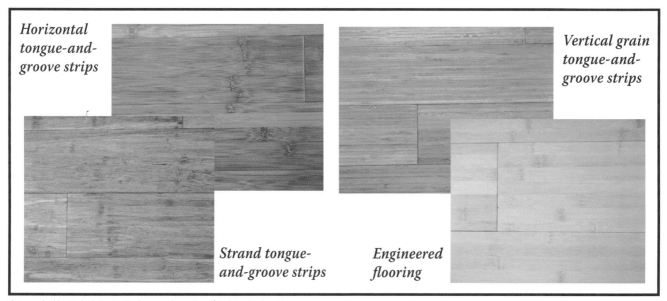

Horizontal tongue-and-groove strips

Vertical grain tongue-and-groove strips

Strand tongue-and-groove strips

Engineered flooring

Photographed by Kimberly Potvin. Bamboo panels courtesy of Ambient Bamboo Floors

Engineered bamboo is available in two forms: (1) tongue-and-groove planks, which are nailed or glued in place, and (2) glue-less click-in-place planks.

Bamboo is available in both light and dark shades. The light-colored product is its natural hue, while the darker color flooring is produced by a heating process. The darker flooring is attractive, but the heating required to produce it softens the fibers, making the flooring slightly less dense and durable.

Hardness Ratings

Bamboo flooring companies rate the hardness of their products in newtons. Strand bamboo is the hardest (approximately 1,360 newtons), reportedly twice as hard as red oak. The next hardest is the natural color bamboo. For example, the Teragren Company's natural bamboo is rated at 1,850 newtons. The softest is the dark bamboo. (Teragren's is rated at 1,470 newtons.)

Bamboo Pros & Possible Drawbacks

Bamboo is a great product, but like any other building material, it's not perfect. Here's a quick recap of the pros and cons:

Pros

- ☑ Bamboo is fairly durable, dimensionally stable, and ideal for low-traffic areas.

- ☑ Bamboo is a rapidly renewable resource.

- ☑ Bamboo is harvested with little, if any, damage to the environment—after as few as three years—with no need to replant, since new shoots emerge from the root system. In contrast, harvesting trees for wood flooring means cutting them down and replanting (or waiting for them to grow naturally from seeds that fall to the earth). For some tree species, it may be more than 100 years before the new growth is harvestable.

- ☑ Bamboo production employs an estimated 6 million people in Asia, and has spawned a lucrative industry in other countries, including the United States and in Europe.

Possible Drawbacks

- ☑ Bamboo may dent and scratch and does not hold up perfectly in high-traffic areas, such as entryways and kitchens.

☑ Bamboo is shipped thousands of miles from Southeast Asia, which requires a lot of energy. (Some proponents point out that because bamboo is transported in large quantities by ship, the amount of energy used to bring this product to market is fairly low.)

☑ Some critics contend that growing bamboo requires a lot of fertilizer and pesticide use. While pesticides and fertilizers are used to grow bamboo, they're used primarily for cultivation of edible bamboo, not the plants used to make bamboo flooring.

☑ Some argue that bamboo production endangers pandas and wildlife and destroys forests. Almost any school child can tell you that pandas dine exclusively on bamboo, but pandas feed on an entirely different species. While some forests are cleared to provide land for bamboo, this is not a common practice. Moreover, experts say that trees removed to grow bamboo tend to be pine, fir, or eucalyptus that are grown in plantations, not biologically rich old-growth forests. Replacing forests with bamboo does, however, reduce biological diversity because bamboo plantations support fewer species of wildlife. Some species of bamboo can also invade native forests if not carefully managed.

☑ Bamboo flooring releases formaldehyde after installation. Many bamboo flooring products are made with urea-formaldehyde glues. However, formaldehyde is released from the finished product at a slower rate than from many other building materials, such as oriented strand board subflooring. You can purchase no-formaldehyde bamboo flooring, glued with isocyanate. While safe for the consumer, isocyanate glues purportedly expose workers in factories to some toxicity.

Shopping Tips

Bamboo flooring is widely available in home improvement centers, such as Lowe's and Home Depot, and large retail flooring outlets. It can also be purchased from green home building suppliers and through Internet suppliers. (See the Resource Guide at the back of the book.)

Unfortunately, the products vary considerably in quality, so shop carefully. Do your research. Key factors to inquire about include the product's hardness rating, formaldehyde content, finish, and warranty. Check out the company's reputation and manufacturing process, as well as their treatment of workers, if possible. You may also want to contact local installers to advise you on products that perform well in your area.

Bamboo contains less natural formaldehyde than wood. However, you may still want to minimize your exposure to this substance. The strand products emit less formaldehyde than either vertical- or horizontal-grain bamboo. (See "Installation" for more on reducing your exposure to formaldehyde.)

Some inexpensive bamboo flooring is finished with multiple coats of polyurethane that may not hold up well over time. According to Green Building Supply in Fairfield, Iowa, "It's difficult to tell which finish is the best just by looking at it. The best manufacturers use a five-coat 'German Klump' finish of aluminum oxide with a super-tough, scratch-resistant ceramic topcoat." Some manufacturers are so confident in their new finish system that they warranty their products for life against delamination, and for 25 years against surface wear (residential).

Go Green!

To improve indoor air quality, use environmentally friendly cleaning products—for flooring and all the other surfaces in your home. You can make your own cleaners from natural ingredients or find natural products in grocery stores and many discount stores and home centers.

Ask about warranties, too, and how claims for defects or failure are handled. "The main problem I see with bamboo is scratches," says green building expert David Adamson from EcoBuild in Boulder, Colorado (**www.eco-build.com**). Bamboo flooring finished with the more dent-resistant aluminum oxide shows scratches fairly easily, he notes.

"The second problem I've encountered," Adamson adds, "is shrinkage—gapping—especially at the butt end or end match in solid planks that are not sufficiently acclimatized in dry climates." In the West, Adamson recommends allowing one to three weeks for planks to adjust to the humidity level in the space where they'll be installed. Engineered products don't need this period, but can still crack later as a result of shrinkage. These products can't shrink at the joints because of the powerful glue used to bond them, so cracks form internally within the material.

Although this discussion may dissuade some from buying bamboo, Adamson points out that wood flooring products do this, too. "Cracking is natural, and I think consumers have an unrealistic expectation that wood and bamboo floors will never gap or crack or scratch."

Instead of buying pre-finished bamboo flooring, Adamson suggests purchasing unfinished bamboo flooring, then finishing it after it's installed. He recommends plant-based finish products, such as AFM Natural Hard Wax Finish. Applying this product can be a little tricky. It may require thinning and may take longer to dry than water-based polyurethane finishes. Few professionals are familiar with this technique, but Adamson believes that it is a superior method.

Installation

Installing a bamboo floor requires a considerable amount of knowledge and skill and is a job best left to the experts. If you want to take the project on, check the manufacturer's website for instructions and follow them carefully. You can find instructions, along with cleaning and maintenance guidelines, at **www.bamboo-flooring.com**

You may want to attend a workshop on installing hardwood flooring, which is similar to bamboo in many respects, at your local home improvement center. Good advice can also be found in many home improvement books.

To reduce exposure to formaldehyde (if formaldehyde resins were used in the product), open the packages and store the planks or tiles loosely in a garage or other outdoor, covered area, for a couple of weeks prior to installation. Be sure that air can circulate around all of the planks. This allows the bamboo to release gases outside your living space. If flooring with formaldehyde is installed during warm weather, leave the windows open during installation. Following these procedures will help reduce formaldehyde exposures initially, when outgassing is greatest.

What Will It Cost?

Cost Estimate: Installation of bamboo flooring for a 12' x 16' room

Cost for materials only: $1,560

Contractor's total, including materials, labor, and markup: $2,300

Flooring options, cost per square foot installed:

Bamboo: $12

Oak strip: $9

Laminate: $8

Cork tiles: $10

Stone tile: $22 to $180

Recycled-content tile: $33

Conventional carpeting: $12 to $60 per square yard

Costs are national averages and do not include sales tax.

Project 3

Reclaimed Wood Flooring

If you're remodeling or building a new addition, consider installing reclaimed wood flooring and giving a second life to salvaged wood. If you're thinking you'll be settling for a lower-quality product, you should know that salvaged, old-growth wood is often tighter-grained, harder, and more dimensionally stable than new-growth wood. Floors made from reclaimed timbers are therefore more durable and stable than those made from newly harvested trees. Reclaimed wood is also generally very attractive, and you may be able to find wood from species such as chestnut that are no longer commercially harvested.

Salvaged wood also puts to good use waste that might otherwise end up in a landfill. It reduces wood harvesting in a world of rapidly increasing demand, which helps save energy, reduce pollution, and preserve wildlife habitat.

Where Can You Find Salvaged Wood?

Reclaimed lumber is available in many varieties of both hardwood and softwood—from fir and hemlock to maple, oak, black walnut, and others.

Salvaged lumber is widely available in many parts of the country. You can search online or locally, or order it through green building material suppliers. (Supplier websites often include product photographs, and some companies will send samples for free or at a nominal fee.) To reduce shipping costs and energy used for

transportation, look for a supplier in your area. Reclaimed wood can be found at local salvage yards and often in the classified section of newspapers. In addition, local demolition companies may sell wood from their projects, although wood from a demolition site might be less practical for a do-it-yourselfer, as it may require a fair amount of refurbishing and preparation before it can be installed.

Some cities have public salvage yards that sell new and used building materials, including lumber left over from construction and remodeling projects. Habitat for Humanity's Building Supply Outlets (**www.habitat.org**), for example, found in many major metropolitan areas, stock donated materials, both new (leftover) and recovered from building demolition.

Go Green!

Save usable lumber from home construction projects for future use or donate it to Habitat for Humanity or a community recycling program.

Flooring made from reclaimed wood can add to the beauty and marketability of your home.

Courtesy of Aged Woods, Inc.

Salvaged Wood Options

Extremely attractive plank reclaimed wood flooring, including tongue-and-groove, comes in widths ranging from 3″ to 24″, although 4″ to 10″ widths are the most common. Reclaimed wood is also used to create an assortment of other useful building materials, such as siding, timbers for posts and beams, molding, paneling, wainscoting, and roof shakes.

Salvaged wood comes from numerous, sometimes unusual sources, including old barns, mills, bridges, and trees removed from urban and suburban neighborhoods, for example, after storms. The Aged Woods company in York, Pennsylvania, recovers wood from 75- to 200-year-old barns slated for demolition. The Armster Reclaimed Wood Company in Madison, Connecticut, salvages wood from water and wine storage tanks, bridge timbers, and old mills. This

company and several others also harvest logs from the bottoms of lakes and rivers, where they sank and remained for decades, preserved by the cool, low-oxygen environment. These "sinker logs" are dried and re-cut into a variety of products, including flooring.

Go Green!

To keep hardwood floors looking their best without using chemical cleaners, some people recommend a mixture of equal parts water and white vinegar, applying with a barely damp cloth and rubbing gently to remove dirt. Never use excess water, which can damage the floor. Check with your flooring supplier for the best advice on cleaning your floor's finish.

Installation

Installing reclaimed wood flooring is basically the same as installing new wood flooring and is a job best handled by professional installers or skilled do-it-yourselfers. Wood planks and tongue-and-groove strips are typically fastened directly to plywood or oriented strand board subfloors.

Shopping Tips

Although there are many sources of reclaimed lumber, supplies are limited, and availability and cost fluctuate. Plan ahead to secure the flooring you need well in advance. While you're at it, check out the supplier's practices. Some companies, like Aged Woods, kiln-dry reclaimed wood to kill insects and reduce shrinkage and warping after installation.

It is a good idea to view the product in person, too, so you know what you're getting. You don't want to buy a load of wood only to find that it contains a lot of useless lumber—planks that are too narrow, too thin, too splintery, or poor quality. Watch out for bargains. You may pay more going with one company, but get a higher-quality product with a lot less waste. Be sure the company's wood is properly kiln-dried, precisely milled, and trimmed to remove unusable materials.

As you shop for reclaimed wood flooring, you will find a variety of finishes. The "distressed" finish provides an antique look and hides minor scratching. Some products are unsanded; others are sanded, but not stained. Still others are stained and finished. Some salvaged lumber may contain nails that will need to be removed. Be sure to check for nails before sawing (to protect your saw blades and yourself).

What Will It Cost?

Reclaimed wood, processed and ready for installation, generally costs more than new wood flooring, often two to four times as much. But remember, you're very likely getting a higher-quality wood product and species that may not even be available anywhere else today—and you're helping recycle a beautiful, natural material that would otherwise take up space in a landfill.

Cost Estimate: Installation of salvaged hardwood flooring for a 12' x 16' room

Cost for materials only: **$2,400**

Contractor's total, including materials, labor, and markup: **$3,050**

Flooring options, cost per square foot installed:

Salvaged hardwood: **$16**

Oak strip: **$9**

Pre-finished oak strip: **$11**

Floating laminate: **$9**

Cork tiles: **$10**

Conventional carpeting: **$12** to **$60** per square yard

Costs are national averages and do not include sales tax.

Reclaimed Wood and Building Codes

Building codes may restrict the use of reclaimed wood as framing members, but there are no restrictions against its use for flooring or other nonstructural applications.

Project 4

All-Natural Linoleum Flooring

Project Rating:

Savings
🍁 🍁 🍁

Environmental Benefit
🍁 🍁 🍁

Health/Comfort
🍁 🍁 🍁

Level of Difficulty
🍁 🍁 🍁

All-natural linoleum is one of the newest trends in home building and remodeling and one of the greenest products on the market. If you're building a new home or addition, or replacing a kitchen or bathroom floor, take a careful look at this product.

Made from virtually all natural ingredients, linoleum is comfortable, colorful, and durable. Although modern vinyl flooring is often referred to as "linoleum," these two products are as different as night and day. (See "Benefits of Linoleum" on the next page.) True linoleum is manufactured from wood and cork "flour," finely ground from waste products. (Wood flour is acquired from lumber mills, and cork flour is obtained from factories that manufacture products such as wine bottle corks and cork gaskets for engines.) In contrast, vinyl flooring is made from chemicals extracted from petroleum.

Linoleum also contains pine resin (extracted from the sap of pine trees) and linseed oil (from flax seed commercially grown in the United States and Canada, among other countries). Other linoleum ingredients include:

- Powdered limestone, which serves as filler
- Pigments for color
- Very small amounts of zinc-based drying agents

These components are mixed, then pressed onto a backing mat made from jute, a plant grown primarily in India and Pakistan. An acrylic sealant is added as a protective topcoat.

Linoleum is currently manufactured in Europe and imported to the United States. It comes in an amazing array of colors, often in mottled patterns. The leading manufacturer, Forbo, produces a product known as Marmoleum. All-natural linoleum is also available from flooring giant Armstrong, which recently purchased a European linoleum manufacturer and is now marketing its own line of natural linoleum flooring products (Marmorette).

Linoleum is often installed in sheets, the edges of which can be heat-welded to hide the seams. Marmoleum also comes in planks and square tiles, known as Marmoleum Click. This product consists of a top layer of Marmoleum mounted on high-density fiberboard and cork under-layers. Like floating floor products, Marmoleum Click simply snaps in place, so it's possible for handy do-it-yourselfers to install. Because no glue is required, you can walk on it immediately after installation.

Linoleum is widely available through conventional flooring outlets and green building retailers, many of which are listed in the Resource Guide of this book. Check manufacturers' websites for dealers in your area.

Marmoleum flooring (here with inlaid pattern) is durable and made from natural and recycled material.
Courtesy of Forbo Flooring B.V.

Benefits of Linoleum

☑ Softer and warmer than ceramic tile floors.

☑ Made from natural *and* renewable materials.

☑ Biodegradable, unlike vinyl. Linoleum could be ground up and composted or burned to generate energy in a waste-to-energy plant. (When incinerated, vinyl flooring products produce toxic dioxin.)

☑ Fire-resistant—won't melt or burn except at very high temperatures.

☑ Resists stains from grease, oils, and solvents.

☑ Resists cracking, scratching, and abrasion, and gets harder over time. It can be expected to last 30 to 40 years, compared to 10 to 20 years for vinyl—an important consideration when weighing its higher initial cost. Durability also results in less extraction and use of natural resources, less energy for manufacturing, and less landfill waste over the long term since the floor won't need replacing as often as vinyl.

☑ Requires less maintenance than vinyl floors. It's cleaned with a damp mop and a neutral detergent, and there's usually no need to apply wax, which is sometimes required to protect vinyl-coated flooring products.

☑ Maintains a "new" look, hiding nicks, scratches, and dents because pigments run throughout the thickness of the material. (Vinyl flooring, on the other hand, has a synthetic wear layer that contains the color and pattern. When it wears away, the floor needs replacing.)

☑ Repairs easily if damaged—by buffing the affected area and resealing.

☑ Safer for workers who produce it in the factory than vinyl flooring. (Vinyl production exposes workers and residents of nearby communities to cancer-causing vinyl chloride.)

Possible Drawbacks

Although linoleum offers many advantages, it does have its downsides. For one, all linoleum is currently produced in Europe, and transportation to the United States consumes energy. But because less energy is used to manufacture natural linoleum than vinyl flooring, this helps offset the energy required for transportation.

Linoleum, like vinyl flooring, releases some noxious odors during and after installation. This "outgassing" can last for several weeks or even months. Although both products release about the same amount of potentially toxic chemicals, there are qualitative differences. Vinyl products outgas plasticizers that act like the female hormone estrogen in the body and are therefore a risk for young girls. Linoleum gives off odors from linseed oil, including fatty acids and aldehydes. Some chemically sensitive people may react to these chemicals, which are otherwise not harmful.

When installing this product, it is a good idea to provide ample ventilation or, for new home construction, to schedule installation of linoleum floors well before moving in.

Installation

Linoleum is thicker and stiffer than vinyl and therefore more difficult to install. Installing sheet linoleum is best done by experts. Even then, be sure to hire installers who have received factory training. Linoleum is typically glued to a concrete or wood subfloor, which must be clean and flat. Voids must be filled in with a leveling compound. As noted earlier, Marmoleum can also be purchased in tiles that click together like pieces of a puzzle, which require no adhesive, a project that handy homeowners can tackle.

Linoleum should be acclimated to the space where it will be installed for at least one week before installation. For flooring that requires adhesive, select a low- or no-VOC type recommended by the flooring manufacturer. This is a healthier option than conventional adhesives. Remember that adhesives used for installing vinyl products won't work for linoleum.

Linoleum should not be installed on moist basement floors. If there is moisture in your basement, be sure that installers moisture-test the subfloor beforehand, preferably after a hard rain. If the moisture level in the concrete is too high, installers may be able to use a commercially available underlayment/sealant, known as Sealflex, to reduce moisture penetration. Forbo manufactures a product known as Moisture Limitor for use with its flooring products. Limitor is a high-strength, latex-based compound that's applied to floors. This low-VOC product does not contain any known hazardous materials.

Maintenance

Linoleum should be cleaned with a damp (not wet) mop, using a mild detergent. Check with the supplier for a list of acceptable cleaning agents. If wet-mopped, manufacturers may recommend periodic application of an acrylic sealer. Armstrong, for example, recommends stripping old acrylic and then re-polishing their linoleum flooring twice a year.

Shopping Tips

When shopping for linoleum, keep in mind that it sometimes has a yellow cast on the surface. This is known as a "drying room film" and will dissipate when the floor is exposed to natural or artificial light. When selecting a product, the folks at Armstrong suggest that you expose linoleum samples to the light in the area where you plan to install it for several hours before making your final design and color choice.

What Will It Cost?

Linoleum can cost more to install than a conventional flooring product made of vinyl, but you get a healthier, much longer-lasting product. (I installed natural linoleum in my bathrooms in 1995, and it still looks brand new.) Expect to pay two to three times more for linoleum than for the most basic vinyl-coated tile, although linoleum costs about the same as high-quality sheet vinyl flooring.

Cost Estimate: Installation of all-natural linoleum flooring for a 12' x 16' room

Cost for materials only: $925

Contractor's total, including materials, labor, and markup: $1,350

Flooring options, cost per square foot installed:

Linoleum: $7

Pre-finished oak strip: $11

Laminate: $8

Ceramic tile: $13

Cork tiles: $10

Costs are national averages and do not include sales tax.

Project 5

Laminate Flooring

Project Rating:

Savings
🍁 🍁 🍁

Environmental Benefit
🍁 🍁 🍁

Health/Comfort
🍁 🍁 🍁

Level of Difficulty
🍁 🍁 🍁

If you want a beautiful, green, and relatively easy to install floor, consider laminate flooring. You don't want just any laminate flooring, though, but an environmentally friendly product made from sustainably grown, harvested, and manufactured wood.

Laminate flooring, also known as *floating floor*, includes such well-known brands as Pergo. It's a relatively new product, introduced in the United States in the early 1990s as an easy-to-install alternative to hardwood flooring. (Green laminate flooring is more recent.)

Unlike conventional wood flooring, which consists of solid lumber, laminate comes in long planks or square tiles composed of three or more layers. On top is a pre-finished thin wood veneer "wear" layer coated with a durable finish material, usually water-based polyurethane. The middle layer consists of engineered wood, such as high-density fiberboard. The bottom layer is a moisture-resistant material, such as foam, rubber, cork, or plastic. When installed, the planks or tiles rest directly on the substrate—either wood subflooring (plywood or particleboard) or concrete (provided the floors are fairly dry). The flooring pieces snap together, which makes it relatively easy for homeowners to install, although some laminate

flooring products are secured with glue.

Regular laminate flooring is a fairly green product in that it uses much less wood than conventional hardwood flooring products. This, in turn, reduces timber harvesting, which protects

Laminate flooring made from certified wood and recycled materials is a great way to green your home.
Courtesy of EcoTimber

forests and wildlife habitats and saves energy. Green laminate flooring is even better. First, it's manufactured from natural, environmentally friendly materials. The top layer is wood veneer made from certified lumber—from trees that have been sustainably grown, harvested, and milled. Certification is provided by independent nonprofit organizations, such as the Forest Stewardship Council (FSC), which certifies lumber companies throughout the world and has the most rigorous standards.

The middle layer is typically high-density fiberboard made from recycled wood fiber—putting a waste product to good use and reducing timber cutting. The bottom layer consists of low- or no-VOC materials (that don't emit harmful chemicals), which, of course, is healthier.

EcoTimber produces a more durable environmentally friendly flooring material, which they refer to as engineered flooring. It consists of a surface layer of high-quality hardwood (not a thin veneer) that's bonded to two wood sub-layers. Cross-ply construction makes the product more stable than solid wood, according to the manufacturer. EcoTimber offers both engineered and solid FSC-certified flooring.

Installation

Laminate flooring is much easier to install than hardwood, and therefore a good project for do-it-yourselfers. Unlike hardwood, laminate does not require sanding, staining, and finishing, which can take a week or more, between the tasks and the drying times. As soon as a laminate floor is laid down, it's safe to walk on it—that is, if you've installed a glue-less variety. (You have to wait until the glue dries when installing glue-down types.)

Manufacturers usually provide detailed installation instructions that should be followed to the letter. Unfortunately, some people gloss over the instructions and end up with an inferior floor. Laminate flooring materials should be acclimated to the temperature and humidity of the space where they'll be installed prior to installation. To do this, you just remove the product from the packaging, and let it sit in the room

for 48 to 72 hours. Failure to do so may cause the floors to buckle. (This is the number one mistake of homeowners and even professional contractors!)

Be sure to leave a gap (usually about 5/16 to 1/2 inch, but follow the instructions) between the flooring and walls—or any other abutting surface. This prevents buckling by allowing for expansion and contraction that occurs naturally in response to changes in temperature and humidity.

The smallest plank should never be less than 8 inches long or 2 inches wide. To avoid this, measure and lay out the flooring before you begin. You may have to cut the first boards to avoid this situation. Joints should be staggered, not lined up. Check the manufacturer's suggestions for offsetting joints.

Be sure to level any low spots in the subfloor before you install laminate flooring. Use a self-leveling compound and let it dry before you install the flooring. (A 72-hour minimum drying time is usually recommended, but check the manufacturer's recommendations.) Check wood subflooring for soft spots or squeaks and correct them before you install the laminate. You may need to screw the subflooring into the underlying floor joists to create a solid surface. Laminate flooring won't correct the problem.

Green laminate flooring samples
Courtesy of EcoTimber

When installing baseboard molding after the floor is in place, don't nail into the laminate, as this could interfere with its expansion and contraction. Follow manufacturer's instructions on doorways, too. It's important not to hammer on the groove end of the board—ever! And, always start the installation of the laminate flooring with the groove side and end toward the walls. A tapping block is used to tighten joints. Don't pound very hard or you may damage the flooring.

Also, bear in mind that even though laminate flooring can be installed over concrete floors, if the floor is moist, you may be heading for trouble. When in doubt, contact a foundation/basement contractor to test the moisture level of the concrete floor. Laminate flooring installation may be ill-advised in damp basements or may require an additional underlayment layer, such as polyethylene, to prevent moisture from seeping into and ruining the flooring. When installing a plastic layer, be sure to tape the seams. You may also need to correct moisture problems on the outside of your house, for example, installing downspout extenders, regrading soil that slopes toward the house (Project 54), or other measures.

If your floor plan is complicated and will require a lot of cutting, you may want to hire a professional installer.

Shopping Tips

Homeowners can find conventional laminate flooring products at flooring retailers and home improvement centers, but the green versions will be more difficult to locate. The best approach is to check the manufacturer's website for a dealer locator. You can also check out the many green building outlets listed in the Resource Guide of this book.

Look for products made without formaldehyde. If the dealer can't tell you for sure, contact the manufacturer and ask for a copy of their Material Safety Data Sheet. It will tell you everything that's in their products. Polyurethane binders such as MDI or PMDI are less harmful than formaldehyde-containing resins.

If you purchase a glue-down product, consider using environmentally friendly adhesives. (Ask for low-VOC glues.) You can purchase these through green building

materials outlets. Check with the manufacturer to be sure they are compatible with the flooring product.

When shopping for laminate products, be sure to compare warranties, which typically range from 5 to 30 years. Check out EcoTimber (**www.ecotimber.com**). As mentioned earlier in this project, they offer an unusually thick wear layer—one of the thickest in the industry, and Brazilian cherry, hickory, maple, and walnut. The thicker layer creates a more durable, longer-lasting product that can be sanded and refinished, ensuring a much longer life.

What Will It Cost?

Because laminate floors are relatively easy to install, you may be able to cut costs by purchasing the materials for about $5 to $7 per square foot and doing the work yourself.

Cost Estimate: Installation of laminate flooring for a 12′ x 16′ room

Cost for materials only: **$1,230**

Contractor's total, including materials, labor, and markup: **$1,700**

Flooring options, cost per square foot installed:

Laminate: **$9**

Oak strip: **$9**

Pre-finished oak strip: **$10**

Cork tiles: **$10**

Conventional carpeting: **$12** to **$60** per square yard

Natural wool carpeting: **$45** to **$150** per square yard

Costs are national averages and do not include sales tax.

Project 6

Recycled-Content Tile

If you're remodeling a kitchen or bath, or simply replacing worn-out or outdated flooring, consider an environmentally friendly recycled-content tile. Made from a number of clean, nontoxic waste materials, recycled-content tile is a healthy flooring option.

Like other tile products, recycled-content tile is highly durable and will outlast most, if not all, other types of flooring. Tile resists scratching and is fire-resistant, and because it's so durable, you will save money over the long haul by not having to replace it. (Consider installing a neutral color that will not become dated.)

Tile is easy to clean and, if glazed, won't absorb liquids or release unpleasant odors like carpeting can. Another advantage over carpet is that tile doesn't harbor potentially harmful mold spores, pollen, dust, or dust mites. And tile doesn't contain toxic chemicals and won't give off fumes (a process known as outgassing) like many other flooring products, even some green options. In fact, tile is arguably as healthy a flooring material as you can buy.

The use of recycled materials reduces waste shipped to landfills and cuts down on mining of clay and other minerals needed to make conventional tile. Recycling also reduces energy use because making a product from waste material typically requires less energy than fabricating one from raw materials. This, in turn, helps to slash fuel use in manufacturing and helps reduce environmental pollution.

Recycled glass tiles are often used for their decorative qualities, as in this colorful backsplash.

Courtesy of Stardust Glass, Portland, OR. www. stardustglasstile.com
(Kitchen design by Natasha Jansz Designs)

Recycled Tile Options

Recycled-content tile can be used for floors, countertops, and walls and may be made from either recycled glass or nontoxic mine or factory wastes. Tiles come in two varieties—ceramic and glass. Ceramic tiles may be made from factory waste (known as *post-industrial waste)* generated by the production of conventional tiles. Some manufacturers, such as GeoStone Ecocycle, produce tiles that contain 50% to 100% in-house manufacturing waste—waste that would otherwise have ended up in landfills.

Other products, such as Fireclay Tile, combine post-industrial *and* post-consumer recycled wastes. Fireclay tile consists of up to 25% recycled granite dust (post-industrial waste) from a granite-cutting operation. It also contains recycled glass—20% of the tile is old windowpane glass, and nearly 9% is recycled brown and green glass bottles (post-consumer waste). The glazes used by this company contain no lead, so they're safer for the workers who apply them.

Recycled-content glass floor tiles from UltraGlas, Inc. contain 15% to 30% recycled glass. Blazestone tiles produced by Bedrock Industries are made from 100% recycled glass, as are the tiles from Sandhill Industries.

Although recycled-content glass tiles are good for the environment, they are also prized by many interior designers because some types have special decorative qualities, such as translucent iridescence, not found in other tiles. Recycled tile for walls and countertops is produced by many of the companies mentioned here and listed on page 23.

Installing Floor Tile

Tile installation is a job best handled by professionals or experienced do-it-yourselfers. A considerable amount of knowledge and skill is required, especially if you're applying tile over uneven wood surfaces or have a complicated design in mind that requires a lot of tile-cutting.

If you plan to hire a professional installer, it's a good idea to line one up before you purchase the tile. Many installers like to order materials themselves so they have enough for the job and can obtain a contractor discount.

Recycled glass tiles set in a decorative pattern add beauty and help green your home.

Courtesy of Stardust Glass Tiles, Portland, OR

GeoStone Ecocycle floor tiles

Courtesy of Crossville, Inc.

Green Adhesives and Grout

When installing tile, consider using nontoxic thin-set mortars and adhesives. Conventional products emit volatile organic chemicals (VOCs) that could cause health problems in sensitive individuals. Look for low-VOC products such as American Formulating & Manufacturing's (AFM) Safecoat 3-in-1 Adhesive, EcoTimber's HealthyBond® flooring adhesive, or Evirotec's Floor Covering Adhesive. Bostik also manufactures two no-VOC thin-set mortars. You may have to order these products online.

One of the most important requirements for a good tile job is a solid base. Concrete is one of the best substrates, provided it's not cracked or uneven, but tile is also routinely applied over wood floors. Be sure that the subfloor is not warped or rotted and is adequately secured to the underlying floor joists. Problems with the subfloor may cause the tiles to come loose within a year or two, depending on traffic. Uneven subflooring can often be leveled using a self-leveling compound.

If the subflooring is severely warped or rotted, tear it out and replace it. Consider using a Forest Stewardship Council (FSC) certified plywood. FSC-certified wood products come from companies that grow, harvest, and mill their woods in a sustainable manner.

In some cities, discarded wood products, including subflooring, can be taken to building materials recyclers that repurpose the material, for example, grinding the wood to make mulch or compost.

Tile is applied using a thin-set mortar. When installing over subflooring, it's a good idea to use a rigid backerboard for a firm base. (Check out recycled-content backerboard. One manufacturer is NyCore.) A coat of thin-set mortar is typically applied over the backerboard to help keep it from flexing. (Flexing may cause mortar joints between tiles to crack and, even worse, may cause tiles to come loose.)

After the backerboard is tightly secured, chalk lines need to be snapped on the floor, and the tiles can be laid out along the lines. When you need to make cuts, use a tile cutter or tile-cutting saw. These can be rented or purchased from a local home improvement center.

After tiles are set and the adhesive has dried, grout is applied in the gaps between tiles. Be sure to seal the grout after it dries to repel moisture and dirt and to prevent discoloration.

If you'd like to tackle the job yourself, and you have no experience tiling a floor, wall, or countertop, it would be wise to take a class or two first. Many home improvement centers, such as Lowe's and Home Depot, offer free classes. If you know a local tile installer, you might consider hiring him or her for a couple of hours of instruction. You can also find detailed instructions online or in one of the many home improvement how-to books, such as Better Homes and Gardens' *Big Book of Home How-To*, Home Depot's *Home Improvement 1-2-3*, or the *Stanley Complete Step-by-Step Revised Book of Home Repair and Improvement*.

Go Green!

To clean tile or other counters without chemicals, sprinkle on baking soda, then rub with a damp cloth or sponge. For stains, make a baking-soda-and-water paste and let it sit on the stain for several minutes. For a natural disinfectant, mix 2 cups of water with 3 tablespoons liquid soap and 20 to 30 drops tea tree oil.

Shopping Tips

Recycled-content tiles are available directly from manufacturers, at some flooring supply stores, and at online green building materials outlets. To locate a specific product, you may want to contact manufacturers to find a local supplier. You can also check with your local home improvement centers to see if they carry recycled-content tile, as it continues to gain popularity.

Choosing recycled over conventional tile is a great way to green your home. Recycled glass tile offers some unique designs you won't find elsewhere.

Some Sources of Recycled-Content Tile

GeoStone EcoCycle, www.crossvilleinc.com

Fireclay Tile, www.fireclaytile.com

Quarry Tile, www.quarrytile.com

Terra Green Ceramics, www.terraggreenceramics.com

Recycled Glass Tiles

Aurora Glass, www.auroaglass.org

Bedrock Industries, www.bedrockindustries.com

Oceanside Glasstile Co., www.glasstile.com

Sandhill Industries, www.sandhillind.com

UltraGlass, Inc., www.ultraglas.com

Eco-Tile, www.quarrytile.com

Stardust Glass, www.stardustglasstile.com

What Will It Cost?

Cost Estimate: Installation of 100% recycled material floor tiles, installed in a 12' x 8' room

Including underlayment (subflooring), spacers, mortar, grout, and sealer

Cost for materials only: **$2,250**

Contractor's total, including materials, labor, and markup: **$3,200**

Flooring options, cost per square foot installed:

Recycled-content tile (from basic, tile-only installation to higher quality tile including new wood underlayment): **$10** to **$33**

Conventional ceramic tile: **$13**

Stone tile: **$22** to **$178**

Bamboo: **$12**

Oak strip: **$9**

Maple strip: **$12**

Cork tiles: **$10**

Laminate: **$8**

Costs are national averages and do not include sales tax.

Project 7

Recycled-Content Carpet

According to the Carpet and Rug Institute, carpeting covers 70% of all floors in homes and commercial spaces in the United States. Although popular, carpet does have some downsides. For example, it can affect a home's air quality by releasing toxic chemicals and by harboring and releasing dust, dust mites, pollen, and mold spores that can lead to allergies and other illnesses.

Carpeting is a challenge to keep clean, too. And since it doesn't last as long as other flooring products, such as tile and hardwood, it costs more in the long run due to more frequent replacement. This, in turn, results in more waste—approximately 2.5 million tons per year of old carpeting ends up in landfills each year. And finally, most carpet on the market today is made from chemicals derived from petroleum, a nonrenewable resource.

If you do select carpeting for your floor, consider an environmentally friendly option—recycled content carpet. It is typically made from plastic soda bottles (PET plastic, a type of polyester made from oil). The bottles are ground up, melted, and then spun into new fibers, which are attached to two layers of backing.

Using recycled plastic to make carpet fibers is better for the environment than using virgin materials. Recycling helps reduce landfill wastes and puts a waste product produced in massive quantities to good use. According to one estimate, approximately 40 two-liter soda bottles are used to produce one square yard of carpet.

Recycled-content carpeting puts an abundant waste product to good use.
Courtesy of Mohawk Industries

Recycled-content carpeting is available in a variety of colors.
Photo by Dan Chiras

The production of recycled carpet also results in lower emissions than manufacturing conventional carpet. Moreover, some manufacturers (such as Mohawk, which produces carpets under the brand names Karastan, Mohawk, and Durkan) have implemented progressive environmental policies at their plants to recycle and reduce waste, pollution, and energy use. They've also redesigned products to eliminate hazardous materials and have replaced many solvent-based materials with water-based alternatives.

Although recycled-content carpeting is greener than most conventional carpet, its backings may be made from a type of plastic (styrene butadiene, known as SB latex) that contains several potentially toxic chemicals. These can be "outgassed"—or released into the air of your home. Find out from manufacturers what is in their backing and padding materials. Several companies claim their backings contain no toxic ingredients such as CFCs, SB latex, formaldehyde, PCBs, or mercury.

Recycled-content carpeting is widely available in many colors and weaves. It looks, feels, and is priced the same as high-quality carpet manufactured from virgin materials (typically polyester, nylon, and olefin).

According to manufacturers, recycled carpet has greater colorfastness, resilience, and stain-resistance than virgin-fiber carpeting. It also comes with the same warranties (covering colorfastness, static control, and resistance to stains, crushing, and matting).

I've installed recycled-content carpet in two of my homes over the past 25 years and have been very satisfied with it. Based on my experience, I wouldn't say it's more stain- or mat-resistant than traditional carpeting, but it's comparable.

Green Carpet Pad

In homes, carpets are typically installed over carpet pad to provide additional cushion or "bounce." Green carpet pads are made from an assortment of natural and recycled materials. The natural materials include animal hair, jute, and rubber. Nature's Choice, for example, produces a cashmere and jute carpet pad.

Go Green!

- Whether or not your bathroom has carpet, moisture and mold are always a concern. Run the exhaust fan while showering or bathing, and for about 30 minutes afterward if windows are closed.

- Recycled carpet, although greener than conventional carpet, may emit some VOCs, so plan on installation when the weather is warm, if possible, so you can open windows to increase ventilation. Leave them open if possible for at least three days. It's even better if you can vacate the premises during this time.

Appleseed Wool Corporation's carpet pads are made from 100% wool felt stitched to a jute backing. This product, known as UnderFleece™, contains no glues, dyes, or chemical treatments. Earth Weave manufactures a natural rubber carpet pad as well.

Some carpet pad is also made from recycled materials. Carpets Inter, for instance, makes a pad that is 90% recycled PET plastic. Earth Weave Carpet Mills produces a pad made from 80% post-industrial waste wool. Other companies use recycled rubber and polyurethane foam.

Installing Carpet & Pad

Recycled-content carpet and green carpet pad are installed just like any other wall-to-wall carpeting. They are tacked down in residential applications, not glued. This is not a job for the do-it-yourselfer because it requires special equipment and expertise provided by professionals.

Shopping Tips

Research your options online, and visit local retailers to see and feel different materials. You may also want to find out the environmental standards each manufacturer employs before you buy.

Also consider recycled nylon carpeting. At least two manufacturers (Shaw Industries and Interface) have developed a process to recycle nylon carpet fibers.

You'll find prices vary considerably. Some discount carpet outlets offer recycled-content carpet, but be sure you know what you're getting—in quality, appearance, warranty, and safe ingredients. Always check carpet in person and try out a sample in the room where you plan to install it. Look at it in daylight and in artificial light in the evening to be sure you will be happy with the color and texture.

What Will It Cost?

Cost Estimate: Installation of recycled-content carpeting and padding for a 12′ x 16′ room

Cost for materials only: **$640**

Contractor's total, including materials, labor, and markup: **$1,100**

Carpet options, cost per square yard installed:

Recycled-content carpeting: **$53**

All-natural wool carpeting: **$45** to **$150**

Conventional carpeting: **$57**

Flooring options, cost per square foot installed:

Pre-finished oak strip: **$11**

Floating laminate: **$9**

Ceramic tiles: **$13**

Cork tiles: **$10**

Costs are national averages and do not include sales tax.

Project

8

All-Natural Wool Carpeting

If you're in the market for carpeting, consider one of the most environmentally friendly materials available—wool. Wool carpet is made from either 100% wool fiber or a blend of wool and synthetics (made from petrochemicals). The most environmentally friendly and healthiest option is 100% wool made without toxic chemicals. Wool carpet is odor-free from the day it's installed and is great for individuals who suffer from allergies or multiple chemical sensitivity.

One-hundred-percent wool is made from a renewable resource and lasts much longer than conventional synthetic carpet materials. The backing materials of 100% wool carpet are all-natural, such as jute. Wool carpet that comes with a natural backing is fully biodegradable when it has reached the end of its useful life and goes to the landfill.

Wool can be a little softer than some synthetic fibers. It also captures and retains dust better than conventional carpet, which is actually a good thing because it holds the dust until it can be removed by a vacuum cleaner. This results in less dust in the air than you'll experience with some synthetic carpets. (The downside is that wool carpeting retains allergens, such as pollen and dander. They can be released back into the room air if your vacuum cleaner does not have a good filter.) All natural wool carpet is also fire-resistant.

Available in a variety of weaves and colors, wool is one of the most durable carpet fibers on the market. It cleans well and, according to retailers, is naturally stain- and soil-resistant. (Be aware though that *Consumer Reports* claims that wool carpet stains easily and that light

Wool carpeting is durable and looks great.
Courtesy of Nature's Carpet

colors tend to yellow in bright sunlight, so be sure to check out warranties for stain- and fade-resistance.)

Wool carpeting can be purchased at major carpet and flooring retailers or on the Internet through numerous green building materials outlets and online carpet retailers.

Wool Carpet Options

Check out Nature's Carpet (**www.naturescarpet. com**), which produces one of the purest wool carpets. No harmful chemicals are used at any stage in its production, including moth repellants. The sheep even graze on organically fertilized fields. The carpet backings and adhesives are made from natural materials, such as jute and recycled wool.

Earth Weave Carpet Mills (**www.earthweave.com**) manufactures wool carpet with 100% biodegradable adhesives that bond the wool to a hemp-cotton primary backing. The secondary backing is made of jute, a vegetable fiber grown without pesticides or chemical fertilizers in developing countries, including

Bangladesh. No harmful chemicals are used in the production of these carpets, and color variation is achieved through the selection of naturally pigmented wool.

Installation

Wool wall-to-wall carpet is installed like other carpets; it's usually tacked down in residential applications, not glued. The job is best left to professionals who have the equipment and expertise to perform the work quickly and correctly.

Go Green!

- If you're replacing carpet that's still in pretty good condition or has good sections, rather than throw it away, try donating it to a charity or to Freecycle, the ReUseIt Network, Sharing Is Giving, FreeSharing, or Craigslist. You can also use it in a dry basement or cut it into small pieces for later use, for example as pads to kneel on when working on the car, doormats, or even scratching posts for cats. Or you could even carpet the dog house!

- If your old carpet is too worn to reuse, explore recycling options before it is removed. Ask the retailer of your new carpet for suggestions. Carpet recycling is in its infancy, but if more of us show we're interested, it could help stimulate companies to take this effort seriously. To see if there is a carpet reclamation center in your area, contact Carpet America Recovery Effort (CARE) at **www.carpetrecovery.org**

Wool carpet comes in many styles.
Courtesy of Nature's Carpet

Shopping Tips

When shopping for wool carpet, research your options first. Study the wealth of information available online. As you compare various products, check manufacturers' environmental standards. Also check their warranties for stain-resistance, fade-resistance, and wear.

Be aware that many companies use chemical dyes or backings made from nonrecyclable and nonbiodegradable latex. Some carpet may also be chemically treated to improve its resistance to carpet moths and beetles.

When checking out options, ask about the fiber content—is it 100% wool or a combination of wool and synthetic fiber? Where does the wool come from? As a rule, New Zealand wool is regarded as superior because their sheep are bred for long fibers. Also be sure to ask whether the backings are natural or synthetic, and whether they contain chemical dyes.

While photos on websites help to illustrate the array of options, it's definitely best to see and feel the carpet at a local retailer *before* you come to a decision. You can also order samples from suppliers.

What Will It Cost?

Cost Estimate: Installation of all-natural wool carpeting with recycled carpet padding in a 12' x 16' room

Cost for materials only: **$2,500**

Contractor's total, including materials, labor, and markup: **$3,350**

Carpeting options, cost per square yard installed:

Natural wool carpeting: **$150**

Conventional carpeting: **$57**

Recycled-content carpeting: **$53**

Flooring options, cost per square foot installed:

Pre-finished oak strip: **$11**

Floating laminate: **$9**

Cork tiles: **$10**

Costs are national averages and do not include sales tax.

Project 9

Healthy Paints, Stains & Finishes

One of the easiest and least expensive ways to spruce up a room is with a new coat of paint. Woodwork and flooring can also be sanded and refinished to give your home a new look. Unfortunately, paints, stains, and finishes are notorious contributors to indoor air pollution. Oil-based paints, for example, release large quantities of potentially harmful volatile organic chemicals (called VOCs) as they dry. The release of VOCs continues for a week or two after painting. Conventional wood stains and finishes also release huge quantities of VOCs, often more than oil-based paints, and much more than water-based wall paints.

VOCs and other chemical ingredients in paints, stains, and finishes may cause short-term health effects, such as headaches, dizziness, nausea, allergic reactions, and sore throats. They may also cause serious, long-term health problems like cancer. The very old and very young are most susceptible, as are those with weakened immune systems. VOCs in paints also contribute to local air pollution, notably photochemical smog that plagues many cities in summer months.

Conventional water-based latex interior house paints are safer than oil paints. They release fewer VOCs, but also emit small amounts of formaldehyde, ammonia, mildewcides, and other potentially harmful chemicals. As these paints dry, the chemicals are released into the room air, creating a distinct odor. The chemicals are inhaled by individuals applying the paint and by the

No-VOC paints look the same, and go on the same but are much healthier than conventional paints.
Courtesy of The Sherwin-Williams Company

home's residents—sometimes for up to several weeks afterward.

Why add chemicals if they can cause health problems? The most dangerous ones, VOCs, are used to make the paint dry faster. Mildewcides are added to prevent mold and mildew, both in the can and when the paint is on the walls. (Generally, interior paints contain less mildewcide than exterior paints.)

Responding to these and other concerns, the paint industry has made dramatic changes in their products. They now offer many environmentally and people-friendly options. What's more, you won't have to break the bank to go green, since these paints don't cost any more than premium conventional paints, and sometimes less.

What Are Your Options?

To begin with, many off-the-shelf interior paints today contain much lower VOC concentrations than in the recent past. Some manufacturers have gone a step further, producing paints with even lower levels of VOCs, labeling the paint "low-VOC." All major paint manufacturers produce a line of low-VOC paints, including Glidden, Sherwin-Williams, Kelly-Moore, and Benjamin Moore. (See sidebar.) They're available in paint stores, home improvement centers, and hardware stores.

No-VOC paints are also available from many of the same companies. Lifemaster 2000, for example, is a no-VOC interior house paint manufactured by ICI paints (parent company of Glidden). It is used in hospitals, schools, and offices. Sherwin-Williams also manufactures a no-VOC paint, known as Harmony® Interior Latex. Several others are listed in the box on this page. No-VOC paints are available in paint stores or can be special-ordered.

No-VOC interior paints can be tinted to produce any color you want, but in many cases pigments are dissolved in solvents (VOCs). The deeper the tint (or more intense the color), the more VOCs are added. When shopping for a no-VOC paint, ask about zero-VOC colorants like those from American Pride.

Low-VOC Paints

Sherwin-Williams – Duration Home® Interior Latex

Glidden – Glidden Spread 2000

Kelley-Moore – Eviron-Cote

Duron – Genesis Odor-Free

Benjamin Moore – Eco-Spec

No-VOC Paints

ICI Paints – Lifemaster 2000

Sherwin-Williams – Harmony® Interior Latex

The Home Depot – The Freshaire Choice

Olympic Paint – Premium Paints (several options available)

Southern Diversified Products – American Pride Paints

Pittsburgh Paints – Pure Performance

AFM – Safecoat

BioShield – Solvent-Free Wall Paint, Clay Paints, Milk Paint, and Kinder Paint

The Home Depot now sells a no-VOC paint, The Freshaire Choice. The can, labeling, and brochures are made from recycled materials.

While low- and no-VOC paints are safer and better for the environment than conventional paints, they often contain ammonia and antimicrobial additives (mildewcides). Another issue to be aware of is that federal regulations that apply to VOCs in paint only cover the types of VOCs that contribute to the formation of smog. Other types of VOCs are not counted, so no- or low-VOC paints may actually contain some VOCs that may pose a health risk. To find out, contact the manufacturer and ask for a copy of the product's Materials Safety Data Sheet (MSDS).

If you suffer from multiple chemical sensitivity (MCS) or simply prefer the healthiest paints on the market, check out paints manufactured by companies such as

AFM, BioShield, and Aglaia. Many of their products are made without any VOCs whatsoever and contain no other potentially harmful chemicals, such as ammonia and mildewcides.

BioShield manufactures a complete line of zero-VOC wall paints in a wide range of colors. Rudolf Reiz, who founded the company, notes, "To me, it seemed like an oxymoron to clean and beautify our home with products that actually made our inner environment unhealthy. I created all of our natural products with my family in mind so I could breathe easier." Reiz adds, "When we say no VOCs, we mean none whatsoever!"

BioShield also produces milk paints made from milk protein, called casein. Milk paints are one of the original paint formulations used in many historic buildings. They come as a powder that is mixed with water as needed, then painted on walls with or without tint.

Milk paints are ideal for hospitals or homes with chemically sensitive individuals. I recently used tinted milk paint in my home and was amazed how easy it was to mix. The paint went on quickly, and required two coats for full coverage. I was also quite pleased with the final results. It looks like any other quality paint I've used over the past 30 years.

Milk paint holds up well and can be wiped clean. Like BioShield's other products, it can be purchased online from one of the two dozen green building material suppliers.

The AFM company in San Diego is another manufacturer of low- and no-VOC paints. Their Safecoat no-VOC paints contain no ammonia, formaldehyde, acetone, heavy metals, or other VOCs—regulated or not. In addition, AFM supplies many of their dealers with zero-VOC colorants.

I recently used AFM Safecoat and BioShield no-VOC paint (untinted) when repainting my living room and entryway. Both products went on easily, covered walls and ceilings very well, and, remarkably, produced little, if any, odor, even with my nose pressed to a newly painted wall!

Test First!

If you are chemically sensitive, it's a good idea to test *all* paint products before you apply them to a room. Most sources recommend painting a block of wood, then placing the block on a nightstand next to your bed for a few weeks to see if you react to it. You can ask for a paint sample from the store.

Safecoat by AFM is one of several truly no-VOC paints.

Courtesy of AFM

Kitchen painted with AFM Safecoat paint.
Courtesy of AFM

Over the years, I've used a number of other AFM products, including their water-based concrete sealer (DynoSeal), stain (DuroStain), and finish (Polyureseal BP), on various projects in my homes. Although they cost more and were not available from local stores, all of them were pleasant to work with—much more so than standard sealants, stains, and finishes. To locate a local dealer or online retailer, log on to **www.afmsafecoat.com** If you're a contractor, be sure to ask for contractor discounts.

Yet another option is paint from the German company, Aglaia. They manufacture natural wall paints in a full range of colors, as well as natural wood finishes for floors, trim, and exposed posts and beams. Aglaia's paints and wood finishes are made with natural plant oils. For example, their water-based wood finish (Aglaia Aquasol) contains a blend of safflower, linseed, and lavender oils. Aglaia's natural oil finishes and paints can be thinned and cleaned up with water. You can find a retailer or online supplier by logging on to their website, **www.aglaiapaint.com**

You may also want to check out stains and wood finishes from Livos, another German company. Livos products are made from citrus oils. I used Livos' Kaldet Wood Stain on the interior wood trim of an attached sunspace. The painter (who'd been in the business for over 20 years) and I were amazed at how pleasant the product smelled. The stain has held up over the years through the heat and direct sunlight. Livos also sells natural wood sealers for interior and exterior applications.

Finally, if you're interested in a natural, earthy look, you may want to consider American Clay's Earth Plaster. Earth Plaster is a practical, environmentally friendly, and beautiful alternative to conventional interior plasters. It is recommended for both historic and new buildings. American Clay's product comes in a dry powder in five-gallon buckets and is pigmented and hydrated on-site. The company sells 35 different pigments. Their plasters can be troweled onto drywall or sprayed on using a drywall hopper and compressor. (Check the manufacturer's recommendations.)

One advantage of Earth Plaster over gypsum, lime, and cement plaster is its longer working time—up to several days if you need it—so you can take your time and work with confidence that the surface won't set before you've achieved the finish you want, according to the manufacturer. (Just be sure to allow for the extra drying time.) In addition, there's no waste, since you can reuse extra plaster by breaking it up and rehydrating it. I've worked with this product and have been amazed at how beautiful it looks and how easy it is to apply. To learn more, see the company's website at **www.americanclay.com**

Painting Your Home

Low- and no-VOC paints apply and clean up like any other water-based paint. The only difference I've found is that certain products may take longer to dry than conventional paint. For example, no-VOC semi-gloss paints used to paint wood trim and cabinetry may take longer than ordinary semi-gloss paints. In fact, it may take several months for this paint to *completely* dry to rock-hardness (though you can touch the walls and hang pictures without any problem after a few days).

When applying paints that contain some VOCs, be sure to ventilate the work area with outside air. Use a fan to ensure greater air circulation. If at all possible, leave the house for a few days after painting; for example, paint just before leaving for a trip or a vacation—if you can manage both trip preparation and painting in the same week! Or, if you are hiring professionals, ask them to apply the paint while you're

Go Green!

To reduce the amount of trash that ends up in landfills, choose reusable paint brushes, rollers, and paint trays, not disposable ones.

American Clay Earth Plaster creates a soft look in this bedroom.
Photo courtesy of Celeste Wegman Interiors

gone—if you can arrange for proper supervision and security. Have the workers leave the windows open, even just a little, while they're painting and when they leave—again, if you can keep your home secure at the same time. You may be able to at least crack some windows in locations not accessible to intruders to create natural ventilation.

If you've never painted before, read up on interior painting tips in a home improvement book or on the websites or the brochures of paint companies. Proper

preparation of surfaces is key to a successful project. Be careful when on ladders. You don't want to end up in the hospital's trauma unit like I did after a ladder slipped out from underneath me while I was staining window trim 15 feet above a tile floor!

Go Green!

Use box fans in windows to draw out the paint vapors if your paint contains even low levels of VOCs. Take frequent breaks to get some fresh air, and use a mask.

Shopping Tips

When shopping for paints, ask questions. If a salesperson is vague or not very knowledgeable, ask for someone who is, or take your business elsewhere. Find someone who really knows the contents of, and application techniques for, the paints they sell. The VOC content of paints is often listed on the label on paint cans or in product literature. If not, call the company (look for a toll-free number on the paint can).

VOC levels are listed in grams per liter. For latex paint, national standards require VOC levels no higher than 250 grams per liter for water-based flat paints. For non-flat (satin or semi-gloss) paints, VOCs should be no higher than 380 grams per liter. Several states, such as California, have adopted more stringent standards of 100 grams or less for flat paints and 150 grams or less for non-flat paints.

 For the best products in the low-VOC category, look for the Green Seal logo on the label. Green Seal is a nonprofit organization that certifies a variety of products, including paints. Their label is on flat interior paint products if they contain fewer than 50 grams of VOC per liter and on non-flat paint products that contain under 150 grams/per liter.

When hiring a contractor, specify that you want them to use either low- or no-VOC paints, and be sure they follow through with your request. You may want to suggest a specific product or purchase the paint yourself to be sure you get what you want. If your contractor hems and haws, find one who will work with you, preferably one who has used the product before.

What Will It Cost?

Low- and no-VOC paints often cost more than bargain brands, but are about the same price as higher-quality conventional paints you'll purchase at paint stores.

Cost Estimate: Painting of 1 door, 3 windows, trim, walls, and ceiling of a 12' x 16' room, using low-VOC paint

Includes prep work, primer, and 2 coats of paint

Cost for materials only: **$280**

Contractor's total, including materials, labor, and markup: **$950**

Cost comparison to traditional paint:

Total cost for professional painting of a 12' x 16' room using conventional paints: **$850**

Costs are national averages and do not include sales tax.

Project 10

Green Cabinetry

If you're replacing kitchen cabinets or planning to install them in a new home or office, consider a healthy alternative to conventional cabinetry. Many cabinets release small amounts of a potentially toxic chemical, formaldehyde, into the air we breathe. Experts on indoor air quality say this can continue over the lifetime of the cabinets.

How Are Cabinets Made?

Many cabinets, as well as bathroom vanities and shelving, are made from particleboard or a similar material known as medium-density fiberboard, or simply MDF. These materials consist of sawdust and wood shavings, both waste products from lumber mills and plywood production. The wood fibers are bonded together by a small amount of plastic resin, which contains formaldehyde.

A thin wood veneer is often glued to particleboard or MDF to give the appearance of real wood. However, many cabinets are also faced with melamine, a plastic sheet that's glued to the particleboard.

Healthy Cabinet Options

To reduce formaldehyde exposure, you can custom-order cabinets made from solid wood or PrimeBoard, an MDF substitute made from wheat straw and a non-formaldehyde-producing resin. (You can also buy low-VOC cabinetry, as well as high-recycled-content cabinetry, made from MDF board [Norbord].) You can request that custom cabinet makers stain and

finish your cabinets with no-VOC products. The entire cabinet should be made from solid wood or wheat straw material, not just the doors. If you choose wood, you may also want to specify that it come from a sustainably harvested source.

Custom-made cabinets are expensive, often two or three times more than conventional cabinetry. If you're on a budget, you may want to check out local building supply salvage outlets for used solid-wood cabinets. In a garage or pantry, where aesthetics are not as much of a concern, consider installing metal cabinets.

Go Green!

If you're planning to install new cabinets, but your old ones are still in decent shape, remove them carefully so they can be donated to a local salvage yard or used building materials retailer. Area builders or remodelers may be willing to dismantle and take old cabinets off your hands if they're well-made and in good condition. Or you can place an ad in the local paper or on a website like **freecycle.org** or **reuseitnetwork.org** and give them away.

Neil Kelly green cabinets—beautiful, healthy, and good for the environment!
Courtesy of Neil Kelly Cabinet Co., By Photo Design, Portland, OR

A leading manufacturer of green cabinets is Neil Kelly Cabinets. This was the first company in the world to offer a full range of healthy, environmentally friendly materials and techniques, including FSC-certified woods, formaldehyde-free agriboard case/drawer material, and low-VOC glues, adhesives, and finishes. They offer optional features such as solid wood for drawers and all-natural oil finishes.

Other manufacturers have followed suit, increasing the availability of green cabinetry for homes and offices. Green Leaf Cabinetry in Ohio, for instance, manufactures cabinets using "Pure Bond Plywood"—a plywood core made from a formaldehyde-free bonding agent. Their wood for doors and drawers is FSC-certified from well-managed forestry operations or locally harvested trees that have been cut down for other reasons, such as clearing lots for buildings or roadways. All of their finishes are low- or zero-VOC.

Yet another option is to purchase cabinets and other types of furniture, like desks, made by manufacturers in Europe, where the use of formaldehyde resins has been banned. Shipping requires additional energy and increases costs, however.

MDI: A Safe Replacement?

Most manufacturers of formaldehyde-free agriboard, particleboard, and MDF use a resin known as MDI (methylene diphenyl isocyanate). While this resin does not outgas hazardous chemicals in finished products and is therefore considered safe to the occupants of a home, it can cause dermatitis (skin rash) and respiratory problems among factory workers. It can also sensitize workers' immune systems, resulting in asthma-like symptoms, although controls are usually in place to reduce their exposure.

Green Leaf Cabinetry looks great and is a healthy choice for new and existing homes.

Green Leaf Cabinetry, Courtesy of Schumann Architectural Photography

Installing Cabinets

Removing old cabinets and especially installing new ones is a job for a professional or an experienced do-it-yourselfer. Special knowledge, skill, and tools are required for this job. Complications can arise if your walls, floor, or ceiling are not level, plumb, and square.

Base cabinets can be particularly challenging because of the extra task of installing countertops. If you're up to the job, consult the manufacturer's instructions and read up on installation, either in one of the many home improvement books or on the Internet. If you don't have the time or patience, however, it's best to hire a professional.

Go Green!

Resist the temptation to upgrade. Whether it's new cabinetry, new skis, new clothes, or a new cell phone, hold on to what you have and use it for as many years as you can. Refinishing or slip-covering furniture rather than tossing it out can improve its appearance and increase its life. Replacing perfectly usable products with the latest fashion wastes a lot of the Earth's natural resources and energy and causes more environmental damage.

Formaldehyde—It's Everywhere!

Formaldehyde has long been used as a preservative by scientists and the medical community for biological specimens. Now formaldehyde can be found in a wide variety of building materials. Most notable are particleboard and medium-density fiberboard.

These products are an economical substitute for solid lumber and help put waste material to good use. As a result, they're found throughout our homes and offices. Particleboard, for example, is used as a core material for interior doors, cabinets, bookcases, desks, vanities, and furniture. Medium-density fiberboard is also used to make furniture and cabinets, as well as molding and picture frames.

All of these products release tiny amounts of formaldehyde, a suspected carcinogen, into the air. In concentrations well below those we can detect through our sense of smell, formaldehyde can also cause a rare, but debilitating autoimmune disease, known as multiple chemical sensitivity (MCS). MCS is marked by allergy-like and other physical reactions to several types of air pollutants, such as outgassed chemicals from plastics, paints, carpeting, and so forth.

Once exposed, people with MCS become highly sensitive to numerous other products, including deodorants, perfumes, and conventional paints, stains, and finishes. Many who suffer from MCS become weak and unable to move when exposed to one of these or other products. To be able to function, they must strip their homes of all offending products. In addition, breathing even small amounts of formaldehyde may also increase risk for nasal and lung cancer.

Shopping Tips

When shopping for cabinets and vanities, be sure to ask store personnel for information on formaldehyde content and finishes. If the salesperson can't provide this data, or is unsure, go elsewhere or contact the manufacturer for detailed information.

To find local retail outlets that carry healthy, environmentally friendly cabinetry, check out manufacturers' websites. Also search online for local retailers that specialize in green building products. Ask local cabinet suppliers if they offer environmentally friendly cabinets. If they hear it enough, they're bound to take notice and may even start carrying a line.

What Will It Cost?

As mentioned, green cabinets, especially if custom-made, can cost two or three times as much as stock cabinets made of conventional materials. If you order cabinetry from one of the few manufacturers that make green cabinets, such as those mentioned in this project, you may also have a few hundred dollars worth of added shipping costs.

There are ways to keep costs down while going green and reducing your use of virgin wood. One is to purchase and refinish old cabinets from a building salvage store. Another approach is to use open shelving in place of some wall cabinets. You can also substitute a free-standing furniture piece, such as an old hutch, a work table with shelves, or a large cart with shelves and casters, for some of the cabinets. One more option to consider: Find a cabinetmaker to build new doors and drawer fronts out of green materials. The cabinet frames can be cleaned and refinished with a low- or no-VOC finish before the doors and drawers are installed.

Project
11

Home Energy Audit

Energy costs have skyrocketed in recent years and are expected to continue on this course well into the future. To combat rising prices, many homeowners replace windows or install new furnaces—or add expensive solar heating or electrical systems. While these and other major improvements can result in huge savings, they also require a substantial investment.

Energy experts agree that the most economical way to cut energy costs is to make your home more airtight and energy-efficient. An energy auditor will reveal inefficiencies and will suggest inexpensive steps you can take to eliminate them, resulting in instant savings—and major savings over time—with very little effort.

Low-cost energy-efficiency measures also reduce your investment in future upgrades. For example, if you seal leaks in exterior walls and add insulation, you may not need as big a furnace when it comes time to replace your old one. The same is true if you decide to purchase a solar electric system in the future—you can reduce its size and cost if you've made your home more energy-efficient in ways recommended by your energy auditor.

A home energy audit can be performed by a trained professional—or by a homeowner who knows what to look for. Most audits uncover numerous opportunities to save energy.

Finding an Energy Auditor

Although energy audits can be performed by homeowners, a certified professional energy auditor has the equipment and is trained to identify all inefficiencies in homes, including appliances and electronics. Professionals also help pinpoint occupants' inefficient practices that, if corrected, can save substantially on energy bills.

A complete audit—without retrofitting—generally costs about $300 and takes only a few hours. You can locate an energy auditor in the Yellow Pages (look under "Energy Conservation" or "Energy Management") or by calling your state's energy office. You can also log on to the Energy Star® website (**www.energystar.gov**) and select *Home Energy Audits*. This site lists home energy raters, many of which also offer audits, and indicates how many home audits each company has performed.

In some cities and towns, local utility companies offer free or low-cost audits (as low as $15 to $25) or rebates to help offset the cost of hiring a professional auditor. (Low-income families may qualify for free energy audits from the state offices of energy conservation or from local nonprofit organizations.)

Why Perform an Energy Audit?

Energy audits themselves won't save you money, but if you carry out the recommended retrofits, you can save a substantial amount on your fuel bills from that day forward. The savings could range from 10% to as much as 50%, perhaps more. Savings depend on how inefficient your home is now and the number of improvements you make.

Besides saving money, energy improvements will make your home much more comfortable, for example, by eliminating drafts. Sealing leaks in the outside walls and foundation makes your home healthier for people with allergies too, by keeping dust, pollen, mold, and outdoor air pollutants out of your living space. And the environment benefits as well, since using less energy means using less fossil fuel and reducing pollution, especially greenhouse gas emissions.

What Does an Energy Audit Involve?

Locating Leaks. The first step is to identify leaks in the building envelope—that is, the walls, foundation, roof, and ceiling. Tiny cracks typically occur around doors and windows, at the junction of exterior walls and floors, and where interior walls and ceilings meet. Leaks are also common where pipes penetrate the exterior walls or where wiring for cable and satellite TV, phone service, and electrical service enters our homes. If these penetrations haven't been properly sealed, they may permit warm air to stream out, or cold air to enter on frigid winter days. In the summer, leaks allow hot air in, and cool, air-conditioned air to escape, wasting energy and money.

Few people are aware of the multitude of energy-wasting leaks in their homes, and how quickly they add up. If all the leaks in the building envelope of a typical older home were combined, they would be equivalent to a 3-foot by 3-foot window left open 24 hours a day—365 days a year! In a newer home of roughly the same size, the leaks would be equal to a 2-foot by 2-foot open window.

To detect leaks, an energy auditor begins with a visual inspection to identify very large openings in the building envelope—for example, missing or cracked window panes in basement windows or openings from coal chutes left over from olden days.

The Energy Detective

Many of us gasp in horror when we open our utility bills. We vow to use energy more carefully next time, but because we have no way to track usage day-to-day, it is difficult to know where our energy dollars are going. To cut energy use, families need to know more than *how many* kilowatts of electricity they use each month. They also need to know *when and how* they're using it. Enter The Energy Detective (TED), a convenient device that lets you monitor your electrical energy use in real time.

The Energy Detective displays electrical energy usage on an LCD screen. That means no surprises! You can see how much power you're using every second, as well as what it has cost you during a day—or so far this month—and take steps to lower your demand. TED can even be connected to your computer so you can log and graph your electrical consumption.

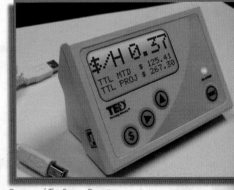

A TED can be wired into a home's main service panel (breaker box) in about 15 minutes by an electrician. (This can also be done by homeowners who are experienced and skilled in electrical work). TEDs start at about $139. For more information, visit **www.theenergydetective.com**

Courtesy of The Energy Detective

Energy auditors examine windows, checking for missing caulk, rotting wood, or gaps around window frames, and noting whether windows are double- or single-pane. They'll also look for storm windows and, if you have them, what condition they're in. If your home is heated by a forced-air furnace, the auditor will inspect the ducts. They will also check for leaks around room air conditioners or where pipes from central air conditioning systems enter a home.

After locating the most obvious leaks, the auditor will then focus on smaller, less visible leaks, which can be pinpointed by performing a blower door test. To run this test, the auditor first closes all exterior doors and windows and fireplace dampers (setting the house in winter mode). He then shuts off pilot lights to water heaters and furnaces and closes dampers of fireplaces and doors to woodstoves. (It is a good idea to remove ash from fireplace hearths or cover them with wet newspapers. This keeps ash from being sucked out of the fireplace into the room.) Interior doors and heat registers are opened to ensure a good flow of air throughout the house. The auditor then installs a blower door device in the opening of one of the exterior doors, typically the front door. This device, shown in the photo on the opposite page, consists of an expandable aluminum frame that fits almost any door. It's covered with nylon fabric and fitted with a large electric fan and a meter.

With outside windows and doors shut, the fan is switched on. It sucks air out of the house. As the fan runs, replacement air rushes in through cracks in the building envelope. The meter on the blower door indicates how leaky the house is, giving a reading in cubic feet per minute.

To identify leaks (so they can be sealed), the auditor switches the fan's direction so that it blows air into the house, forcing air out through the cracks in the building envelope. Using an artificial smoke gun, the auditor inspects every room. If the smoke is whisked out through a crack, the auditor marks the spot or makes a note in a notebook. If you've hired the auditor to also seal the leaks, an assistant may follow along with a caulk gun, sealing small cracks, or a foam applicator to seal larger openings.

By carefully examining every room in the house, starting in the basement and ending in the attic or uppermost story, the auditor identifies all the leaks that need to be sealed.

If your home is heated by a forced-air heating system, the auditor may also perform a duct blast test in conjunction with the blower door test to measure leakage in the duct system. (You may be surprised to learn that you can lose up to 35% of your heat or cooled air through leaky ductwork.)

Appliances and Electronics. The auditor's next task is to check the age, condition, and efficiency of appliances, such as refrigerators, furnaces, boilers, stoves, water heaters, and air conditioners. Auditors should also test for carbon monoxide emissions from combustion appliances and check for back-drafting before sealing the cracks in the building envelope. They do this by running all bath fans, range hood fans, and dryers, which can pull air from a house down through vent pipes of appliances like water heaters and furnaces. (This is known as back-drafting.) They'll also look for an extra refrigerator or freezer—old models homeowners move to their garages because they can't bear to dispose of them. The auditor will make note of light fixtures and the type of lightbulbs you use. (Lighting typically accounts for at least 10% of a home's electric bill.)

Go Green!

• Recycle old refrigerators and freezers that are taking up space in the garage or basement. Old models typically consume a huge amount of electricity—often only to cool a six-pack or two of beer or soda.

• One of the easiest, most cost-effective ways to make your home more energy-efficient is to seal up large air leaks like broken or missing window panes or holes in exterior doors. Replace window panes and use foam caulking or wood to seal up large openings.

Blower door test device used by home energy auditors to determine how leaky our homes are and to identify leaks for sealing.

Minneapolis Blower Door™ Courtesy of the Energy Conservatory

Energy Use Patterns. Auditors also typically ask questions about your family's patterns of energy use, for example, whether you prefer baths or showers, whether you leave lights and electronics on when you leave the house, or whether you turn the thermostat down in the winter when you leave the house or at night when you sleep.

Insulation Levels. The auditor also inspects insulation in the walls and ceilings surrounding living space, and in attics, basements, and crawl spaces. A few auditors use infrared (heat) cameras to photograph walls, ceilings, and windows to detect leaks and uninsulated or under-insulated areas where heat is escaping in the winter and entering in the summer.

Final Report. When the energy audit is complete, auditors return to their offices and prepare a written summary of their findings, including steps that should be taken to reduce energy use and improve comfort. Their report may recommend:

- Sealing leaks in the exterior walls with caulk or expanding foam sealant.

- Sealing leaky ducts.

- Adding insulation to the attic floor, basement walls, and exterior walls of your living space.

- Insulating ductwork that passes through un-conditioned air spaces, such as an unheated and un-air-conditioned attic.

- Replacing the furnace/air conditioning filter every other month.

- Adding an insulation blanket to the water heater.

- Insulating hot water pipes, if they're accessible.

- Replacing old and inefficient appliances.

- Adding foam insulation behind the face plates of electrical outlets and light switches.

- Closing the fireplace damper when not in use or adding a glass door to prevent air leakage.

- Taking shorter showers and installing water-efficient showerheads and faucet aerators that save not only water, but also the energy required to heat it.

Auditors provide information on the savings you'll achieve from various efficiency measures, including caulking. They also typically rate their recommendations according to the energy savings they'll produce and their cost-effectiveness. This helps homeowners select measures that yield the greatest energy and cost savings with the least investment. Auditors often use computer software to analyze the performance of a home and to project potential savings.

With the report in hand, you can get started on your home's energy retrofit yourself, or you can hire a professional. As noted, companies that perform energy audits sometimes do retrofits or can recommend someone who does.

Performing an Energy Audit Yourself

You can follow the same steps as a professional auditor, although without a blower door device. Begin by looking for large openings in outside walls, then smaller, less visible leaks. These can be detected on windy days by systematically walking through your home and feeling around doors and window frames, at the base of walls, and anywhere else there is an opening from outside to inside walls. Leaks can also be detected with a stick of burning incense. Air leaking into a home will deflect the smoke. Be sure to check around electrical outlets, light switches, and ceiling fixtures, especially recessed lighting and whole house fans, both major sources of heat loss in the winter.

To work efficiently, be prepared to seal up leaks as you uncover them with caulk or foam or weather stripping (used on doors, windows and large cracks). Leaky light switches and electrical outlet plates can be sealed with foam insulators. (Turn off the circuit that services that room or area before removing a switch or outlet plate.)

During your energy audit, inspect insulation in walls, especially basement walls, and ceilings. Foundation insulation may be applied to the outside of your home. (It's rarely found in older homes.) Details on insulation inspection and installation can be found in Project 13.

Check the condition of heating/air conditioning system filters. As noted earlier, they should be replaced once a month or every other month when these systems are in operation. Also check and vacuum the coils on the back of your refrigerator and at the same time, make sure there are no water leaks underneath.

Assessing the performance of furnaces, water heaters, or older kitchen appliances is tricky. It is a job best left to professional auditors who have the tools to measure combustion efficiency. Some utility companies will check the performance for free or at an economical rate.

If all of this seems overwhelming, you may want to download a home energy analysis tool, such as the Energy Quotient at: **www.accuratebuilding.com/ publications/energy_guide**

This site allows you to rate your home on a scale of 1 to 1,000 and identify potential energy-saving changes. Look for more advice on home energy audits at the U.S. Department of Energy's website: **www.energystar.gov**

What to Watch Out For

If you perform your own energy audit, consider wearing a dust mask and eye protection when inspecting attic insulation or looking for air leaks in dusty, damp crawl spaces or basements. In older homes, you may encounter asbestos insulation around pipes and ducts running from your furnace or boiler in the basement, or vermiculite insulation, which may contain asbestos, in the attic. Vermiculite is a brown, gray, or yellow granular (small pebbles) insulation that's no longer in use. If inhaled, asbestos fibers can lead to lung cancer, especially in smokers, or asbestosis, a debilitating lung disease, in nonsmokers. Be sure to consult a professional insulation installer if you encounter what you suspect may be asbestos or vermiculite insulation—and don't touch it!

Inspecting insulation levels in exterior walls can be tricky. One way is to access wall cavities via electrical outlets and light switches. Turn off the electricity to

Go Green!

Make sure the ducts for your heating, ventilating, and air-conditioning system are properly sealed. This one step can save well over $100 per year and reduce the circulation of mold and dust in your home. While you're at it, have a professional service your system.

that circuit at your home's electrical panel or subpanel. Make sure the power is turned off by checking with a voltmeter or plugging a lamp or other device that you know is working into an outlet on that circuit. Then remove the cover plate with a screwdriver. Poke around in the cavity with a wooden ruler or stick, not metal, illuminating the area with a flashlight, to determine if there is any insulation in the wall.

One energy auditor offered a description of how he detects the amount of insulation in walls: "I use small 8-inch, wood meat skewers to probe walls: First, I insert the blunt end and feel for resistance. If there is fiberglass insulation in the wall cavity, the skewer may spring back a little. I then mark how far the skewer traveled before it hit the insulation, then factor out the thickness of the drywall. Then, I insert the skewer back into the test area, sharp end first, until it hits the sidewall. By measuring that depth, I can calculate the thickness of the insulation. By determining the depth of the wall cavity and how much insulation is in it, I can find out if there is room to add more."

Checking wall insulation this way isn't foolproof because many electricians trim insulation back around outlets. As a result, professional auditors often cut a few test holes in walls in out-of-the-way places, for example, in closets against outside walls, to see if the builder installed insulation. They may also use infrared cameras to detect the presence of insulation in walls. Be sure test holes are filled.

Indoor Air Quality Concerns

To keep indoor air healthy in a well-sealed house, minimize pollutants such as paint with VOCs and furniture/cabinets with formaldehyde. Avoid chemical cleaning agents and aerosol sprays. Use bath and kitchen fans to remove steam and smoke.

What Will It Cost?

As noted, an energy audit typically costs about $300, though you can often get low- or no-cost audits through utility companies or your state or local government.

What Will You Save?

Acting on the items identified in an energy audit—that is, insulating, caulking, upgrading appliances, and more—will save you money immediately. The amount of money you save will be determined by factors such as your climate, your lifestyle, the age and condition of your home, your local utility company's rates and billing practices, and any available rebates.

The U.S. Department of Energy and the Environmental Protection Agency estimate savings in energy costs of 20%—just by sealing a home and insulating properly. Installing Energy Star appliances and Energy Star-qualified heating or air conditioning equipment can save at least another 20%.

For more information, visit the Home Energy Saver online at **www.hes.lbl.gov** and the Energy Star Home Energy Yardstick at **www.energystar.gov** for tools to calculate your energy use and savings. The Energy Star website will show you energy costs for similar homes around the country and offer tips to reduce your costs.

The retrofits you make will reduce your utility bills, so long as you don't add new appliances/electronics or use the ones you have for longer periods.

Caulking & Weather Stripping

Most older homes are riddled with holes in the "building envelope"—the outside walls, roof, and foundation. Although some are quite large, like broken or missing window panes in the basement or basement doors that don't close properly, most gaps in the building envelope are very small. Collectively, however, these small gaps can add up and allow huge amounts of air to move freely in and out of our homes—24 hours a day, 365 days a year. A one-eighth inch wide, six-foot-long crack between a door and a door jamb, for example, is equivalent to a 9-square-inch opening.

On cold winter days, leaks in the building envelope let heated air escape and cold air enter. In the summer, cool, air-conditioned air leaks out of gaps on calm days, while on blustery days, hot air may force its way in through these openings.

Air leakage costs us dearly in higher fuel bills. Most people pay 30% to 50% more to heat and cool their homes than they have to as a result of the leaks in their homes, according to the Energy Star program.

Air movement through walls not only increases heating and cooling costs, it also increases dust levels, which results in more frequent cleaning. Leaks can also impact our health since dust and pollen may aggravate allergies. In addition, leaks allow moisture to enter walls and ceilings, which may condense on insulation and the inside surface of exterior sheathing and drywall. These may become a breeding ground for mold, the spores of which enter our living spaces, triggering allergic reactions and causing a host of other health problems.

But that's not all—water in walls may eventually lead to structural damage, because framing, if kept wet, begins to rot over time. Replacing rotted framing is expensive, as a neighbor of mine recently discovered. After having made his last mortgage payment, he discovered moisture damage in the home's framing members. Fixing the mess cost him a whopping $125,000!

Sealing leaks saves energy, cuts fuel bills, and leads to a healthier, more durable home. This project is about as easy as it gets—and it's one of the least expensive.

How to Seal a Home

To seal leaks, you need to first identify them, a process described in Project 11. If you haven't done so, take a few moments to read it. Once you've found the leaks in your home, either on your own or with the help of a professional energy auditor, you can hire a professional retrofitter to seal them, or you can perform the work yourself. If you choose to go it alone, you'll need some inexpensive supplies and simple tools, including clean rags, rubbing alcohol, a caulk gun, clear or paintable caulk, liquid spray foam (expanding foam), weather stripping, foam gaskets for sockets and light switches, a utility knife or scissors, a screwdriver, and a stepladder.

Sealing Leaks

When sealing a home, the basement and crawl spaces are good places to begin. They are also the most important places to seal because air tends to move into our homes at the lowest openings and exit at the highest points—upper-story rooms or attics.

Start by sealing the largest and most visible cracks in your basement or crawl space, such as broken or missing panes of glass, or gaps around dryer vent exhaust pipes or plumbing. Replace missing or broken panes of glass or install rigid foam insulation over the openings. Gaps like those around dryer vent exhausts can be sealed with caulk or expandable liquid foam, discussed shortly.

Next, seal cracks between the top of the foundation and the wall. These are often so large that light shines through them. Turn off the basement lights and look at the walls from inside to locate gaps, then seal them up with foam or caulk. (You can usually seal cracks from inside, though some may have to be sealed from the outside if they're easier to access that way.)

This is also a good time to insulate the cavity formed by the floor joists and the rim joist. (The floor joists rest on top of the sill. The ends of the joists are attached to the rim joist.) Batt or blanket insulation can be placed into the cavity, or rigid board insulation can be cut to size and friction-fit into the space. Another option is to use expanding foam insulation.

For large cracks, those wider than 3/8" and deeper than 1/2", professionals often use backer rod, a tubular foam that's used to fill large cracks. Backer rod can be purchased in hardware stores. It is stuffed into gaps with a screwdriver or a small putty knife. It's a good idea to vacuum or brush dust and dirt out of openings first.

Liquid foam insulation can also be used to seal large gaps. It is applied via a narrow tube attached to the spray can. The foam quickly expands to fill the gap.

Insulating foam sealant
Courtesy of The Dow Chemical Company.

Once dried, excess can be trimmed off. Exposed foam can also be sanded and painted. Like backer rod, liquid foam seals large openings, preventing air flow, and adds insulation, further reducing heat loss or heat gain.

Liquid foam insulation (also called expanding foam) is available in home improvement centers and hardware stores. Two types are used: polyurethane and latex. Polyurethane expands rapidly and extensively. It sticks to your hands and clothing and is hard to clean up. Latex foam expands less and is a bit easier to clean up.

For openings over a half inch, I use Dow's Great Stuff Big Gap Filler. This polyurethane insulating foam sealant fills, seals, and insulates. For cracks up to a half inch, I use Dow's Great Stuff Gaps and Cracks insulating foam polyurethane sealant. Smaller cracks can also be sealed with a clear or a paintable caulk (if you want the caulk to blend in). Caulk comes in small tubes or cartridges for use in caulk guns. When caulking, cut the plastic tip off the cartridge at an angle (a small opening is better) using a utility knife, then insert the cartridge in the gun, push the plunger forward, and engage it. Then pierce the seal at the tip and advance the plunger. (To save partially used caulk cartridges, you can wrap the tip with electrical tape.)

Caulks come in three basic varieties: (1) pure silicon, (2) a silicon and modified polymer formulation, and (3) latex. Silicon and silicon/modified polymer are the best products. Although they cost a bit more, they're more flexible and can expand and contract with changing temperatures without cracking. This, in turn, means they last longer than the less expensive latex caulks.

Latex caulks are a bit easier to apply, but are less flexible and won't last as long. They should be painted when applied on exterior surfaces to protect them from ultraviolet radiation in sunlight.

When sealing with foam or caulk, be sure to clean the surfaces first. Vacuum or blow dust out, then use a wet rag to remove the remaining particles. Some people wipe the surface with rubbing alcohol (isopropyl alcohol). Once the surface has dried, fill the gap with caulk. I use my finger to smooth the caulk out (or you can smooth it out with the back side of a plastic spoon).

Apply caulk slowly and carefully so you deposit a steady, consistent bead. Smooth it out and wipe up any excess immediately. If you want, you can apply painter's masking tape on both sides of the gap, for example, around windows and doors, for a nice, neat job. I've never found that necessary.

While you're in the basement, be sure to seal gaps in the ceiling that open into the first story. Openings are often cut in the floor to allow plumbing, electrical, and ductwork to pass from the basement to the next level. Cold air can enter your home through these openings, causing considerable discomfort. (They can also allow insects and rodents to access main living areas.)

Be sure to seal heating, cooling, and ventilation ducts that run through the basement, as well as openings in the foundation wall where plumbing pipes exit. When sealing leaky ducts, many heating and air conditioning professionals use mastic sealant, not the cheaper, less durable duct tape or metallic tape. (The only thing duct tape does not stick to is ducts; the adhesive dries, and the tape usually falls off.) Mastic is by far *the* best product on the market for sealing leaky ductwork. Mastic is a paste that's painted over the seams between sections of metal ductwork. It outlasts duct tape and metallic tape and creates an excellent seal. (You can

also use UL-approved butyl-back foil tape like mastic products to seal ducts. The butyl-back tapes expands and contracts, with heating and cooling of ducts like mastic products.)

Unfortunately, duct mastic may be difficult to locate at home improvement centers or hardware stores. When inquiring, tell the retailer that you want mastic for sealing ducts, not laying tile floors. They are entirely different materials. If you have trouble locating mastic, call a professional energy auditor/retrofitter or heating and air conditioning installer and ask them where they purchase theirs.

Basements are filled with openings, so start in one corner and work methodically. After you have sealed the basement, move up to the next level of your home.

Key areas in basements that should be addressed for sealing against air leakage are bulkheads, and crawl space accesses. Drafty by design, most bulkhead doors are made of sheet metal or wood and do not seal tightly; thus they can be a major source of heat loss. The U.S. Department of Energy's weatherization programs specify a basement door to be built at the base of bulkhead stairs. The door frame should be constructed of 2 × 4 lumber. The door should be made of ½" plywood, Z-framed and hinged to the door frame, and insulated with 1" high-R-value board on the basement side. The door should be weather-stripped, including a door sweep. Barrel bolt locks should be installed (one high, one low) to create a tight seal.

Go Green!

One simple, inexpensive way to reduce air leakage is to place an old rolled-up towel or a "draft dodger" against the thresholds of exterior doors. Draft dodgers, popular a few decades ago, are usually sand-filled, snake-shaped sacks, heavy enough to stay in place. They're not as effective as weather stripping, but are better than nothing as a quick, if temporary, remedy.

Sealing Walls, Doors & Windows in Main Living Areas

Walls

Walls in living spaces often have numerous cracks—typically around doors and windows and along baseboards. These openings can usually be sealed with clear or paintable caulk. If the walls are painted, use a paintable caulk, as noted earlier, although clear silicon hardly shows.

Air leakage is very common at the base of walls, so pay special attention to these locations.

Doors & Windows

Exterior doors are also one of the biggest sources of air leakage, which typically occurs between the door and the jamb. These leaks can be sealed with weather stripping. This product comes in several varieties and is usually placed against the door stop, the piece of wood against which a closed door rests—on the top and sides of the finished opening. First remove the old weather stripping and clean the surface well, being sure to remove all remnants. You may want to also wipe the area down with rubbing alcohol to remove remaining residue and dirt.

The cheapest, most widely available, and easiest weather stripping consists of self-adhesive foam strips. Simply cut foam from the roll with a pair of scissors and then apply to clean, dry surfaces. Peel the paper backing to expose the sticky surface, then press in place. Follow the directions on the package. Manufacturers usually recommend applying this product in warmer weather, above 50°F. Although self-adhesive foam is easy to use, in my experience, it doesn't last very long.

Another option is felt weather stripping. It's also relatively inexpensive and easy to apply, but is the least effective in stopping air flow. It also doesn't last as long as other options.

Metal V-strips are a considerably more durable option, for doors. They are nailed down using tacks. Metal V-strips outlast other weather stripping materials, but can be difficult to find. Check hardware stores and home improvement centers. They may have this product in stock or may be able to special order it for you. If not, call a local door and window installer.

Yet another type of door seal is made of durable, UV-resistant, polyethylene bonded to resilient urethane foam. (One brand is Q-Lon.) It seals against air and water infiltration, and paint and varnish does not adhere to it. Many new exterior doors come with this type of weather stripping, though you can also buy kits for retrofitting an existing door.

Tubular rubber and vinyl gaskets are also used to seal doors. A variation of these that I've used on doors in my home is the universal door weather strip manufactured by M-D (Macklanburg-Duncan). It consists of a tubular rubber gasket attached to a metal strip. The metal strip is tacked onto the door jamb stop so that the rubber portion abuts the closed door. This product is easy to install and has worked well for me. I purchased it at a home improvement center.

Windows also often need sealing. In fact, they may account for half or more of the total air leakage in a home. Double-hung windows are notoriously leaky, especially older models. To seal up these windows, use a self-adhesive vinyl V-strip weather stripping. Follow installation directions on the package.

Seal Your Fireplace

Unbeknownst to many of us, a great deal of heat is lost through fireplaces. Many flues do not fully close and therefore allow huge amounts of warm air to escape in the winter. If your flue won't close all the way (you can tell because you can reach up and feel cold air leaking in on winter days), consider installing a "chimney pillow," or "chimney balloon," a device that inflates and seals off the chimney. A small tag on the pillow hangs down into the fireplace reminding you that the chimney is sealed.

Foam weather stripping is widely available and easy to install, but not as durable as other products.
Courtesy of M-D Building Products

Another way to seal leaky windows is with rope caulk, a removable, putty-like cord that comes in a roll. It's applied before the winter sets in, and then removed in the spring, if you want to open the windows. If not, rope caulk can be left in place during the summer to reduce leakage and cut air conditioning costs. It's great for painted windows, but the oil in the caulk that keeps it flexible may stain wood. In Projects 49 to 51, you'll find more ways to address leaky windows, including installation of storm windows and complete replacement.

Air leaks also occur in unusual locations—places you'd never think about checking, for instance, beneath the bathroom vanity where pipes enter and behind kitchen cabinets and cupboards mounted on outside walls. As noted earlier, light switches and electrical outlets, even on interior walls, also leak air.

To seal electrical outlets and light switches, use foam gasket insulators made especially for this purpose, available at hardware stores and home improvement centers. Be sure to turn off the power at the breaker

box before you remove the screws holding the cover plate in place. Then insert a foam gasket and replace the cover plate. You can block the slots in electrical outlets that are not being used by inserting child-safety plugs.

Attic Doors & Ceilings

When sealing a home, be sure to check the attic access door. Often located in back hallways or inside closets, these openings (whether with fold-down stairs or just a plywood hatch cover) are usually uninsulated and unsealed. They're a major source of air leakage. Using a stepladder, remove the access panel. If uninsulated, glue a two- to four-inch layer of rigid polystyrene foam on the upper surface. (Blanket insulation is a poor choice for this application because it's difficult to hold it in place.)

Most home improvement centers sell 4 × 8 foot, and half sheets of rigid foam insulation. Pink board or blue board offer the highest R-value per inch of the polystyrene products and are easy to cut. After

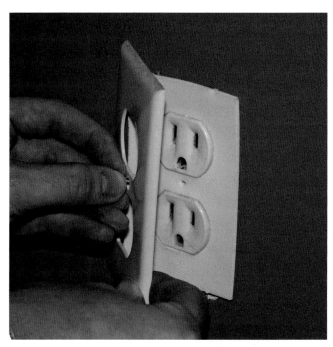

Foam gaskets for outlets and switches help to reduce energy bills.
Photographed by Kimberly Potvin

attaching the foam, apply a layer of self-adhesive foam weather stripping along the perimeter of the access hatch that rests in the opening. If your attic access is through a pull-down staircase, you can purchase a cover for it at hardware stores or home improvement centers.

You can also weather-strip knee-wall access hatches. Apply foam weather strip to the inside of the hatch along the perimeter. Thumb locks or barrel bolts can be used to create a tighter seal as well.

As a final note, be sure to check other openings in the ceiling for leakage. Recessed ceiling light fixtures are notorious for leakage. Leaky cans should probably be replaced with new, air-tight recessed light fixtures, a job you may want to delegate to a professional electrician. Whole-house fans are also notorious sources of air leakage. Buy or make an airtight fabric cover to place over the opening in the winter, when it is not in use.

What to Watch Out For

Because most of our homes have leaks in places where we might not even think to look, it's usually worth the extra money to hire a professional to inspect and seal a home. An energy auditor may seal the house while the blower door test device is running, so they know exactly where the leaks are. They also typically measure air leakage before and after they seal the house to assess how well they've sealed your home.

When shopping for caulk, don't save a buck or two by purchasing a cheap product. You want this stuff to last, and the more expensive caulk will outlast less expensive ones!

Many people worry that sealing up a home will cause problems with indoor air pollution. This is rarely a problem in older homes. They're so leaky that efforts to seal them, while effective, typically won't make a house so airtight that indoor air pollution becomes a problem. If you're concerned, seal your home, but take steps to

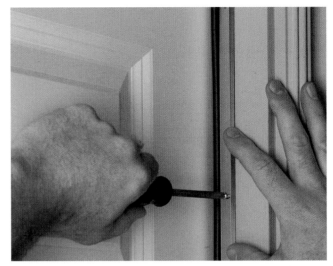

Universal door jamb weather stripping
Courtesy of M-D Building Products

prevent indoor air pollutants. For example, avoid the use of potentially toxic chemicals such as hair sprays, paints containing volatile organic compounds (VOCs), building materials with formaldehyde, cigarette smoke, perfumes, and chemical cleaning agents. Run the bathroom ceiling fan while bathing or showering and after you're done for at least 30 minutes (when windows are closed in the winter). By taking these steps, you can minimize problems with indoor air quality. (The cost of running a fan is pretty minimal.)

When sealing up your home, you also want to be sure that there's ample air to feed combustion appliances, such as natural gas or propane water heaters and furnaces. Again, this is rarely a problem. If you hire a professional to run a blower door test before and after sealing up the home, he or she can address this issue.

What Will It Cost?

The cost of this project varies widely depending on the size of your home, its age and condition, and whether you do the job yourself or hire a professional. You will need a variety of products, as mentioned throughout this project. Individually, many of them, such as weather stripping tape or a can of foam sealant, cost $5 or less. To figure out material quantities, measure and add the dimensions of cracks and window and door perimeters that need to be weather-stripped, allowing a little extra for waste.

Cost Estimate: Installation of caulking and weather-stripping for a 2,500 square foot home

This estimate of cost includes all windows, doors and vertical trim boards, assuming there is no caulking already in place. (Generally, the only time this amount of caulking and weather stripping has to be applied is when the exterior of a home is repainted. If only some areas need replacing on your home, the job, and the cost, will be smaller.) The estimate also includes installation of vinyl weather stripping and door sweeps.

Cost for materials only: **$150**

Contractor's total, including materials, labor, and markup: **$750**

Costs are national averages and do not include sales tax.
If you have one contractor do several small projects, you'll save money overall.

What Will You Save?

Sealing a home can result in savings in heating and cooling, ranging from as little as 5% to 10% in a house that's already well sealed—to as much as 30% to 40% or even more; it all depends on how leaky the house was in the first place.

Project 13

Insulating Your Home

Few of us would go outdoors on a cold winter day for hours on end without a warm coat. But many of us live in homes that are, for all intents and purposes, standing out in the cold, day after day and night after frigid night, with nothing more than a light sweater on. Inside our under-insulated homes on cold winter days, we either freeze or crank up the heat to make up for the lack of insulation. Turning up the heat, of course, costs us dearly in fuel bills.

This project outlines ways to assess the insulation levels in your home and explains how to beef them up if you find they're inadequate. If you live in a cold climate, these steps can save you a fortune on your heating bills. However, they're just as important for those of us who live in hot climates where air conditioning costs can be even higher than heating bills in colder regions.

What Are Your Options?

When insulating a home, no part of the building envelope—that barrier between you and your family and the great outdoors—should be ignored. In addition to the attic and walls, you may need to add insulation on the inside of the foundation walls and the underside of the bottom floor of your house above unheated or cool spaces such as crawl spaces or basements. Not all parts of the building envelope require the same type or amount of insulation.

In new construction, attics and ceilings are typically insulated with fiberglass blankets (rolls) or batts—or loose-fill insulation, such as cellulose (recycled newspaper) or fiberglass blown into the spaces between framing members. In some new homes, attics and ceilings are insulated with a spray foam product. This material is sprayed between framing members

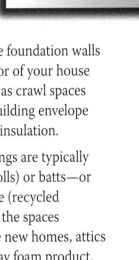

Homes in both hot and cold climates should be well insulated.
Photos by Dan Chiras

as a liquid, which quickly expands and dries, filling the cavities and creating a tightly sealed and insulated space.

Because hot air rises, and because the roof represents a huge surface area exposed to the cold in the winter, attic and ceiling insulation typically needs to have the highest R-value. (R-value is a measure of the ability of a wall or ceiling to resist heat movement; the higher the R-value, the greater a material's ability to reduce heat loss.) The roof is also a source of significant heat gain in the summer, so insulation in the attic or ceiling helps to reduce cooling costs as well.

In newer homes, walls are insulated similarly, that is, with blankets, batts, loose-fill, and/or liquid foam insulation products. Floors over heated spaces, such as finished basements, are typically not insulated unless sound-proofing is required. Floors over unheated spaces, such as unfinished basements or crawl spaces, are usually insulated with fiberglass batts. Foundations in new housing are insulated with rigid foam board, typically made from polystyrene.

In older homes, the story is quite different. Foundations and floors, especially over crawl spaces, are rarely insulated. Walls of living spaces are often woefully under-insulated or not insulated at all. Attics tend to be the one spot you'll find insulation in an older home, though even these are typically under-insulated.

If you live in an older home, even one built as recently as 1980, chances are it's under-insulated. The lack of insulation, combined with rising utility rates, could easily explain your high utility bills. Even in newer homes, insulation levels tend to be well below those required for optimal comfort and efficiency.

Why Insulate?

Adding insulation greatly improves a home's energy efficiency, reduces fuel use and energy bills, and increases comfort. It's one of the most cost-effective measures a homeowner can take to save energy and money. And, like other energy-saving measures, it has huge environmental benefits! The less energy your home consumes, the less pollution will be produced from power plants, and the cleaner the skies and

healthier the environment for all living beings—you and your family included.

Assessing Insulation Levels in Your Home

Before adding insulation, you need to find out what you have in place now. You'll also need to seal the cracks in the building envelope before you insulate (Project 12). Failing to seal air leaks can reduce the value of your insulation efforts. In fact, even a tiny amount of moisture entering the walls or ceilings through unsealed openings can decrease the R-value of many types of insulation by half. If you hire an energy auditor, he or she will assess your home's insulation needs and will make recommendations on the proper amount and types for the different parts of your home.

The Attic

To check the level of insulation, begin in the attic, the most likely place you'll find insulation. It is also the easiest to retrofit and one of the most important locations to insulate, as noted earlier. Most attics can be accessed through an opening in the ceiling, a door hatch or pull-down stairs, usually in a back hallway or a closet. Tools that will help you in this project include a stepladder, flashlight, probe, ruler, screwdriver, hole saw, dust mask or respirator, and proper eye protection.

With a ruler, measure the depth of the insulation and note what type you have. You'll most likely find fiberglass, either in blankets or loose fill. If you have roll- or blanket-type insulation, pull up a piece and look at the backing. It should have the R-value printed on it. Record this number on your notepad. In very old homes, you may find loose, brownish material known

Go Green!

When shopping for a new home, look for one whose long axis runs east to west and whose south side has plenty of shade-free windows in winter to allow the low-angled sun to naturally heat the home.

as vermiculite. Be careful, as vermiculite is sometimes contaminated with hazardous asbestos. (Call an insulation specialist when in doubt.)

If the attic is finished living area, you may need to remove a floor board or cut a small hole in the floor to check the insulation between the ceiling joists. If your finished attic has a cathedral ceiling, insulation may have been applied between the roof rafters overhead, under the sheetrock. If the ceiling is finished, you may need to remove a ceiling light fixture to check for insulation. Be sure to turn the power off to this circuit beforehand. (Test an outlet on the circuit by plugging in a lamp or other small device that you know is working, or by using a voltmeter—whenever you are planning to perform a task involving electrical wiring.)

Outer Walls

After assessing the ceiling insulation, turn your attention to the outer walls of your living spaces—the bedrooms, living room, dining room, and so on. The easiest way to check insulation in these walls is to remove the cover plates on a few electrical outlets or light switches located on outside walls in different parts of the home. First turn off the circuit to the outlet or switch. Peek into the wall cavity to check for insulation.

Using a wooden ruler, pencil, or wood skewer, probe the wall cavity next to the outlet or light switch to see if it's insulated. If the probe passes through the cavity without resistance, there's no insulation in that part of the wall. If you run into some resistance, it's insulated. Bear in mind, however, that electricians sometimes trim the insulation away from electrical outlets and light switches (for fire safety). Even though you may not encounter insulation near a light switch or electrical outlet, it doesn't mean the rest of the wall is uninsulated. Professional energy auditors and insulators often drill a small hole in an out-of-the-way place, for example, in a closet against an outside wall. They use a hole saw to cut the holes, and then special wall plugs from an insulation supply company to repair the damage after making their inspection.

Crawl Spaces and Basements

If your home is built over a crawl space or unheated basement, check the insulation under the floor from below. If you're lucky, the builder or previous owner has applied some insulation batts between the floor joists. Make sure there's a vapor barrier (plastic or paper backing) on the fiberglass batts. If the spaces between the floor joists are not insulated, measure the depth of the joists (so that you know the thickness of the batts you need to purchase).

Next, check the foundation insulation. Begin by looking at the exterior of the foundation wall for rigid foam that may be applied to it. You may need to dig a little, but do so carefully so as not to damage insulation that may be there. Chances are, you won't find any.

If your home has a basement, insulation may have been applied to its inside walls. Interior insulation is common in finished basements and is applied in the space between framing members attached to the foundation wall (behind the drywall or paneling). As mentioned earlier, you can remove a few electrical cover plates to check. Once again, make sure to turn off the power to the circuit first.

Installing Insulation in Your Home

If parts of your home are uninsulated or under-insulated, you'll need to determine how much insulation to add. The easiest way to do this is to hire a professional insulation contractor who will recommend the amount and install it. If you want to

Go Green!

In the summer, turn the thermostat up a little at night and when you're away from your home or apartment. In the winter, turn the heat down a little when you're sleeping or away. This easy adjustment can make a substantial dent in your heating and cooling costs. If you have trouble remembering, consider installing a programmable thermostat (Project 15).

do the project yourself, you can call your local building department and ask them for their recommendations. For attics, the current standard in most parts of the United States is around R-30 to R-38—which translates into 10 to 14 inches of insulation, depending on the material. Energy-smart builders often exceed these recommendations by at least 30% to 50%.

You can also log on to the EPA's Energy Star website to check recommendations for your area. This site provides a map of temperature zones with an accompanying table that lists recommended R-values for walls and ceilings.

Another option is to log on to the Zip Code Insulation Program website sponsored by the Department of Energy. After entering your zip code, the site will make recommendations for insulating your home: **http://www.ornl.gov/~roofs/ZIP/ZipHome.html**

The Attic

When insulating an attic, you can use fiberglass batts or blown-in insulation. For blown-in cellulose insulation (with an R-value of about 3.5 per inch), you can hire a professional or rent or borrow a blower from a local home improvement center. (They often lend blowers to homeowners who purchase a certain amount of cellulose insulation from them.) Cellulose insulation is an environmentally friendly product made from recycled newspaper and wood fiber.

If you choose to lay fiberglass blankets over the existing insulation, and the old insulation comes to the top of the ceiling joists, lay the new insulation perpendicular to the joists, covering them entirely. (If you need to walk around in your attic in the future, you can always peel back the top layer of insulation in that area so you can see where the joists lie, so as not to step through the ceiling below. Yet another approach is to blow liquid foam insulation between the rafters (the framing members that support the roof deck). This is a job for a professional.

Walls

To insulate exterior walls, you can also "fur out" the wall using 2 × 4s, 2 × 6s, or smaller furring strips, that is, apply framing lumber to the inside of the walls to create spaces to add insulation. You can then install cellulose, fiberglass blankets or batts, or spray-in liquid foam insulation between the furring strips. Once the insulation is in place, new drywall or paneling is attached to the framing. This method can be used on all walls and is especially applicable to solid brick and concrete block walls, but it is a job best handled by professionals.

If you'd like to use rigid foam insulation, which has the highest R-value per inch, you can attach the material directly to the wall, then secure new drywall over it, using long drywall screws. While effective, these techniques reduce interior space, making rooms a bit smaller. Base and ceiling moldings, as well as window and door trim, will also have to be removed and reinstalled.

If your walls are not insulated, professional installers can blow cellulose insulation into the stud cavities through 2-inch holes drilled every 16 inches in the siding or the interior wall surface at the top and bottom of the walls. Another option is to spray liquid foam

Cellulose insulation blown into attics helps reduce heating and cooling costs and increases year-round comfort.

Courtesy of Cellulose Insulation Manufacturers Association (CIMA)

insulation into wall cavities through small holes drilled in the wall. This type of insulation generally does a better job of filling spaces than cellulose, especially in older homes with plaster-on-lathe walls. Both of these are jobs that should be done by an experienced installer—one who can also patch up the holes when the job's done.

While attics are relatively easy to insulate, walls can be quite difficult. If the space between framing members is already filled or partially filled with insulation, it is difficult to blow in additional loose-fill material. Your best option in this case is to apply rigid foam insulation to the interior or exterior surface of the wall. On the outside, rigid foam insulation can be attached directly to existing siding. New siding can then be installed over the insulation. Of course, window and door openings will have to be extended ("re-trimmed") to adjust for the thicker wall. Insulating this way is a good idea if you are planning to re-side your home anyway, but it is a job best left to professionals. (Be sure that the installer takes steps to prevent moisture from accumulating between the old siding and the insulation.)

Floors

If your home's floors lie over unconditioned space (that is, an unheated and uncooled area like a crawl space), and the floor is not insulated, it's a good idea to insulate it. (Do not insulate walls in a crawl space that is damp or ventilated with outdoor air.) This will keep you and your family much more comfortable and lower your heating bills. A college professor friend of mine who lives in rural western New York recently installed insulation under the floor of his 100-year-old farmhouse upon my recommendation. He reported a 10-degree increase in interior temperature at the same setting as before (with the heat running) and a dramatic increase in comfort.

Batt insulation can be installed between the floor joists beneath the finished floor. Although effective, this is not the most pleasant task since you'll be working in a dark, damp, and dirty space for quite a while—probably around obstacles like water and sewer pipes, electrical wires, and heating and cooling ducts.

To hold batts in place, use metal insulation supports. Use paper- or foil-backed batts under floors. The backing serves as a vapor (moisture) barrier. In cold climates, the vapor barrier side of the insulation batt should be against the floor to prevent moisture from the house from penetrating the insulation. In warm climates, the vapor barrier should face down toward the basement or crawl space to prevent moisture from those areas from entering the insulation. (In cold climates, moist air tends to move from the home's interior to the outside; in moist, warm climates, moisture moves in the opposite direction.)

After installing insulation batts in a crawl space, lay 6-mil polyethylene plastic sheeting over the dirt floor to reduce the amount of moisture entering the space. Tape or otherwise attach the plastic to the foundation wall. Doing so will help to keep the insulation dry and will help retain its R-value.

For uninsulated basements, it is best to install insulation against the concrete foundation walls on the inside—so long as they are dry. Never insulate walls that are soaked by moisture from the ground outside

Environmentally Friendly Insulation Options

When insulating, use environment- and people-friendly products. Cellulose, for instance, is made from recycled newspaper and wood fiber. Some types of fiberglass insulation are made from recycled glass. And some fiberglass insulation batts are encapsulated to prevent workers from inhaling the fibers. Some manufacturers are using safer binders that replace formaldehyde resin in fiberglass batt insulation. Many of the rigid foam insulation products are no longer made with ozone-depleting chemicals.

There are also a number of new products you may want to consider, including cotton batt insulation (made from waste from blue-jean factories), loose-fill wool insulation, and liquid foam insulation made from chemicals derived from soy.

Fiberglass batt insulation (with backing) installed in the floor over unconditioned (unheated or uncooled) spaces can reduce bills substantially.

Courtesy of Johns Manville

the home. Moisture creates a breeding ground for mold and mildew. Always fix moisture problems *before* you insulate. This may require some regrading—sloping the ground around your home away from the foundation so water flows away from the basement. It may also require installation of new gutters and downspouts or repair or replacement of old, leaky ones. It's always a good idea to install downspout extenders, pipes that attach to the downspouts and carry water six or more feet from your home. If these measures don't solve the problem, you may want to hire a foundation specialist to correct it (Projects 53 and 54).

Insulation can be applied to the inside of the basement/foundation walls much the same way it's applied to the inside of walls in the main living space, as described previously. (You don't have to cover the insulation with drywall unless you're planning to finish the basement.) While you need to correct any moisture problems first, you should also choose a type of insulation that's impervious to moisture, such as liquid or rigid foam.

What to Watch Out For

Installing insulation can present challenges for beginners and even experienced do-it-yourselfers. If you're working in the attic, pick a cool day. When walking about in the attic, be careful to step on the ceiling joists. Stepping between them could send you through the ceiling into the living space below and result in a major repair job of the ceiling—and you! It's best to take some lightweight planks (e.g., 1 x 6) into the attic, if the space is unfinished and the joists are exposed (not covered with plywood flooring). Place the planks perpendicular to and across the joists to create more places to step.

If your attic is inadequately lighted, find a way to provide good lighting for the job, such as a couple of reliable shop, or "trouble" lights. (You can even get cordless LED work lights for super energy efficiency, longevity, and convenience.)

You should wear eye protection and a respirator or a high-quality face dust mask when applying insulation—especially cellulose and fiberglass products—to prevent inhaling dust and fibers. When working with fiberglass, wear a long-sleeved shirt, long pants, and gloves to protect your skin.

Do not apply insulation over old or frayed wiring. If your home is older than 20 to 30 years, check with the building department to see if the wiring needs to be brought up to code before insulating. Do not apply insulation against light fixtures (cans for recessed lights) that penetrate the ceiling if they are not rated for insulation contact (and most are not), or against flues from wood stoves. Doing so could cause a fire.

When insulating an attic, do not cover the soffit vents, openings on the underside of the eaves (roof overhang), if you have them. These vents allow air to circulate from the outside into the attic, then out through a roof or gable-end vents. This circulation removes moisture that may collect in the insulation from the living space below. To optimize air flow through the soffit vents, install plastic rafter vents. They create an air channel that allows air to flow between the soffit vents and the attic.

If you notice stains in ceilings, mold in insulation, or even rotting wood in your attic, this is an indication that the roof is leaking. Get it fixed *before* you insulate! If existing insulation is wet, remove it, fix the leak, and then install new insulation.

Finally, when installing fiberglass insulation, don't compress it. This lowers its R-value. Also, don't leave gaps between insulation and framing members.

What Will It Cost?

The cost of this project will depend on the levels of insulation you already have in your home, how much you need to add, and whether you do the job yourself or hire an installer. There are a couple of helpful websites with charts indicating how much R-value you need for the insulation in various parts of your home, based on your location and climate, and the type of heating and cooling system you have. http://www. eere.energy.gov/consumer/tips/insulation.html and http://www.energystar.gov/index.cfm

Cost Estimate: Installation of unfaced R-38 fiberglass floor and attic ceiling insulation

Includes supports and rafter vents for a 2,500 square foot, two-story home

Cost for materials only: **$2,400**

Contractor's total, including materials, labor, and markup: **$5,500**

Insulation options, costs per square foot installed:

Fiberglass	Cellulose
R-13: **$.84**	R-13: **$.58**
R-19: **$.92**	R-19: **$.80**
R-30: **$1.42**	R-22: **$1.04**
R-38: **$1.69**	

Costs are national averages and do not include sales tax.

What Will You Save?

Insulation substantially increases energy efficiency. It is even more effective when coupled with weatherization. Savings in energy costs range widely from 5% to as much as 50% or even 75%, depending on how leaky and under-insulated the home is. With rising fuel costs, this project becomes a more and more attractive investment and will add to a home's resale value.

Project 14

Insulate While You Paint

Insulating and sealing your home to improve energy efficiency (Projects 12 and 13) and reduce energy consumption can save a substantial amount of money. While adding insulation to attics is usually pretty straightforward and fairly inexpensive, adding insulation to finished walls can be much more difficult and costly.

If your walls are uninsulated or under-insulated, or you don't have an attic and can't easily add insulation to your ceiling, here is one way you can improve energy efficiency. Repaint walls with a paint containing an insulating additive. These additives are available online from several companies, among them, Insuladd® and Hy-Tech Thermal Solutions®. Additives can be mixed with ordinary interior or exterior paints. Or you can buy premixed insulating paint from the same companies.

How Does It Work?

Insulating paint additives consist of a fine, white powder containing hollow ceramic microspheres, developed by researchers at NASA for use in spacecraft. When mixed into paint, the microspheres form a tightly packed layer that minimizes the transfer of heat through a wall.

In exterior paints, the microspheres reduce summer heat flow *into* a home, making it more comfortable and cutting cooling costs. In the winter, insulated paint applied to interior ceilings and walls keeps heat from moving *out* of your home, again saving on fuel bills, according to manufacturers. Besides reducing energy use and energy bills and making our homes more comfortable, insulating paint additives are nontoxic and easy to use. They deaden

Insuladd insulating paint additive is used in exterior and interior paints to lower heating and cooling costs.

Courtesy of Tech Traders, Inc. "The Insuladd Company"

sounds, resist mold growth, and increase fire-resistance of walls. The painted surface is easy to clean, and lasts longer than conventional paints.

Insulating paint additives can also be used in attics, basements, and even on roofs. They can be used on the outside of metal buildings to improve their energy performance. If you live in a mobile or prefabricated home that needs an insulation upgrade, this product could work well. To view test data and learn more about Insuladd, log onto the company's website (**www.insuladd.com**). To learn more about Hy-Tech Insulating paint additives, visit: **www.hytechsales.com**

Application

Applying insulating paint is one of the easiest projects you can undertake—and yields some of the greatest energy savings. Simply brush, roll, or spray on the premixed paint, or mix the additive into the paint of your choice, preferably an environment- and people-friendly paint product such as those described in Project 9.

Because insulating paint additives come in powder form, be sure to remove all filters from spray equipment before use. Otherwise, the filters will remove the additive from the paint during application. When applying paint with a sprayer, manufacturers recommend the use of a larger-than-normal spray tip to allow maximum coverage and boost the insulation value of your walls.

Use one package of insulating paint additive for each gallon of paint. For larger projects, you may want to purchase a 5-, 10-, 25-, or 50-gallon kit to save money. I've used both brands with three no-VOC interior house paints, Bioshield, Safecoat, and Sherwin-Williams Harmony in my house. I found that insulating paint additives mixed well with all three paints and did not settle out. Paints containing the additives went on the walls well, but were a bit thicker than "unadulterated" paint. The finished walls feel a little rougher than when painted with ordinary wall paint.

For best results, the manufacturers recommend two coats of paint. Applying more than two coats will result in only a marginal increase in performance. Remember: when applying an insulating paint to interior walls, you only need to paint the walls and ceilings facing the outside where heat losses could occur. You can paint over paint that contains additives if you want to change the room color, although this will slightly decrease the insulating effect.

Go Green!

- To save energy, close curtains, shades, and blinds on cold nights. You can lose up to 20% of your heat through uncovered windows. If your home does not have window coverings, consider installing insulated shades or curtains (Project 16).

- Never discard paint cans containing wet paint. Open the lid outside, and let the paint dry. It can then be safely disposed of. Check with your town's waste management program for instructions for disposing of paint and other hazardous materials.

The exterior of a two-story brick and masonite home located in Lexington, KY was painted in April 2001 with INSULADD. The data was taken from copies of utility bills supplied by the homeowner from the utility company (KU). Electrical usage shows primary air-conditioning months. Energy savings are 12% over the previous year. (This figure would even be greater if adjusted for the hotter summer temperatures of 2001.)

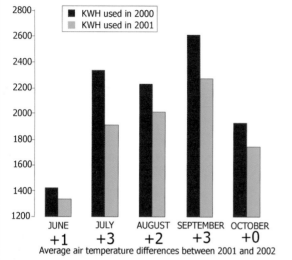

Average air temperature differences between 2001 and 2002

Electricity used in a home with and without insulating paint

Courtesy of Tech Traders, Inc. "The Insuladd Company"

Shopping Guide

Both Hy-Tech and Insuladd offer a number of insulating paints and sealants in addition to their paint additives. Hy-Tech, for instance, manufactures interior and exterior wall paints for wood, stucco, and cement board. They also manufacture clear sealants for wood, stone, stucco, and concrete.

Insuladd also offers a number of interior and exterior paints and sealants for different applications. Their Insuladd E-Coat IX, for instance, is an insulating, heat-reflecting satin-finish paint for interior and exterior walls. It can be applied to a variety of metals, wood, and masonry products such as stucco, and even roof tiles and shingles.

Putting Insulating Paint Additives to the Test

To test the performance of these products, a friend's daughter and I conducted a science project together. We first painted the insides of two cardboard boxes, one with ordinary household paint and another with an insulating paint additive. We then placed temperature sensors and heat sources in each box and closed them off. We measured temperature rise for 40 minutes and found that the temperature inside the box painted with insulating paint additive was consistently more than 10°F higher, proving that the paint is indeed an effective insulator.

What Will It Cost?

A package of insulating additive for one gallon of paint costs about $12 to $15. You can buy the premixed paints for about $30 per gallon, when purchasing five gallons at a time, but need to also allow for shipping costs.

Cost Estimate: Professional surface preparation and painting

Two coats of paint (with an insulating additive) to the exterior and outermost interior walls of a 2,500 square foot home. Includes siding, trim, doors, windows, walls, and ceilings.

Cost for materials only: **$1,300**

Contractor's total, including materials, labor, and markup: **$8,100**

Costs are national averages and do not include sales tax.

Project 15 Programmable Thermostat

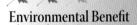

Some people keep the thermostat in their homes set at a constant level, day in and day out, thinking that maintaining a consistent temperature saves energy. The reality is that most homes take only 15 to 30 minutes to heat up or cool down, so running the air conditioning or heating system at the same temperature 24 hours a day can waste a lot of energy—and costs a lot of money. It's a little like keeping a kettle running on the stove 24-hours a day in case you might like a hot drink sometime during the day! Homeowners can of course control heating and cooling by manually changing the thermostat as they come and go—or before they head off to sleep. But even the most conscientious person can forget at times.

To simplify your life and save energy, consider installing a programmable thermostat. These devices monitor and control heating and cooling systems automatically, based on your schedule. For example, they can be programmed to turn down the heat at night a half hour before you and your family head off to bed, say to $55°F$ to $60°F$, and then turn it back up to $68°F$ to $70°F$ a half hour before you awaken. You can also program your thermostat to turn the heat down again as you and your family head off to work and school, then turn it up again a half hour before you arrive home. Programmable thermostats can also be used to control air conditioning. You can even program in a separate weekend setting. Programmable thermostats typically come with a manual override, so you can set the temperature differently on days when your routine changes.

Home improvement centers and hardware stores carry a variety of programmable thermostats ranging in price from about $50 to over $250. Features vary, so shop carefully, and for best performance, select an Energy Star®-rated thermostat.

Programmable thermostats are easy to install and can reduce your energy bills by 10% or more per year, if properly programmed. They're also good for the environment—less energy use means less environmental pollution from power plants, especially greenhouse gas emissions.

Convenience is a great feature of these thermostats, since you'll no longer need to adjust the temperature when going to bed or leaving the house. And lastly, your heating and air conditioning equipment won't run as often, meaning less noise and reduced wear and tear—which results in lower maintenance, repair, and replacement costs.

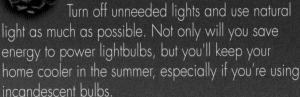

Go Green!

Turn off unneeded lights and use natural light as much as possible. Not only will you save energy to power lightbulbs, but you'll keep your home cooler in the summer, especially if you're using incandescent bulbs.

Programmable thermostats come in many models. Chooose one that is easy to program.

Courtesy of Honeywell International, Inc.

Installation

Installing a programmable thermostat normally takes about 20 to 30 minutes. You'll need a screwdriver, wire cutter/stripper, drill with 3/16" drill bit, and a level. Follow the manufacturer's printed instructions.

First, shut off the power to the circuit to which the thermostat is to be connected *and* circuits for the furnace or boiler and air conditioner. Warn household members, and tape off the fuse or circuit breaker. Adjust the thermostat setting way up or way down to see if the heat or AC kicks in, depending on which setting it's turned to. If it switches on, you have not shut off the correct circuit breaker.

With the power switch shut off, remove the cover (typically on a mounting plate attached to the wall) from the old thermostat. If wires are screwed into terminals in the front of the plate, disconnect them. The wires should be color-coded—for example red and white. If not, the terminals should be labeled.

Disconnect the wires, one at a time. If not color-coded, label them (with the same markings on the terminal) using masking tape. Now remove the back plate, making sure the wires don't slide into the wall. (To prevent this, roll the wires around a pencil.)

If there are no wires attached to terminals on the face of the back plate, the connections are on the back. To access them, remove the screws that attach the wall plate to the wall. If color-coded, you're in good shape. If not, label the wires (which terminal they're attached to) *before* you unscrew them.

After removing the wall plate, lay out holes for the new thermostat using the template provided by the manufacturer. If there's no template, use the back plate of the new thermostat and mark the location of the new screw holes with a pencil.

Drill holes according to the manufacturer's specifications and insert the plastic anchors provided with the thermostat. They're required to hold the screws in plaster and drywall. (You won't need them if you can drill into a wall stud, but this is unlikely.) Insert the plastic anchors carefully. Now attach the back plate of the programmable thermostat to the wall by driving the screws into either the plastic anchors or the studs. Attach the wires to the terminals.

Install batteries in the new thermostat for backup power to protect the program in case of a power failure, then attach the cover and turn the power back on. Program it according to the manufacturer's directions.

Installation Tip

The number of wires attached to a thermostat varies. If the thermostat controls only a heating system, you'll find two wires. If it controls a furnace and a central air conditioner, there will be more wires. They should be color-coded, or the screws to which they're attached should be labeled.

What to Watch Out For

Before you head out to buy a new thermostat, be sure to check the number and type of wires that are attached to the old one so you know what type to purchase (that is, a high-voltage or low-voltage thermostat). You'll have to remove the faceplate from the wall to do this. (Once again, be sure to turn the power off first.)

If the wires are thin and come directly out of the wall, they're usually carrying low-voltage current. Low-voltage thermostats are typically used for forced-air, baseboard hot water, and radiant floor heating systems. With proper precautions, this should be a relatively safe job for an experienced do-it-yourselfer.

If your home is heated by an electric baseboard heater, however, the situation may be different. The thermostat is operating off of 120 volts of electricity, which can cause a significant shock. Don't try to replace the thermostat yourself unless you've had significant experience with electrical wiring. Hire a professional.

Shopping Tips

Features to look for in a programmable thermostat:

- ☑ Storage capacity—ability to store multiple settings; most programmable thermostats offer six settings, including weekday/weekend programs.
- ☑ Manual override—allows overriding settings without affecting the daily or weekly program.
- ☑ Battery backup—to save the program in case of a power outage.
- ☑ Easy-to-read and logical digital display.
- ☑ Temperature accuracy—within one degree.
- ☑ Good instructions—Easy to follow and printed on the inside cover of the unit, so you don't need to consult the owner's manual for programming.

Old thermostats may have a sealed tube containing mercury, a hazardous substance. Contact your town's waste management agency to obtain instructions for proper disposal.

What Will It Cost?

Programmable thermostats cost anywhere from $50 to $250, depending on the features. Thermostats designed to work with heat pumps cost more because of the requirement for two-stage heating.

Cost Estimate: Installation of a new programmable thermostat

Cost for materials only: **$120** (mid-priced unit)

Contractor's total, including materials, labor, and markup: **$210**

Costs are national averages and do not include sales tax. If you have an electrician do more than one project in one visit, you'll save money overall.

What Will You Save?

A programmable thermostat can easily pay for itself within a year. Every degree a thermostat is set back over an eight-hour period will cut your heating bill by about 1%. If you turn down the heat 5 degrees at night, for example, you can cut your bill by 5%. Turning it down 10 degrees during the day while you're at work will cut the bill an additional 5%.

Go Green!

- Whenever possible, use rechargeable batteries. They have economic and environmental benefits compared to disposable batteries. They cost more and can have more toxic ingredients than disposable batteries, but can be recharged many times, resulting in less toxic landfill waste overall. Manufacturers of some NiMH rechargeable batteries claim these can be recharged up to 3,000 times.

- Some used thermostats can be donated to used building materials outlet stores.

Project 16

Insulated Shades & Curtains

Windows are a major contributor to high energy bills. In the winter, they allow heat to escape, driving up utility bills. In the summer, they let hot air in, increasing cooling costs. Fortunately, there is something you can do to reduce this waste of energy without having to invest in expensive replacement windows: install insulated curtains or shades.

This is a simple, effective way to block the flow of heat out of windows in cold winter weather, especially at night, and reduce unwanted heat gain in warm weather. With a tug on the cord, you can cut energy use, sometimes substantially, and increase your home's comfort. And anytime you reduce power use, you help lower environmental pollution caused by power plants.

Window shades come in many varieties, and almost any product you choose will help reduce energy use and increase comfort. Even mini blinds are better than no window coverings at all. However, for maximum benefit, consider installing one of several types of insulated shades or curtains.

Cellular shades are the most widely available insulated shade on the market (see photo on right). Also known as honeycomb shades, they come in single-, double-, or triple-cell styles and half a dozen different pleat sizes, ranging from 3/8 inch to 1-1/4 inch. Generally, the more cells, the higher the insulation value.

Cellular shades are typically installed over windows, but also work well on French doors, sliding glass doors, and skylights. Many manufacturers offer top-down, bottom-up opening options, which allow you to open the shades

Cellular shades' honeycomb construction reduces heat loss in the winter and heat again in the summer—saving energy and cutting utility bills.
Courtesy of Gordon's Window Décor and SymphonyShades.com

Top-down, bottom-up cellular shades over French doors and windows help keep you warm in the winter and cool in the summer.

Courtesy of Gordon's Window Décor and SymphonyShades.com

either from the bottom, as in a conventional window shade, or from the top down for light and views with some privacy. This feature is especially useful in south-facing windows, because it allows you to block the late summer/early fall sun, to prevent overheating, while still allowing some light to come in. Cellular shade fabrics and colors can be selected to filter incoming light a little or a lot, or to block light entirely.

Cellular shades can be purchased from curtain retailers, some department stores, and home improvement centers. Most of these outlets offer installation. You can also purchase cellular shades online from a rather mind-boggling list of vendors. When ordering, be sure to provide accurate window measurements, taken according to the retailer's instructions.

Another type of insulating shade is made by the Warm Company. This product is composed of two layers of insulating material (polyester batting) with a layer of mylar in between. These layers are sandwiched between two layers of fabric—an inside layer (provided by the manufacturer) and an outside decorative fabric that

Go Green!

Putting on a sweater, or even long underwear, indoors allows you to stay comfortable while turning down the thermostat, saving energy and helping protect the environment.

Warm Window shades dramatically reduce heat loss in the winter.
Courtesy of The Warm Company

materials needed to fabricate and install shades. The company also sells a DVD with instructions, and fabric stores often carry a complete line of accessories needed to make curtains.

If you're not up to the task, you may be able to hire a professional to custom make Warm Window shades for your home (call local curtain suppliers for referrals). You can also purchase premade window quilts from The company's other website (**www.1windowquilts.com**). Many of their insulated window shades are mounted on a roller. The edges of the shade are attached to a tracking system that creates a very tight seal. (The shades clean easily by vacuuming or using a spray-on upholstery cleaner.)

Plow and Hearth and other Internet suppliers also offer a variety of insulated shades and curtains, including some attractive insulated Roman shades. Some insulated curtains come with one or two layers of acrylic foam insulation backing.

Installation

To install cellular shades, you'll need screwdrivers (flat and Phillips-head), a cordless drill, a pencil and tape measure, a 1/4" hex nut driver, and a level. Consult the manufacturer's information for special tools you may need.

you select to go with your décor and the color scheme of your home.

Potentially more effective at blocking heat than many cellular shades, Warm Window fabric shades also darken rooms, which is helpful for those who work at night and sleep during the day, or who simply like to take an afternoon nap in a dark room.

If you are skilled in the art of sewing, you can even make your own shades using Warm Window fabric, available through major fabric outlets. For guidance, check out the worksheet and hardware buying guide posted on the manufacturer's website (**www.warmcompany.com/wwpage.html**). The worksheet provides tips on measuring windows, determining finished shade size, and creating a list of

Go Green!
In your efforts to save energy and cut costs, don't forget ceiling fans. If set to turn in the proper direction for each season, they help keep a home warmer in winter and cooler in summer.

Insulated curtains don't provide a tight air seal, but do help save energy and look great, too.
Courtesy of Smith & Noble, LLC

Cellular shades are fairly easy to install even if you have only a modest amount of skill and patience. I installed a dozen large shades in my home in one day without assistance, with no problems whatsoever. Shades can be mounted in one of two ways: inside the window recess or outside (on the window trim or directly on the wall above the window). Be sure to follow the manufacturer's recommendations.

Cellular shades require installation of plastic or metal mounting hardware. If you're mounting on wood trim, the hardware is attached with wood screws. If you're mounting the brackets in drywall or plaster and can't screw directly into studs, which is often the case, you'll need to install plastic anchors to hold the screws in place. When mounting in concrete, stone, brick, or tile,

drill holes first, using a carbide-tipped drill bit, then insert expansion anchors. Screws are used to attach the brackets to the wall or to anchors, and the shades are snapped in place.

For optimum performance, cellular shades should be installed so they fit snugly in window openings. This reduces air flow behind the shade, resulting in a more efficient covering. To create an airtight seal, consider installing cellular shades with a side track system like those offered by Symphony Shades. Side tracks attach to the window frame and the window shade.

Installing Warm Window shades can be more challenging. I've installed them in two different homes—once hiring a professional to make and install the shades, and another time starting from scratch with the help of my partner Linda who is very good with a sewing machine.

If you're making the shades yourself, you need to be patient, detail-oriented, and have a lot of time on your hands. Each six-foot shade in my home took about 10 hours to sew, string, and hang. If you're thinking about doing the job yourself, you may want to buy the materials to make and install one shade first to decide whether you're up to the task.

What to Watch Out For

When ordering shades, be sure to measure carefully, and measure the correct openings. Check the manufacturer's recommendations for this procedure and follow their guidelines carefully. You may need an assistant to help hold the tape measure for precise measurements. Measure two or three times to be sure.

Shopping Guide

Window shades come in a huge array of colors, styles, and materials, so shop around. It's always a good idea to check curtains and shades out in person to be sure you know what you're getting.

One of the problems I've encountered when buying window shades online is that when repairs were needed later, local retailers/installers were not willing to do them. So, if you're considering an online purchase, call local shops in advance to see if they will restring or repair cellular shades from other manufacturers should the need arise.

If you're going to install cellular shades to repel summer heat, purchase a type with a white or silver reflective backing. Remember, too, the tighter the fit, the more energy you'll save. With inside mounts, you do, however, need to leave a little room for movement between the shade and the window opening.

Hold-down brackets can be installed to prevent cellular shades from swaying on doors. These brackets are often provided at no additional cost, but ask for them when you place your order.

When shopping for cellular shades, check out special features such as continuous cord loop, which makes opening and closing shades easier. Because cords can pose a choking hazard to young children, be sure to tie them out of reach (cleats are available for this purpose), or select cordless models. Check with the manufacturer for recommendations.

For hard-to-reach windows or for individuals who have reduced mobility, look into motor-driven shades. (They're controlled by an electrical switch.)

What Will It Cost?

The cost of insulated window shades varies widely since there are so many different features, fabrics, weaves, sizes, and degrees of insulation and light filtration. They start at as little as $15 for a small 23" x 64" foam-back Roman shade and go up from there to $200 or more per window.

What Will You Save?

Energy savings from insulated shades varies with the construction of the product and how tightly the shade device fits into or over a window opening. The Symphony Shades company claims their shades "are so energy-efficient that they pay for themselves in less than three years (in Vermont, in a house without air conditioning). Add in air conditioning costs, and they pay for themselves in less than two years. In parts of the country where heating and cooling costs are greater, the savings will be greater."

The Window Quilts company (www.WindowQuilts.com) claims their product has an R-value of 4.9, which translates into 67% energy savings over insulated glass alone. If you have conventional single-pane windows, the savings are even more dramatic. Each shade is custom-made for your home.

Don't forget that insulated shades will also increase your comfort level by reducing cold drafts in winter and excess heat in summer.

Project 17

Solar Hot Air Collector

Project Rating:

Savings

🍁🍁🍁

Environmental Benefit

🍁🍁🍁

Health/Comfort

🍁🍁🍁

Level of Difficulty

🍁🍁🍁🍁

If you've already made your home more airtight and added insulation, but you'd still like to do more to reduce your heating bills, you may want to consider installing a solar hot air collector.

What Is a Solar Hot Air Collector?

This technology is about as simple as solar gets. Most of the collectors on the market consist of an insulated metal box containing a black metal plate, known as the *absorber plate*. It absorbs sunlight on cold winter days and, like the interior of your car, turns sunlight into heat. Solar hot air collectors are insulated, and most are covered with single- or double-pane glass (glazing). These features trap sunlight inside the collector, raising the temperature even on the coldest winter days, provided the sun is shining.

Solar hot air collectors are typically mounted on south-facing exterior walls. Air from inside the house is drawn into the collector by a small fan or blower. As the air flows through the collector over the solar-heated absorber plate, it is heated—anywhere from 40°F to 90°F. Solar-heated air is then blown into the house via a pipe that passes through the exterior house wall.

Solar hot air systems are controlled automatically. When the sun shines on the collector, and the temperature inside it reaches 110°F, the fan turns on, blowing warm air into the home. To prevent overheating, the fan turns on only when room temperature drops below the setting on a thermostat, which is also connected to the collector. Solar-heated air warms the room, and the thermostat shuts the unit off when the room temperature reaches the desired setting.

Solar hot air systems primarily provide daytime heat, although heat gained during the day may linger into the evening hours if it's absorbed by thermal mass inside the home. (Thermal mass consists of solid heat-absorbing materials like drywall and floor tile.) At night, the heat stored in thermal mass radiates into the rooms, providing additional comfort. Generally, the more thermal mass, the greater the nighttime benefit.

Go Green!

To really stop heat flow through windows at night, cut out a piece of rigid foam that exactly fits the whole window opening and place it in the window when the sun goes down. A decorative cloth covering makes the inserts more attractive. This is a very inexpensive way to block heat loss.

Solar hot air collectors, like this vertically mounted one, reduce winter heating bills and tap into a clean renewable energy source.
Courtesy of Your Solar Home Inc.

What Are Your Options?

At least eight companies in North America manufacture solar hot air collectors. For most homes, the best choice is a glazed collector. These come in two basic varieties: back-pass and front-pass. In a back-pass collector, room air flows behind the absorber plate. In front-pass collectors, air passes in front of the absorber plate. Back-pass models come with single-pane glass; front-pass models require two-panes of glass to reduce heat loss.

Of the two types of glazed solar hot air collectors, back-pass models are the most common. They're cheaper to manufacture and are about 50 pounds lighter than front-pass collectors, which makes them a little easier to install.

To heat sheds, barns, and workshops, you may want to consider the newer *transpired solar hot air collector*. Rather than warming room air, these collectors extract cold air from the outside, heat it, and then blow the solar-heated air into the building.

A transpired collector consists of a dark-colored metal absorber plate. The sides and back of the collector are metal, insulated to reduce heat loss. On sunny days, sunlight heats the collector's absorber plate. When the unit turns on, heated air is drawn into the interior, then blown into the home.

Why Install a Solar Hot Air Collector?

Solar hot air systems allow homeowners to tap into free energy. They also reduce dependence on increasingly expensive fuel. Combined with other renewable energy technologies, solar hot air systems could help us stretch declining supplies of home heating fuels, such as natural gas and oil, giving us more time to develop other clean, affordable, and reliable renewable energy resources. Solar hot air systems also help reduce pollution, since fossil fuels are not being burned to produce heat or energy at power plants.

Installation

This is definitely *not* a job for a beginner. Unless you've got lots of experience in carpentry and are familiar with electrical wiring, it is best to hire a factory-authorized installer. For best results, solar hot air collectors should be mounted on vertical south-facing walls to absorb the low-angled winter sun. The eaves protect them from the high-angled summer sun. Collectors can also be mounted on roofs or on the ground next to your home, provided the area is not shaded.

New Construction

Although solar hot air collectors are typically added to existing buildings, they can also be integrated into walls of new buildings during construction, reducing their profile. DeSoto Solar is one manufacturer of these units.

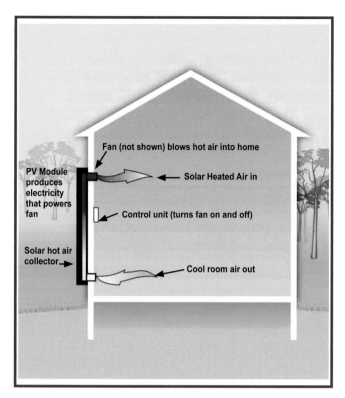

PV Module produces electricity that powers fan

Fan (not shown) blows hot air into home

Solar Heated Air in

Control unit (turns fan on and off)

Solar hot air collector

Cool room air out

Solar hot air collectors capture sunlight to heat room air.
Illustration by Anil Rao

Although ground and roof mounts are sometimes desirable, they're typically more complicated and expensive than wall mounts. In homes with attics, for instance, installing a collector on the roof requires the use of flexible insulated ducts to transport air to and from the collector. It also requires a much more powerful fan than a wall-mounted collector. Moreover, both roof- and ground-mounted collectors are typically mounted flush with the roof or at a slight angle and are therefore exposed to sunlight year-round, which could reduce their life expectancy. Collectors can be covered during the off season, though, to ensure a longer life.

Installation of a glazed solar hot air collector on a wall requires first cutting two large holes (5- to 7-inch diameter depending on the manufacturer's specifications) in the south-facing wall where the collector will be mounted. (Transpired air collectors require only one 9-inch diameter hole.) Before cutting through the wall, the installer needs to be sure there are no water pipes or electrical wires running through that area.

The next step is to mount the collector on the wall using hardware supplied by the manufacturer. This will take a couple of strong workers. Once the collector is mounted, the thermostat and fan can be installed.

Most solar hot air systems require the installer to connect the collector to household 120-volt alternating current electricity using a step-down transformer, which feeds lower-voltage electricity to the fan or blower. If you're not experienced in electrical work, wiring diagrams can be very difficult to understand and, of course, electrical work can be dangerous. To simplify matters, two manufacturers provide wiring alternatives. Your Solar Home's solar hot air collector, the SolarSheat series, comes with its own source of electricity, a small solar electric module. This provides electricity to the built-in fan. This collector is installed the same way as the others, but in this case, the only wiring involves attaching the two wires from the panel to the thermostat (mounted on a wall inside your home). That's it. The fan is pre-connected to the collector in the factory.

I installed a solar hot air collector from Your Solar Home on the roof of my garage to provide a little heat during the winter months and have been very pleased with it. The unit is quiet and has functioned without incident for two years.

Another solution to simplifying the wiring has been provided by Cansolair, which makes a glazed solar hot air collector called Solar Max. Air flow is supplied by an indoor fan in an attractive console that plugs into a 120-volt wall outlet. The fan unit also includes a washable filter that helps purify room air.

Solar-powered fan unit by Cansolair
Courtesy of Cansolair Inc.

Solar hot air collectors work best in places with sunny, cold climates such as Colorado and New Mexico, although they also provide a fair amount of heat in cold, but less sunny, locations such as the Midwest.

Shopping Tips

When shopping for solar hot air systems, be wary of outlandish claims that seem too good to be true. "Marketing departments can make anything look good," says Bill Hurrle of Bay Area Home Performance, a company in Wisconsin that installs solar hot air systems. "One panel won't heat a home," says Hurrle, despite what some sales people may tell you. Several companies have submitted their collectors for testing by the Solar Rating and Certification Corporation, an independent testing lab. SRCC tested collectors provide a level of assurance.

Glazed collectors are ideal for most applications. In my view, transpired collectors are of limited value in most homes, as they can supply too much fresh air into a home—far more than is required to meet fresh air requirements. This high rate of air flow into and then out of a home through openings in the exterior walls and roof can cause moisture buildup in the insulation

behind walls and ceilings—and even a tiny amount of moisture in insulation can decrease its R-value (its ability to retard heat flow) by half. Moisture can also promote mold growth and cause wood framing and wood sheathing to rot, leading to costly structural damage.

Although transpired collectors may not be suitable for homes in many climates, they can work well for structures that are not insulated or airtight, such as barns, garages, and workshops, providing a little comfort on a cold winter day.

Before you purchase a system, check with your local building department to see if you need to obtain a permit to install a solar collection system. Also check with your neighborhood association, if your home is part of one, to make sure there are no covenants restricting solar installations.

Manufacturers of Solar Hot Air Collectors

Solar hot air collectors can be ordered online or purchased through a growing list of solar suppliers—companies that install solar hot water and solar electric systems. Here are some manufacturers and their websites:

Cansolair – www.cansolair.com

ClearDome Solar Systems – www.cleardomesolar.com

DeSoto – www.iedu.com/DeSoto

Northern Comfort Solar Systems, Sunsiaray Manufacturing– www.sunsiaray.com

Solar Unlimited – www.solarunlimited.net

Solarsheat – www.yoursolarhome.com

SunAire – www.aaasolar.com

SunMate – www.environmentalsolarsystems.com

What Will It Cost?

The cost of solar hot air collectors varies tremendously, depending on your climate, the square footage of your home, and other factors. Keep in mind that the first step is always making your home energy-efficient in every other way. Doing so will substantially reduce the capacity, and therefore the expense, of a solar system.

Cost Estimate: Installation of two solar hot air collectors

Cost for materials only: **$1,700**

Contractor's total, including materials, labor, and markup: **$2,500**

Costs are national averages and do not include sales tax.

What Will You Save?

Solar hot air collectors can reduce heating costs, often substantially, although most models require a small amount of electricity to operate the fans. Manufacturers estimate paybacks on an investment in solar collection systems of four to eight years, based on current energy prices. When retrofitting homes in a cold, cloudy climate, expect about a 25% to 35% annual reduction in heat bills. In cold, sunny climates, you can expect much greater savings.

Project 18

Energy-Efficient Furnace

Although more homes are being heated by clean, renewable solar energy, the vast majority still rely on fossil fuels (natural gas and fuel oil) or electricity generated by nuclear and coal-fired power plants. With the cost of these fuels on the rise, it's becoming increasingly expensive to stay warm in the winter. Fossil fuel combustion also contributes to global warming and global climate change, as well as acid rain and air pollution.

Concern for these issues has caused many people to replace old, inefficient furnaces with energy-efficient models. If your furnace is more than 15 years old or is frequently in need of costly repairs—or if you're planning to add on to your home and need to upgrade your furnace to heat the additional space, consider installing an Energy Star-qualified model.

An energy-efficient furnace will cut your utility bill substantially, saving you hundreds of dollars a year. By reducing energy use, efficient furnaces help reduce air pollution produced by conventional power plants. They also can help to improve the air quality of your home.

Before you invest in a new furnace, it always pays to make your home more energy-efficient—for example, by sealing the leaks in the exterior walls and roof, adding insulation, and installing insulated window shades (Projects 11–16). These and other projects in this book will save you money over the long haul and could even reduce the size (heat output) of your new furnace. Smaller furnaces cost less.

What Are Your Options?

Gas Furnaces

Numerous companies manufacture high-efficiency furnaces for forced-air heating systems. Let's review the options and features you should look for.

Conventional gas furnaces, like those found in many older homes and in newer tract homes, are usually located in a basement, utility room, or a well-vented closet. They contain a combustion chamber where natural gas or propane is burned. The burner is ignited by a pilot light, a flame that burns 24 hours a day.

In a conventional furnace, heat generated in the combustion chamber is transferred via a heat exchanger to room air that enters the furnace via the cold-air return ducts. The heated air is then distributed

Go Green!

Furnaces and boilers can be modified to improve their efficiency. Learn how by logging on to the Department of Energy's Consumer's Guide located on their Energy Efficiency and Renewable Energy website, **www.eere.energy.gov/consumer**

High-efficiency furnaces save money and reduce pollution, both inside the home and outdoors.

Courtesy of Coleman® Heating & Air Conditioning

High-efficiency furnaces produce a lot more heat from the fuel they burn, saving homeowners substantially over the long haul. Most high-efficiency gas furnaces are induced-draft models—so named because they contain an energy-efficient electric fan. It draws air from outside the home into the combustion chamber and propels exhaust gases from the combustion chamber out of the house via the flue pipe.

The efficiency of induced-draft furnaces results from the use of more efficient heat exchangers, but also from an electronic ignition, which eliminates the need for a standing pilot light.

The most efficient gas furnaces on the market today are condensing models. These furnaces contain a second heat exchanger, which extracts additional heat from the flue gases, cooling them until the moisture they contain condenses. (Condensation of moisture releases additional heat.) Because so much heat is removed by the heat exchanger, waste gases can be vented through plastic pipe, which is barely warm to the touch. The condensed moisture is drained into a nearby floor drain.

Both condensing and non-condensing furnaces are equipped with sealed combustion chambers. This feature prevents dangerous exhaust gases, such as carbon monoxide and nitrogen dioxide, from entering our homes. Replacing your old gas furnace with a highly efficient model, therefore, could also improve indoor air quality in your home.

When shopping for a new furnace, look for Energy Star-qualified models. Their efficiencies, which are listed as annual fuel utilization efficiency, or AFUE, run from approximately 83% to 97%. As a rule, the induced-draft furnaces have efficiencies in the 80% range, and induced-draft condensing furnaces are in the 90% range.

throughout the home by a warm-air duct system. Heated air is propelled through these ducts by a fairly powerful (and sometimes noisy) blower.

Waste gases (containing toxic pollutants) from the combustion chamber are vented to the outdoors through a flue pipe. As the hot gases rise, they create a partial vacuum in the combustion chamber. This draws room air into the fire, ensuring a continuous supply of oxygen required for proper combustion. The rise of hot air, together with the inflow of room air, is known as *draft*.

Conventional natural-draft furnaces are the least efficient of all furnaces. Those manufactured before 1992 have efficiencies below 78%. Many are only 55% to 65% efficient, which means that they convert only 55% to 65% of the fuel they burn into heat. The rest is wasted.

To view a list of Energy Star-qualified furnaces, log on to the Energy Star website (**www.energystar.gov**), and click on *Products* then *Heating and Cooling* and *Furnaces*. Be sure to check out the product lists.

Oil Furnaces

Fuel oil, a product of petroleum, is burned in home furnaces in many parts of the country. It is injected into the furnace's combustion chamber through a nozzle that produces tiny droplets that mix with air to promote combustion. Many oil furnaces are designed to enhance air turbulence, which boosts combustion efficiency.

Most Energy Star-qualified oil furnaces boast efficiencies in the 83% to 86% range, with condensing oil furnaces at about 95% efficiency. All of these are much higher than oil furnaces made before 1992. (Older furnaces are typically only 50% to 60% efficient.)

Although condensing models are more efficient, they're not very common. The main reason for this is that fuel oil contains many more contaminants (such as sulfur) than natural gas or propane. Condensing out of the combustion gases, these contaminants produce a fairly corrosive liquid that can damage the internal components of a furnace. For this reason, contractors often recommend against these models.

While sealed combustion chambers are widely used in high-efficiency gas furnaces, very few high-efficiency oil furnaces come with this feature. Why? Experience has shown that cold outside air drawn into the combustion chamber of an oil-fired furnace reduces combustion efficiency and may impede start-up.

Installation

Installing an energy-efficient furnace requires removing your old equipment. (In old houses, watch out for asbestos, which may be wrapped around boilers, furnaces, and hot water or steam pipes, as well as around old furnace ducts. Asbestos is a hazardous material that should be removed by a hazardous-waste specialist.)

Installation may also require a new flue and air intake for induced-draft models. Electrical and gas service must be temporarily disconnected and then reconnected. All of these steps require considerable knowledge and skill and should be performed by professional installers. (Working with gas lines carries with it a high risk of explosion, too.) In many locations, installers must be licensed by the state. Professional installers will secure permits, if required.

Shopping Tips

Although energy-efficient furnaces are typically more expensive than less-efficient models, the higher initial cost is typically offset within a few years through lower energy bills. After this period, the new furnace becomes a source of tax-free "income." Remember, too, that the higher up-front investment also provides a hedge against rising fuel costs.

Go Green!

• If your home is heated by a forced-air system, it's a good idea to hire an energy auditor to test for leaks in your ducts. Leaky ducts can lose up to 35% of the hot air produced by a furnace. You can seal the ducts with mastic or hire a professional to do the job for you.

• According to the EPA, dirt and neglect are the main causes of heating system inefficiency and failure. To prevent problems and lower heating costs, the EPA recommends periodic professional servicing of your system. Also clean or replace air filters in forced-air systems every month or two during the heating and cooling seasons.

When considering a new energy-efficient furnace, ask installers/suppliers about state and local tax incentives or rebates from local utilities. Many incentives are available to homeowners and can help you lower the initial cost of a more efficient furnace. Log on to the Database of State Incentives for Renewables & Efficiency at **www.dsireusa.org** and check with your energy provider.

When buying a new furnace, be sure that the system is properly sized to your home, especially if you have retrofitted your home for energy efficiency. Contractors often oversize furnaces based on the misconception that this will ensure plenty of heat. Unfortunately, oversized furnaces tend to cycle on and off more frequently than properly sized systems. This, in turn, results in less-efficient operation. (It takes a while for a furnace to reach maximum efficiency, so if it is cycling on and off, it runs at peak efficiency less often.) Start-ups also require more fuel. All of these factors mean more fuel consumption—which may offset new furnace efficiency gains.

According to the United States Department of Energy, it is not uncommon for heating systems to be two or three times larger than required to meet the demand for heat. As a rule, a heating system should be no more than 25% larger than the calculated heat load (heat requirement).

Be sure to hire a reputable contractor who is capable not only of properly installing the new equipment, but also accurately calculating your heat demand, taking into account energy efficiency measures you've taken, such as added insulation. Also follow maintenance recommendations and hire a professional to periodically inspect and maintain your system.

Call several reliable installers in your area to see what kinds of systems they offer, and what they recommend. Check their customer satisfaction by looking up complaints through the Better Business Bureau and by calling references. You can find a contractor by searching through the Yellow Pages or, better yet, ask a general contractor or electrician you trust for recommendations.

The table below gives some examples of what the energy cost savings might be, in different parts of the country, if you upgrade from a 60% or a 78% efficient furnace to a 90% efficient model.

Savings from a High-Efficiency Furnace

Annual savings projected for a 2,500 SF home with replacement of a less efficient gas furnace with a new 90% efficient gas unit (assuming a gas price of $1.17/therm)

	vs. 60% efficiency	vs. 78% efficiency
Portland, ME	$1,227	$355
Pueblo, CO	$1,227	$298
Albuquerque, NM	$1,040	$263
Orlando, FL	$277	$56
San Diego, CA	$146	$59

Annual savings projected for a 2,500 SF home with replacement of a less efficient oil furnace with a new 83% efficient oil unit (assuming an oil price of $2.41/therm)

	vs. 60% efficiency	vs. 75% efficiency
Portland, ME	$1,634	$580
Pueblo, CO	$1,634	$551
Albuquerque, NM	$1,401	$505
Orlando, FL	$310	$112
San Diego, CA	$200	$96

Calculations based on the Department of Energy's "Life Cycle Cost Estimate for an Energy Star Qualified Residential Furnace" found at www.energystar.gov

What Will It Cost?

The cost to replace a furnace will vary according to the size of your house, energy efficiency measures you have in place (such as high R-value wall and attic insulation, properly sealed vents, efficient windows, a programmable thermostat), and the features and the efficiency of your new furnace. The cost to remove the old equipment may be higher if hazardous materials, such as asbestos insulation, have to be removed.

> ## Removal of an old furnace and installation of a new, high-efficiency gas furnace with 3-ton capacity, for a 2,500 square foot home
>
> Cost for materials only: **$2,525**
>
> Contractor's total, including materials, labor, and markup: **$3,900**
>
> *Costs are national averages and do not include sales tax.*

What Will You Save?

Although highly efficient gas furnaces typically cost $500 to $1,000 more than less-efficient models, they will easily make up the difference in fuel savings because they're up to 15% more efficient. To calculate your potential cost savings, check out the savings calculator on the Energy Star website. You can also calculate return on investment through the DOE's Energy Efficiency and Renewable Energy website: **http://www.aceee.org/ consumerguide/heating.htm#contractor**

Project
19

Energy-Efficient Boiler

Is your boiler more than 15 years old? Does it often require repairs, or is it in need of a single, costly repair job? Or are you planning to add on to your home and need to upgrade your boiler to heat the additional space? If any of these situations apply, consider a new Energy Star-qualified boiler.

An efficient boiler will reduce your utility bill—often considerably—saving hundreds of dollars a year. It can be one of the most cost-effective ways to improve energy efficiency in your home. It will also produce much less pollution and help to improve your home's indoor air quality.

If your home is heated by an in-floor or baseboard hot-water system, your hot water (and therefore your heat) is generated by a boiler (versus a furnace that produces hot air that is circulated through vents). Typically located in basements or utility rooms, boilers burn natural gas, propane, heating oil, or, in some cases, electricity. The combustion of these fuels heats water that circulates in pipes around the combustion chamber.

In homes equipped with radiant floor systems, also known as in-floor heating, hot water is circulated through pipes beneath the finished floor. Heat is absorbed by the floor and radiated into the room. In homes with hot-water baseboard systems, water is circulated throughout the house to baseboard heat

exchangers. Located at the base of walls, they contain a series of aluminum fins that are heated by hot water flowing through copper pipes attached to the fins. The heat transferred from the pipes to the fins is then radiated into the rooms. Both in-floor and hot-water baseboard systems are referred to as hydronic heating systems.

While in-floor and baseboard heating systems are more efficient than forced hot air, and therefore more cost-effective, the cost of fossil fuels to run these systems is rising rapidly, making them more and more expensive to operate. One way to address concerns for rising

Go Green!

Be sure to adjust your thermostat whenever you leave your home during the day and at night when you sleep. If you have trouble remembering, consider installing a programmable thermostat. When used properly, they can save $150 or more per year on utility bills, according to the EPA.

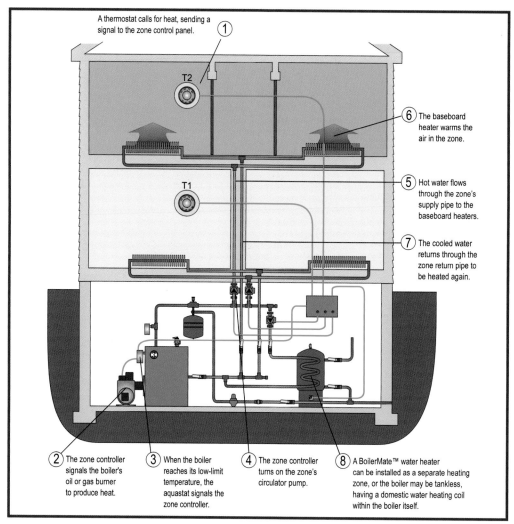

A thermostat calls for heat, sending a signal to the zone control panel. ①

⑥ The baseboard heater warms the air in the zone.

⑤ Hot water flows through the zone's supply pipe to the baseboard heaters.

⑦ The cooled water returns through the zone return pipe to be heated again.

② The zone controller signals the boiler's oil or gas burner to produce heat.

③ When the boiler reaches its low-limit temperature, the aquastat signals the zone controller.

④ The zone controller turns on the zone's circulator pump.

⑧ A BoilerMate™ water heater can be installed as a separate heating zone, or the boiler may be tankless, having a domestic water heating coil within the boiler itself.

Components of a typical baseboard hot-water system

Reprinted with permission from *How Your House Works*, by Charlie Wing

prices and pollution generated by conventional heating systems is to upgrade your boiler to make it more efficient or replace it with a newer and considerably more energy-efficient model. (To learn about possible efficiency upgrades to existing boilers, log on to the DOE's Consumer's Guide on their Energy Efficiency and Renewable Energy website at **www.eere.energy. gov/consumer**)

What Are Your Options?

As noted elsewhere in this book, the first thing to do before investing in a new boiler (or any expensive new heating equipment) is to make your home as energy-efficient as possible. Projects 11–15, for instance, can help you reduce your home energy bill dramatically

and, in the process, will significantly reduce the size/ capacity of a new boiler if you end up replacing your old one. The more efficient your home is, the less heat your heating system will need to produce. This means you can purchase a smaller boiler with a lower initial cost.

A lot of companies manufacture high-efficiency boilers for radiant floor heating systems and hot-water baseboard systems. Most achieve combustion efficiencies in the 85% to 90% range. Some are as high as 92% to 95%.

High efficiency is achieved in a number of ways. Most boilers contain an electronic ignition that produces a spark that is used to ignite the burner, so there's no

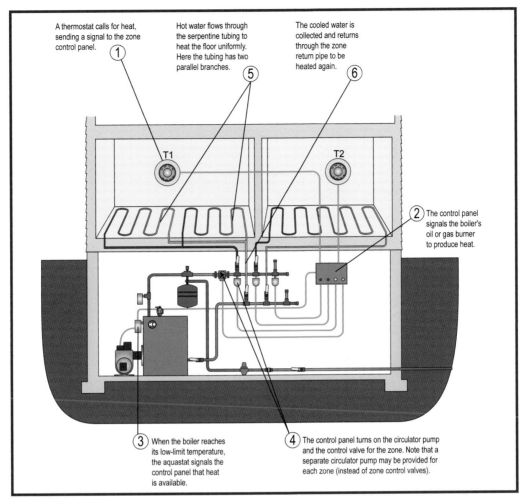

A thermostat calls for heat, sending a signal to the zone control panel. ①

Hot water flows through the serpentine tubing to heat the floor uniformly. Here the tubing has two parallel branches. ⑤

The cooled water is collected and returns through the zone return pipe to be heated again. ⑥

② The control panel signals the boiler's oil or gas burner to produce heat.

③ When the boiler reaches its low-limit temperature, the aquastat signals the control panel that heat is available.

④ The control panel turns on the circulator pump and the control valve for the zone. Note that a separate circulator pump may be provided for each zone (instead of zone control valves).

How an in-floor radiant heat system works
Reprinted with permission from *How Your House Works,* by Charlie Wing

need for a standing pilot light. These boilers also burn fuels and extract heat from combustion gases more efficiently than older models.

Like energy-efficient furnaces, energy-efficient boilers also improve indoor air quality by using closed combustion chambers—sealed chambers where gas or oil burns. Replacement air is derived from outdoors, not room air. A small fan draws air into the combustion chamber and forces the exhaust gas out through the flue. (These are known as induced-draft boilers.)

To check out your many options, log on to the Energy Star website (**www.energystar.gov**). Click on *Heating and Cooling* under products, then click on *Boilers.* You'll find a consumer product list on this web page.

Installation

Installing an energy-efficient boiler will require removing your old boiler first. Induced-draft boilers may require a new flue and air intake. Electrical and gas service must be temporarily disconnected, then reconnected. Installation should be carried out by a professional heating contractor. If your boiler—or the pipes connected to it—are very old, they could have an asbestos coating. This material should be removed by an asbestos-removal specialist.

Shopping Tips

When shopping for a new boiler, look for an Energy Star-qualified model. Although they are typically more expensive than less efficient models, fuel savings will offset the higher initial cost. To calculate the return on your investment, log on to **www.aceere.org/consumerguide** and click on *Heating*. Don't forget to factor in federal, state, and local incentives, including utility rebates, that are available on energy-efficient boilers. For information on incentives in your area, log on to the Database of State Incentives for Renewables & Efficiency at **www.dsireusa.org**

AFUE Rating

AFUE stands for Annual Fuel Utilization Efficiency. A high-efficiency system has an AFUE of at least 90%.

Like gas furnaces, boilers should be properly sized, especially if you have retrofitted your home for energy efficiency. Oversized heating equipment is much less efficient and won't last as long because it cycles on and off more frequently than correctly sized equipment. As a rule, a boiler system should be no more than 25% larger than the calculated *heating load* (heat requirement).

Hire a reputable heating contractor who can accurately calculate your requirements, considering all the energy-efficiency measures you have taken.

Call several installers in your area to see what boilers they offer and what they recommend. Ask friends or colleagues for recommendations of heating/air conditioning contractors. You can also find contractors who install Energy Star appliances at **www.natex.org** or **www.acca.org**

Installing a Carbon Monoxide Detector

Sealed combustion chambers can make our homes safer by preventing harmful pollutants generated during combustion from leaking into the living space. However, it is still a good idea to install carbon monoxide detectors in areas of the home where they can be heard. One unit on each floor is a good idea. Be sure to install one in or near the master bedroom, so if carbon monoxide levels rise in the night, you will hear the alarm.

What Will It Cost?

Boilers, including installation, generally cost more than $4,000, as shown in the estimate below. They require their own pipe and radiators, separate from the duct system for air conditioning. So, for a new home, this is an extra cost consideration. If you're replacing your old boiler, however, the pipe should already be in place, so this should not be a cost factor unless it, too, needs upgrading.

Cost Estimate: Installation of new high-efficiency gas boiler for a 2,500 square foot home

Includes removal and disposal of old boiler

Cost for materials only: **$2,575**

Contractor's total, including materials, labor, and markup: **$4,500**

Costs are national averages and do not include sales tax.

What Will You Save?

Although an efficient gas boiler can cost $500 to $1,000 more than a less efficient one, the difference will be offset fairly quickly in fuel savings—very quickly if you have an old, extremely inefficient model now. According to the EPA, new Energy Star boilers are up to 15% more efficient than new standard models. To calculate your potential cost savings, check out the Savings Calculator on the Energy Star website **www.energystar.gov**

Project

20 Heat Pump & Solar Hot Water

With warnings about the dangers of global warming and the continually rising cost of home heating fuels, many people are looking for ways to heat their homes with clean, renewable energy. Two excellent options are heat pumps and solar hot water systems.

What Is a Heat Pump?

Heat pumps are devices that use refrigeration technology to extract heat from the outside environment—either from the air surrounding your home (air-source heat pump) or from the ground (ground-source heat pump, otherwise known as geothermal). The heat is then concentrated and distributed throughout a home through ducts in a forced air system or through pipes in radiant floor or hot-water baseboard systems.

In ground-source, or geothermal, heat pump systems, pipes buried in the ground (either vertically or horizontally) circulate a fluid that absorbs the Earth's heat. (The ground below the frost line remains a constant 50°F.) In air-source heat pumps, heat is drawn directly from the outside air, then transferred to the home. This works even on cold winter days because the refrigerant in the heat pump is colder than the air temperature (in locations that are well suited to these systems).

The equipment in both geothermal and air-source heat pumps is powered by electricity. For every unit of electricity a ground-source heat pump consumes when in operation, it produces about four units of heat. (An electric heater produces only one unit of heat for every unit of electricity it consumes.) Air-source heat pumps are slightly less efficient than ground-source pumps, producing about three units of heat for every unit of electricity they consume.

Because they run on electricity, heat pumps require no in-home combustion of fossil fuel. This eliminates the risk of combustion gases such as carbon monoxide spilling into the rooms of a house and results in healthier indoor air. It also reduces the chances of a house fire.

As an added bonus, heat pumps can be used to cool your home in the summer. Running them in reverse extracts heat from the house and deposits it into the outdoor environment—either the air or ground. In addition, some of the heat from a heat pump can be used to warm water for in-home use.

Go Green!

Ceiling fans can reduce cooling costs by as much as 40% and heating costs as much as 10%.

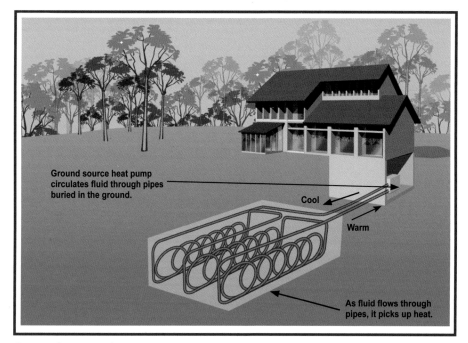

Ground-source heat pump

Illustration by Anil Rao

As a result, heat pumps can serve three purposes: they provide heat in winter, cool your home in the summer, and heat water.

Air-source and ground-source heat pumps replace conventional furnaces and boilers and are tied into existing heating distribution systems in houses. As a rule, air-source heat pumps are typically installed in milder climates, although at least two manufacturers (Mitsubishi and Fujitsu) now produce them for use in cold climates. Geothermal systems (ground-source heat pumps) are typically installed in colder climates.

Additional Considerations

Ground- and air-source heat pumps require electricity, which is generated by power plants, many of which burn coal or natural gas. When these fossil fuels are burned, they produce greenhouse gases and a number of other harmful pollutants. Even so, ground- and air-source heat pumps produce *less* pollution than conventional home furnaces and boilers because the heat comes from the air or ground.

While heat pumps are more efficient and cleaner than conventional furnaces and boilers, geothermal systems cost more to install—about 25% to 100% more

than a high-efficiency boiler or furnace (depending on location, local labor costs, and difficulty of the installation). Even so, they can save a substantial amount of money over the long term. Air-source heat pumps are fairly economical to install and provide excellent savings, but may not be appropriate for very cold climates.

Installation

The installation of a heat pump will first require removing old heating equipment (but not the duct system or pipes used to distribute heat throughout the house). Installation of a ground-source heat pump is easiest in new home construction, as it requires extensive excavation and/or drilling to lay the heat-absorbing pipes in the ground. This can be performed

Some Product Options

Look for the SEER rating on heat pumps. SEER stands for Seasonal Energy Efficiency Rating. A high-efficiency unit has a rating of at least 12 SEER.

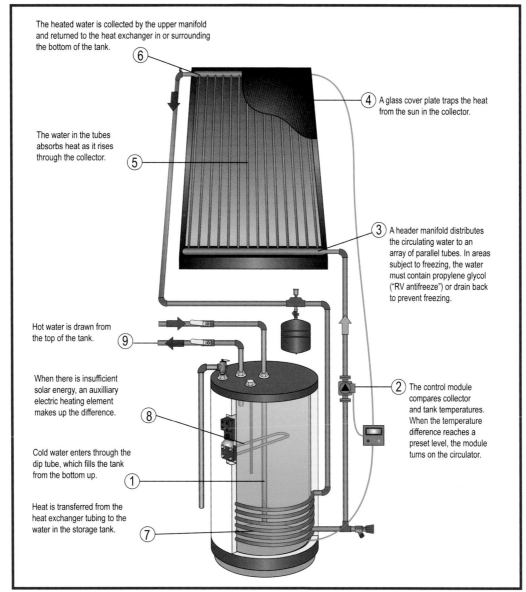

The heated water is collected by the upper manifold and returned to the heat exchanger in or surrounding the bottom of the tank.

6

4 A glass cover plate traps the heat from the sun in the collector.

The water in the tubes absorbs heat as it rises through the collector.

5

3 A header manifold distributes the circulating water to an array of parallel tubes. In areas subject to freezing, the water must contain propylene glycol ("RV antifreeze") or drain back to prevent freezing.

Hot water is drawn from the top of the tank.

9

When there is insufficient solar energy, an auxilliary electric heating element makes up the difference.

8

2 The control module compares collector and tank temperatures. When the temperature difference reaches a preset level, the module turns on the circulator.

Cold water enters through the dip tube, which fills the tank from the bottom up.

1

Heat is transferred from the heat exchanger tubing to the water in the storage tank.

7

Solar hot-water system
Reprinted with permission from *How Your House Works*, by Charlie Wing

while a home is being built, before the finish grading is completed. Installation in an existing yard, especially a small one, is often more difficult and considerably more expensive. Pipes may need to be installed vertically to a depth of 200 feet, which requires a drill rig. Getting a drill rig into a backyard in an urban or suburban setting may be difficult or impossible. In such cases, a solar hot-water system may be more economical, provided there's sufficient sun-bathed roof area for installation of the solar collectors.

When talking to installers, be sure to ask about local building code restrictions on this equipment.

Solar Hot Water Used for Space Heating

Another renewable-energy option for heating your home is a solar hot-water system. These systems are typically installed to provide domestic hot water, as shown in Project 35, but larger systems can also provide space heat.

As shown in the drawing above, a solar hot-water system consists of collectors that are typically mounted on the roof. They absorb sunlight, even on cold winter days, as long as the sun is shining. In many systems, the solar heat is drawn off by a fluid (usually propylene glycol) circulating through pipes in the collector. The heat is then transferred to a solar storage tank, typically located in the basement. Hot water from the reservoir may be circulated through the pipes in a baseboard hot-water system or in a radiant floor heating system. Or it can be extracted by a heat exchanger installed in a forced-air heating system. (For more details on solar hot-water systems, see Project 35.)

Installing a Solar Hot Water System

Solar hot-water systems require installation of rooftop collectors and a storage tank, with pipes connecting the two. The solar storage tank is connected to the existing heating distribution system. System design and installation require considerable knowledge and skill and, in some cases, a license, and are therefore best performed by a professional installer.

Shopping Tips

Whether geothermal or solar, be sure that your new system is properly sized to your home, considering the steps you've taken to increase your home's energy efficiency, such as adding insulation and caulking air leaks in outside walls. Some contractors tend to oversize heating systems, which results in lower operating efficiencies of heat pumps, as explained in Project 18 (and higher purchase costs in the case of both solar heating systems and heat pumps).

When shopping for a heat pump, look for an Energy Star-qualified model. Although more expensive, the difference in initial cost will be offset by lower energy bills. To calculate your return on investment, log on to **www.aceee.org/consumerguide** and click on *Heating*.

It's best to research the various products in advance and compare their performance records. You can find a heat pump or solar hot-water system installation contractor in the Yellow Pages or by logging on to **www.natex.org** or **www.acca.org** Ask for references and follow up with them. Be sure to check with the Better Business Bureau to see if there have been any complaints.

What Will It Cost?

As noted earlier, geothermal systems typically cost about 25% to 100% more to install than an equivalent conventional high-efficiency boiler or furnace, depending on access, location, and the size/capacity of the system. Air-source heat pumps are less expensive than geothermal, but not suitable in all climates. Below is a sample estimate for a solar hot-water system.

> ## Cost Estimate: Installation of a closed-loop solar hot-water heating system for a 2,500 square foot home
>
> Cost for materials only: **$4,500**
>
> Contractor's total, including materials, labor, and markup: **$9,700**
>
> *Costs are national averages and do not include sales tax.*

What Will You Save?

Solar hot-water systems and heat pumps rely principally on no-cost renewable energy. These systems tend to have the highest return on investment of any solar technology, except passive solar design (which requires no electricity to operate). Both geothermal and solar systems provide a hedge against rising fuel costs well into the future. When calculating installation costs, check federal, state, and local incentives, including possible rebates from local utilities that can reduce the initial cost of installing these systems. Log onto the Database of State Incentives for Renewables & Efficiency for more information at **www.dsireusa.org**

Project
21

Wood Stoves

As the price of home heating fuels continues to rise, and the impacts of global warming become more obvious and costly, more and more people are turning to renewable energy to heat their homes. One option is wood. If you're going to burn wood, a clean-burning wood stove is a far better device than notoriously inefficient fireplaces. That said, wood has plusses and minuses as a fuel.

Why Heat with Wood?

Although modern wood stoves are designed to minimize smoke and other pollutants, they still produce more pollution, both indoors and outdoors, than modern high-efficiency furnaces and boilers. However, they do offer several benefits over conventional home heating systems. In rural areas, wood can be economical since it tends to be readily available and inexpensive. It can be surprisingly abundant in many cities and towns as well. For example, factories and retail outlets often discard hundreds, sometimes thousands, of pallets and shipping crates each year. Construction sites dispose of lumber as well, and landscapers or city workers may be willing to part with wood if they're not chipping it up for their own use. As long as this wood is not infested with insects or treated with dangerous chemicals or finishes, it could be used (with permission from the source, of course) to heat homes with wood stoves.

Burning wood instead of oil or natural gas also helps us reduce emissions of the greenhouse gas carbon dioxide, provided trees are replanted to replace the wood you

burn. In this case, wood is as close to carbon neutral as any fuel can be. Any wood that replaces fuel oil can help us reduce our costly reliance on Middle Eastern oil and environmental issues resulting from oil extraction.

Although wood burning has its advantages, it is arguably the dirtiest of all renewable fuels. Wood smoke contains hundreds of air pollutants, including nitrogen oxides, carbon monoxide, organic gases, and particulate matter, many of which have adverse health effects, according to the U.S. Environmental Protection Agency. The EPA notes that smoke from burning wood is a major contributor to air pollution in many urban and rural areas. Some municipalities restrict wood-heating appliance use at all times or when the local air quality reaches unacceptable levels.

Wood stoves can also contribute to indoor air pollution. While modern wood stoves are tightly sealed to reduce this problem, a leaky stove can release carbon monoxide and other pollutants into a room. Pollutants can also enter a room when the door of the stove is opened. Even with the most efficient wood stoves on the market, burning wood produces more pollution than the combustion of natural gas or home heating oil in a modern energy-efficient furnace or boiler.

Wood stoves also heat unevenly. (It's warmer in the immediate vicinity of the stove than in distant rooms.) In addition, wood stoves produce a fairly dry heat (though this can be offset by keeping a pot of water on the stove). They can also pose a fire hazard if not properly installed and operated. Moreover, wood stoves require frequent refueling and cleaning. You'll need to remove ashes every day or so. All in all, wood stoves are rather messy. And count on a considerable amount of labor—cutting and splitting wood and hauling it into the house to supply your wood stove.

Although wood does have its downsides, improvements in wood-burning technology make it a renewable fuel worth consideration. Wood stove installation is usually pretty straightforward. A well-made stove will provide decades of service.

What Are Your Options?

Wood stoves come in many shapes, materials, sizes, styles, and colors. Those designed for serious home heating fall into two categories: *radiant* and *circulating*. Radiant wood stoves are made from welded steel or cast iron. Heat from the fire is absorbed by the walls of the stove and then radiates into the room. Circulating stoves also have a welded steel or cast-iron shell, but surrounding the inner shell is a second layer of metal with an air space in between. The fire heats the inner shell, which then warms the air in the space between it and the outer shell. Warm air then flows out of this space into the room—either passively (by convection) or actively (by a fan).

Modern radiant and circulating stoves achieve efficiencies from 60% to 80%, much lower than boilers and furnaces, but much higher than older wood stoves. Manufacturers achieve these efficiencies, in part, by creating openings that introduce air into the combustion chamber at strategic locations. The more air (oxygen), the more efficient combustion becomes.

Some manufacturers also boost efficiency by using a catalytic burner, a ceramic honeycomb device through which exhaust gases flow from the fire as they leave the combustion chamber. Like the catalytic converter in an automobile, exhaust gases from a wood fire

Radiant wood stove
Courtesy of Regency Fireplace Products

contain unburned hydrocarbons. These gases contain a significant amount of energy, but only ignite at the higher temperatures present in the catalytic burner.

Although catalytic burners boost the efficiency of a wood stove, they add to its cost, and they also need to be replaced every three to six years. You can expect to pay a couple of hundred dollars to replace one.

Efficiency can also be boosted by an internal baffle, which is less expensive and more durable than a

Go Green!

Don't throw away leftover wood from projects around the house. Donate larger pieces to neighbors who need wood for building projects or to nonprofits like Habitat for Humanity that resell it. Or, place unwanted lumber by the side of the road with a "free" sign. If you have a wood stove or a clean-burning and efficient fireplace, cut the wood up and burn it yourself. If you heat with wood, ask neighbors to save clean, non-treated scrap wood and pruned limbs for you.

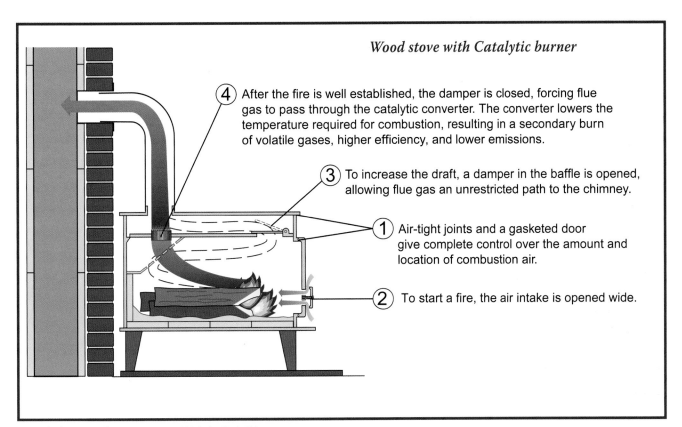

Wood stove with Catalytic burner

④ After the fire is well established, the damper is closed, forcing flue gas to pass through the catalytic converter. The converter lowers the temperature required for combustion, resulting in a secondary burn of volatile gases, higher efficiency, and lower emissions.

③ To increase the draft, a damper in the baffle is opened, allowing flue gas an unrestricted path to the chimney.

① Air-tight joints and a gasketed door give complete control over the amount and location of combustion air.

② To start a fire, the air intake is opened wide.

Reprinted with permission from *How Your House Works,* by Charlie Wing

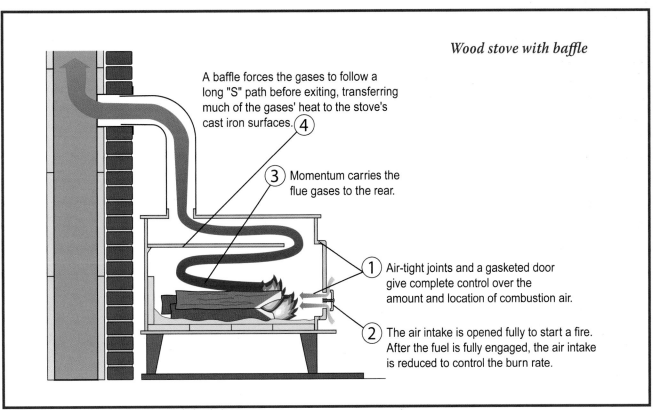

Wood stove with baffle

A baffle forces the gases to follow a long "S" path before exiting, transferring much of the gases' heat to the stove's cast iron surfaces. ④

③ Momentum carries the flue gases to the rear.

① Air-tight joints and a gasketed door give complete control over the amount and location of combustion air.

② The air intake is opened fully to start a fire. After the fuel is fully engaged, the air intake is reduced to control the burn rate.

Reprinted with permission from *How Your House Works,* by Charlie Wing

catalytic burner. Baffles direct exhaust gases back over the fire where they ignite, wringing more Btus from wood.

Baffles and catalytic burners not only increase combustion efficiency, they also result in cleaner-burning stoves, which means less air pollution and less creosote build-up in the flue pipe. Creosote is a mixture of organic compounds that deposits on the inner surface of chimneys and flue pipes. If it ignites, it creates a very hot, intense fire that can ignite nearby combustibles, such as wood framing in an attic. The fire can then spread to the rest of the house.

Installation

Wood stoves can be installed by very handy homeowners, but the job is best performed by a professional installer for several reasons, the most important of which is safety (fire prevention). Some local building departments may require a professional installer. Virtually all will require a building permit and a final inspection to be certain the installation complies with the local building code.

If you elect to undertake this job, read the instructions provided by the manufacturer or supplier, and consult with your building department for guidance and permits. Don't cut corners. Proceed carefully, paying attention to detail, especially when cutting a hole in your roof to accommodate the flue pipe. Be sure to properly flash the flue pipe to prevent roof leaks.

Ideally, wood stoves should be centrally placed in a home for optimal heat movement through the structure. If you can, avoid placing a wood stove against an exterior wall since the heat will warm the interior surface of the wall and flow to the outside. (Building code will require you to install a heat barrier, such as brick veneer, against the wall if it contains combustibles [such as wood framing]. Although the heat barrier will reduce heat flow through the outside wall, a central location is still best.)

When installing a wood stove, also consider its location in relation to the fuel supply—your wood pile. Make it as easy as possible to haul wood to the stove.

Preventing any chance of a house fire should be the top priority in wood-stove installation. The wood stove and the flue pipe must be placed at a correct distance from combustible materials in floors, walls, and ceilings. Proper installation also generally requires the use of specified materials to shield the floor and walls from the intense heat given off by the stove. You can obtain this information from your local building department as well as the manufacturer's installation instructions. Also check with your insurance company to be sure they will still cover your home (and not increase your premiums) if you install a wood stove.

Professional installers not only have the knowledge and experience to do this job safely and correctly, but are familiar with building codes and can save you the trouble of having to learn them.

Shopping Tips

Wood stoves are sold at a few large hardware stores, but primarily at wood-stove specialty retailers. These companies often employ their own installers or can recommend qualified ones.

When shopping for a wood stove, be sure to look for models certified by the U.S. Environmental Protection Agency (EPA). These certified stoves may include a catalytic combustor or baffle system, mentioned earlier, which reduce pollution emissions and increase efficiency. (The more efficient a stove is, the more heat

Go Green!

• To reduce air pollution and creosote formation (in flues and chimneys) when heating your home with a stove, a fireplace, or a wood-burning stove insert, burn only dry, well-seasoned wood. It burns much cleaner than "green," newly harvested and unseasoned wood.

• If you heat with wood, use ceiling fans or table-top fans to move warm air around your home. Close doors to rooms you're not using.

it produces.) All wood stoves sold today should carry an EPA certification sticker and indicate efficiency and emissions. This information is a great tool for comparing various models and selecting the most efficient and cleanest-burning stove. High-efficiency stoves not only produce fewer emissions, they are also often safer, since complete combustion helps to prevent a buildup of creosote in the flue pipe. Visit the EPA website for helpful information on wood-stove safety, ratings, and even retailers and installers in your area: **www.epa.gov/woodstoves**

When shopping, one of your most important considerations is the size of your wood stove. Manufacturers provide information, such as heat output per hour (in Btus) or the number of rooms (or the room or house size in square feet or cubic feet) their stoves are designed to heat. This information can help you select a model. Unfortunately, not all manufacturers test their stoves under the same conditions, so these statistics aren't helpful when comparing wood stoves from different companies. They do provide a rough basis for comparing different stove models.

For best results, ask a reputable wood stove retailer—one who is familiar with your area and heating requirements—to make a recommendation. He or she should first look over your home and understand its heating needs. One thing to be aware of is that many retailers consider all homes of a certain size to be the same with respect to heating requirements. However, if you've added insulation and taken other steps to improve your home's efficiency, you won't need as big a wood stove. While oversizing a furnace or boiler is a bad proposition—it results in a much less efficient heating system—oversizing a wood stove does not cause problems; it's just more expensive. You can always burn smaller fires or reduce air flow to the combustion chamber to adjust the intensity of the fire.

Before investing in a wood stove, be sure to make your home as energy-efficient as possible. Seal leaks in the building envelope. Add insulation to walls and ceilings, if needed, and use insulated shades over windows on cold nights.

What Will It Cost?

Wood-stove prices range from about $500 to $2,500, depending on size/heat output, features, and special finishes (other than black cast iron). Other costs include installation, which will vary based on your home's design and the wood to fuel the stove, if you don't have a free supply available. Wood stoves require installation of a full-height chimney or flue if you don't already have one in place. Cords of wood vary widely in cost from under $100 up to $300, depending on your location.

Cost Estimate: Installation of a wood-burning stove, chimney, and protective surround

Includes cutting a flue opening through the ceiling and roof, all fittings and flashing, and brick and brickwork

Cost for materials only: **$3,750**

Contractor's total, including materials, labor, and markup: **$6,900**

Costs are national averages and do not include sales tax.

What Will You Save?

Heating your home with wood can greatly reduce or even eliminate your heating bill, paying for itself over a few years' time. Your savings will depend on factors such as access to free or low-cost firewood, the model of stove you select, and the type of construction required to install it, especially if your home doesn't have a chimney. A bonus if you're in an area with frequent power failures is a reliable backup heat supply.

Project 22 Pellet Stoves

Project Rating:

Savings
🍁🍁🍁

Environmental Benefit
🍁🍁🍁

Level of Difficulty
🍁🍁🍁

If you'd like to trim your home heating bill and are thinking about purchasing a wood stove, you might want to consider another option. Pellet stoves offer several advantages over wood stoves. The fuel they burn is less messy than firewood and burns more cleanly. Wood pellets are also made from abundant wood waste material.

What Is a Pellet Stove?

Pellet stoves are the lazy man's wood stove. They are easier to load, less messy, and can provide hours of heat without reloading. Pellet stoves are more sophisticated combustion devices than wood stoves, allowing for more precise control of the combustion, and therefore heat output.

Pellet stoves are made from steel or cast iron and resemble wood stoves in many respects. They burn dry, compressed pellets typically made from sawdust and wood chips. Pellet stoves also burn cleaner than wood, and because natural resins and binders (lignin) in the sawdust hold the pellets together, manufacturers don't need to use potentially toxic glues to make their product.

Pellet stoves are available in free-standing models and as fireplace inserts (Project 23). Some companies also manufacture pellet-fueled furnaces and boilers designed to replace or supplement conventional gas, oil, and electric furnaces and boilers.

Sawdust and wood chips used to make pellets come from sawmills throughout the United States and Canada. Sawmills produce millions of tons of sawdust every year as they convert trees into finished lumber. For years, sawmills burned this waste in huge, inefficient incinerators. These smoldered for days on end, producing clouds of gray, smelly smoke that sullied the skies of many a rural town. (I know from experience, having lived near one in Montana for a year.)

Today, many sawmills convert this abundant waste product into pellets for wood stoves. This has helped to bolster rural economies while providing a clean-burning fuel for millions of people in North America. This is an excellent example of how waste can be transformed from an economic liability to an asset.

Not All Pellets Are Wood

In some areas, nut hulls and other plant materials are pelletized. Unprocessed corn kernels and fruit pits can also be burned in some types of modern pellet stoves.

Pellet stoves burn cleanly and are direct-vented so they don't require a chimney.

Courtesy of Quadra-Fire, a brand of Hearth & Home Technologies, www.quadrafire.com

Pellets are sold in 40-pound (18 kilogram) bags in numerous retail outlets, including wood-stove dealers, many hardware stores, some home improvement centers, grocery stores, feed and garden supply centers, and large discount stores. Homeowners who rely on a pellet stove as their primary source of heat in cold climates can purchase pellets by the pallet to save money. You may need two to five pallet loads to make it through the winter in particularly cold areas. Local suppliers will deliver them. If you use the pellet stove only occasionally, you may want to buy a few bags of pellets at a time.

Pellets should be stored in dry areas, such as the garage or basement or under waterproof tarps alongside the house. Bags can be hauled into the house, one at a time, and the pellets fed into a hopper in the back of the stove. From here, the pellets flow into a small combustion chamber where they are burned. Most pellet stoves produce a relatively small, but hot fire (much smaller than a wood-stove fire).

Why Install a Pellet Stove?

Pellet stoves offer many advantages over wood stoves. Like wood stoves, they burn a renewable fuel, but their fuel is a waste product that was once incinerated at the expense of the local air quality. (Since wood pellets burn more cleanly than the incinerators once used to dispose of mill waste, pellet stoves help reduce air pollution.) The use of pellet stoves also helps to support local economies and the wood-products industry.

Another advantage of pellet stoves is that the rate of combustion, and therefore heat output, can be easily regulated by adjusting the rate at which the pellets are fed into the combustion chamber. (Although combustion in wood stoves can be regulated by adjusting the air flow to the combustion chamber, they can't be as finely controlled as pellet stoves.)

Pellet stoves are equipped with small, relatively quiet fans that blow hot air from the surface of the stove into the room. This helps improve the efficiency of heat transfer (meaning you get more heat from the fuel) and also helps distribute heat throughout the house.

Yet another advantage is that pellet stoves are easier to load and nowhere near as messy as wood stoves. Pellet stoves can provide heat for many hours without reloading. (Some models can burn a day or two at a low setting on a full hopper.) Many pellet stoves can be thermostatically controlled, too, so they ramp up when room temperature drops.

On the downside, pellet stoves require electricity to operate—for the auger that delivers pellets from the hopper to the combustion chamber and the blower fans that come standard on many models. Pellet stoves need to be plugged into a 120-volt electrical outlet. Although they require electricity, they don't use much. According to the Department of Energy, under normal usage, pellet stoves consume about 100 kilowatt-hours (kWh). That's about $9 to $15 worth of electricity per month, depending on local utility rates. The gains in efficiency easily offset this small amount.

In addition, pellet stoves usually cost more than similarly sized wood stoves. (That said, you could save on installation, since most pellet stoves are direct-vented—that is, exhaust gases are vented through a pipe in the wall behind the stove rather than through a long pipe that exits through the roof via a chimney.) Wood pellets cost more than firewood, too, and you'll also generate a lot of plastic waste since pellets come in plastic bags, even when ordered in bulk.

Another drawback of pellet stoves is that they're more complex than wood stoves. Moving parts like the fan and the motor that operates the auger that delivers pellets to the combustion chamber require occasional maintenance by you or the installer. Most wood stoves require very little, if any, maintenance.

Installation

Pellet stoves, like wood stoves, can be installed by handy, knowledgeable do-it-yourselfers with good carpentry skills and the patience to read and follow detailed instructions. Check this information before you buy, so you can see what is involved. Also check with your local building department to determine their requirements, including building permits, before you purchase a pellet stove. They may require professional installation.

Shopping Tips

Pellet stoves vary in size, style, and heating capacity (8,000 to about 90,000 Btus per hour). To select the appropriate size, consult a knowledgeable dealer/installer—one who will take into account *all* of the factors that affect the stove size you need, including the energy efficiency of your home.

As noted earlier, most pellet stoves produce a much smaller fire than a wood stove, so if you like the look of

Go Green!

• Reuse the plastic bags pellets come in, for trash or other purposes. You can also check local recyclers or http://earth911.org to find out where the bags may be recycled.

• If you buy pellets by the pallet, you or one of your neighbors may be able to use the pallet's wood for construction projects (such as the compost bin in Project 59) or for firewood.

• Thinly scatter cold ashes from your stove on your gardens or lawn, or add them to your compost pile—not too much at once though, as ash is a strong alkaline. Ash can help restore soil nutrients to very acidic soil. Don't put ash on acid-loving plants though, like rhododendrons, azaleas, or blueberry bushes. Use protective gloves when handling ash and store it in a metal container with a lid.

a conventional fire, shop for a stove with a good flame pattern and a large viewing glass. Some models contain ceramic logs that disperse the flames and create a more traditional-looking fire.

Pellet stoves come in two basic types: bottom or top fed. Each has pros and cons. With a top-fed stove, for example, there's less chance of a fire burning back into the hopper. However, the combustion chamber is more likely to become blocked by ash (created when pellets burn) and clinkers (deposits that form when ash is reheated) than those in bottom-fed stoves. Be sure to burn high-grade (low-ash) pellets in top-fed pellet stoves. Bottom-fed models can burn a lower-grade pellet because both ash and clinkers are deposited into an ash pan.

Remember that ashes need to be removed once or twice a week if a pellet stove is being used daily. If you anticipate frequent use, look for a model with a large-capacity ash pan that is easy to access.

Also look for a pellet stove that permits easy access to parts that need occasional repair or replacement. You may want to sign a service contract with the stove retailer to cover routine maintenance and repair. To learn more, log onto **www.hearth.com**

What Will It Cost?

Prices for pellet stoves range from about $1,700 to $3,000 or more, according to the Department of Energy. Installation costs roughly $150 to $400, depending on the difficulty of the job, the amount of flue pipe that must be installed, and labor costs in your area. If you are debating between a wood stove and a pellet stove, and you don't already have a chimney in place, a pellet stove will save on installation costs since it does not require a full-height chimney or flue.

Cost estimate: Installation of a pellet-burning stove, and protective brick surround

Cost for materials only: **$2,400**

Contractor's total, including materials, labor, and markup: **$4,900**

Costs are national averages and do not include sales tax.

What Will You Save?

To calculate the savings if you use a pellet stove as your home's main heat source, visit the Wood Master website, which provides a calculator for comparing the cost to run a pellet stove to other fuels, such as, oil, natural gas, electricity, and propane (http://www.woodmasterplus.com/whyus-costsaving.php).

Project 23

Fireplace Insert

A wood-burning fireplace adds to a home's ambiance and, as a result, increases its market value. Unfortunately, conventional fireplaces are notoriously inefficient—they sometimes lose more heat than they radiate into a room! In fact, they are one of the least efficient of all heating technologies ever invented! Most older wood-burning fireplaces achieve only 5% to 10% efficiency. In other words, only 5% to 10% of the heat generated by the fire actually makes its way into the adjoining rooms. Most of the heat is lost up the chimney. In addition, conventional wood-burning fireplaces are a well-documented source of air pollution.

If you want to improve your fireplace's energy efficiency, one thing you can do is install a sealed glass door over the opening. Tightly sealed glass doors reduce heat loss through the chimney when the fireplace is not operating and are much more effective than simply closing the damper, since dampers are leaky.

Another option is to install a fireplace insert. According to the Hearth, Patio, and Barbeque Association (HPBA), "the installation of a fireplace insert can turn an occasional source of warmth into a convenient and easy-to-use supplemental zone heater that can help control high home heating bills, while protecting winter air quality."

What Is a Fireplace Insert?

A fireplace insert consists of a firebox surrounded by a steel or cast-iron shell. The unit fits into an existing wood-burning fireplace. Inserts are designed to burn wood, wood pellets, coal, natural gas, or propane.

Room air circulates between the firebox and an outer shell, absorbing heat. The shell ensures that the heat is delivered to the room and not absorbed by the brick or masonry material. The combustion chamber of a wood-burning insert is accessed through a tightly sealed steel door or, more commonly, a self-cleaning glass door that permits a view of the flame.

Fireplace inserts increase the efficiency of wood-burning fireplaces about 65% to 70%, while reducing pollution emissions. Many inserts are equipped with

Project Rating:

Savings
🍁 🍁 🍁

Environmental Benefit
🍁 🍁 🍁

Level of Difficulty
🍁 🍁 🍁

Go Green!

If you heat with wood, ask neighbors to save clean scrap wood and pruned tree limbs for you. Make sure the wood is aged at least six months before burning. Green wood burns less efficiently and produces less heat and more pollution than dry, aged wood.

Wood-stove inserts help improve the efficiency of fireplaces.

Courtesy of Quadra-Fire, a brand of Hearth & Home Technologies, www.quadrafire.com

small, relatively quiet fans that circulate room air around the outside of the stove. Fans improve the rate at which heat is removed from the combustion chamber. They also help circulate warm air through the house.

Installation

In the 1980s, many wood-burning inserts used the existing chimney to vent exhaust gases, provided the chimney was in good shape. As a result, fireplace inserts were relatively easy and inexpensive to install. To prevent chimney fires, however, modern inserts require installation of an approved stainless-steel chimney liner—a flexible or rigid (sometimes a combination of the two types) pipe that runs the length of the chimney flue. The liner exhausts combustion gases to the outside and protects the flue. It also prevents the accumulation of creosote in the flue,

protecting against house fires. The liner should be continuous from the fireplace insert to the top of the chimney.

Fireplace inserts that burn wood, wood pellets, and coal are relatively easy to install, but installation of the chimney liner, wiring to the electrical fan (if it doesn't plug into a nearby outlet), and other components typically require a professional. Besides, your local

Fireplace Efficiency

Although conventional fireplaces are extremely inefficient, many newer ones (made from standard brick or other masonry) come with a prefabricated steel lining and a blower that circulates air around the fire, drawing off heat and boosting the efficiency.

building code may require a licensed professional for this work. Be sure to check with the building department for requirements, including permits and inspections.

Before installing a fireplace insert, be sure to clean the hearth and chimney flue. Hire a professional so it's done properly. (A chimney installer will normally offer this service.) The first step is often attaching weatherproof flashing at the top of the existing chimney and installing the chimney liner, starting from the top. Once the liner is in place, the installer will secure a rain cap on the chimney. The fireplace insert is then installed, and the chimney liner attached to the insert. If the unit comes with a thermostatically controlled fan, it may need to be wired into your existing electrical supply. To install a natural gas or propane insert, a gas line will need to be run to the insert. (This is definitely a job for professionals!)

Shopping Tips

Fireplace inserts are widely available through wood-stove retailers and on the Internet. Determining the type of insert you want to install involves several considerations, including cost and the type of available fuels in your area—and your goals. For example, if your goal is to burn a renewable fuel, choose a wood or wood pellet insert. Also compare units by efficiency and heat output, level of maintenance required, and, of course, appearance, including the size of the window that allows you to view the flames.

Wood-burning fireplace inserts vary with respect to heat output, ranging from 30,000 to nearly 85,000 Btus per hour. The larger the space you need to heat, the more Btus you'll need. Oversizing a wood or pellet fireplace insert won't hurt. You can always burn smaller fires by putting in less fuel or adjusting either the air

intake (of wood-burning fireplace inserts) or the rate at which pellets are delivered to the combustion chamber (in pellet-burning inserts).

When purchasing a fireplace insert, look for an Energy Star-qualified unit for the best energy efficiency and lowest pollution emissions. Also look for a model with a blower. Before you shop for an insert, be sure to carefully measure and record the height, width and depth of your fireplace.

What Will It Cost?

Fireplace inserts for burning wood or pellets start at about $1,000 and go up to about $2,500, without installation, depending on features and finishes, including door frame materials and handles. Pellet-burning fireplace inserts tend to be more expensive than wood-burning models.

Cost Estimate: Installation of a fireplace insert and accessories

Cost for materials only: **$1,800**

Contractor's total, including materials, labor, and markup: **$2,600**

Costs are national averages and do not include sales tax.

What Will You Save?

Installing a fireplace insert, like a wood or pellet stove, involves the initial cost, then ongoing expense to provide fuel, as well as a modest amount of electricity to run the fan. Over the long term, however, a wood-burning fireplace insert can help cut utility bills, as wood is cheaper than conventional home heating fuels. Ask local retailers for their input on the economics of this venture.

Project 24
Radiant Barrier

Project Rating:

Savings
🍁 🍁 🍁

Environmental Benefit
🍁 🍁 🍁

Health/Comfort
🍁 🍁 🍁

Level of Difficulty
🍁 🍁 🍁

When most people think about staying cool in the summer, they immediately think of air conditioning or evaporative cooling. Although effective, these systems are fairly expensive to install and, with rising fuel costs, expensive to operate. Generating that energy also contributes to global warming and other environmental problems.

If you want to find a way to stay cool without polluting or burning fossil fuels, consider installing a radiant barrier in your attic. This simple, inexpensive measure could help cool your house and, if you use air conditioning, reduce your energy costs. Radiant barriers are especially effective when combined with other energy-efficiency measures such as adding attic insulation (Project 13), sealing the leaks in exterior walls (Project 12), and other improvements (especially Projects 14 and 16).

What Is a Radiant Barrier?

As the name implies, a radiant barrier blocks heat. (Technically speaking, it reflects infrared radiation.) Radiant barriers are installed in homes primarily to reduce summer heat gain. Heat entering your house through the roof and ceiling can account for up to 15% to 25% of summer heat gain, according to the U.S. Department of Energy. (Some other sources suggest higher levels of heat gain through the roof.)

Radiant barriers consist of a thin sheet of a reflective material, usually aluminum, applied to a paper or plastic backing. Some products are fiber-reinforced to make them more durable and easier to handle.

Radiant barriers are installed in attics in existing homes in one of several ways. The simplest is to lay it on top of the existing insulation—with the reflective side facing up (toward the roof). This is referred to as an *attic floor application*. Radiant barriers can also be stapled onto the underside of the roof rafters, again with

Radiant barrier
Courtesy of Radiant GUARD

the reflective side up. An easier option is to have a liquid radiant barrier sprayed on the underside of the roof decking. This product is made by Efficient Attic Solutions (**http://efficientattic.com**) and is currently available in Texas through Home Depot and TXU Energy. It should be available soon in Arizona, Nevada, California, and Florida. Check with your local Home Depot or Lowe's for an installer.

In new construction, radiant barriers can be attached to the upper surface of the roof rafters prior to installation of the roof deck (usually plywood or OSB). Or, they can be installed on the underside of the roof deck. Some roof decking comes with a radiant barrier already attached.

Radiant barriers may be available at home improvement centers and lumberyards, so ask around. If not, a local insulation contractor or supplier can probably help you. You can also locate these products on the Internet.

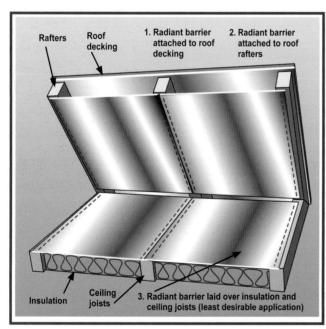

Radiant barrier installation options
Illustration by Anil Rao

Why Install a Radiant Barrier?

Roofs are bathed in intense sunlight during the summer. The hot underside of the roof deck radiates heat into the attic. As the attic heats up, heat flows through the ceiling insulation into the living space below. The hotter the attic, the more heat is gained.

Radiant barriers prevent the flow of heat into the living space and, therefore, help cool our homes passively. This, in turn, reduces cooling costs, saving homeowners a significant sum year after year. The Florida Solar Energy Center estimates that, in their state, radiant barriers can reduce cooling costs by 8% to 12% per year.

By reducing energy demand, radiant barriers also reduce air pollution and habitat loss from mining coal and nuclear fuels used to generate electricity. And they increase comfort in our homes.

Radiant barriers are typically installed in the hottest climates, for example, the southern United States. However, homeowners in many parts of the world could benefit from installing a radiant barrier, considering rising fuel costs and increasing summer temperatures caused by global warming.

Installing a radiant barrier in a home cooled by an air conditioner or an evaporative cooler could reduce the run time of these appliances. This, in turn, not only saves energy and lowers your utility bills, but can reduce maintenance costs and increase the equipment's life span, meaning fewer replacements over the lifetime of a house. When combined with other passive cooling

Go Green!

Next time you paint, re-side, or re-roof your home, consider a lighter-colored product for the job if you live in a sunny, hot climate. Lighter colors reflect heat from the sun, whereas darker colors absorb heat. Energy savings in southern climates can range from 10% to 50%.

measures (such as weatherizing and insulating a home), radiant barriers could eliminate the need for air conditioning altogether. Although installed primarily to aid in cooling, radiant barriers also reduce heat loss through the ceiling in the winter, saving you even more money.

Installation

As noted earlier, you can lay the radiant barrier over existing insulation or tack it to the underside of the roof rafters (the framing members that support the roof deck). Tool requirements are minimal in either case. You will probably need only a flashlight or electric lights, staple gun and staples, scissors or utility knife, a dust mask, and a stepladder.

No matter how you install the product, be sure that the reflective side faces up, so it can reflect heat upwards and away from the living space below.

The job will go faster with an assistant. It will also be safer and easier if you choose a relatively cool day—for example, in the spring or late fall—as attic spaces can become swelteringly hot in the summer. If your attic is unfinished, watch where you step. If you place your foot between ceiling joists or trusses, you could punch a hole in the ceiling below and fall through. You can use a piece of wood or plywood to distribute your weight over the joists.

When building a new house or adding on to an existing home, you can install a radiant barrier as described in this project, or ask the builder to install one over the rafters (beneath the decking). Better yet, you could request roof decking that comes with a pre-applied radiant barrier.

Radiant barrier over attic floor insulation—an easy way to install a radiant barrier, although dust buildup on the membrane can reduce its effectiveness.

Courtesy of Energy Efficient Solutions

Safety Recommendations from the Department of Energy:

- Wear proper protective clothing and equipment as recommended by the manufacturer. Working around some types of attic insulation may irritate the skin, eyes, and respiratory system and may require long sleeves and pants, gloves, eye protection, and a dust mask.

- Be especially careful with electrical wiring, particularly around junction boxes and with old wiring. Never staple through, near, or over electrical wiring. Hire an electrician to repair or replace frayed or defective wiring in advance of radiant barrier installation.

- Watch your head. In most attics, roofing nails penetrate through the underside of the roof decking. A hard hat can help prevent injury.

- Make sure that the attic space is adequately ventilated and lighted.

- Do not cover recessed light fixtures or vents with a radiant barrier.

What to Watch Out For

For retrofits, I recommend tacking radiant barriers to roof rafters rather than laying them directly over insulation on the attic floor. There are several reasons for this. One is because a radiant barrier laid over insulation accumulates dust over time, which can reduce its effectiveness by as much as half, according to the Department of Energy. Another problem with applying the barrier over the insulation is that it makes it difficult, and even potentially dangerous, to move about in the attic, since you can't see where joists are. It's also harder to access ducts, heating and air-conditioning equipment, and electrical wires for service, if they're covered.

If you place a radiant barrier on the underside of roof rafters, it will not accumulate so much dust. It also allows for freer passage of water vapor that rises up through the ceiling and attic insulation, so it can more easily exit the home. During the winter, water vapor from interior spaces can penetrate ceilings—especially around light fixtures—and enter the attic space. This moisture may condense on the underside of a radiant barrier applied over insulation if the material is not moisture-permeable. The moisture may drip onto the insulation, reducing its R-value. Moisture could also damage the ceiling and could promote mold growth in the insulation.

If you are shopping for a radiant barrier to lay over insulation on the attic floor, look for a product that allows water vapor to pass through it, either through tiny holes or through a special vapor-permeable material. Water vapor permeability is not a concern when applying a radiant barrier to the roof or roof rafters.

Although radiant barriers help reduce heat gain, roof-mounted radiant barriers may increase shingle temperatures by 2°F to 10°F, potentially reducing the life of asphalt shingles. Radiant barriers on the attic floor cause smaller increases of 2°F or less, according to the U.S. Department of Energy.

To comply with building code fire safety requirements, radiant barriers must be rated Class A by the National Fire Protection Association. When shopping for a radiant barrier, be sure to look for these ratings. They are either printed on the product or listed on material data safety sheets provided by manufacturers or vendors.

When installing a radiant barrier, be careful not to compact existing loose-fill or batt insulation, as this will reduce its R-value.

The Importance of Attic Ventilation

Attic ventilation helps us stay cool in the summer and removes damaging water vapor in the winter. (See Project 26.) If you install a radiant barrier, you'll find that it performs better in summer if your attic is well-ventilated.

How much ventilation is required? Unfortunately, there are no specific recommendations for homes with radiant barriers. But as manufacturers point out, building codes have established guidelines for ventilation of one square foot of net free ventilation area for each 150 square feet of attic floor area. A 900-square-foot attic will require 6 square feet of open vent. This ratio may be reduced to 1 to 300 if a vapor barrier was installed on the rafters, or if the builder installed a ridge or gable vent and soffit vents.

Because part of the vent area is typically blocked by mesh material or louvers, its net free area is slightly smaller than its overall dimensions.

What Will It Cost?

The costs for a radiant barrier depend on a few different factors. One is the type of material, e.g., reinforced or perforated sheets versus the most basic type of sheet material—or a spray-on barrier. (If you choose to install the sheet material yourself, you can purchase one roll of reinforced, perforated radiant barrier material, 48" x 125', for about $85 to $120.)

For professional installation, costs will be higher if the radiant barrier is applied to the rafters, as opposed to the less time-consuming job of laying it over the attic floor insulation. Material costs for the rafter application are also higher since the total area of the roof and gables is greater than the area of the attic floor—it will take about 7% to 50% more material for the rafter application, depending on the roof configuration. Extra costs can also accrue if other measures need to be taken, for example, installing attic and roof vents.

It is easier and cheaper to install a radiant barrier when you build a new home or addition, than when retrofitting an existing attic. Radiant barrier installation is sometimes offered as part of an energy upgrade, along with insulation and weatherization (sealing) of homes.

Cost Estimate: Installation of a radiant barrier on the attic floor of a two-story, 2,500 square foot home

Cost for materials only: **$560**

Contractor's total, including materials, labor, and markup: **$1,060**

Costs are national averages and do not include sales tax.
If you have one contractor do several small projects, you'll save money overall.

What Will You Save?

According to the Department of Energy, the savings on heating and cooling bills, resulting from a radiant barrier, depend on many factors. These include the type and placement of the radiant barrier, your home's size and style, and the amount of attic insulation. Other influences include the color (light versus dark) of the roof, the ambient temperature in your location, and your thermostat settings.

Project 25

High-Efficiency Cooling Systems

Summers seem to be getting hotter every year. To stave off heat waves, more and more homeowners are purchasing window air conditioners, central air conditioning systems, or evaporative coolers—even in northern areas of the country. If you're in the market for an evaporative cooler or air conditioner, look for an energy-efficient model.

Evaporative Coolers

If you live in a dry, hot climate, such as the desert Southwest or the mountain states, the cheapest and most environmentally friendly option for cooling your home is an evaporative cooler, also known as a "swamp cooler" or a "desert cooler." If you live in a more humid climate, you may want to skip this information and read about energy-efficient air conditioners later in this project.

Evaporative coolers have fewer moving parts than central air conditioners and, as a result, cost about half as much. Standard models require much less energy to operate—up to 75% less than an air conditioner. Evaporative coolers also provide a steady supply of fresh air, unlike central air conditioning systems, which simply circulate room air through the cooler. As an added bonus, these devices don't require ozone-depleting chemicals like those found in older-model air conditioners.

Evaporative coolers are relatively simple devices that are usually mounted on the roof, although wall-, window-, and ground-mounted units are also available.

They come in two basic designs. The first and simpler one is the *direct evaporative cooler*. As shown in the illustration below, it draws outside air in through a moistened mat and then blows it into the house. As the outside air flows through the mat, it is humidified. The heat in the incoming air causes this moisture to evaporate—to enter a vapor state. Evaporation draws heat out of the incoming air, cooling

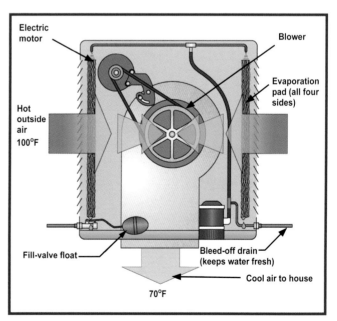

Direct evaporative cooler
Reprinted with permission from *How Your House Works*, by Charlie Wing

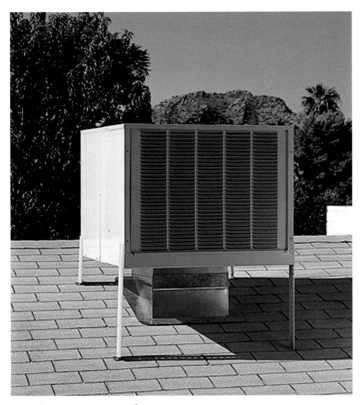

Evaporative cooler
Courtesy of AdobeAir, Inc. www.adobeair.com

drawn into the unit from the outside as shown below. One stream passes through a wet mat and is cooled. It then passes through a device known as a *heat exchanger*. The cool air cools down the heat exchanger. This air, however, does not enter the home. It's discarded—returned to the outdoors.

A second stream of outside air also flows into the cooler. It passes through the other side of the heat exchanger and is cooled. This air is then blown into the house.

Two-stage evaporative coolers cost more than direct coolers and are slightly less efficient, but they offer the advantage of not adding moisture to room air. (Humidity can cause problems in some homes.) A sophisticated—and considerably more efficient—version of this technology is now being produced by a company in Colorado. This new unit, the "Coolerado Cooler," achieves the same results as a two-stage cooler, but uses much less energy. It's probably the most efficient mechanical cooling system on the planet.

it down by as much as 40°F. (This evaporation process is what makes you feel cooler when you step out of a swimming pool on a hot summer day.)

The cool, slightly moistened air is then distributed throughout the house, either through ducts to individual rooms or via a single duct to a central location. The cool air circulates through the home and exits via open windows, screen doors, or a special vent. The house stays cool because of the continuous supply of air moving through it. Moisture levels usually aren't sufficient to cause condensation. (If you don't open windows or a vent though, the moist air will leak out through gaps in the building envelope, and could accumulate in insulation and cause all kinds of problems.)

The second type is an *indirect evaporative cooler*, also known as a *two-stage evaporative cooler*. These units are a bit more complicated. Two-stage evaporative coolers are designed to cool incoming air, but not humidify it. To achieve this, two streams of air are

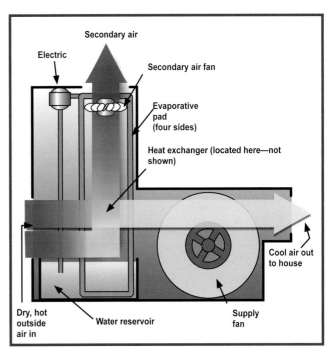

Indirect evaporative cooler
Illustration by Anil Rao

The Coolerado 2-stage evaporative cooler
Courtesy of Coolerado Corporation

Many evaporative coolers incorporate a bleed-off valve that drains water from the reservoir at the base of the mat approximately every six hours. Although the bleed-off feature consumes about five gallons of water or more per hour, it is a desirable feature because it helps to reduce mineral build-up in the system and reduces maintenance.

Evaporative cooler sizing is based on air flow—how many cubic feet of air a unit can deliver to a home per minute (cfm). Models range from about 3,000 to 25,000 cubic feet per minute. Manufacturers typically recommend providing enough air-moving capacity to ensure 20 to 40 complete air changes per hour, depending on the climate. To calculate the size of the unit you'll need, first determine the cubic footage of your home, then divide that number by two. For example, a 2,000 square-foot home with 8 foot ceilings has a volume of 16,000 cubic feet. Divide that by 2 and you get 8,000 cubic feet, which determines the size of the evaporative cooler you need.

Sizing is important, so be sure to hire a professional who knows what he or she is doing. Oversized direct evaporative coolers waste water and energy and may even cause excess humidity to build up in your home. While researching your options, you may want to consider a two-speed cooler or a variable-speed evaporative cooler. Both designs are more efficient and help you more precisely meet your needs.

Installation

Installing an evaporative cooler is a job best handled by a professional heating, ventilating, and air-conditioning contractor. Steps include constructing and attaching a platform to support the cooler, cutting an opening to connect the cooler to the ductwork below, flashing the roof, and connecting tubing to the water supply and code-approved electrical wiring to the circuit box.

What to Watch Out For

Evaporative coolers are ideally suited for hot, dry climates, as noted earlier. They don't work well in humid climates since they can't significantly cool moist air. (There's already too much moisture in the outside air to effect evaporation.) If you live in a climate where an evaporative cooler works, consider yourself lucky.

Although evaporative coolers offer many advantages over air conditioners, they consume a fairly large quantity of fresh water, a resource that is often in short supply in the regions for which these systems are best

Go Green!

• Close windows and drapes on hot days to reduce heat gain. Run heat-producing appliances like dryers, clothes washers, and dishwashers during the evening, the coolest part of the day. Use a ceiling fan to make the temperature feel cooler. For every degree you can turn the thermostat up, you save 1% to 5% on air conditioning costs.

• Seal and insulate leaky ducts in your heating and cooling system (Project 12). This reduces the loss of heated or cooled air to unconditioned spaces, such as attics, and can reduce energy used for cooling by 10% to 15%.

suited. Evaporative coolers use between 3.5 and 10.5 gallons of water per hour while running. Systems with bleed-off valves, consume the most water.

Evaporative coolers work best if maintained properly—and regularly. Drip pans (reservoirs) should be emptied and cleaned if the cooler is shut off for an extended period to eliminate bacteria and mold. The drip mats should also be replaced or cleaned per manufacturer's instructions.

Another issue worth noting is that two-stage evaporative coolers force large amounts of outdoor air into a home. This may bring in pollen and other particulates that affect people with allergies.

Air Conditioners: What Are Your Options?

Unlike evaporative coolers, air conditioners can be used in all climates. They cool and dehumidify air simultaneously using the same technology that makes your refrigerator operate. Instead of removing heat from stored food, however, air conditioners remove heat from indoor air and dump it outside.

Central air systems are generally more efficient than window or wall units. They circulate cool air through the same ducts used to distribute heat in the winter via a forced-air heating system.

Because of growing interest in energy efficiency, changes in federal law requiring more efficient appliances, and America's Energy Star program, air conditioners have improved dramatically in recent years. By law, all new air conditioners must have a seasonal energy efficiency ratio (or SEER) of at least 13. (The higher the number, the more efficient the unit.) Energy Star appliances have a SEER of 15 or higher. Air conditioners may also come with an energy-efficiency ratio (EER) that indicates their efficiency when operating in higher temperatures. Energy Star-qualified central air conditioners must have an EER of at least 11.5. Wall and window air conditioners have lower ratings because they're less efficient—EER ratings range from 9.4 for larger units to 10.7 for smaller ones.

If you're building a new home and have taken steps to reduce its cooling needs (for instance, by making it airtight and well-insulated), and an evaporative cooler isn't right for you, consider an Energy Star-qualified air conditioner.

If your home is currently equipped with central air, and the equipment is 12 years old or older, it's a good idea to replace it with an energy-efficient system. It's likely on its last legs—since central air conditioners don't last much longer than this. It is also very likely inefficient and costing you a lot more money to operate than a modern energy-efficient model. You may also want to consider replacement if your system needs frequent repair. (If you have home repair insurance that covers replacement, you may want to wait until the air conditioner expires, so the new one will be covered by the plan, though your choice of new equipment may be limited.)

If your window unit air conditioner is between 10 and 15 years old, it may also make sense to replace it. Although it may have a few good years left, it's also very likely inefficient—with a SEER around 7 or 8. Installing a moderately efficient model with a SEER of 13 can cut fuel costs by 30%. Installing an Energy Star-qualified air conditioner with a SEER of 15 could cut your cooling costs by half!

With rising fuel costs, an energy-efficient air conditioner may be one of the best investments you've made in a long time. Rather than dumping an old air conditioner in the landfill, be sure to call around to

Go Green!

Use energy-efficient lighting and appliances to reduce waste heat and keep your home cooler in the summer. Install compact fluorescent lightbulbs in fixtures near the thermostat. Waste heat from ordinary incandescent lights may cause the air conditioner to run more often than necessary.

appliance recyclers in your area to see if they will take it off your hands. They should be able to remove the ozone-depleting freon gas, too.

Installation

Removing an old central air conditioner and installing a new one is a job for professionals. Window units can be installed by homeowners who are strong enough to lift them into place. You should be able to replace a window unit in a half hour or so.

What to Watch Out For

Before you rush out to buy a new air conditioner, be sure to take steps to reduce heat gain. Doing so can significantly lower your cooling load, so much so that you may no longer need an air conditioner. Or, you may only need to install one or two wall or window units, which are cheaper, though slightly less efficient, than central air conditioning. If you decide to install room air conditioners instead of a central air system, bear in mind that wall units are generally a little better than window units since they're more airtight and won't leak as much air (in summer and winter) as window units. They also don't obstruct views or reduce daylight like window units. They do require cutting a hole in an exterior wall, however.

When replacing an old, worn-out, or inefficient central air conditioner or installing a new one, shop carefully. Find a reputable, well-qualified dealer/installer to calculate your cooling needs. Don't let a salesperson talk you into a particular unit without a detailed calculation of your home's actual cooling load, taking into account all improvements you have made in energy efficiency. Don't base the size of the new unit on your old, inefficient one or general rules of thumb. Insist on a thorough analysis based on local climate and calculations of heat gained through the windows, walls, and ceilings of your home. A qualified installer or energy auditor should perform an ACCA Manual J load calculation to determine the size of the central air conditioner you need.

Air conditioners are typically rated in Btu/hour—how much heat they can remove per hour. The cooling capacity of some units, however, is rated in tons. One ton is equal to 12,000 Btu/hour. The cooling load analysis is used to determine the size of the unit.

Whatever you do, don't fall into the trap of oversizing your air conditioner. Oversizing may seem like a good idea, but it makes about as much sense as buying oversized shoes. Having too much capacity results in frequent on-and-off cycling of an air conditioner—that is, the air conditioner turns on and off frequently. This wastes energy. In addition, because it takes time for an air conditioner to dehumidify air, frequent cycling on and off fails to reduce humidity levels. Lower humidity makes us feel cooler and thus improves comfort.

"When replacing heating, ventilation, and air-conditioning equipment, bigger doesn't always mean better," according to the EPA. "If the unit is too large for your home, you will be less comfortable and might actually have higher utility bills." The goal in all of this is to right-size the air conditioner—to determine the size needed to do the job.

Air conditioners are fairly noisy, so be sure to install the equipment for a central air unit away from living spaces, bedrooms, porches, and patios, if possible. For optimal function, the outside components should be located in a cool, shaded area, preferably on the north side of your home. Excess heat reduces the air conditioner's efficiency

Go Green!

Properly cleaning and maintaining an air conditioner will extend its life and help it operate more efficiently. Replace the filters in a central air system every other month. Dirt can interfere with air flow and efficiency and damage the equipment. Check and rinse filters in room air conditioners every two months. Have a professional clean and inspect your central system or window unit as recommended by your owner's manual.

Be sure that air can circulate around the unit, too. You may need to clear shrubs or other plants that block air flow. If not, the air conditioner won't be able to dissipate heat as effectively. By all means, avoid rooftop installations unless the unit is shaded.

Shopping Tips

Look for a model that includes a fan-only switch. This feature allows you to save energy and money by using the air conditioner's fan on its own to cool your home. This can work well at night to draw cool air into your house, so long as it is not too humid.

You might also want to buy a unit with a filter check light that indicates when the filter needs replacement. Variable-speed fans allow for more efficient operation than the one-fan-speed-for-all-temperatures option. Yet another option on some air conditioners is a thermal expansion device or TXV. Factory-installed, a TXV helps boost performance under high temperatures.

Finally, if your furnace needs replacement, and you're in an area with relatively mild winters, you may want to consider installing an air-source heat pump discussed in Project 20. These devices serve as air conditioners in the summer and heaters in the winter. Like ground-source heat pumps, air-source heat pumps remove heat from the air in the winter—even when temperatures are quite low. The heat pump concentrates that heat and delivers it to the home using refrigeration technology. In the summer, these remarkable devices remove heat from the air inside our homes and dump it outside.

Installing Central AC

If your home is not equipped with central air conditioning, but you'd like to install a new system, contact a local HVAC expert for advice. If your home is equipped with a forced-air heating system, you may be able to use its ducts to distribute cool air. If you don't have ductwork in place, you might want to consider a ductless mini-split system, a device known as an air-source heat pump. These operate on electricity, are fairly efficient, are easier and less costly to install, and also distribute warm air in the winter.

What Will It Cost?

Direct evaporative coolers run about $700 to $1,000. Indirect (two-stage) evaporative coolers cost about twice as much. Other cost factors include the size of the cooler, whether you have ductwork already in place, and the type of mounting (roof or ground). Another cost (and environmental) consideration is the water used by indirect evaporative coolers, between 3.5 and 10.5 gallons for each hour they operate.

Cost Estimate: Replacement of a central air-conditioning system with a new indirect, evaporative cooler for a 2,500 SF home

Includes removal of old air conditioning equipment and an allowance for connections. Does not include ductwork.

Cost for materials only: **$3,725**

Contractor's total, including materials, labor, and markup: **$5,200**

Costs are national averages and do not include sales tax.

What Will You Save?

Replacing an inefficient central or room air conditioner with an Energy Star-qualified model will save energy and money. To get an idea of how much you will save, based on your local utility costs, visit **www.energystar.gov** and search for the air conditioner calculator.

Evaporative coolers, if appropriate (and allowed) in your area, will save money over conventional air conditioning systems. Operating costs are between 25% and 30% of conventional air conditioning. Replacement parts are more expensive than for conventional air conditioning, but you can save money by performing most of the maintenance yourself.

Indirect (two-stage) evaporative coolers are less efficient and more expensive to operate than direct coolers, but use only about 1/4 the electricity of a conventional air conditioner.

Project 26

Ceiling & Solar Attic Fans

One of the easiest ways to keep your cool in the summer is to use fans. In addition to moving air around, which makes us feel cooler, fans can, if properly located, purge heat from a house and draw cool outside air in. Moreover, they use a lot less energy than central air conditioners and evaporative coolers and are much less expensive to install. Fans can dramatically lower utility bills by reducing our use of air conditioning. In this project, we'll look at two options that work well together: ceiling fans and attic fans, including solar-powered models.

Ceiling Fans—How They Work, and What Are Your Options?

Ceiling fans don't cool homes, they cool people. They do so without changing indoor temperature one degree! How? By moving air. The movement of air over the surface of your skin removes heat from a region physiologists call the *boundary layer*—a warm layer of air that surrounds us at all times. By stripping heat from the boundary layer, a ceiling fan makes us feel as if the room air is around 4°F cooler without lowering the room temperature. Ceiling fans are especially effective early or late in the cooling season when all you need is a slight temperature decrease.

If you've made your home energy efficient by implementing other measures presented in this book (such as sealing cracks in the building envelope, adding insulation and insulated window shades, painting your house a light color, and installing energy-efficient lights

and appliances) a few strategically placed fans may be all you need to stay comfortably cool in the summer. Even if you still need air conditioning, ceiling fans will save energy allowing you to raise the thermostat setting. This will lower your electric bill and help the environment by reducing the demand for power generation.

Ceiling fans come in a wide assortment of styles and colors, with and without lights, in a wide price range. Some are operated by remote control, others by wall switches in combination with pull chains. Most ceiling fans come with a switch to change the speed. In addition, most have two settings so you can control the direction in which the blades turn—one setting for winter (to push warm air down) and another for summer (to lift warm air up).

Go Green!

One of the most effective ways to stay cool in the summer is by planting shade trees around your home. To get results sooner, plant a fast-growing variety—or spend more up front for a larger, more mature tree.

Installation

Ceiling fans can be mounted close to the ceiling for low ceilings, or on a down rod (a piece of pipe that positions the fan away from the ceiling) for cathedral ceilings. (If the fan is too high, it may not have much effect.)

Installing a ceiling fan can be fairly easy *if* you're experienced in electrical work and *if* there is a ceiling light fixture whose electrical connections you can use for the fan. If you're installing a ceiling fan in a room without an overhead light fixture, you've got a much bigger project—one that may require the services of a professional installer.

When installing a ceiling fan in a room with a ceiling light fixture, you will have to remove the existing ceiling-mounted electrical box and replace it with a fan-rated box. (See sidebar later in this project.) Be sure to turn off the circuit at the breaker box to avoid

Ceiling fan alternatives: with light
Courtesy of Monte Carlo Fan Company

shock. Test the circuit with a voltmeter to be certain you turned off the correct one before starting the job. Other tools needed for this project include a drywall saw, reciprocating saw or metal-cutting keyhole saw, hammer, wire stripper, lineman's pliers, needle-nose pliers, wire cutters, a screwdriver, and a stepladder.

Once the fan box is in place, attach the mounting plate and thread the electrical wires through it. Use a sturdy

Ceiling fan alternatives: without light
Courtesy of Monte Carlo Fan Company

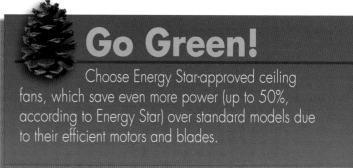

Go Green!

Choose Energy Star-approved ceiling fans, which save even more power (up to 50%, according to Energy Star) over standard models due to their efficient motors and blades.

stepladder. It's a good idea to ask a friend or family member to stabilize the ladder and hand you tools as you need them.

After the mounting plate is installed, assemble the fan (without blades) on the floor, following the manufacturer's instructions. Suspend the fan temporarily on the mounting plate using a hook. Connect the wires from the electrical service to the wires that supply the motor in the fan. If you're installing a fan with a wireless remote switch, wire the receiving unit into the fan, following manufacturer's instructions. When the electrical connections are secure, attach the canopy to the mounting plate. (The canopy is the base of the fan.) Then install the blades. For further guidance beyond the manufacturer's instructions, check out detailed installation information in a home improvement book.

When installing a ceiling fan in a room without an overhead light fixture, you'll need to cut a hole in the ceiling, install a fan box and attach it to the ceiling joists, and then run electrical wire to the fan. Wire can be run from the breaker box (main service panel) or from a nearby circuit, so long as the fan won't overload the circuit. This is generally a job for an electrician.

Shopping Tips & What to Watch Out For

Before shopping for a ceiling fan, measure the volume of the room (length × width × height), and then consult with the folks at your local home improvement center to select the right size.

When installing a ceiling fan, be sure that fan blades are at least 10 inches from the ceiling. If mounted closer, they will not be able to circulate air as well. Also note that ceiling fans should be mounted so the blades are at least seven feet off the floor to avoid injury. Even then, a person who is six feet tall runs the risk of bruising a hand when dressing or stretching beneath a low-hanging fan.

Attic Fans

You can achieve even greater savings—and improve the comfort of your home even more—by installing an attic fan. Like radiant barriers discussed in Project 24, attic fans reduce heat buildup in attics. How?

Conventional attic fans remove warm air through openings (attic vents) typically located on the gable ends or on the roof of the house, as illustrated in the drawing on the previous page. The air that's vented from the attic is replaced by slightly cooler outside air drawn in through soffit vents (openings on the underside of the eaves). Reducing air temperature in the attic reduces heat gain through the ceiling below, as explained in Project 24, and can take a huge chunk out of your energy bill (by reducing cooling costs). But how does an attic fan cool your home when the outside temperatures on a hot summer day are extremely high?

If outside temperatures are in the 90°F to 110°F range, the attic temperature can easily climb to 140°F to 150°F. Even 105°F outside air, when circulated through a 140-degree attic, will dramatically lower its temperature. Doing so will reduce heat gain through the ceiling into the living space below.

Go Green!

In many climates, it is possible to cool homes simply by opening secure windows at night. Cool evening breezes purge heat from the house. Close the windows and draw the shades during the day to keep heat out.

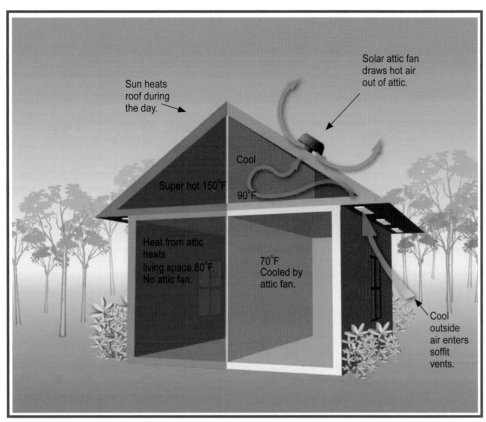

Attic fans reduce attic temperatures, which lowers the temperature of living space.

Illustration by Anil Rao

Installing an Attic Fan

Installing an attic fan is a job best handled by professionals. If you are an experienced do-it-yourselfer with electrical and carpentry skills (for example, running wire and cutting and flashing holes in the walls or roof of your home), you could tackle this job yourself. Here's a rough outline of what you'll need to do. (Necessary tools include a reciprocating saw to cut the hole, an electric drill, fish tape to run wires through walls, a screwdriver, lineman's pliers, wire strippers, a utility knife, utility lighting, a ladder, and a safety harness.)

Conventional thermostatically controlled attic fans are typically installed in a screened or louvered opening in the attic (on the gable ends of your home) and are wired into a 120-volt electrical circuit. If your attic is not supplied with electricity, wires will need to be run into it—either from an existing household circuit or via a brand new circuit connected to the breaker box. Electrical wires are typically pulled up through interior or exterior wall cavities. Before connecting to an existing electrical circuit, check the amperage on the attic fan to be sure that the attic fan won't overload the circuit (exceed its rated amperage) when operating with other electrical devices. (The allowable circuit amperage is printed on the circuit breaker or fuse in older homes.)

After running the wiring, mount the fan in the gable vent opening. If the attic is not equipped with an opening, you'll need to cut one. You may want to install a louvered attic vent—one that closes when the fan shuts off—rather than a screened opening.

Attic fans should be securely attached to studs on either side of the opening. If the existing studs are too far apart, you can mount the fan on two horizontally placed 2 × 4s properly attached to nearby studs.

Once the fan is mounted, the thermostat is secured to a nearby stud. The thermostat senses attic temperature and turns the fan on when the attic reaches a preset level.

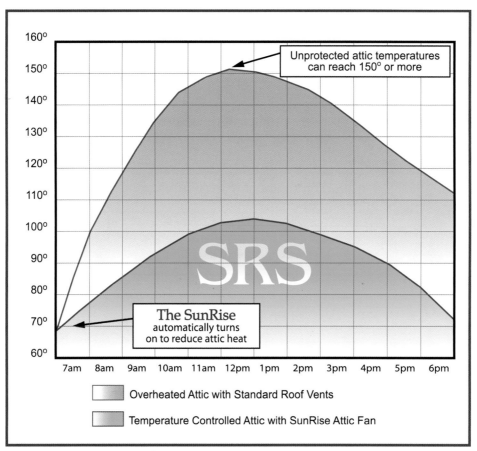

Attic temperatures— with and without a fan.
Courtesy of SunRise Solar Inc.

Connect the wires from the fan and the electrical supply from the circuit to the thermostat, according to the manufacturer's directions. Screw on the cover plate of the thermostat, turn on the power, and adjust the temperature setting.

Solar Attic Fan

To achieve even greater savings and to simplify installation, you may want to consider a solar attic fan. These are typically mounted in the roof and powered by a built-in 10- to 20-watt solar electric module (panel). The module generates direct current (DC) electricity to run the fan. The fan exhausts air at a rate of 800 to 1,200 cubic feet per minute, depending upon the model.

Solar attic fan
Courtesy of SunRise Solar Inc.

Solar gable fan—shown from the outside with a solar panel (left) and from inside the attic (right)

Courtesy of Solatube International, Inc.

Installing a Solar Attic Fan

Solar attic fans are much easier to install than conventional electric attic fans since you don't have to run electrical wires. All you'll need to do is cut an opening in your roof from the outside, according to the manufacturer's specifications, and mount the fan with flashing to prevent leakage. Although that sounds easy, it can be a challenge. Working on a roof, especially a steeply pitched one, can be dangerous. Correct installation of flashing is crucial to prevent roof leaks that can cause costly damage to your home.

Also remember that attic fans require openings to draw outside air into the attic to replace the hot air they're purging. Vents are usually located under the eaves (overhangs). A gable-end opening may also suffice. When in doubt, consult a professional contractor and check the manufacturer's requirements.

To operate effectively, the solar electric module should be in a sunny area so that it is either not shaded at all, or shaded for only a small amount of time during the day.

When installing a solar attic fan or roof fan, do not cut structural framing members. And remember, when cutting holes in roofs, measure two or three times and cut once. Be careful when climbing ladders and working on roofs, too. It's always a good idea to have an assistant.

While most solar attic fans are integrated units, at least one manufacturer makes a model that can be mounted in a louvered gable-end opening like a conventional attic fan (shown above). The solar electric module is not part of the fan, as in the roof-mounted solar attic fan, but is mounted separately on the roof in a sunny location. Wires from the solar electric module connect to the fan in the attic.

Shopping Tips

Before you buy a solar attic fan, measure your attic carefully and then check with the manufacturer's specifications to be sure the fan you're considering will be sufficient. When selecting a ceiling fan, bear in mind that larger rooms may require two or more ceiling fans. Homes with large attics may need at least two attic fans.

Why Use a Fan-Rated Box?

Regular ceiling-mounted electrical boxes should always be replaced by fan-rated boxes, attached to ceiling joists or to a support bar that attaches to joists. In most cases, ordinary electrical boxes aren't strong enough to support a heavy ceiling fan and the force of its motion. Fan-rated boxes have deep-threaded holes or very strong bolts that create a sturdy attachment for the fan.

What Will It Cost?

Ceiling fans range from $35 to $250. Solar attic fans cost between $300 and $700. Regular attic fans start at around $90.

> ## Cost Estimate: Installation of 2 ceiling fans and 2 solar attic fans, controls, and wiring
>
> Cost for materials only: **$750**
>
> Contractor's total, including materials, labor, and markup: **$1,500**
>
> *Costs are national averages and do not include sales tax. If you have a contractor do several small projects at once, you'll save money overall.*

What Will You Save?

A regular attic fan uses electricity, but saves about 10% on air conditioning costs by keeping your attic (and, as a result, your living space below) cooler. Solar-powered attic fans cost more up-front, but produce the same cooler attic with no energy cost.

A ceiling or portable floor fan will cut your energy costs if you have central air conditioning, as long as you raise the thermostat setting. For every degree you turn it up, you can cut 7% to 10% from your cooling costs. Fans use 90% less energy than air conditioning.

According to the Progress Energy Company, which serves customers in the Carolinas and Florida, "a 1,500-square-foot house with air conditioning using two ceiling fans and raising the thermostat setting could save about $70 to $200 over a six-month cooling season." Actual savings depend on the local climate and energy costs.

Here are some examples of minimal savings that you might attain by using ceiling fans instead of air conditioning in different parts of the country.

(Based on Department of Energy data, costs are rapidly escalating so, depending on your climate and AC use, you may save much more than indicated in these examples.)

Annual savings using a ceiling fan instead of AC to cool, based on average cooling hours by U.S. region:

	vs. room AC	vs. central AC
Portland, ME	$75	$200
Pueblo, CO	$135	$378
Charlotte, NC	$210	$578
Tucson, AZ	$285	$798
Miami, FL	$420	$1,176

Project
27
Whole-House Fan

Project Rating:

Savings

🍁 🍁 🍁

Environmental Benefit

🍁 🍁 🍁

Health/Comfort

🍁 🍁 🍁

Level of Difficulty

🍁 🍁 🍁

There are many ways to cool a home that are considerably less expensive and more environmentally friendly than conventional air conditioning: adding insulation to walls and ceilings; sealing leaks in the building envelope; and installing window shades, energy-efficient lights and appliances (that release less heat), energy-efficient windows, ceiling fans, and solar attic fans. Another efficient way to cool your home is with a whole-house fan.

What Are Your Options?

Whole-house fans are high-capacity fans mounted in a central hallway in the first-floor ceilings of single-story homes and in the top-floor ceilings of multiple-story houses. They draw cool outside air into our homes through open windows. The air flows through the house and is vented out through the attic. Whole-house fans bring huge quantities of cool, fresh air into a home. As one manufacturer of a line of quiet whole-house fans (AirScape) notes, "it just makes sense to harness the cool air that Mother Nature has to offer, rather than expensively manufacturing your own."

Whole-house fans are not the same as attic fans featured in Project 26. Attic fans cool the attic during the day, effectively reducing heat gain through the ceiling below. They draw air in through roof vents in the eaves. In contrast, whole-house fans ventilate and cool the entire house. They do so by pulling outside air into the home through open windows. They vent all this air out through the attic.

Whole-house fans are used in a variety of climates—from moderate ones where cooling demands are low, to desert areas with hot summer days and cool nights. They're even helpful in hot, humid climates like the southeastern United States, where they can be used in the spring and early fall, when cooling demands are lower.

Whole-house fans are typically run early in the morning and in the evening when outside temperatures fall below indoor temperatures. They can also be used to cool your home during the day if you have a

Go Green!

• One way to cool your home is to install compact fluorescent lightbulbs in your most commonly used fixtures. Not only are they more efficient and longer-lasting, they produce a lot less waste heat than ordinary lightbulbs.

• Be sure to cover and seal your whole-house fan during cold weather. The louvered opening is a major source of heat loss during the winter. You can install the cover on the attic side, or on the ceiling in the living space. You can buy or make a cover out of fiberglass duct board and duct tape.

Whole-house fans draw cool outside air into homes, purging heat.

Illustration by Anil Rao

Whole-house fans were fairly popular in the early- to mid-1900s, but the early designs were crude and rather noisy. "People who grew up with one in their house often remember it like the monster in the attic," note the folks at the AirScape fan company. Fortunately, many new models are a far cry from those loud, industrial-looking units.

Installation

Installing a whole-house fan is a fairly difficult project best left to professionals, since it involves electrical work and carpentry. If you tackle the job yourself, be sure to follow the manufacturer's instructions. You'll find installation guidelines in many home repair books as well.

cool, dry, non-musty basement. Warm outside air is drawn in through basement windows, then is cooled as it passes through this naturally cool underground space. The air then flows up the basement stairs into the main living areas and is vented through the attic. (Be sure there are no toxic fumes or radon in the basement, and that it is free of mold; otherwise this can be an unhealthy strategy. You also won't want to leave windows open in areas at risk for break-ins.)

AirScape whole-house fan

Courtesy of HVACquick.com

Safety First

When working in an attic, be sure to stand on ceiling joists so you won't step through the drywall ceiling below. You may want to lay a piece of plywood over the joists to serve as a work platform.

When operating a whole-house fan, be sure to open a sufficient number of windows. If you don't, you may have a problem known as back-drafting—a situation in which outside air is drawn into your home through vent pipes such as the water heater flue pipe. This introduces polluted air into your home. Check with the installer for recommendations on the safe operation of your system.

Remember, too, for a whole-house fan to work, your attic must be adequately vented. That is, it must provide a sufficient amount of roof venting to allow air to escape as quickly as it is being blown into the attic. Consult the manufacturer for recommendations. A good rule of thumb is to make sure your attic has the same amount of venting as the size of the hole you've created in the ceiling to mount the fan.

Whole-house fans are usually used when the temperature of the outdoor air is lower than the indoor air. Also, the incoming air is not filtered or dehumidified in any way (just drawn in through open windows) and therefore can introduce dust, pollen, and humidity into your home.

What to Watch Out For

Bear in mind that, because whole-house fans operate with the windows open, they should not be used at the same time as an air conditioner. But, as mentioned earlier, they are useful even if you do have an air conditioner. They provide a cheaper alternative early and late in the cooling season, or at night, if it's cool enough. The air conditioner can be used when the fan is not running.

Before arranging to have a whole-house fan installed, check with your local building department to see if a permit is needed. Also, check the type of wiring that's required. You may need to use armored cable or more flexible NM cable.

Shopping Tips

When shopping for a whole-house fan, pay close attention to air-flow ratings of different models. Air flow is rated in cubic feet per minute, or cfm for short. The larger the home, the greater the air flow needed to cool it. The minimum required to cool an entire home is equal to three times the square footage. (For a 1,200 square-foot home, you'll need a whole-house fan that moves 3,600 cfm.)

Other features to consider in a whole-house fan are variable speeds—high for quick cooling, and low (quieter) for a less forceful air circulation. Different models also offer different controls—from wall switches or pull cords to timers. Louvers (or dampers) should open and close automatically when the fan is turned on and off. You can also choose between a direct-drive fan and a belt-driven fan. The direct-drive models are noisier, but the belt-drive fans require more maintenance.

What Will It Cost?

The materials cost (whole-house fan and other supplies) can be anywhere from about $300 to more than $1,000, depending on the fan's size and features, the framing and electrical work required, whether a new circuit needs to be installed, and the type of fan cover.

This compares with window air conditioners at about $250 to $750, and $2,000 to $4,000 for a central air-conditioning system.

Cost Estimate: Installation of a whole-house fan

Includes a high-quality 36" square, 6,500 cfm, 2-speed fan with switch, wiring, and new circuit breaker, as well as an allowance for framing and drywall repair materials

Cost for materials only: **$1,200**

Contractor's total, including materials, labor, and markup: **$1,450**

Costs are national averages and do not include sales tax.

What Will You Save?

Using a whole-house fan when the temperature cools off in the evening and early morning hours—instead of air conditioning—can save significantly on energy costs. Not only does a whole-house fan cost much less to run than air conditioning, but it can cool a house down in just a few minutes, once the outside air temperature has decreased. Actual savings will depend on current power costs in your area.

Project

28

Radon Test & Mitigation

Many homes are plagued by a silent, but deadly killer—radon gas. Although radon is found in almost all parts of the country, most of us are unaware of its presence, since it is a colorless and odorless gas. (See map below.)

Radon is a radioactive gas released by the decay of a naturally occurring element, uranium, found in the Earth's crust. According to the EPA, radon is "present in almost all rock and all soil and water." Radon seeps into some of our homes from the ground below and is present in the air we breathe.

Inhaled radon gas releases radioactivity, but the bigger concern, according to health experts, is that when it undergoes radioactive decay, the gas is converted to a radioactive form of lead. Lead atoms deposited in lung tissues continue to release radiation. This can cause mutations in the DNA of cells that can lead to lung cancer.

How serious is this problem? According to the World Health Organization and the EPA, radon is responsible for about 15% of all lung cancers and 21,000 deaths each year in the United States—more than the number

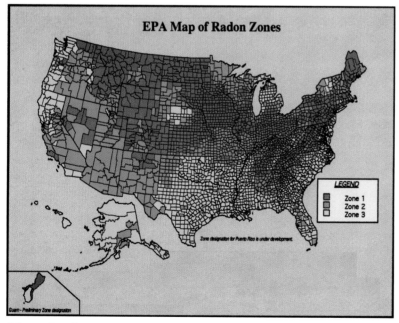

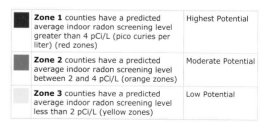

	Zone 1 counties have a predicted average indoor radon screening level greater than 4 pCi/L (pico curies per liter) (red zones)	Highest Potential
	Zone 2 counties have a predicted average indoor radon screening level between 2 and 4 pCi/L (orange zones)	Moderate Potential
	Zone 3 counties have a predicted average indoor radon screening level less than 2 pCi/L (yellow zones)	Low Potential

Map of radon zones in U.S.
Courtesy of EPA

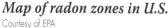

of people who die from accidents caused by drunk drivers. Smokers exposed to radon have a much higher risk of developing lung cancer than nonsmokers.

To protect yourself and your family, you should test your home for radon—or hire a professional to do the job. If radon is detected at levels higher than those recommended by the EPA (see "Radon Mitigation" later in this project), you should take action.

How to Test for Radon

Radon is usually present in outdoor air at very low levels, but is typically more concentrated indoors. According to the EPA, nearly 1 out of every 15 homes in the United States has radon concentrations that exceed their standards. To see if you might be in a radon-rich area, log on to **www.epa.gov/radon/ zonemap.html**

Because radon occurs so widely, it is a good idea to test your home. Even if a neighbor tested his or her home and it turned up negative, you should test yours, because levels vary from one home to another depending on the soil conditions and potential points of entry. "Testing is the only way to know if you and your family are at risk from radon," notes the EPA.

Radon testing falls into two categories: short-term and long-term. By far the quickest and easiest is the short-term test, which takes two to three days. One of the simplest is a small metal canister or plastic vial that contains charcoal that absorbs radon gas from the air in your home or office.

Kits can be obtained through local home improvement centers and hardware stores. You can also purchase them from companies that perform radon mitigation. The kit I purchased (Pro-Lab) from a home improvement center cost about $10 and included a self-addressed, stamped envelope to return the vials for analysis (measurement of radon levels). Analysis costs an additional $20. You can also purchase a radon test kit online from the National Safety Council at **www.nsc.org/issues/radon** Their short-term kits cost $10, as of this book's printing, including the analysis.

To use a test canister or vial, simply remove the lid and place it on a solid surface. It should be at least 20 inches off the floor and three feet away from exterior walls and should be located in the basement or the lowest lived-in level of your home, where it won't be disturbed or accidentally covered.

If your home has a finished basement that is frequently used, this is a good location for the test. If you don't have a basement or the basement is rarely used, place the radon test kit in a first-floor room that's regularly used, for example, a living room, playroom, office, or bedroom. Do not place it in a kitchen or bathroom, as moisture can alter the results. Place the canister away from drafts and high heat as well.

Be sure to leave the kit in this location for the entire period. When the test is over, place the lid on the canister or vial and return it to the lab specified on the package. Send it in right away. Results are typically sent back within a couple of weeks.

Keep doors and windows closed during the test period. (If you're planning to be away for a weekend, run the test then.) Close windows and outside doors at least 12 hours *before* you start the test. Although it's important to "button up" your home during the test, you can run heating and air-conditioning systems, so long as they only recirculate air in a home. The EPA recommends

How Does Radon Get In?

- Cracks in floors and walls in the basement
- Gaps in suspended floors (over crawl spaces or basements)
- Openings around sump pumps and drains
- Cavities in walls
- Joints in construction materials
- Utility penetrations—gaps around pipes and wires
- Crawl spaces that open directly into a building

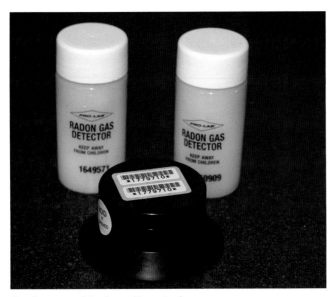

Radon test kit from Pro-Lab
Photo by Dan Chiras

that you not operate fans, heating systems, or other equipment, such as whole-house ventilators, that draw fresh air in from outside, as this will alter the results. Direct-vent furnaces and boilers should be fine. Small exhaust fans that operate for short periods (for example, bathroom or kitchen exhaust fans) may be run during the test. The EPA recommends that you not conduct short-term radon assessments during unusually severe storms or periods of unusually high winds. High infiltration rates (air leakage into your home) will lower radon values.

Because radon levels vary from day to day and from one season to the next, short-term tests are less likely to provide accurate readings of radon levels than long-term tests. However, if you need results quickly—for example, as part of a home inspection to sell a home—a short-term test may be your only option. If you're planning on selling your home within a year or two, it is wise to perform a radon test long before you put the for-sale sign up, so you take steps to mitigate problems, if any, and show the results to prospective buyers. If you're buying a home, you might want to make sure a test is run—and ask that the owner include the basement if you're considering finishing it later as living space.

Long-term home radon tests are available from the National Safety Council and through professional

radon mitigators. Like short-term kits, they contain absorbent charcoal, but require continuous sampling for 3 to 12 months. (The EPA recommends at least three months for long-term tests.) For my home, I used an Alpha Track radon test kit from the National Safety Council. Unlike Pro-Lab vials, theirs came in a sealed pouch. The test unit did not require removal of a cap.

Which Test Should You Use?

The EPA recommends starting with a short-term test. If the results show radon levels over 4 picocuries per liter (pCi/L), a follow-up test is recommended to confirm the results. (Picocuries are a measure of radioactivity.) The follow-up test can be either a long-term test or another short-term test.

To accurately determine the year-round average radon level in your home, the EPA recommends the long-term test. If it reveals higher than acceptable levels, you should call in a specialist to analyze the problem and recommend solutions. If the work needs to be done by a professional, you can find a radon specialist through the Yellow Pages, checking for certifications, experience and references, as well as ratings with the Better Business Bureau. (To learn more about the effects of radon, radon testing, and mitigation, check out the EPA's radon website, **www.epa.gov/radon**)

Preventing Radon Problems in New Construction

Before building a new house, it is a good idea to test for radon first, using a land test device. They're available online or through local radon mitigation contractors. If the test indicates that radon could be a problem, radon mitigation equipment and appropriate construction methods and materials should be incorporated into your plan. It's a lot cheaper to do this up front than install a radon mitigation system after a house is built.

The Surgeon General of the United States recommends testing all homes below the third floor for radon. Fortunately, testing is inexpensive and easy to do. It will take only a few minutes of your time—and costs very little.

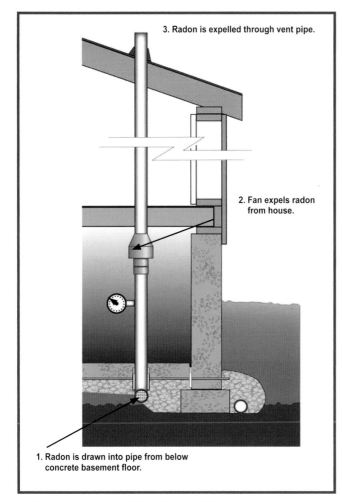

3. Radon is expelled through vent pipe.

2. Fan expels radon from house.

1. Radon is drawn into pipe from below concrete basement floor.

Sub-slab radon mitigation: soil suction
Illustration by Anil Rao

Radon Mitigation

Radon levels in outdoor air average about 0.4 pCi/L—ten times lower than the "action level" for homes. To protect your family's health, it would be ideal to reduce radon inside your home to this level. Because this is difficult to achieve in most cases, most radon experts recommend lowering the risk of exposure by reducing radon levels in homes below the 4 pCi/L EPA-designated level.

Radon levels can be lowered in one of several ways. A common method is the soil suction system shown in the illustration above. In this technique, porous pipes are installed underneath the basement floor or in the crawl space. A fan attached to the pipes pumps radon gas from underneath the house, releasing it outdoors.

To improve the system's efficiency, you'll need to seal all cracks and openings in the basement walls and floors that rest on, or are suspended over, the ground—for example over a crawl space. Sealing helps to block the flow of radon gas into a home.

Radon levels can also be reduced by installing an energy recovery ventilator (Project 29). This device removes room air and replaces it with fresh outdoor air. It operates more or less continuously. To save energy in the winter, the warm indoor air passes through a heat exchanger, which transfers heat from the stale, polluted outgoing air into the fresh, clean indoor air. To learn more about this option, call a local radon contractor or your state radon office or log on to EPA's radon website.

Additional Considerations

Radon may not be on your radar screen, but it's on the minds of many home buyers and real estate agents. Since a radon test is often required by the sales contract, it's a good idea to test for radon well before you put your house on the market. You don't want to lose a prospective sale because a buyer can't wait for a test or possible radon mitigation efforts. For more information, refer to the EPA's pamphlet, *Home Buyer's and Seller's Guide to Radon.* It's available through regional offices of the EPA and online at their radon site.

Radon may also enter a home through the water supply—for example, from a domestic well or a municipal water system supplied by well water. Radon in water can be inhaled when you are taking a shower

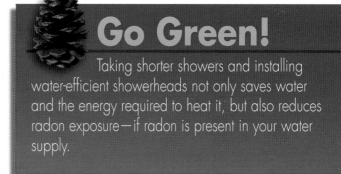

Go Green!

Taking shorter showers and installing water-efficient showerheads not only saves water and the energy required to heat it, but also reduces radon exposure—if radon is present in your water supply.

or washing dishes. Radon can also be ingested in drinking water, although this type of exposure poses a much lower risk than breathing radon, according to the EPA.

If you want to know if radon may be entering your home from a public water supply, contact your water provider. If your home is supplied by a well, you can test the water using a kit available online through numerous retailers, including companies that sell land and home radon test kits. If results show that radon in your water supply is a problem, it can be removed at the point-of-entry by an aeration or filtration treatment system.

In aeration systems, air is bubbled through the water, stripping out the radon. An exhaust fan is used to vent the radon outdoors, so it's not inhaled by the home's occupants. Filters contain activated carbon granules that absorb radon passing through them. Carbon filters tend to cost less than aeration devices, but because radioactivity collects in the filter, contaminated filters may require special (more costly) disposal methods.

Radon can also be removed at the point-of-use, that is, at the tap, by a filter. While cheaper, these filters only treat the water coming out of faucets on which they're installed. As a result, they're not as effective as point-of-entry treatment, which treats all water in the house and is recommended by the National Safety Council.

What Will It Cost?

According to the EPA, hiring a professional to reduce radon levels in generally costs between $800 and $2,500, depending on the home's design and construction and radon reduction methods. The average cost is about $1,200.

Most radon reduction systems require a small amount of electricity to operate. They could also result in the loss of some heated or air-conditioned air. The energy used depends on factors including climate and the type of radon reduction system. However, radon mitigation, where needed, is not an optional expense, but essential protection.

Conventional Radon Mitigation Methods and Costs				
Method	Typical Radon Reduction	Typical range of installation costs (contractor)	Typical operating cost range for fan electricity and heating/cooled air loss (annual)	Comments
Sub-slab suction (sub-slab depressurization)	80%-99%	$800-2,500	$75-175	Works best if air can move easily through the soil under the slab.
Drain-tile suction	90%-99%	$800-1,700	$75-175	Works best if drain tiles form a complete loop around the house.
Block-wall suction	50%-99%	$1,500-3,000	$150-300	Only in houses with hollow block walls, requires sealing of openings.
Sump hole suction	90%-99%	$800-2,500	$100-225	Works best if air can move easily to sump under slab or if drain tiles form complete loop.
Caulking of radon entry routes	0%-50%	$100-2,000	none	Normally used in combination with other techniques.
House (basement) pressurization	50%-99%	$500-1,500	$150-500	Works best with tight basements that can be isolated from outdoors and upper floors.
Natural ventilation	Variable	$200-500 if additional vents are installed; $0 with no additional vents	$100-700	Significant heat and conditioned air loss; operating costs depend on utility rates and the ventilation.
Heat recovery ventilation	25%-50% if used for full house; 25%-75% if used for basement	$1,200-2,500	$75-500 for continuous operation	Limited use; works best in a tight house and when used for basement; less conditioned air loss than natural ventilation.

Excerpted from U.S. Environmental Protection Agency's *Consumer Guide to Radon Reduction*, http://epa.gov/radon/pubs/consguid.html

Project 29 Energy-Recovery Ventilator

Clean air is essential to good health—not just outdoors, but the air we breathe in our homes. How do we ensure clean, healthy indoor air? The first and most important approach is prevention—banning or reducing smoking and the use of harmful chemicals, such as cleaning agents, perfumes, hair sprays, and nail polish, as well as building materials that produce potentially harmful fumes. We can also reduce exposure to these hazards by ventilating spaces where chemical products are used—for example, running a bathroom fan or opening the window when applying hair spray.

Many toxic products can be replaced by healthy ones. You can, for instance, choose a natural fiber or PET plastic shower curtain instead of vinyl, or install wool carpeting, recycled ceramic tile, cork flooring, natural linoleum, or green laminate flooring instead of conventional carpeting or vinyl flooring. You can also use natural cleaning agents and low- or no-VOC paints, stains, and finishes. Radon mitigation efforts, described in Project 28, are another important component in preventing indoor air pollution.

If prevention is the first line of defense in cleansing our air, removal of hazardous substances is the second. An energy-recovery ventilator, or ERV (sometimes incorrectly referred to as a heat-recovery ventilator, or HRV, which I'll explain shortly), provides one means of removing stale, unhealthy air.

What Is an Energy-Recovery Ventilator?

ERVs are mechanical ventilation systems that remove stale, polluted air from our homes and replace it with fresh outdoor air. ERVs are often installed in new airtight, energy-efficient homes to ensure an adequate supply of fresh air. They can be operated in the winter when the furnace is running, as well as summer when the air conditioner is on (although they're not quite as effective with AC).

Go Green!

• Improve your home's air quality by using true HEPA (high-efficiency particulate air) filters for your furnace/air-conditioning system. Although they reduce air flow somewhat, HEPA filters also diminish the circulation of allergens and dust by trapping 99.97% of particles, versus the 10% to 40% trapped by regular fiberglass filters. So-called "HEPA-type" filters may be far less effective.

• Whether installing new ducts or utilizing existing ones, be sure to insulate those that run through unheated spaces. All joints should be sealed with duct mastic. Don't use duct tape. It won't last long.

An energy-recovery ventilator.
Courtesy of Fantech, Inc.

To conserve energy in the winter, ERVs pass the outgoing warm air through an internal component known as a heat exchanger. In the heat exchanger, heat from the outgoing air is transferred to the cool incoming air. This exchange (heat recovery) prevents the home's occupants from being blasted with cold winter air and also saves considerably on the heat bill. In the summer, outgoing room air cools the incoming warm air, helping to maintain comfort. Energy-recovery ventilation systems, therefore, provide a controlled way of ventilating a home while minimizing energy loss, according to the Department of Energy's online publication, *A Consumer's Guide to Energy Efficiency and Renewable Energy.*

Energy-recovery ventilators can be operated by timers or controlled by humidistats, sensors that detect humidity levels in a home. ERVs often remove excess humidity, but can also be set to add humidity.

When researching ERVs for purchase, don't be confused by the terminology. An ERV is not the same as a heat-recovery ventilator. In an ERV, the heat exchanger transfers a certain amount of water vapor—along with heat energy—to the incoming air, while a heat-recovery ventilator transfers only heat. Because an ERV transfers some of the moisture contained in the exhaust air to the usually less humid incoming winter air, the humidity of homes with ERVs tends to stay more constant. This feature also keeps the heat exchanger core warmer, minimizing problems with freezing.

Installation

Although you can purchase a small wall- or window-mounted ERV, most are fairly large units that are suspended from the ceiling—usually in attics, utility rooms, basements, and crawl spaces.

Installation is a job for professionals. ERVs require two connections to the outdoors—one to exhaust stale indoor air, and the other to bring in fresh outside air. According to the *Sustainable Building Sourcebook.* "The inlet and outlet on the building exterior need to be distanced from each other to avoid cross-contamination." Ideally, they should be located on different sides of the house.

If your home has a central heating and air-conditioning system, an ERV can be integrated into your existing ducts to remove stale indoor air and circulate fresh

Go Green!

• To improve your indoor air quality, avoid dry cleaning clothing that can be safely hand-washed. Or consider buying a steam cleaner you can use at home. If you do dry-clean, avoid cleaners that use PERC, a substance that can affect our health and pollute ground water. Look for organic cleaners that use the carbon dioxide process, not the hydrocarbon solvent called DF-2000, which is petroleum-based, so contributes to global warming.

• To save energy, close doors to unoccupied rooms and partially close registers.

air to each room. If your home is not equipped with a central air or a forced-air heating system, installation can be considerably more challenging. The installer may need to build chases (channels to transport air) or install ducts to deliver stale air to the ERV for removal and to distribute fresh air throughout the home. A cheaper alternative is to have the ERV ducted to one central spot in the house. It's best to choose a location that won't result in cold (or hot) air blowing on people, since the incoming air can be slightly cooler or warmer (depending on the season) than room air. For optimum performance, stale air is usually removed from the most humid locations in our homes, such as kitchens and bathrooms.

Could Your Home Benefit from an ERV?

Energy-recovery ventilators are ideal for airtight homes. If your home is new and fairly airtight, or if you've spent time and money reducing leakage through the building envelope (Projects 11 and 12), an ERV may be useful.

How do you know if an ERV is suitable for your home? One way is to have a blower door test performed as part of an energy audit (Project 11). If the air exchange calculated from this analysis is 0.5 air changes per hour (ACH) or less, an ERV is probably a good idea. Another way to determine if an ERV is worth installing is to assess how long odors linger in your home. The longer an odor lingers, the more airtight a home is. The more airtight, the more essential it is to create a supply of fresh air. ERVs may also be advisable in homes in which the heating and/or cooking equipment is not adequately ventilated, for instance, if there's no hood over the gas range, or if the stove does not vent to the outside. An ERV may also make sense if your garage is attached to the house and is not adequately vented, a common situation in some older homes that can result in car exhaust fumes entering your home. (To address this, you can also install a simple exhaust fan that is automatically or manually controlled in the garage to remove exhaust fumes.)

Indoor Air Quality and Health

As you've seen and heard in advertisements for home air filters and duct cleaning services, the air inside our homes can be polluted—sometimes at levels higher than outdoor air. Indoor air pollution comes from a variety of sources. Some pollutants come in from outdoors—chemicals emitted by cars, lawn mowers, leaf blowers, factories, and power plants. Naturally occurring allergens, such as mold and pollen, can also enter our homes from outside.

The pollutants of greatest concern, however, come from harmful chemicals inside our homes. Carbon monoxide, for instance, is released by various combustion appliances, such as wood stoves and gas-fired furnaces, fireplaces, ovens, stoves, and water heaters. Tobacco smoke and burning candles also cause indoor air pollution. Other pollutant sources include pet dander, perfumes, deodorants, cleaning agents, nail polish, paints, stains, and finishes. Even new furniture, cabinets, carpeting, vinyl flooring, shower curtains, and some forms of insulation can emit harmful chemical pollutants. High levels of humidity can also promote mold growth.

Indoor air pollution is responsible for many illnesses, including allergies, asthma, and flu-like symptoms that occur in some individuals when they are exposed to molds. Some pollutants are irritants; others contribute to more serious illnesses, such as emphysema and lung cancer. Reducing indoor air pollution helps create a healthy environment for children and the elderly, who are typically more sensitive to pollutants.

ERVs may be advised if household chemicals and paints are stored indoors (or in an attached garage or basement) and, of course, if formaldehyde levels are high. Formaldehyde is present in many common household materials, including furniture, kitchen cabinets, flooring, and some window treatments. ERVs are also advisable if radon levels are high. Note, however, if radon levels are 15 pCi/liter (picocuries per liter) or higher, an ERV will not generally be adequate to reduce them sufficiently. (See Project 28 for more on radon.)

What to Watch Out For

ERVs work best if there's a supply and return duct for each bedroom and for all common living areas such as family rooms and kitchens. For optimal performance, duct runs should be as short and straight as possible. Duct size is important, to allow air to flow freely through the system.

If you live in a cold climate, choose an ERV equipped with a device to prevent freezing and frost formation. Frost forms as very cold supply (incoming) air flows through the heat exchanger. Frost buildup reduces the system's efficiency and can damage the unit.

ERVs need to be cleaned periodically to ensure adequate performance and to prevent the build-up of mold and bacteria in the heat exchanger. It's a good idea to have a professional service the unit annually.

Homeowners can handle other maintenance, such as cleaning or replacing filters every couple of months, and cleaning outside screens and condensate drains and pans. Check the owner's manual for instructions.

What Will It Cost?

ERVs are a well-developed technology. The prices range from about $500 to $1,700. ERV systems typically cost more to install than other ventilation systems—those that simply bring fresh air into a home through filters and pump stale air out without recovering heat.

What Will You Save?

ERVs pre-cool or pre-warm (depending on the season) the incoming air. This reduces the demand on a home's heating and cooling system and can save energy, depending on your climate and the tightness of your home.

Most energy-recovery ventilation systems on the market today recover about 70% to 80% of the energy in the outgoing air, transferring it to the incoming air.

According to the DOE, ERVs are "most cost-effective in climates with extreme winters or summers, and where fuel costs are high. In mild climates, the cost of the additional electricity consumed by the system fans may exceed the energy savings from not having to condition the supply air." The other factor to consider is the health benefit of freshening your indoor air.

Project 30

Flushing Your Water Heater

Most of us pay a lot more for energy than we need to. Why? Because we waste so much of the energy we consume in our daily lives. One area where we waste a lot of energy is in our use of hot water. In fact, you could easily meet your hot water needs with 20% to 50% less energy. How?

If you're like most people, your hot water is supplied by a storage water heater—a 40- to 60-gallon tank heated by natural gas, propane, oil, or electricity. These units are inherently inefficient. They maintain a huge reservoir of hot water 24 hours a day, 365 days a year. Unfortunately, a substantial amount of heat escapes through the walls of the tank. In gas-fired units, heat also escapes out the flue pipe.

Fortunately, there are many ways to get the hot water we need more efficiently. You can, for instance, lower the temperature setting on the water heater or set it to vacation mode (or completely off) when you're away from your home for more than four or five days (Project 32). If you have an electric water heater, you can install a timer that turns your water heater off any time hot-water demand is low. You can also install an insulated "blanket" made for a water heater and insulate the hot water pipes (Project 31). Water-efficient showerheads will also save you a bundle on your energy bill (Project 37).

Another important way to improve your water heater's efficiency is to flush out sediment that accumulates in the bottom of the tank. This is an easy, no-cost measure that will reduce the water heater's energy requirements.

It will also vastly extend the life of this appliance, saving you additional money by reducing replacement costs.

Besides saving you money, this project will help your family reduce its contribution to greenhouse gas emissions and global warming. By using less energy, you'll also help extend the nation's rapidly declining supplies of natural gas—providing more time to develop clean, reliable, and renewable alternatives. Like other efficiency measures, a water-heater flush requires very little, if any, investment in materials, tools, or equipment, and begins to reward you for your efforts immediately! The only tools, you'll need are a garden hose, a bucket or four-quart pot, and possibly vinegar and a funnel.

How Flushing Improves a Water Heater's Efficiency

Each year thousands of gallons of cold water enter a water heater—either from a well or a municipal water supply. The water often carries tiny amounts of sand, rust, and dissolved minerals that settle to the bottom of the tank. These materials are collectively referred to as sediment.

In gas- and propane-fired water heaters, the build-up of sediment slowly insulates the water in the tank from the heat source—the flame beneath the tank. Sediment may harden over time as it is repeatedly heated and cooled. As it thickens and hardens, sediment

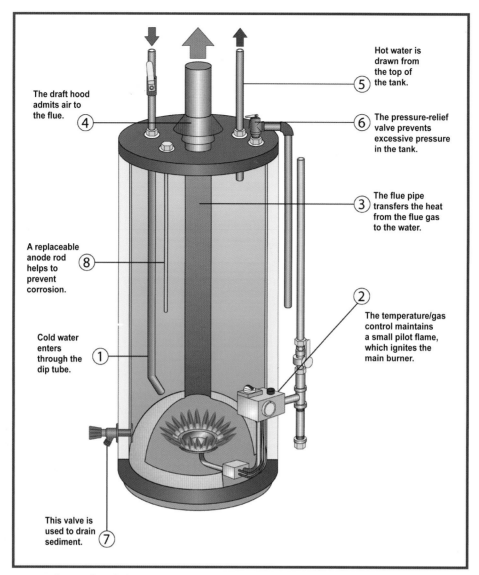

The draft hood admits air to the flue. ④

Hot water is drawn from the top of the tank. ⑤

The pressure-relief valve prevents excessive pressure in the tank. ⑥

The flue pipe transfers the heat from the flue gas to the water. ③

A replaceable anode rod helps to prevent corrosion. ⑧

The temperature/gas control maintains a small pilot flame, which ignites the main burner. ②

Cold water enters through the dip tube. ①

This valve is used to drain sediment. ⑦

Typical gas-fired water heater
Reprinted with permission from *How Your House Works,* by Charlie Wing

increasingly reduces the transfer of heat to the water. As a result, it takes more energy to meet your hot water needs.

In an electric water heater, sediment also accumulates on the electric heating elements. Electric resisters are mounted in the side of the tank—one near the top, the other near the bottom. Electricity flowing through these elements produces heat. (Like the heating elements in an electric stove, the elements in a water heater produce heat as electricity flows through them.) In this case, the heat is transferred to the water.

As impurities accumulate on the heating elements, heat is transferred less efficiently to the water. In addition, sediment buildup on heating elements can cause them to overheat and break, resulting in a costly replacement. While the elements are being coated with impurities, sediment also builds up on the bottom of the tank and may, over time, bury the lower heating element, dramatically reducing its efficiency.

How do you know if sediment has accumulated in your water heater? In gas-fired water heaters, bottom sediment traps hot water. When it reaches a certain temperature, hot water is suddenly released from the sediment, bursting out and creating a boiling or popping sound. If you hear these sounds coming from your water heater, it's well past time to flush the tank. Even if your water heater isn't making a racket, you may need to flush the tank—for example, if it has never been drained and is more than a couple of years old.

How to Flush Your Water Heater

To flush an older tank, one that may contain a fair amount of sediment, first shut off the power to the unit. For an electric water heater, turn off the electricity at the breaker box (also known as the main service panel) or at a nearby fuse box or cut-off box. The latter is typically mounted on a wall near the water heater. For a gas burner, turn the gas setting on the hot water heater to "pilot" or turn it off completely. The pilot control is separate from the temperature control. Whether gas or electric, consult your water heater manual for instructions and follow them carefully—as incorrect actions can be dangerous. Be especially careful when relighting the pilot light.

Next, turn off the cold-water supply to the water heater. This valve is located on a cold-water line that enters at the top of the tank. Now, open a hot-water faucet somewhere in the house, for example, in a nearby bathroom or kitchen. This will allow air into the tank of the water heater, so it can drain quickly and completely.

Next, attach a hose to the drain valve at the base of the tank and run it outside or to a nearby floor drain, if there is one. You could also empty the tank into a one- or two-gallon bucket, but it must fit under the drain valve at the base of the water heater.

Now, open the drain valve. If you are using a hose, it will automatically empty water into a floor drain. Be careful. This water is hot and could burn you. If you're using a bucket, you'll need to empty it numerous times until the tank is empty.

As the tank begins to drain, expect the water to be cloudy. That's the sediment you're purging from the tank. When the tank has drained, water will stop flowing. When this occurs, open the cold water valve at the top of the tank. This will allow clean, cool water in to rinse out additional buildup, known as scale. You may also want to turn the cold water on and off—pulsing water through the tank—to purge the tank of scale.

If it's been a few years since your tank was installed, you may also want to rinse it with white vinegar before refilling. Vinegar contains acetic acid that dissolves calcium deposits in water heaters. In a gas-fired unit, close the drain valve (at the bottom of the tank) and then unscrew the union coupling (a threaded plumbing connection where the cold water enters, or hot water exits). Pour a quart or two of vinegar in from the top, using a funnel. To remove scale from an electric water heater, close the drain valve, then carefully remove the lower heating element and pour the vinegar in the opening.

For best results, you may want to let the vinegar sit in the tank for an hour or two. When the time is up, open the cold-water line once again. Pulse the water. Then drain the tank. Repeat this procedure until the water draining from the tank is crystal clear. After you have rinsed the tank with vinegar, rinse it several times with water (until you can no longer smell vinegar). When done, close the drain valve, remove the hose or bucket, open the cold-water line, let the tank fill, and turn on the power. You should be back in business, but this time, making hot water more efficiently.

Periodic Draining

To maintain a new water heater tank or one that has been recently flushed, drain sediment at least once a year. This is a simple process compared to the complete flush just described. You don't need to turn off the power or the cold water. Simply attach a hose to the drain valve or position a pot or a bucket under it, then

Safety Tip

If you plan ahead, you can let the water sit for several hours after turning off the water heater, so it can cool a bit before you open the drain valve. Even then, be careful, as the water may still be hot.

open the valve and remove a couple quarts of water. When the water comes out clear, you're done. This will take only a minute or two. (First read the instruction manual for manufacturer's recommendations for draining your water heater.)

Mark the next date when flushing will be needed on your calendar—so you don't forget. It's amazing how fast the months and years go by, and how easy it is to forget such simple, money-saving procedures.

What to Watch Out For

While flushing a water heater is pretty simple, you can run into complications. If, for instance, you open the drain valve and nothing comes out, sediment has probably built up and hardened in the bottom of the tank and is blocking the drain valve. At this point, many people replace their water heaters. Before you retire yours, however, you may want to try removing the hardened sediment. To do this, turn off the power. Then shut off the cold-water supply, open the drain valve, and let the tank drain, if it will. To remove hardened sediment in an electric tank, remove the lower heating element and chip out the sediment using a long, thin metal rod, which you can purchase at a hardware store. Work very carefully, however, so as not to damage the tank's glass lining.

In a gas-fired tank, remove (unscrew) the drain valve. Using a long, thin rod, chip away at the hardened sediment. Work carefully, gently, and slowly, as the tank may be weakened, and you risk knocking a hole in the tank wall. If this happens, you'll need to purchase a new tank or upgrade to a tankless water heater (Project 34). (You may want to shop around a bit before you begin this process to find out what your options are, just in case you end up needing a water heater replacement.) Keep in mind that a plumber would probably recommend buying a new water heater at this point, so you don't have much to lose by trying this measure.

What Will It Cost?

Flushing your tank to remove sediment costs nothing but a little of your time and possibly the cost of some vinegar. If you have to replace the water heater, the cost could range from about $200 for very small capacity storage tank heaters to upwards of $1,000, plus installation, depending on the size and whether it's a storage or tankless model. If you purchase a new storage water heater, check the Energy Guide label to compare FHR (first hour rating, or capacity), EF (energy factor), and expected life span, to get the most for your money. The least expensive water heaters are often the most costly to operate. Gas water heaters generally last about 12 years with regular maintenance. Electric models can last twice as long, though they are less economical to operate.

If you hire a plumber to flush your water heater, you'll pay the going labor rate for a visit to your home, which can be $100 or more. Since it's a pretty straightforward task that doesn't take much time, it makes sense to do it yourself, as long as you're careful and follow the manufacturer's instructions.

What Will You Save?

Flushing your tank can save a significant amount of money. According to one source, every half-inch of sediment on the bottom of a tank boosts the energy required to heat water by 70%—very significant when you consider that water heating accounts for about 17% of the typical home's annual energy bill. Proper water heater maintenance, including periodic flushing, could also lengthen this appliance's life by a few years.

Project 31 Water Heater Blanket & Pipe Insulation

Conventional water heaters operate day and night to provide a supply of hot water for you and your family. When you need hot water, it is available any time. However, maintaining a constant supply of hot water requires a lot of energy. In fact, water heating accounts for about 17% of an average home's energy consumption. A good portion (20%) of that energy is wasted. Heat escapes through the walls of the water heater and out the flue pipes. To perform its job more efficiently and economically, your water heater could use a little help.

In this section, we'll look at two projects to save energy and lower your utility bill: installing a water heater blanket and insulating the hot-water pipes in your home. These projects reduce fuel use and greenhouse gas emissions and can save you a fair amount of money over the long term. Although the savings are modest, so is the cost of these projects. Both measures will easily pay for themselves in a year or so. As a side benefit, they may also improve your hot-water supply, reducing complaints about cold showers. The tools for each are minimal: scissors, foam pipe insulation, the water heater blanket, and a tape measure.

Installing a Water Heater Blanket

The first step in making a water heater more efficient is to wrap it with an insulating water heater blanket, which will cost you around $20. Water heater blankets, also known as "jackets", are available at home improvement centers, such as Home Depot, Lowe's, and Menards; numerous independent building supply stores; hardware stores; and the Internet. The most common insulation blankets are made from fiberglass with a vinyl plastic facing (on one or both sides) and are rated at R-10. Choose one with an insulating value of at least R-8. (R is a measure of resistance to heat movement; the higher the R-value, the better.)

Insulation blankets are especially helpful in homes with older water heaters, whose tanks are often inadequately insulated, but they're even more important for water heaters located in unheated spaces, such as basements, garages, and crawl spaces. If the insulation in the water tank's wall is less than R-15, it's generally worth adding an insulation blanket.

Water heater blanket in package
Photo by Dan Chiras

The R-value may be posted on the water heater. If not, check with the installer or the manufacturer's customer service department. If neither can help, try this test. Place your hand on the side of the tank. If the tank feels warm, it needs an insulation blanket. You can also place a folded towel on the top of the tank and let it sit for a half hour or so. When you return, feel the towel. If it's hot, add a blanket.

To begin, remove the one-size-fits-all blanket from the packaging, and then wrap it around the tank, keeping the free ends near the front so they can be taped together. If your water heater's tank is small (for example, only 30 gallons), overlap the ends or trim off some of the excess insulation with a pair of sharp, heavy-duty scissors. Once trimmed or overlapped, the ends are taped. (Tape is provided with the water heater blanket.) For best results, the blanket should fit snugly against the tank.

When installing a water heater blanket, be sure to read and follow the manufacturer's directions very carefully. There are some important details you don't want to miss, especially with oil- or gas-fired water heaters, for example, making sure not to block air flow to the combustion chamber, discussed shortly.

You can make your own water heater blankets using reflective insulation—one of my favorite insulating products. It consists of a single or double layer of bubble wrap—plastic containing air bubbles. This layer is sandwiched between two thin, yet durable layers of aluminum foil or silver (reflective) plastic.

Reflective insulation can be purchased in 48-inch-wide rolls—a perfect size for most water heaters—at home improvement centers. To make your own water heater blanket, measure the circumference of the water heater, then cut a piece of insulation of the same length from the roll. Wrap it around the tank. Be sure to cut openings for the pressure release valve on the side of the tank (and for the thermostat if you have a gas-fired water heater). Also make sure the insulation does not

Water heater blanket made of reflective insulation
Photo by Dan Chiras

impede air flow at the top or bottom of a gas- or oil-fired water heater. Tape the ends using paper-backed metallic tape, usually displayed next to water heater blankets in home improvement centers.

I have found that making your own water heater blanket costs about the same as buying a commercially available fiberglass blanket. However, reflective insulation is easier—and safer—to work with than

Go Green!

• To save money and help create a greener world, take 5 to 10 minute showers instead of baths and install water-efficient showerheads.

• If you wash dishes by hand and have a double sink, fill one basin with rinse water and the other with hot, soapy water. You can use two plastic tubs that fit into your sink to save even more water. When finished, the rinse tub can be used to water plants. Rinsing dishes with the faucet on wastes a tremendous amount of water.

fiberglass. In recent years, some manufacturers have eliminated the inner plastic lining of their fiberglass water heater blankets to save money. Unfortunately, this means you have to handle fiberglass, which can cause skin irritation. Reflective insulation water heater blankets are thinner and especially useful when insulating water heaters that are mounted close to a wall or in small spaces such as closets.

Although pre-made reflective insulation water heater blankets were once sold in hardware stores, I haven't seen this product in any retail outlet for many years. If you would like to purchase a water heater blanket made from reflective insulation, you can order online from one of several manufacturers, such as Canada's EcoTech Hydronics and Heating at **http://ecotechhydronics. com/insul.html**

Installing Pipe Insulation

Insulating hot-water pipes is another relatively easy project that will save energy and money. (You'll need to be able to access the water pipes to insulate them, which is not always possible.) This project will also help provide more hot water faster since it will take less time to deliver hot water if pipes are not so cold. (This is especially true if your pipes run through unheated spaces, such as a basement or crawl space.)

Begin by measuring the length of the hot-water pipe runs in the basement or crawl space leading from your water heater to each faucet, bath, shower, and appliance in your home. Hot-water pipes are pretty easy to identify, especially if you start at the water heater. Here you will find a cold-water line that delivers city or well water to the water heater, and a hot-water pipe from which heated water flows to various faucets and appliances in your home. Follow this pipe, if it's exposed, to the various end uses, measuring all pipe runs.

Hot-water pipes typically run alongside cold water pipes. If you're having trouble determining which is which, turn on the hot water in a sink, shower, or tub for a minute or so and feel the pipes. Hot-water pipes in our homes come in two sizes: ½- and ¾-inch diameter. You will find both ½- and ¾-inch in the same

house with ¾-inch hot-water pipe feeding ½-inch pipe runs. While measuring pipe lengths, be sure to check the diameter of the pipe as well, and separately list the lengths of ½-inch and ¾-inch pipe, so you can buy the right amount of insulation. For reference, a ¾-inch pipe comes directly off the water heater.

Pipe insulation comes in two basic varieties, foam sleeves that fit over hot-water pipes and small rolls of fiberglass that are wrapped around the pipes. Both types can be found in hardware stores and home improvement centers. Foam sleeves fit on pipes quickly and easily and are therefore the product of choice for most homeowners. They come in 6-foot sections for ¾- and ½-inch pipe, split down one side, which makes it easy to fit them around the pipes. Once you've installed a section of insulation, pull the clear plastic tape off the seam so the sides stick together. If you need to cut the insulation, use a sharp serrated knife or a pair of heavy-duty scissors. When you encounter angles in your pipes, cut a piece of insulation to fit to the corner. Cut the ends at a 45° angle so that they fit snugly against each other where pipes bend.

Some water heaters have a heat trap, an S-shaped flexible copper pipe that leads from the top of the water heater to the hot-water lines. (Its purpose is to reduce convective heat loss.) You can insulate that portion of the hot-water pipe with fiberglass wrap insulation.

Insulate all the hot-water pipes you can locate in your basement or crawl space. You may even want to insulate cold-water pipes to eliminate condensation that occurs when cold water runs through warm, damp spaces. This will prevent water from dripping on the floor and perhaps on valuables stored in boxes—and will reduce the chance of mold growth.

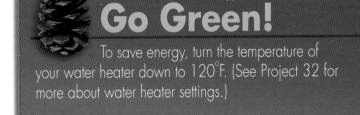

Go Green!

To save energy, turn the temperature of your water heater down to 120°F. (See Project 32 for more about water heater settings.)

What to Watch Out For

When installing a water heater blanket on a gas- or oil-fired water heater, you'll need to cut openings in the blanket for the thermostatic controls at the base of the unit. You may also need to cut a slotted opening for the pressure-release valve on the side of the water heater if it is not precut. Do not cover the valve. If it blows, you'll need to replace it.

Also, when installing a water heater blanket, do *not* insulate the top of the tank, as this may block air flow into the draft vent. Air enters at this point and joins the hot gases escaping from the combustion chamber (at the base of the water heater), ensuring adequate ventilation. If blocked, carbon monoxide can escape— with potentially lethal consequences. Moreover, insulation on the top of the tank can be scorched by hot gases in the flue pipe.

Be careful not to block the air intake at the bottom of the tank near the pilot light and combustion chamber. A good air supply is essential for efficient combustion. The insulation blanket should be at least two inches above the floor to ensure adequate air flow into the combustion chamber. (Check the water heater and blanket manufacturer's recommendations.)

The insulation blanket should fit snugly against the tank. Gaps reduce its effectiveness. It's a good idea to inspect the water heater blanket from time to time to be sure that it has not come loose. After a few years, I had to re-tape mine because the tape had given out, and the blanket was no longer snug against the water heater.

Insulating an electric water heater is a bit easier than insulating gas-, propane-, or oil-fired water heaters. Because there are no flue pipes, pilot lights, or oxygen-consuming combustion chambers in an electric water heater, you can insulate the entire tank. However, make sure not to cover the access to the heating elements. No matter what type of tank you have, the pressure-relief valve and drain pipe leading from it to the floor should not be covered by the insulation.

Also keep the warranty, safety, and operations information and instruction manual uncovered. (They may be on a label attached to the tank or located in a pouch taped to the side of the water heater or a nearby wall.) You want your plumber to be able to see them. Also, some manufacturers may void their warranties if these labels are not visible.

When measuring pipe and installing pipe insulation, be prepared to get a little dirty, especially when working in crawl spaces.

What Will It Cost?

Pre-made water heater insulation blankets cost about $16 to $22. Some utility companies sell them at a reduced price, offer rebates, and even install them at low or no cost to qualified homeowners. You can buy a 48" x 10' roll of reflective insulation, if you choose to make your own insulation blanket, for about $22. Foam pipe insulation pieces cost about $4 to $5 for a 6' length. As long as you can access the pipes, it's a fairly simple project, and doing it yourself will save a substantial amount of money over hiring a plumber.

What Will You Save?

According to the U.S. Department of Energy (DOE), "unless your water heater's storage tank already has a high R-value of insulation (at least R-24), adding insulation to it can reduce standby heat losses by 25% to 45%. This will save you around 4% to 9% in water heating costs."

The DOE also reports that insulating hot-water pipes reduces heat loss and can increase water temperature by 2°F to 4°F versus uninsulated pipes. This allows you to adjust your water temperature to a lower setting, which will reduce energy costs. You should also use less water since you won't have to run the faucet or shower so long, waiting for water to heat up.

Project 32 Adjusting Water Heater Temperature

Heating water for showers and baths, washing dishes, and washing clothes constitutes about 17% of a family's annual energy demand, according to the U.S. Department of Energy. One of the simplest ways to reduce energy use from these activities is to lower the temperature setting on your water heater. There is a good chance you will be able to do so without sacrificing comfort, convenience, or health, because many water heaters are set much too high. A simple adjustment will very likely not be noticed by anyone in your household, except the bill-payer.

Lowering the temperature setting on a water heater just ten degrees can reduce your water heating costs by 3% to 5%. Although that doesn't seem like much, over the long haul, it can save a significant amount of money. When combined with other projects—like periodic flushing of the hot-water tank, adding a water heater blanket and pipe insulation, and installing water-efficient faucets and showerheads—the savings are quite substantial.

Saving energy also reduces your family's "carbon footprint," the amount of carbon dioxide (the main greenhouse gas) released from energy resources to meet your needs. Lowering the water temperature also lessens the chance of accidental scalding. It may increase the life of your water heater as well, saving you even more money over the long haul. Like some other projects in this book, this one costs nothing more than a few moments of your time, and it begins to save you money immediately.

How to Lower the Temperature

Water heaters are typically pre-set in the factory or by plumbers who install them to a temperature range of 115°F to 150°F. According to the U.S. Department of Energy, however, 120°F is sufficient for most homes. (Experts on home energy use suggest a setting between 110°F and 120°F.) Hot water for a shower, for example, is typically adjusted down to around 104°F for comfort. Although dishwashers typically function best at 140°F, most have a temperature booster, a heating element that quickly raises the temperature of the incoming water to the desired level. It's cheaper to use this feature than to maintain household water temperature at 140°F. In addition, clothes washers, using cold-water detergents, can run on cold-water for most loads quite well.

Go Green!

Use Earth-friendly detergents—that is, biodegradable, phosphate-free detergents—for washing clothes. They're available in many stores and often come in concentrated form, which means less packaging. Be sure to recycle empty boxes and plastic containers, too.

It's also a good idea to remove the sediment from your tank (Project 30). This quick and fairly simple procedure will improve your water heater's efficiency, increase its useful life, and reduce your energy bills. It's also wise to install a water heater blanket and pipe insulation on hot-water pipes (Project 31). These steps will enable you to reap even greater savings without any loss of comfort.

Before you turn the temperature down, take a moment to measure the temperature of the water delivered to hot-water taps in your home. You'll need a cup or a glass and a thermometer (a candy thermometer works well). This task is best performed shortly after a shower or after dishwashing—that is, when the water in the tank is hottest. Be sure to wait until the water heater turns off. You can tell a gas-fired water heater is off by the absence of flame in the combustion chamber. Gas water heaters are also quieter once the flame shuts off. Waiting ten to fifteen minutes after a shower should ensure an electric water heater has brought the water temperature back up to the thermostatic setting.

After the burner has shut off, or the heating element has turned off, go to a nearby sink or tub. Place a thermometer in a cup, then turn on the hot water. Let the water run until the temperature peaks at a steady high temperature. This may take a few minutes. If it is over 120°F and your dishwasher contains a temperature booster, you can probably lower the setting without any loss of comfort or effectiveness.

To lower the temperature setting on a gas-fired water heater, locate the dial near the bottom of the water heater. Most have several temperature settings—from high to low. Mine reads "hot," "warm," and "vacation." Each one offers a wide range for fine-tuning. If the water temperature in your home is much higher than 120°F, and the temperature is set on hot, turn it down to the lower range of "hot." Recheck the temperature at a faucet in a day or two, using the same technique. If

the temperature is still too high, lower it a little more—perhaps into the upper end of the "warm" range. (That's where I set mine to achieve a 120-degree temperature.) Continue this procedure until you achieve the desired temperature setting at the faucet. Lowering the temperature gradually—over a period of two weeks—helps family members get used to adjusting the cold-hot water mix.

Lowering the temperature setting in an electric water heater is a bit more involved. These water heaters have two elements, one near the top of the tank and one near the bottom. Each is protected by a metal cover that must be removed to access the temperature setting. Before you remove the screws holding the plate in place, *turn off the electricity to the unit* either at the breaker box (the main service panel) or at a nearby fuse box or cut-off box. Fuse boxes and cut-off boxes are typically mounted on a wall near the unit. Test the circuit with a volt meter to make sure you've turned off the power.

Once the covers have been removed, lower the setting. Consult the owner's manual for specific instructions, as units vary. Most thermostats on electric water heaters

Temperature setting on gas water heater

Temperature setting on electric water heater

include a small dial or screw-type adjustment that allows you to raise or lower the temperature setting. If the temperature measured at a nearby faucet is greater than 120°F, lower the setting a bit, equally on both heating elements. Turn the power back on, and then check the water temperature in a day or two, following the same procedure outlined earlier.

After resetting the thermostat, it is time to wait for feedback. If family members complain that they are running out of hot water when showering, you may want to raise the temperature a little. You should also strongly consider installing more efficient showerheads (Project 37). If you receive no complaints, you may want to lower the setting a tiny bit more.

You can save even more by lowering the temperature further—or shutting the water heater completely off—when heading out of town for an extended vacation. On a gas water heater, turn the temperature setting to the "vacation" mode or to the lowest setting. (Don't forget to reset the temperature as soon as you return.) To shut the water heater completely off, turn the second dial on the top of the control unit (located at the base of the water heater) to the "off" position. This shuts the pilot light off. When you return, you'll have to relight the pilot light according to the manufacturer's instructions. For an electric water heater, it is much easier—and much quicker—to turn the power to the water heater off than to turn the temperature down on the top and bottom heating elements.

What to Watch Out For

Lowering the temperature setting on a water heater is pretty simple, although there are a few things you should keep in mind. When measuring water temperature, be sure to use the cup method. Don't hold a thermometer under a stream of hot water. Aeration may lower the temperature, leading to an inaccurate reading.

When adjusting the temperature controls on an electric water heater, be sure that the top and bottom elements are set for the same temperature. This prevents one

heating element from doing more work and possibly wearing out before the other. For safety, always turn off the electricity before adjusting the settings.

Go Green!

- If you have an electric water heater, you can save an additional 5% to 12% of energy by installing a timer that turns it off at night when you don't use hot water and/or during your utility's more expensive peak demand times, according to the DOE. You can install a timer yourself. They cost around $60, but can pay for themselves in about a year.

- To save energy and water, wash only full loads of clothing or adjust the setting on the washing machine according to the size of the load. Also, avoid the automatic wear-it-once-then-wash-it mentality. Some clothes, lightly used, like towels and jackets, don't need to be washed every time.

What Will You Save?

There is no cost for this project other than a few moments of your time. According to the U.S. Department of Energy, for every 10°F you reduce your water temperature, you can save between 3% to 5% in energy costs.

Project 33
Water Heater Anode Rod Replacement

Project Rating:

Savings
🍁 🍁 🍁

Environmental Benefit
🍁 🍁 🍁

Level of Difficulty
🍁 🍁 🍁

Storage water heaters serve us well but, compared to other appliances, they die rather young— usually only 8 to 12 years after they are installed. Fortunately, cost- and resource-conscious homeowners can take some steps to dramatically increase a water heater's useful life. One is to periodically flush sediment from the tank, a fairly simple task that takes only a few minutes every year (Project 30). Another measure, one that takes a little more planning and effort, is to periodically replace the anode rod inside the tank.

Anode rods are installed in all electric and gas water heaters. These three- to four-foot long metal rods are made from magnesium or aluminum and are suspended from the top of the tank. They protect the water tank from its worst enemies, rust and corrosion.

Although replacing an anode rod won't reduce household energy use, it will extend the life of your water heater—perhaps even doubling its lifespan. This can result in big savings, since water heater replacements (including installation) usually cost at least $900.

There is typically one anode rod in a household hot water heater. "A 6-year-warranty residential tank will have one, while a 12-year-warranty tank will have two, or an extra-large primary anode," according to the experts at **www.waterheaterrescue.com** "Special aluminum/zinc sacrificial anodes or powered anodes may be used to resolve odor problems caused by bacteria in some water."

Like other projects in this book that extend the lifespan of household appliances, this one helps your family reduce its contribution to greenhouse gas emissions and global warming. How? By reducing your material consumption, in the form of more frequently replaced water heaters. Whenever you replace old or worn-out products, it takes natural resources, energy, and materials to make the new ones.

Anode rods protect storage water-heaters from rust, ensuring a longer life.
Courtesy of Rheem Water Heating

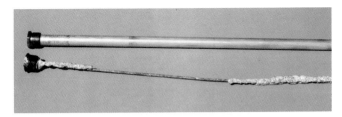

Corroded anode rod compared to a good rod
Courtesy of www.waterheaterrescue.com

As an anode rode corrodes, it becomes thinner. Once the magnesium or aluminum is gone, rust and corrosion set in, and the steel tank begins to deteriorate. Once this happens, a water heater's days are numbered. If you replace the anode rod before it's worn to nothing, however, your water heater could provide many additional years of service. How often the rod needs replacing depends on your water quality. Salty or overly softened water accelerates corrosion.

Longer product life also means less waste being dumped into rapidly filling landfills. And, also like many other projects in this book, this one requires only a modest financial investment if you do the work yourself.

How Do Anode Rods Protect Water Heaters?

Hot water in most homes is supplied by gas or electric storage water heaters—welded-steel tanks that hold between 30 and 60 gallons of hot water. To protect the steel from rust and corrosion caused by minerals in the water, manufacturers install glass linings in their tanks. Without this lining, the steel tank would last only a few years, and the water would be rust-colored and would stain sinks, tubs, and shower stalls.

Although glass linings protect the steel, they rarely form a perfect seal. Tiny imperfections in the lining, which may be caused by damage during shipment, can result in leakage. This causes the steel to rust, and it is for this reason that anode rods first came into use.

Anode rods are typically made of magnesium or aluminum, as noted earlier. These metals corrode more easily than steel. In other words, they corrode before the steel does. As a result, the anode rod is sacrificed to protect the steel tank.

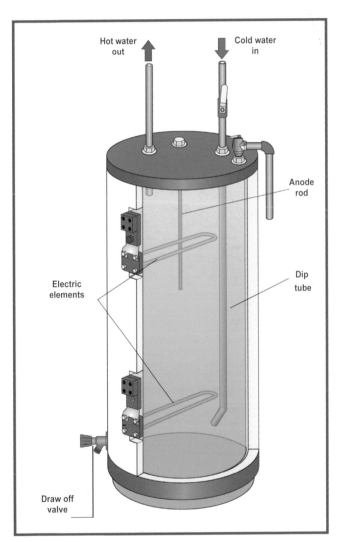

Typical electric water heater showing anode rod
Reprinted with permission from *How Your House Works* by Charlie Wing

Replacing an Anode Rod

Anode rods should be inspected every three years. If your home is equipped with a water softener, check the anode rod every year and replace it when necessary.

Before you inspect the anode rod, it's a good idea to have a replacement on hand. If you don't need it right away, chances are you will within a year or two. You can purchase one online or from a local plumbing supply outlet or a solar hot water system dealer/installer. The supplier can look up the model of your water heater and tell you what size you'll need. Be sure to give details on the location of the water heater, too. If there's not much room above your hot water heater, you may need a flexible rod.

To replace an anode rod, first turn off power to the water heater. For an electric water heater, turn off the electricity to the unit at the breaker box (main service panel) or at a nearby fuse box or cut-off box. For a gas-fired unit, turn the gas down to the lowest setting or to pilot. You can even turn the gas off completely, if you know how to safely relight the pilot.

Next, turn off the cold-water intake. It's controlled by a valve located in the cold-water line, which enters at the top of the tank.

Now drain a small amount of water—a quart or two—from the bottom of the tank via the drain valve (a spigot used to drain the tank). Be careful; this water can be very hot. Drain the water into a cooking pot.

Once you've turned off the power and drained a little water from the tank, locate the anode rod. Anode rods are situated on the hot-water side of the water heater—that is, near the hot-water outlet. In many tanks, they're attached to a separate square or a hex-headed plug located in the top of the tank. The word "anode" may be stamped into the metal on the top of the tank right next to the plug.

Being very careful, unscrew the fitting by turning it counterclockwise. If the plug is difficult to move, be patient and apply leverage. Using an adjustable wrench or a pipe wrench, loosen the anode rod and then carefully lift it out of the tank. Compare it to the new rod. If the anode rod is more than half gone (if the diameter is half the size of the replacement rod, or less) or has any exposed bare steel core, it's time to replace it. If not, slip the existing rod back into the tank and store the new one.

With the new rod in place, apply Teflon tape or pipe sealer to the threads on the threaded end of the anode rod. Tighten the rod by turning it clockwise. When the anode rod is installed, open the cold-water valve and watch for leaks. Tighten the rod if the valve leaks. If not, restore the power.

What to Watch Out For

If your water heater is more than ten years old, chances are the anode rod needs replacement. In most locations, magnesium is the material of choice. In some areas, however, aluminum rods are used because magnesium reacts with chemicals in the water and produces noxious odors.

When inserting a bendable anode rod in an electric water heater tank, don't bend it any more than you have to, or you could damage the electric heating element near the top of the tank.

Go Green!

- To save both water and energy, fix any leaky faucets in your home, no matter how small. One drip per second adds up to 5 gallons a day, or 1,800 gallons per year. If your hot water faucet is leaking, you'll waste energy, along with the water.

- When the time comes to retire your old water heater, check local scrap-metal companies and recycling centers to see if they will take it, before you have it hauled to the landfill.

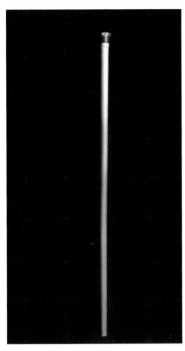

Water heater anode rod replacement
Photo by Kimberly Potvin

However, even though you can increase a water heater's efficiency and lifespan, there are other downsides to an older water heater. For one, their tanks tend to be oversized. They may also backdraft (allow pollutants such as carbon monoxide from the combustion chamber to enter your home). New, more efficient water heaters could eliminate these problems and may be worth the investment.

Replacement is advised if sediment on the bottom of an electric water heater tank has hardened on the lower element or has formed a thick, hard layer on the bottom of a gas-fired water heater. If you can't remove the sediment, a process described in Project 30, replacing the water heater is probably a good idea. You may want to consult with an energy-efficiency expert, such as a home energy auditor, to get his or her opinion.

When to Replace Your Water Heater

Replace your water heater if it has begun to leak, or if you see signs of rust in the water. These are indicators that the glass tank liner has been breached, and the steel casing is corroding. It won't be too long before the corrosion leads to a major leak.

What if your tank is old, but is not rusting or leaking? Should you replace it or improve its efficiency? The most cost-effective way to boost its efficiency is by installing a water heater blanket and flushing sediment from the tank. Replacing the anode rod will prolong the water heater's life, saving you money. Installing water-efficient showerheads and pipe insulation will also help improve efficiency and reduce fuel bills. These measures are much cheaper than replacing your water heater with a new, more efficient model and can, when combined, reap substantial savings.

What Will It Cost?

Anode rods cost between $20 and $50—and up to $150 for a flexible one. If you hire a professional to install it, expect to pay an additional $150 or so for labor and the visit to your home.

What Will You Save?

Your savings, if you replace the rod yourself, can be substantial, when you think that the biggest factor in the longevity of a water heater is probably the condition of its anode rod.

Project 34

Tankless Water Heater

Most homes are equipped with storage water heaters like the ones described in the previous projects. Although some newer models are more efficient, older and many lower-priced models waste about 20% of the energy they consume. Much of the heat they produce escapes through the wall of the tank as the hot water sits unused for many hours at a time. (This is known as *standby loss*.)

Besides being inefficient, storage water heaters don't last very long—between 8 and 12 years. Homeowners can increase the life of their water heater by lowering the temperature to a more reasonable setting, by periodically flushing sediment from the bottom of the tank, and by replacing the anode rod, as described in Projects 30, 32, and 33. Some of these measures also save energy.

If your water heater is more than ten years old and has not been maintained, it may be approaching the end of its useful life. If it's leaking or showing signs of rust, it definitely needs to be replaced. This might be a good opportunity to install a tankless water heater (TWH).

Also known as *instantaneous* or *on-demand* water heaters, tankless water heaters are surprisingly compact units. Most are designed to meet the needs of either an entire household, or a laundry room or bathroom. Even smaller, point-of-use models, commonly referred to as *under-the-sink* units, supply individual faucets.

Like conventional storage water heaters, TWHs provide hot water 24 hours a day, 365 days a year. However, they meet this need without the standby losses of storage tank heaters. How?

A tankless water-heater provides hot water for this laundry room.
Courtesy of Bosch Thermotechnology Corporation

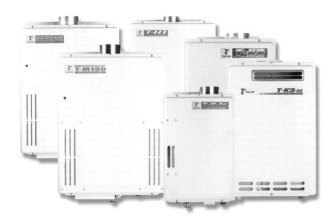

Tankless water heaters come in many sizes.
Courtesy of Takagi Industrial Company

As shown in the drawing below, tankless water heaters do not suffer from standby losses because they do not store hot water. They generate it as it's needed. When a hot water faucet is turned on, cold water begins to flow into the water heater. A flow sensor inside the TWH detects water flow and sends a signal to a tiny computer inside the unit. It, in turn, sends a signal to the gas burner or electric heating element in the water heater, turning on the heat source. As a result, water flowing through the heat exchanger in the TWH is rapidly brought up to temperature—increasing it from around 50°F to 120°F in a matter of seconds.

Because tankless water heaters eliminate standby losses, replacing an old, inefficient water heater with a compact TWH will reduce your annual energy bills. Most sources, such as the EPA, project savings on the cost of heating water of around 20%, compared to a storage water heater.

Savings depend on several factors, primarily the efficiency of the water heater and the amount of hot water a family uses each day. For homes that use up to 41 gallons of hot water daily, the U.S. Department of Energy (DOE) estimates savings of 24% to 34% on the cost of providing hot water compared to a conventional storage tank water heater. In homes that use substantially more hot water, around 86 gallons per day,

the DOE estimates reduced savings, about 8% to 14%. This is because there is less idle time and less standby loss with a conventional water heater when a lot of hot water is used throughout the day. For large families, then, it may make more sense to stick with an energy-efficient conventional water heater and implement other hot-water saving ideas, such as water-efficient showerheads, dishwashers, and clothes washers, to cut down the quantity of hot water used, rather than to change the way water is heated.

Even greater energy savings can be achieved by installing a tankless water heater at major points of use—for example, near the master bathroom or a washing machine or kitchen. (This reduces the length of the pipe run, which reduces the amount of hot water left in the line when the faucet is turned off.) This strategy could yield savings ranging from 27% to 50%, although savings could be offset by the cost of purchasing and installing additional TWHs.

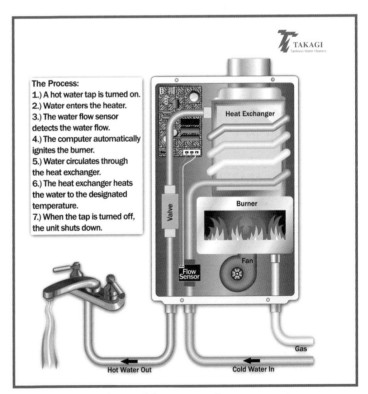

The Process:
1.) A hot water tap is turned on.
2.) Water enters the heater.
3.) The water flow sensor detects the water flow.
4.) The computer automatically ignites the burner.
5.) Water circulates through the heat exchanger.
6.) The heat exchanger heats the water to the designated temperature.
7.) When the tap is turned off, the unit shuts down.

Cross section of a tankless water heater
Courtesy of Takagi Industrial Company

Do Tankless Water Heaters Reduce Water Consumption?

Contrary to popular misconception, tankless water heaters do not reduce water demand in a home, unless they're installed at the point of use. In most instances, you still have to run the water for a while until the hot water from the water heater purges all of the cold water that's been sitting in the hot water line between the tank and the end use. As a result, tankless water heaters are primarily installed to save energy, not water.

Additional savings also result from the long life expectancy of TWHs. According to DOE's Office of Energy Efficiency and Renewable Energy, most TWHs last at least 20 years. In addition, they are made from easy-to-replace, off-the-shelf parts, so repairing a TWH (not an option with leaking storage water heaters) can leaking result in even longer service. In fact, a tankless water heater with periodic maintenance could outlast two or three storage water heaters. So if you're considering a TWH and comparing costs versus a new storage water heater, be sure to take longevity into account.

By reducing your energy demand, a tankless water heater also reduces your family's contribution to local, regional, and global air pollution, including carbon dioxide, a pollutant that is fueling costly global climate change. Because they're smaller, easy to repair, durable, and last longer than storage water heaters, TWHs also reduce resource consumption and landfill waste. Using fewer natural resources means less environmental disruption from mining, as well as pollution.

Possible Downsides

Although tankless water heaters offer many benefits over storage water heaters, they do have a few disadvantages worth noting. One problem is that although they produce a steady stream of hot water, they may not be able to produce enough hot water to meet everyone's needs at once when household demand is high. If hot water is being used at several locations simultaneously, water temperature at the various points of use may decline. Someone taking a shower may experience a drop in water temperature if another family member is also showering, washing clothes, or running the dishwasher. (The same can occur, however, when using a traditional storage water heater.)

This problem can be corrected or at least mitigated by simple, cost-effective efficiency measures, for example, installing water-efficient showerheads, taking shorter showers, replacing old appliances with water-efficient models, washing clothes with cold water, and coordinating hot water use.

Another, more costly way to ensure plenty of water from a TWH is to purchase the highest output model you can find (more on this shortly). Or, you can install two tankless water heaters, although this will cost more and is a less efficient use of resources. When connected in parallel, two TWHs dramatically increase the availability of hot water, meeting your family's needs in times of heaviest hot water use. A third option, again more costly, is to install a TWH at each point of use, for example, near bathrooms, the laundry room, and the kitchen.

Go Green!

Operating appliances such as clothes washers and dishwashers only when full can save up to 600 gallons of water each month. New water-efficient washing machines can save up to 20 gallons per load, and are energy-efficient as well.

Installation

Replacing a storage water heater with a tankless model is a major project, especially if the installation requires rerouting the exhaust (flue) pipe or increasing the size of the opening though which the flue pipe exits your home. (Some TWHs require larger flue pipes than those used for storage water heaters.) This project requires a high level of skill and considerable knowledge of plumbing and electricity and is best done by a professional.

Point-of-use tankless water heaters are more compact than whole-house units, and are typically powered by (and must be connected to) electricity. (They contain an electric heating element.) Incoming cold- and outgoing hot-water lines will need to be connected to the water heater.

Shopping Tips

If you're replacing a conventional water heater, you may want to consider buying a more efficient storage water heater—instead of a more costly TWH, because of the initial cost or for reasons mentioned earlier, such as a big family with a lot of water use throughout the day. Some manufacturers have made dramatic efficiency improvements. Check out the yellow energy tag, which indicates energy use of the model you are considering versus the average for models in its size range. A side-by-side comparison of an efficient storage water heater and a tankless water heater is worth the time.

By maintaining a new storage water heater—replacing the anode rod as needed, and annually flushing the sediment from the tank—you can dramatically increase its life. Installing energy-efficient faucet aerators and showerheads will also lower your water and energy bill.

Tankless water heaters can be purchased through home improvement centers (which offer installation services) and by plumbers. When shopping for a tankless water heater, be sure to consider the physical size of the unit and whether it will fit in the location you have in mind.

Also, pay close attention to the output of the TWH—that is, the rate at which it produces hot water versus your demands. Most tankless water heaters supply 2 to 5 gallons of hot water per minute, which is sufficient for energy- and water-efficient end-users.

Gas-fired TWHs typically produce higher flow rates (more hot water per minute) than electric units. Tagaki makes a TWH that delivers nearly 7 gallons of hot water per minute, which should be enough for several simultaneous uses, especially water-efficient ones.

Some manufacturers, such as Paloma, rate their units on heat output, measured in Btus (British thermal units). Paloma recommends its 118,000-Btu TWH for homes with one bathroom, and with two bathrooms, 141,000 to 145,000 Btus. The 199,000-Btu units are recommended for two-to-three bathroom homes.

Go Green!

Most laundry can be washed effectively in cold water, but if you suffer from allergies caused by dust mites, you may want to wash your bedding in hot water, a measure recommended by allergists.

When shopping for a TWH, pay attention to fuel type. As a rule, power from natural gas and propane produces fewer pollutants than electric models, if they are powered by nuclear or coal-burning plants. (Burning natural gas and propane is nearly twice as efficient as making electricity.) While you're at it, look for a TWH with high energy efficiency (called the "fuel factor"). For greater savings, purchase a model with an electronic ignition instead of a pilot light.

In addition to the cost of the unit, get an estimate of installation costs before you lay your money down. Like a conventional water heater, a tankless water heater requires a flue pipe to remove unburned gases and pollutants, among them carbon monoxide, which is generated from the combustion of natural gas or propane.

Venting is not required for electric water heaters, which slightly lowers installation costs. Unfortunately, electricity is a much more costly way to heat water.

Finally, if you're thinking about installing a solar hot-water system or already have one in place, purchase a TWH designed to work with these systems. Solar hot-water systems, described in Project 35, feed solar-heated water to the TWH.

What Will It Cost?

Tankless water heaters aren't cheap. Prices range from around $600 to $1500, depending on the size of the unit and its output. Installation can run from a few hundred dollars to $1,000 or more for difficult projects. In contrast, a conventional natural gas or propane water heater costs roughly $300 (for a small tank) to $700, plus around $200 to $300 for installation, depending on the size and any complications. Electric water heaters are typically the more expensive models.

What Will You Save?

Is the extra cost of a TWH worth the investment? A family of four spends about $2,100 a year on energy (the average fuel bill in 2007). With water heating constituting 17% of a family's monthly fuel bill, they'll spend more than $350 per year for hot water. If they use water wisely, a TWH could save 24% to 34%—$70 to $100 (or substantially more as energy costs continue to rise). Although these savings may seem modest, in ten years' time, they come to at least $700 and $1,000, which makes up for the additional initial investment. The rate of return on your investment is about 10%. Over the 25-year life of the unit, savings could turn the water heater into a money-maker, netting $1,750 to nearly $2,500 in tax-free savings. Not a bad return, especially considering you're also saving natural resources and reducing pollution.

When running the math, be sure to include any rebates offered by local utilities and/or tax incentives from the federal government or some state governments. Rebates lower the initial cost, resulting in greater lifetime savings. Check into financial incentives by contacting your state's office of energy conservation. Every state has one. You can also find log onto the Database of State Incentives for Renewables and Efficiency at **www.dsireusa.org**

Project 35

Solar Hot-Water Systems

To reduce energy costs and dependence on power plants, many homeowners are installing solar hot-water systems. After all, heating water is a significant energy-consumer—about 17% of an average residential energy bill.

Since solar systems are not inexpensive, it's a good idea to first improve the efficiency of your home—for example, by installing water-efficient showerheads. You can also turn the thermostat down on your water heater, insulate the tank and your hot-water pipes, and periodically flush sediment from the tank (Projects 30–32 and 36). These measures produce substantial savings at very little cost. You can also replace an inefficient water heater with a more efficient (conventional) one—or with an on-demand tankless water heater. If you'd like to cut your fuel bill and reduce your carbon footprint even more than these measures will achieve, consider a solar hot-water system.

What Are Your Options?

The simplest solar hot-water system is the *batch solar water heater*. This extremely cost-effective technology is best suited to hot, sunny climates (like southern parts of Florida, Texas, and California), where winter freezes are something you only read about in the newspaper.

Batch water heaters consist of a black water tank inside an insulated collector box, or a well-insulated solar panel containing large-diameter black copper pipe filled with water, like the one shown in the photo below. Either unit may be mounted on the roof—if it's capable of supporting the weight—or on the ground in a sunny location.

Unlike most other solar systems, batch water heaters contain no pumps (to move water from the collector to the house) and require no electronic controls. Solar-heated water is released from the tank when a hot water faucet, shower, or dishwasher is turned on. Hot water flows from the collector to the water heater. From there, it flows to the point of use, via line

Solar batch water heaters work well in southern climates.

Courtesy of SolarDirect.com

pressure. Replacement water is supplied to the batch hot-water heater by cold line water, either from your local utility or domestic well.

In climates where freezes occur, more elaborate and costly pump-driven solar hot-water systems, called *active systems*, are recommended. Shown in the drawing to the right, an active solar hot-water system consists of a collector mounted on the roof or alongside the house, together with a storage tank located inside the house, next to the water heater (to protect it from the cold).

In many active systems, nontoxic or food-grade antifreeze, known as propylene glycol, circulates through the pipes in the collector on sunny days. It is heated as it flows through the collector. The heat is then transferred to water in a solar storage tank, via a heat exchanger, which is installed next to the water heater These systems are known as *active glycol-based systems*.

Water is used as a heat transfer fluid in *drainback systems*. Like active glycol-based systems, these can be installed in both warm and cold climates. Water will not freeze in the collector or pipes connecting to the storage tank because it drains automatically into the tank when the system is off, for example, at night.

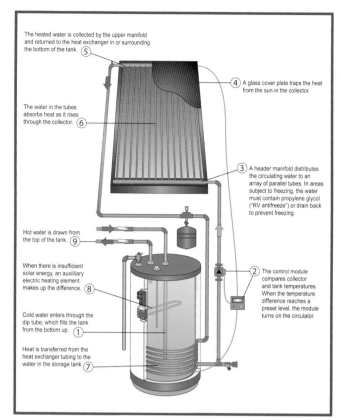

The heated water is collected by the upper manifold and returned to the heat exchanger in or surrounding the bottom of the tank. ⑤

④ A glass cover plate traps the heat from the sun in the collector.

The water in the tubes absorbs heat as it rises through the collector. ⑥

③ A header manifold distributes the circulating water to an array of parallel tubes. In areas subject to freezing, the water must contain propylene glycol ("RV antifreeze") or drain back to prevent freezing.

Hot water is drawn from the top of the tank. ⑨

When there is insufficient solar energy, an auxilliary electric heating element makes up the difference. ⑧

② The control module compares collector and tank temperatures. When the temperature difference reaches a preset level, the module turns on the circulator.

Cold water enters through the dip tube, which fills the tank from the bottom up. ①

Heat is transferred from the heat exchanger tubing to the water in the storage tank. ⑦

Domestic solar hot-water system
Reprinted with permission from *How Your House Works* by Charlie Wing

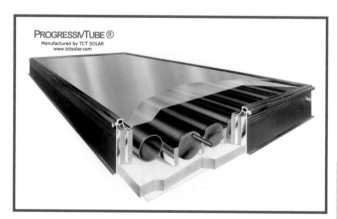

Batch water heater—an inside view
Courtesy of SolarDirect.com

By far the most popular active solar systems are glycol-based. Several types of collectors are available for these systems, including flat-plate collectors, evacuated-tube collectors, and tracking collectors. Evacuated and tracking collectors are more costly, but considerably more efficient than the older flat-plate collectors. Savings from their higher efficiency may offset the higher initial costs. Evacuated-tube collectors work fairly well, even on cloudy days.

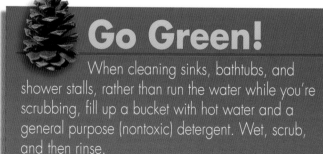

Go Green!

When cleaning sinks, bathtubs, and shower stalls, rather than run the water while you're scrubbing, fill up a bucket with hot water and a general purpose (nontoxic) detergent. Wet, scrub, and then rinse.

(a) Flat plate collectors

(b) Evacuated tube solar hot-water heaters

Courtesy of (a) Heliodyne Inc. and (b) Hills Solar

Installation

Solar hot-water systems require sunny locations, typically a south-facing roof with good solar exposure from at least 9 a.m. to 3 p.m. throughout the year. Collectors for active systems are mounted flush on the roof or on racks angled so that they achieve maximum solar gain throughout the year.

Most active solar hot-water systems are fairly complicated, requiring pumps, storage tanks, sensors, controls, and other components. As a result, they're typically installed by professionals who will also procure a permit from your local building department.

When installing a batch solar hot-water system, pipes must be run from the collector to the water heater. For an active system, pipes are run from the collectors to the solar storage tank, which is connected to the household water heater.

As noted, the storage tanks for glycol-based and drainback systems are typically installed next to the water heater—either a tankless model or a storage

water heater. Heat exchangers, which transfer heat from the solar collectors to the storage tank, are mounted inside the solar storage tank, in the wall of the tank, next to it, or underneath it. Heat exchangers can even be installed inside the tank of storage water heaters, eliminating the need for a solar storage tank. While this may save money, such systems have much less storage capacity for hot water you'll need on cloudy days.

Pumps are required in active systems to circulate the heat transfer fluid from the solar storage tank to the collector. In most systems, the pumps are powered by AC electricity. In others, they're powered by DC

Installation Tip

Although solar hot-water systems can tolerate some shade, it's best to ensure full access to the sun throughout the year. This may require mounting a system on a garage or trimming trees on the south side of the home.

An evacuated solar hot-water collector can be attached to the side of a house when roof mounting is problematic.

Courtesy of Solar Direct.com

electricity supplied by a solar electric module mounted alongside the solar hot-water collector. The latter are typically easier and less expensive to install.

What to Watch Out For

The cost of a solar hot-water system varies with the type of system and the difficulty of installation, which is affected by the type and slope of the roof and the amount of work required to run pipes. Shop around and get references from local installers.

It's best to hire an installer who has been in the business for at least 5 to 10 years and has installed numerous systems. You can locate installers at **www. findsolar.com** Check to see if the installers you have in mind are certified by the North American Board of Certified Energy Practitioners (NABCEP), and ask whether they've received training provided by solar-system manufacturers. Ask how many installations they've completed. You can check out certified installers in your region on the NABCEP website (**www.nabcep.org**).

Choose a system that has been on the market for at least 5 to 10 years, too. Tried and tested systems and reliable dealers are worth their weight in gold! Also,

purchase a system with a good warranty, and consider an annual service contract that provides routine inspection and maintenance. Glycol-based systems must be drained and recharged every five years, a task best performed by a professional.

You'll find considerable competition among dealers/installers, each one touting the superiority of their product. To avoid confusion, you may want to learn more about solar hot-water systems from *Home Power* magazine, the DOE, or my book, *The Homeowner's Guide to Renewable Energy*. You can also compare the performance of solar collectors on the website of the Solar Rating and Certification Corporation. This nonprofit organization tests the performance of solar hot-water systems. They post the data at **www.solar-rating.org** Shop around. Get several estimates.

Go Green!
When brushing your teeth, use cold water and don't leave the faucet running. Installing a faucet aerator will dramatically lower water use, too.

As a final note, ask the installer in advance how they plan to attach the racks for solar collectors that will be mounted on the roof. You want to make sure measures are taken to properly flash the roof and prevent leaks. Your local building department might be able to give you some helpful guidance.

Rebates & Incentives

The economics of solar batch water heaters and active solar hot-water systems are improved by state, local, and federal financial incentives. (Even more generous incentives may be available for businesses.) Your local utility company may also offer rebates. At this book's printing (August 2008), the U.S. government extended its 30% tax credit (with a maximum of $2,000 for a residential solar hot-water system) through 2008. To check the latest state and federal incentives, log on to the Database of State Incentives for Renewables & Efficiency at **www.dsireusa.org**

Some cities offer their own incentives (Austin, Texas, for example, currently offers $2,000) or low- or zero-interest loans to complete the work. Solar Rating and Certification Corporation (SRCC)-certified residential system in the country are eligible for state and federal rebates. Check out other incentives and rebates available for purchasing energy-efficient products and services offered through The Energy Policy Act of 2005: **www.energy.gov/taxbreaks.htm**

What Will It Cost?

A batch water heater costs between $2,000 to $3,000. An active system costs more, roughly $5,000 to $7,000, minus rebates. Installation costs range widely based on complexities of each job, including site access and the extent of piping.

> ## Cost Estimate: Installation of a high-quality closed-loop solar hot-water heating system with a heavy-duty solar storage tank
>
> Cost for materials only: **$4,500**
>
> Contractor's total, including materials, labor, and markup: **$9,700**
>
> *Costs are national averages and do not include sales tax.*

What Will You Save?

A solar hot-water system is a significant investment, but it can last for 40 years, provided it's well installed and maintained. Solar hot-water systems are designed to supply about 70% of a household's hot-water requirement. They may meet 100% of a family's needs in the summer. In the winter they may produce only 40%. In ideal solar locations, solar hot-water systems can supply 80% to 90% of a family's total hot water.

Solar batch heaters, installed in the warmest climates, almost always make economic sense. They're the cheapest and easiest systems to install and will save you a ton on your energy bill.

Active solar water systems make sense in many applications as well, but they're most appropriate for homes in which water is heated with electricity (assuming electrical rates are above 8 cents per kWh) or propane, which costs about 30% more than natural gas. Homeowners whose water is heated with natural gas should perform a careful cost-benefit analysis, but as natural gas prices rise, it's likely that an active solar hot-water system will make sense for them as well. Local dealers can help you run the numbers.

Project 36

Faucet Aerators

If you're looking for a quick, easy, and inexpensive way to reduce your utility bills, consider installing aerators on your faucets, if you don't already have them. Like the efficient showerheads in the next project, faucet aerators yield savings with almost no effort or cost—starting the second you install them and use your faucet.

Besides saving water, faucet aerators reduce the amount of energy needed to heat water, since less is used, and thereby help to reduce air pollution from power plants. Reducing water use also helps combat water shortages and helps protect our rivers and lakes.

What Is a Faucet Aerator?

New faucets come equipped with aerators, small screen-type devices that reduce water flow. By adding air into the water, aerators produce a flow/pressure sufficient for household uses, while reducing the amount of water we consume.

Faucet aerators can be purchased at hardware stores, home improvement centers, or online through green building materials/green living retailers. Aerator flow rates range from 0.7 to 2.5 gallons per minute (gpm). Prices range from as little as $2 for basic models to around $10 for fancier ones—such as the swivel-or dual-flow types.

As a rule, bathroom sinks generally require slightly lower flow rates than kitchen sinks.

If your faucet flow rate is 2.0 gpm or higher, consider installing a 0.7, 1.0, or 1.5 gpm aerator. By installing 0.7 gpm aerators in the bathroom sinks in my house, I cut water flows by approximately two-thirds—and with no complaints from my family. The 0.7 gpm may take a little getting used to—especially if you and family members have grown used to a torrential flow. It takes a little longer to fill up containers to water plants or to fill a pitcher of water. Nevertheless, the 0.7 gpm aerators work perfectly fine and can make a big difference—especially in homes where people are not very conscientious about saving water, for example, running the faucet when brushing their teeth.

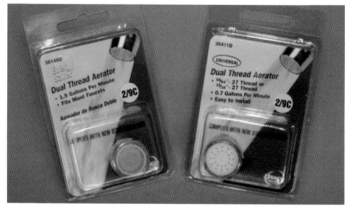

Faucet aerators can dramatically reduce water use when installed on inefficient faucets.
Photo by Dan Chiras

Kitchen sinks generally require a stronger flow. I recommend 1.5 to 2.5 gpm aerators. One model that I like is the Danco 2.0 gpm swivel aerator. It works extremely well and fits most types of faucets, especially older ones that don't have pull-out sprayers attached. The Danco aerator can be operated in two modes—spray or stream. I installed one in my kitchen and a friend's kitchen, and we've both been very pleased with them.

Installation

First, check each faucet to see if it already has an operable aerator. If it does, the flow rate should be stamped on the side of the unit. If it's two gallons per minute or higher in a bathroom sink, consider replacing it. If you can't read the flow rate, or if it's not stamped on the aerator, you can check it by placing a four-quart saucepan under the faucet and timing how long it takes to fill. If it fills in less than 30 seconds, water is flowing at a rate of two gallons or more per minute. If so, you can save water and energy (for hot water) by installing a new lower-flow aerator.

Installation of faucet aerators is a snap. First unscrew the old aerator, if any, using a pair of pliers. Remove the old washer from the faucet and then screw the new

aerator in by hand. Turn on the water. If it leaks around the aerator, tighten it again, this time using pliers. Place a rag over the grip of the pliers to prevent scratching the aerator. (You can also wrap the aerator in masking tape or a rubber band to prevent damage.) When tight, move on to the next sink.

What to Watch Out For

Installing faucet aerators is one of the easiest projects in this book. It will only take a few minutes per faucet. Most aerators screw directly onto the faucet. Others may require an adapter to convert a spout with standard inside (female) threads to standard outside (male) threads. Take a good look at each faucet before you shop to determine which type you'll need. If your

Danco swivel aerators are ideal for kitchen sinks.

Go Green!

• Fix dripping faucets! One drip per second adds up to 5 gallons a day or 1,800 gallons per year. If the hot water is leaking, you'll waste a lot of energy, too. Most leaky faucets can be fixed with a new washer.

• When shopping for aerators or other devices that use water—from bath fixtures to washing machines to landscape irrigation systems—look for EPA's new WaterSense label. These products are water-efficient and provide adequate flow.

• Place a pitcher or gallon jug of water in the refrigerator rather than running the tap until the water gets cold each time you want a drink of water.

old faucet doesn't have threads into which you can screw an aerator, you're out of luck.

Over time, sediment, calcium, and rust may build up inside a faucet aerator, which can reduce the flow and result in an irregular spray pattern. To fix this problem, remove the aerator. Brush out sediment and back-flush the screen and perforated discs inside the aerator with a strong stream of water. Be sure to close the drain first so that you don't lose the parts.

Then dry all parts and brush them with a fine-, soft-bristled, but fairly stiff brush. Reinstall and test the faucet. If this hasn't improved the aerator's performance, remove it again and soak it in vinegar for a couple of hours. Back-flush the aerator once again, and then replace it. If the unit still malfunctions, repeat the procedure one more time or replace it with a new one.

What Will It Cost?

As mentioned earlier, aerators are very inexpensive—about $2 to $10 each. If you need an adaptor to convert the threads, they are usually around $2. If your old faucet is worn out, see below for the cost to replace the entire unit.

Cost Estimate: Average charge for a plumber to remove an old kitchen faucet and replace it with a water-efficient one

Cost for materials only: **$75**

Contractor's total, including materials, labor, and markup: **$200**

Costs are national averages and do not include sales tax.

What Will You Save?

According to numerous conservation, plumbing, and other sources, faucet aerators save water as well as energy used to heat water. The online *California Energy Efficiency Guidebook* indicates that a kitchen aerator can save about 3 gallons of water per day in a typical household, while bathroom aerators can save 2.4 gallons of water each day. Although this may not seem like much, over a year's time, one kitchen and two sink aerators will save nearly 2,900 gallons! If everyone in your city or town joined in, the savings could be phenomenal.

Project 37 Water-Efficient Showerheads

Project Rating:

Savings
🍁 🍁 🍁

Environmental Benefit
🍁 🍁 🍁

Level of Difficulty
🍁

One of the quickest, easiest, and cheapest things you can do to save energy, water, and money is install an efficient showerhead. Of all the energy- and water-saving ideas in this book, water-efficient showerheads yield the greatest return with the least amount of effort—and the savings start with your first shower. An efficient showerhead can cut water use by half, sometimes more, and pay for itself 10 to 20 times over *every year*—potentially saving a family of four up to $250 per year. It is probably one of the best financial investments you'll ever make. (If only our retirement accounts performed as well!)

Showering is one of the biggest uses of water in the home, representing approximately 17% to 25% of residential indoor water use, or more than 1.2 trillion gallons of water consumed in the United States each year, according to the U.S. Environmental Protection Agency. Besides saving water, efficient showerheads reduce our demand for the energy required to heat water for showers, and thus lessen our contribution to local, regional, and global air pollution. Cutting water use in our homes helps combat ever-more-frequent droughts, created, in part, by global climate change. Water conservation also helps protect rivers and lakes, valuable recreational resources and vital habitat for thousands of species.

If your showerhead is old and inefficient, consider replacing it with a modern, efficient model. The tools you will need are minimal: a replacement showerhead; channel locks, vice grips, or large pliers; and teflon tape.

How Are these Showerheads Different?

Water-efficient showerheads restrict water flow to 1.5 to 2.5 gallons per minute, compared to older models that consume up to 5 gallons per minute, sometimes even more. Replacement showerheads can be purchased at home improvement centers, hardware

Europa Elite water-efficient showerhead—one of my favorites.

Courtesy of Alsons Corporation

stores, and discount retail outlets, such as Wal-Mart, Target, and Kmart. The most efficient models—those that use 1.5 gallons per minute—can be purchased online through a variety of sources. (Check out the list of green building suppliers in the Resource Guide.)

Installation

Replacing an inefficient showerhead is about as easy a job as you will find. It will take a beginner 20 to 30 minutes. If you need to hire a plumber, you'll be paying a lot more for installation than the showerhead costs. (But even if you have to hire a plumber, the savings should easily pay for the visit in a year or so!)

Before installing a new showerhead, you may want to test the efficiency of your existing showerheads. To do so, you'll need a stop watch or a wrist watch with a second hand and a gallon bucket. Turn the shower on, holding the bucket right under it. Start timing the second the water is turned on. (You'll probably need a helper to assist with the timing.) Repeat this once or twice, and record the time it takes to fill the bucket. If, on average, the bucket fills in 30 seconds, the flow rate is 2 gallons per minute, which is good. It won't be necessary to replace the showerhead. If it fills in less than 30 seconds, consider replacing it. As an example, if the bucket fills in 15 seconds, the showerhead is delivering 4 gallons of water per minute. If it fills in 10 seconds, the showerhead is putting out 6 gallons per minute.

To remove an old showerhead, clamp a pair of channel locks (or vice grips or pliers) onto the old showerhead while holding the pipe to which it is attached (called a shower arm) with your free hand. Turn counterclockwise, slowly but surely. The showerhead should come off, though not always without some complaint on its part and struggle on yours.

If the old showerhead is difficult to remove, be persistent. It will usually come off with a little persuasion. Be sure to hold onto the shower arm (the pipe to which the showerhead is attached), but don't hang on it while unscrewing the old showerhead. If the shower arm is rusting, you should probably replace it, too. Shower arm replacements can be purchased

at hardware stores or home improvement centers for about $7. They screw into a pipe behind the wall. To remove the old shower arm, turn it counterclockwise using a pair of channel locks or vice grips or pliers. When in doubt, call a plumber to replace it for you.

After removing the showerhead, clean off the threads on the end of the shower arm with a rag. Wrap teflon tape on the threads to ensure a tight fit. Screw on the new showerhead. Be sure the washer is in place when you install it. Now, tighten the showerhead with a pair of pliers or channel locks. When tightening with a wrench, place a rag over the showerhead where the pliers contact it, so you don't scratch the metal. When it's tight, turn the water on to be sure there are no leaks. If the showerhead leaks, tighten it a little more until the leaking stops.

Go Green!

• Use environmentally friendly soaps and shampoos when showering or bathing. They'll help reduce water pollution. Be sure to recycle the bottles and packaging.

• Use a natural fabric, such as cotton or bamboo, for your shower curtain. Plastic (PVC) curtains and liners release a chemical (DEHP, a phthalate) that may be carcinogenic and acts like the hormone estrogen. Check plastics for the recycle symbol #3 or the letter V, which indicate PVC. A safer plastic alternative is PEVA (non-chlorinated vinyl), which is also biodegradable.

• Place a two-gallon bucket under the shower to capture water while you're waiting for it to reach the desired temperature. Use this water for plants inside or outside your home or to flush the toilet. (A half gallon poured directly into a toilet bowl should flush it very nicely.)

Shopping Tips

When shopping for water-efficient showerheads at home improvement centers, you'll find a wide assortment of styles and prices. Although all models, even the most luxurious-looking showerheads on the market, are required by law to use no more than 2.5 gallons of water per minute, performance varies considerably. Some showerheads may be labeled "WaterSense," the EPA's designation to "help consumers find quality showerheads that save water without sacrificing performance." Otherwise, read the package for the gpm and compare.

Over the past 20 years, I've tested numerous showerheads in the 0.5-to-2-gallon range in my home. My personal favorite is the Europa Elite. It's rated at 2 gallons per minute at 60 psi (pounds per square inch) water pressure. I've also tested Peerless Power showerheads and like them a lot. Both the Europa Elite and the Peerless Power showerheads come with a "soap-up" valve (activated by a button or a lever) that allows you to turn the water off at the showerhead while you soap up, and then turn it back on to rinse off. (The water stays hot in the pipe, even though you turn it off for a minute or two.) This procedure can save several gallons of water per shower. I also find it easier to lather up with the water momentarily shut off.

I've also tested Delta's Water Amplifying showerhead, which uses 1.6 gallons per minute at 60 psi. Although the manufacturer says it feels like a 2.5 gpm shower, it will take some getting used to. Personally, I find it less comfortable than other models I've tested. (It produces an almost too-vigorous stream.) But it's all a matter of individual preference.

Niagara's Earth showerhead is rated at 2 gpm. It is adjustable and produces a "broad, rain-like spray—or a focused, pulsating, massaging spray," according to the manufacturer. This unit is self-cleaning and non-aerated, which means less temperature loss between the showerhead and you. (You might even be able to turn the water temperature down at the water heater as a result.) This showerhead is heavenly and ideal for those who are accustomed to a lavish shower. My children love it, though I prefer the more water-miserly Europa Elite because tests in my home show that it uses half as much energy and water, even though the two showerheads are rated similarly.

My suggestion is to buy a showerhead based on the features described on the package and/or reviews you find online. If you don't like it, take it back and try another model. (You can usually return a showerhead if you're not satisfied.) Find the model that gives you energy and water savings and a great shower.

What Will It Cost?

Low-flow showerheads generally cost between about $10 to $50, depending on whether they are hand-held and have adjustments for flow. There are more expensive models with high-tech or designer features. For example, Bricor showerheads have a "vacuum flow restriction" technology and use as little as one-half gallon of water per minute. These cost about $60 to $80 each. Other water-conserving showerheads with a designer look can cost hundreds of dollars.

Replacing a showerhead is a simple project that most homeowners are capable of doing themselves. If you choose to hire a professional, expect a service call charge of $100 or more, in addition to the cost of the showerhead. If you have a plumber do several small projects at once, you'll save money overall.

What Will You Save?

Water-efficient showerheads can reduce your hot-water consumption by 30% or more, which helps cut both your energy and water bills. Inexpensively priced showerheads could easily pay for themselves many times over in one year.

Project 38

Water-Efficient Toilets

With drought and water shortages becoming more and more common, numerous states and nations have enacted regulations to conserve this precious resource. Their efforts have centered primarily on water-efficiency—ways to meet our needs with the least amount of water. One popular approach is the installation of water-efficient toilets to replace old water-intensive ones, which consume as much as 3.5 to 7 gallons per flush. If your home has an older toilet, it makes good sense—economically and environmentally—to replace it with a water-conserving model.

Installing a water-efficient toilet can save you a substantial amount of money by reducing your water bills. If you use well water, an efficient toilet will also reduce the run time of your well pump, reducing electrical consumption. (Plus, the less your pump runs, the longer it will remain in service.)

Efficient toilets reduce our collective demand on limited water supplies and, in urban/suburban areas, the amount of waste flowing to sewage treatment plants. This lowers the plants' operating energy and costs. In rural areas not served by municipal wastewater treatment plants, water-efficient toilets reduce the amount of waste flowing into septic tanks and leach fields, lengthening the lives of these systems.

Dual-flush toilet; inset shows the two buttons used for different flushes.

Courtesy of Caroma. Used with permission.

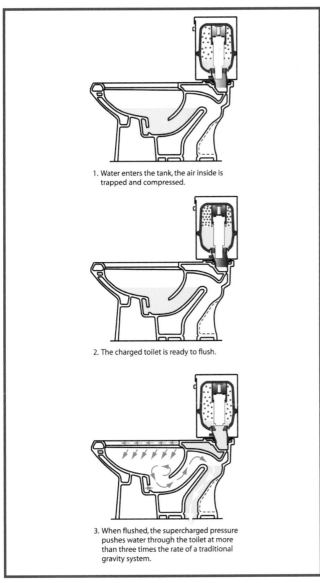

1. Water enters the tank, the air inside is trapped and compressed.

2. The charged toilet is ready to flush.

3. When flushed, the supercharged pressure pushes water through the toilet at more than three times the rate of a traditional gravity system.

How a Flushmate® toilet works
Courtesy of Sloan FLUSHMATE®

As their name implies, dual-flush toilets provide two flushing options. Solids are flushed with 1.6 gallons of water. Liquids are flushed by about half that volume— 0.8 to 0.9 gallons per flush. Most manufacturers offer at least one dual-flush toilet.

The third option is a toilet equipped with Flushmate pressure-assist technology, available from all leading manufacturers. Most common in hotels, restrooms, and commercial buildings, these toilets can also be installed in homes. The Flushmate pressure-assist system consists of a plastic pressure tank mounted inside the toilet tank. It uses pressure from the water supply line to compress air inside the pressure tank, shown in the drawing at left. This system traps and compresses air as it fills with water. The compressed air forces the water into the bowl when the toilet is flushed. The pressure-assist unit uses this force to "push" waste out, creating a vigorous flushing action that whisks waste away and cleans the bowl with only one gallon of water per flush.

The pressure-assist system offers several other benefits. One is that the flush water is contained in a plastic tank inside the ceramic tank, which eliminates the potential for condensation (sweating) on the outside of the tank. This prevents water from dripping onto your floor, causing mold and damage to the flooring. Pressure-assist toilet bowls also have a larger water surface than standard toilets. Having less dry area inside the bowl means a cleaner bowl and less cleaning. These toilets

What Are Your Options?

Water-efficient toilets fit into three categories: (1) single-flush at 1.6 gallons per flush (gpf), (2) dual-flush toilets, and (3) Flushmate-equipped toilets.

Water-efficient single-flush toilets use 1.6 gallons per flush, a standard required by law in all new home construction and bathroom remodels. Although the earliest water-efficient toilets had some problems (such as too-small tanks on standard toilets, which lacked sufficient flushing power), most water-efficient toilets on the market today work extremely well.

Go Green!

Check your toilet periodically for leaks. Slow leaks allow water to flow from the tank to the toilet bowl, and can waste about 200 gallons of water every day, according to the American Water Works Association. To check for leaks, place a few drops of food coloring in the toilet tank. If it appears in the toilet bowl within 30 minutes, there is a leak. Repairs are often simple—like replacing the ball cock valve.

are a bit noisy, however, and you have to buy a whole new toilet if you want this technology. You can't install the Flushmate components in a standard, gravity-fed toilet.

How Much Water Do They Save?

Water-efficient toilets save water, but are they really worth it? According to the American Water Works Association, on average, Americans flush the toilets in their homes five times per person per day. In a home with 3.5 gallons per flush (gpf) toilets, this translates to about 17.5 gallons per person per day—just to flush the toilet. Annually, that's nearly 6,400 gallons per person.

In homes equipped with single-flush toilets that use 1.6 gallons per flush, daily water use is 8 gallons per person, or about 3,000 gallons per year. A single-flush water-efficient toilet will therefore save nearly 3,500 gallons of water *per person* per year compared to a conventional 3.5 gpf toilet. For a family of four, using 1.6-gallon toilets saves about 14,000 gallons saved per year.

In homes equipped with dual-flush toilets, the savings are even greater—as they use only 4.8 gallons per person per day instead of 8 gallons, according to the American Water Works Association. A dual-flush toilet saves over 4,600 gallons per person per year compared to the old 3.5 gpf models and nearly 1,200 gallons per person per year (or 4,800 gallons for a family of four) when compared to the 1.6 gpf model.

Toilets equipped with the power-assisted system require 1 to 1.6 gpf, depending on the model. Those

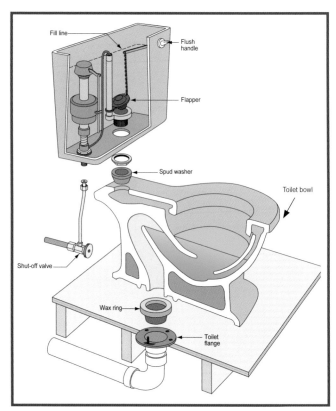

Components of a conventional-flush toilet
Reprinted with permission from *How Your House Works* by Charlie Wing

using one gallon per flush perform as well as the dual-flush toilet. Those that consume 1.6 gpf perform as well as the single-flush toilet.

Installation Tips

If you've never removed or installed a toilet, you may want to hire a plumber. If you're moderately handy, however, you can probably tackle the job yourself. The only tools you should need are pliers, a screwdriver, a wrench (adjustable or socket), a hacksaw, a bucket, and a small cup and rag.

The first step is to remove the old fixture. (Instructions should come with the new toilet.) Turn off the water supply to the toilet by turning the shut-off valve. (See drawing). Flush the toilet to drain the tank and bowl, then remove the remaining clean water with a small

Savings from Water-Efficient Toilets

Toilet Types	Daily Water Use*	Annual Water Use*
Conventional 3.5 gpf	17.5	6,387
Single-flush 1.6 gpf	8	2,920
Dual-flush Average 1 gpf	4.8	1,752
Pressure-Assisted 1 or 1.6 gpf	4.8 to 8	1,752 to 2,920
*gallons per person		

cup and bucket, sopping up the rest with a rag or sponge.

The next step is to disconnect the supply line at the base of the tank. You may need a pair of pliers to loosen the plastic coupling. Be gentle. You don't want to crack it. Next, remove the nuts on the two bolts (concealed by plastic caps) that connect the toilet to the floor. Loosen the nuts with an adjustable or socket wrench, applying some lubricating oil to the threads above the nuts if they're rusted. If that doesn't work, saw through each nut from above using a hacksaw. Don't worry about damaging the nut or the bolt. You're going to replace both of them.

Next, lift the toilet (bowl and tank) off the flange. (Get help if needed, as toilets are heavy, especially one-piece models.) For two-piece toilets, you can remove the tank from the bowl (by disconnecting two bolts inside the tank) and lift each piece out separately.

After removing the toilet, stuff an oversized rag (that can't fall into the hole) into the opening in the floor to block gas from the sewer line or septic tank. Scrape off the wax, putty, and caulk around the flange (the attachment of the toilet to the floor) with a putty knife. If the flange is damaged, pry it off, and then clean the area beneath it. Screw the new flange into the floor. If your floor is concrete, use self-tapping screws.

If the flange can't be removed, you can install an adaptor (sometimes called a "superflange"). It fits over the existing flange, creating a secure attachment for a new toilet. Follow the directions that come with the adaptor.

Next, insert new 3.5-inch flange bolts into the flange or adaptor. Place a new wax ring on the flange or tip the new toilet onto its side and place the wax ring around the opening at the base of the toilet. (Be sure to install the correct size wax ring.)

If the toilet comes in two parts, lift the bowl and place it on the flange, making sure the bolts go through the openings in the base. When the toilet bowl is in place, give it a slight twist to seal the wax ring. Place the washers and nuts on the bolts and tighten them by hand. Be sure to alternate tightening, a little on each side, to prevent cracking.

Now, press down hard on the bowl to create a tight seal. Tighten the nuts with a wrench until they are snug on both sides. Repeat this procedure a couple of times until the nuts no longer "loosen" when you put your weight on the bowl. You've now created a tight seal. Using a hacksaw, trim the bolts off just above the nuts. Replace the decorative caps.

To install the tank, place the gasket, known as the spud gasket, into the bowl inlet. The spud gasket forms a tight seal between the toilet bowl and the tank, preventing leakage. Next, place the tank anchor bolts and washers in the base of the tank. Set the tank on the bowl, making sure the bolts slip into the holes in the back of the tank. Attach the nuts to the anchor bolts and tighten them. To prevent cracking be careful not to over-tighten. With the tank securely in place, reattach the water line.

Shopping Tips

Although water-efficient toilets have improved since their early days in the 1980s, it's a good idea to ask an experienced plumber, or even friends or neighbors, if they have had success—or problems—with any particular brands and models. You can also look online; www.terrylove.com is one website that includes contractors' and homeowners' ratings of water-efficient toilets. (Click on *Toilets* at the top of the page for recommendations as well as a few models to avoid.) Some of the cheaper models may require a couple of flushes to do the job. Paying a few extra dollars for a better unit is worth it in the long run.

Go Green!

If you are getting rid of an old, inefficient toilet, check local resources to see if it can be recycled. If it's too inefficient to be accepted for reuse, look for a recycling facility in your location that crushes ceramic fixtures for use in construction materials, such as road base.

One of the sure-fire ways to assess the effectiveness of a toilet is its gram rating. Gram rating is a standardized laboratory test to determine how many grams of solid waste (using a soy product, not the real McCoy!) a toilet satisfactorily flushes. A rating greater than 500 grams is good.

To be sure the toilet you purchase will fit, check the distance from the wall to the center of the toilet's outlet (the pipe into which the toilet drains) in your bathroom. This is often referred to as the "rough-in." It's usually either 10 or 14 inches.

Also check for rebates. Many water departments, especially those in areas with water shortages, offer rebates ranging from $60 to $80—sometimes as high as $200—toward the purchase price of a water-efficient toilet. Dual-flush toilets often command a slightly higher rebate since they're more efficient.

The Ultimate in Efficiency

As of this book's printing, the most efficient dual-flush model in the world is the Sydney Smart toilet, manufactured by Caroma, an Australian company. This toilet received EPA's WaterSense label and uses the least water of any toilet available in America. It can save an additional 2,975 gallons of water per year compared to other high-efficiency toilets (HETs). Its small flush option uses 0.8 gallon per flush (gpf), and an optional larger flush uses 1.28 gpf, averaging 0.89 gpf. The toilet's "wash-down" flushing (versus siphonic action), along with a larger trapway, promote clog-free performance.

What Will It Cost?

Water-efficient toilets range in cost from about $50 to a few hundred dollars, but most of them are $100 to $200. If you can save a little more water while still getting a good flush (check the model's ANSI flush rating), it will be worth a little extra money, since you'll save over the long haul on your utility bill.

Cost Estimate: Installation of a new, 1.6 gallon flush toilet.

Includes removal of existing toilet

Cost for materials only: **$200**

Contractor's total, including materials, labor, and markup: **$470**

Costs are national averages and do not include sales tax.

What Will You Save?

As noted earlier, 1.6-gallon toilets can save 3,000 gallons per year per person versus older 3.5 gpf toilets. Dual-flush toilets save over 4,600 gallons compared to 3.5 gpf models. If you have a water-guzzling 5 or 7 gpf toilet (older than 1980), you will really save by replacing it! The EPA's WaterSense website notes that "Retrofitting your house with high-efficiency toilets can save a family of four roughly $1,000 over the next 10 years without compromising performance."

Project 39

Eliminating Phantom Loads

Although very few of us know it, our homes are haunted. Not by ghosts, but by phantoms of another sort, known as phantom loads. Phantom loads come from electrical devices that draw power when they're switched off. And they're everywhere. Televisions, satellite receivers, DVD players, cordless phones, and stereo equipment all continue to consume electrical energy when switched off. Battery chargers for a wide assortment of electronic devices, such as iPods, notebook computers, flashlights, chargeable drills, and even portable battery-powered vacuum cleaners are all phantom loads. (Even when the batteries are charged, they continue to draw power.)

That's not all. Transformers for electronic keyboards, printers, fax machines, and small appliances such as coffeemakers also create household phantom loads. All of these devices, and many more, continue to draw power, night and day, when the devices are not in use.

Not all phantom loads are created equal, however. Some are quite high, others barely noticeable. Satellite receivers, for example, may consume 14 to 15 watts when operating, and 12 watts when not operating. Televisions may consume 30 to 60 watts when operating, but under one watt when shut off. Phantom loads also differ with respect to function. Some devices, like televisions, draw power when off to ensure the instant-on capability: when you press the power button on the TV or the remote, the TV turns on immediately. Modems and satellite receivers for televisions provide the same benefit. Other phantom loads, created by devices like TiVo and programmable VCR and

DVD recorders, are required to retain settings in memory for recording television programs. Others perform functions of more dubious value, such as the LED clocks on microwaves and coffeemakers. Still others, like battery chargers, continue to draw power if they're plugged in, while performing no function whatsoever when the device being charged is not connected.

Although phantom loads are not always obvious—for example, cell phone chargers—others, like modems and routers, are quite conspicuous. The small red or green LED lights on these devices tell you the device is drawing power, even though it is not turned on.

Together, though, the electrical consumption of the various phantom loads can add up—often substantially.

Go Green!

A simple way to cut down on power usage is to make sure your computer is set to an energy-efficient power-saving mode. Setting your computer to go into sleep mode when idle for a short time can save as much as $80 a year.

Not All Phantom Loads Are Created Equal

Some phantom loads are extremely high—nearly as high as the operating wattage of the electronic device itself. My satellite receiver, for example, uses 15 watts (0.20 amps) when operating. When turned off (but still plugged in), it consumes 14 watts (0.19 amps). Most electrical devices, however, experience a huge increase in energy demand when switched on. My DVD/VCR player, for example, uses 3 watts (0.05 amps) when turned off and 20 watts (0.28 amps) when playing a DVD or video tape. My 19-inch color television uses 32 watts when operating, but only 1 watt when shut off.

the photo below) or "Watts Up?" (about $110 to $140) meters. (Both can be found on the Internet.) Although they're helpful, it's probably not worth investing in one of these meters just to check for phantom loads. Using the guidelines just mentioned, you can pretty much locate all significant phantom loads in your home. These meters, however, are helpful for home energy audits (Project 11); they're plugged into outlets next to appliances or electronic devices that you want to test. The device or appliance is then plugged into the socket in the meter, as shown below. If the meter indicates power usage when the device you're testing is switched off, it is a phantom load. The meter also shows the size of the phantom load in watts and amps. (Another home energy monitor you might find useful, known as The Energy Detective, is described in Project 11.)

According to the U.S. Environmental Protection Agency, phantom loads account for about 40% of the total energy consumed by household electronic devices. In a home equipped with many electronic devices, especially a large screen television set, DVD players, computers, printers, and cordless phones, phantom loads could easily add up to 200 watts at any given time. That's the equivalent of leaving two 100-watt lightbulbs running 24 hours a day, 365 days a year. If you pay 10 cents per kilowatt-hour, 200 watts of phantom load will cost about 48 cents a day, or nearly $175 per year.

Eliminating Phantom Loads

Purging phantom loads is about as easy as it gets. But first you'll need to locate them. As a general rule, any device that's operated by a remote control or has a clock or a little red or green LED light that stays on all of the time draws power when shut off. Virtually all battery chargers and transformers also continue to consume energy when not in use if plugged into an electrical outlet.

To test for the not-so-obvious phantom loads, you could purchase a digital power meter with a clever name such as the "Kill A Watt" (about $30, shown in

Kill A Watt™ meter measures phantom loads and energy use of all kinds of electrical devices in our homes.

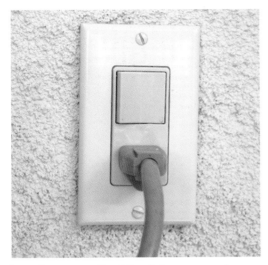

Switch and receptacles like this one can be used to completely turn off microwaves and other appliances without unplugging them.

Photo by Dan Chiras

Once you've identified phantom loads, it's time to eliminate them. Strategies vary by device, and some phantom loads should not be eliminated. For battery chargers used with personal electronic devices, such as cell phones, digital cameras, and laptop computers, and transformers for electronic keyboards, the best way to eliminate the phantom loads is to unplug the chargers from the electrical outlet when they're not in use. When you're done charging your cell phone or digital camera, for example, unplug the charger from the wall. You may also want to purchase a solar battery charger for such devices.

For televisions, stereos, desktop computers, printers, modems/routers, and satellite tuner boxes, it's best to plug the devices into a power strip. When you turn off these devices, also turn off the power strip to terminate the flow of electricity to them. These devices can also be plugged into outlets that are controlled by wall switches. I plug the television, satellite receiver, and DVD/VCR in my bedroom into a power strip that's plugged into an electrical outlet controlled by a wall switch. When I'm done watching TV or a video, I flip the switch and turn them all off at once. The phantom load falls from 33 watts to 0 watts with the flip of a

switch. I also plug my computer and printer into a power strip that is turned off when I'm done working.

Electronic devices, such as microwaves, can be controlled by installing a "switch-and-receptacle" (as shown in the photo). This is an electrical outlet that's controlled by its own on-off switch. When the switch is turned off, the flow of electricity to the plug is terminated. Any device plugged into the outlet is therefore turned off.

Switch-and-receptacles are available in hardware stores and home improvement centers. They're easy to install, if you're experienced and capable in electrical wiring. If not, it's best to hire a licensed electrician. The circuit will need to be turned off (and tested with a voltmeter to make sure it's off) before disconnecting the electrical outlet and installing the switch and receptacle.

Phantom loads in portable stereos and other devices can be controlled by installing cord switches on their electrical cords. Cord switches are available at home improvement centers and hardware stores. They're quite easy to install, after the device has been unplugged, of course.

What to Watch Out For

While it's easy to eliminate phantom loads, it's not always a good idea. If you record TV programs,

Go Green!

To eliminate a common household phantom load, consider replacing a cordless phone with a corded model. Cordless phone recharging cradles draw power 24 hours a day, 365 days a year. Corded phones use a fraction of the power, and the electricity they need to operate is delivered by the telephone line, not from your household circuits. In addition, when the power goes out, you can still use a corded phone. Look for Energy Star-qualified models.

Recycle Those Electronics!

Keep your cell phone for as many years as possible. If you must replace it, recycle it. Up to 100 million cell phones are discarded each year. Recycling helps reduce hazardous chemicals (arsenic, copper, lead, and zinc) released into landfills and leached into groundwater. It also helps wildlife. According to National Geographic, cell phones contain coltan, a mineral extracted illegally from rainforests of the Congo. Coltan mining is reducing the endangered gorilla population.

To recycle your cell phone, look for Eco-Cell collection places at zoos and other locations. They refurbish phones, raising money for conservation. **www.eco-cell.org**

Some electronics stores offer free recycling for phones, rechargeable batteries, and appliances. Cell phones can also be recycled through some charities or **www. recyclemycellphone.org** (which provides free pre-paid mailing labels). **www.mygreenelectronics.org** identifies local drop-offs by item and zip code. Apple, Dell, Sony, Hewlett Packard, and Gateway have recycling programs. Check their websites.

completely switching off the VCR or TiVo will erase your settings. Garage door openers require a small input of electricity for the remote control, so it's best to leave the power on unless you'll be away for several days. I switch mine off (at the breaker box) at night and when leaving home. (Check with your garage door opener manufacturer to ensure safe practices.)

In many newer homes, smoke detectors and burglar alarms are hard-wired—connected to the electrical wiring in your home. While these devices will operate on backup battery power alone, the electrical connection is required by building codes and should not be disconnected.

Although phantom loads can't be eliminated, they can be reduced by use of Energy Star-appliances, whose phantom loads are 50% less than other models.

What Will It Cost?

Eliminating phantom loads costs very little—or nothing—if electronic devices can be plugged into existing electrical outlets with wall switches or power strips, or if you just unplug them. With very little effort, you can easily cut phantom loads by half. The purchase of a power strip can pay for itself in less than a year if you plug your television and stereo system into it and turn it off when these devices are not in use.

Cost Estimate: Installation of four switch/outlet electrical fixtures

Cost for materials only: **$95**

Contractor's total, including materials, labor, and markup: **$290**

Costs are national averages and do not include sales tax.

What Will You Save?

Phantom loads are often individually small, but add up to about 5% of a household's overall electrical demand. If your family uses 800 kilowatt-hours of electricity per month (roughly the national average), phantom loads in your home come to about 40 kWh, or about $4 per month, or $48 per year. In many homes, however, with entertainment centers, numerous TVs and satellite receivers, and computers, phantom loads can be much higher—easily 200 watts. In such homes, phantom loads will cost a lot more—about $250 per year. Nationwide, it's estimated that phantom loads cost Americans more than $4 billion a year.

To calculate your savings, collect your utility bills for the past year and add up the electrical usage. It's listed in kilowatt-hours. Now multiply this amount by 5%. If you cut phantom loads by half, divide this number by two and then multiply the savings by your electrical rate to determine your savings.

Project 40

Energy-Efficient Lighting

Indoor and outdoor lighting make our lives more productive, enjoyable, and safe. It can even improve the ambience, or the mood, of our homes. But lighting doesn't come cheaply. It is responsible for 6% of the average home energy bill—$126 of an annual $2,100 electric bill in 2007. As energy prices continue to rise, that number is going to get bigger and bigger. Fortunately, there are several simple, inexpensive ways to reduce the cost of lighting our homes.

What Are Your Options?

One way to save money on lighting is to use **compact fluorescent lightbulbs** (CFLs). CFLs can replace standard incandescent lightbulbs in most light fixtures. Although conventional incandescent lightbulbs are less expensive than CFLs, they're much less efficient. Only about 5% to 10% of the electricity flowing through them is converted to light; the rest is converted to heat.

CFLs, on the other hand, use about one fourth (sometimes even less) as much energy to produce the same amount of light as an incandescent bulb—and they also produce a lot less waste heat. Their higher initial cost is easily offset by savings resulting from their much greater efficiency and much longer lifespan—which reduces replacement costs.

Compact fluorescents are widely available—at home improvement centers, numerous chain discount stores, and even grocery stores. CFLs come in many shapes and sizes. Most are designed to replace indoor

incandescent lightbulbs, although standard CFLs cannot be used in dimmable or three-way light fixtures. (Those bulbs must be replaced by CFLs specifically designed for such purposes, which are more expensive and can be difficult to find. You may also have to replace dimmer and three-way switches to work with these CFLs.)

CFLs are also available for outdoor light fixtures, including spotlights. I use them in my garage and in the

CFL lights come in many shapes and sizes to meet a variety of needs.

Courtesy of OSRAM SYLVANIA. Used with permission.

LED lights are super efficient but still fairly expensive.

Courtesy of C. Crane Company, Inc.

floodlights that illuminate my front walkway. However, because they take a few minutes to warm up and reach full intensity, and because they should remain on for 15 minutes or more, CFLs are not advisable for motion-sensor security lights.

You may also want to consider replacing standard lightbulbs with the even newer and more efficient LED lights. They're 90% more efficient than incandescent lights and considerably more efficient than CFLs. LEDs are currently more expensive, and your options are somewhat limited, but prices are expected to come down, and more varieties should become available as they gain popularity. LEDs also last longer than any other type of bulb. Where can you buy them? Home centers such as Lowe's (and their websites) offer a selection of LED lights, especially outdoor ones—from lanterns to grill lights. Lighting stores and websites, such as Lamps Plus, offer a wide variety of LED desk lamps, easy to install battery-powered under-cabinet lights, and solar and battery-powered outdoor lights, including lanterns, motion-sensor floodlights, and even floating lights for ponds.

To improve the energy efficiency of a new or existing home, you may want to install Energy Star-qualified light fixtures. They come in many styles including portable table, desk, and floor lamps—and hard-wired options such as porch, ceiling, under-cabinet, wall sconces, bathroom vanity, and other fixtures, according to the EPA. Some indoor models offer dimming, and many outdoor fixtures have automatic daylight shut-off and motion sensors. They're available at home improvement centers and lighting retailers and typically carry a two-year warranty—double the industry standard.

Why Install Energy-Efficient Lighting?

Energy-efficient lightbulbs save money because they produce more light with less electricity. A CFL replacement for a 75-watt incandescent lightbulb, for example, produces the same amount of light (measured in lumens) but uses one-fifth the energy, only about 15 watts. An LED replacement uses a fraction of that—only about 2 or 3 watts to produce same amount of light as a 75-watt incandescent or a 15-watt CFL (75-watt equivalent).

Energy-efficient lightbulbs also save money by reducing summer cooling costs. Because CFLs produce 75% to 80% less waste heat, they can actually decrease the demand on your air conditioner. LED lights produce even less waste heat, around 90% less, and can have an even greater impact on air conditioning. CFLs and LEDs also make heavily lighted rooms, such as bathrooms and kitchens, more comfortable in the summer.

Nationwide, the savings created by the widespread use of energy-efficient lighting could be phenomenal. According to the EPA, "If every American home replaced just one lightbulb with an Energy Star-qualified bulb, we would save enough energy to light more than 3 million homes for a year, more than $600 million in annual energy costs."

How long do these bulbs last? An incandescent bulb lasts 750 to 1,000 hours. A CFL will last 8,000 to 10,000 hours. (I've had several CFLs in my house since 1988

Energy Star-qualified light fixtures like these are attractive and efficient.

Courtesy of American Fluorescent

and they're still working!) An LED lightbulb will last 6 times that long—approximately 60,000 hours. Installing longer-lasting bulbs reduces your replacement costs and time required to shop for and install new bulbs.

Energy-efficient lighting also helps reduce pollution, such as greenhouse gas emissions. If every home in the United States replaced four high-use lightbulbs with CFLs, the EPA estimates that it would prevent greenhouse gases equivalent to the emissions of more than 800,000 cars per year.

Installation

CFLs and LED lightbulbs screw into standard electrical fixtures, so replacement is easy. Rather than replacing all lightbulbs in your home with CFLs or LEDs, most energy experts suggest replacing only the incandescent lightbulbs in the most commonly used light fixtures— lights that are on for a substantial amount of time each day. At a minimum, the EPA recommends installing CFLs in fixtures that are used at least 15 minutes at a time or several hours per day. This strategy yields the greatest savings. According to the EPA, the best fixtures to use CFLs in are usually found in family

and living rooms, kitchens, dining rooms, bedrooms, and outdoors. Home offices are another location to consider, since lights there tend to be left on for long periods.

Although you may also want to install CFLs in less-commonly used light fixtures, for example, in closets or pantries or rarely lighted hallways, turning the bulbs on and off for less than 15 minutes reduces their life span. Nevertheless, you may want to consider installing them in lights that are accidentally left on from time to time, for instance, in garages, sheds, or barns.

What to Watch Out For

When purchasing a CFL, I've found it helpful to go up one step—that is, if you're replacing a 60-watt incandescent lightbulb, buy a 75-watt-equivalent CFL. If you are replacing a 75-watt lightbulb, buy a 100-watt-equivalent CFL. The light of the next-higher wattage CFL seems to more closely match the incandescent bulb it is replacing.

Go Green!

• If you decorate your home over the holiday season, use LED lights for outdoor lighting and Christmas trees. They are widely available and use a fraction of the energy of conventional decorative lights.

• When building a new home, remodeling an existing one, or redecorating, consider Energy Star light fixtures. Replacing the five most frequently used light fixtures in your home with Energy Star-qualified models could save you more than $65 per year in energy costs, according to the Environmental Protection Agency, and costs are rising.

Also note that when some CFLs are switched on, there may be a very slight delay (a fraction of a second) between the time you flip the switch and the time the bulb comes on. (This was especially common in the older style CFLs.) It's barely noticeable and won't cause any inconvenience. CFLs for home lighting also take a few minutes to reach full intensity. Older CFLs blink when they're powering up. Newer models should not.

Most CFLs produce a pleasant yellowish light similar to an incandescent lightbulb. For reading, you may want to purchase a bulb that emits a bluer light like those produced by SunWave. These bulbs emit light similar to midday sunlight and help increase visual acuity. The manufacturer also claims they reduce eye strain. I use them in my office, where I read a lot, and have been extremely pleased with them. They do make the print appear sharper, which is especially appreciated as my eyes age!

When shopping, avoid really cheap CFLs with lower lifetime ratings (under 8,000 hours). I've found that they are not as reliable. I recommend purchasing bulbs only from major manufacturers, such as GE and Sylvania. In my experience, they have a longer life and are much higher-quality bulbs.

"CFLs perform best in open fixtures that allow airflow, such as table and floor lamps, wall sconces, pendants, and outdoor fixtures," according to the EPA. "For recessed fixtures, it is better to use a reflector, floodlight type of CFL, rather than a regular CFL, since the design of the reflector evenly distributes the light down to your task area." Never enclose a regular lamp-type CFL in a recessed light fixture. It will work, but will burn out long before its time is up.

CFLs contain a small amount of mercury vapor, which has caused some critics to question the wisdom of their use. Even though CFLs do contain mercury, these concerns are greatly overblown. Consider these facts: a CFL contains about 4 milligrams of mercury, while, a watch battery contains 5 to 20 milligrams of mercury (although some might say it's better contained in a battery and won't leak out, whereas a bulb could break if dropped, releasing mercury).

Bear in mind that mercury is also produced by coal-fired power plants that produce electricity to power lightbulbs. Electrical production required to power an incandescent lightbulb over a period of five years will produce 10 milligrams of mercury. This pollution is released into the environment. It can then enter aquatic food chains, and end up in fish. Electricity used to power a comparable CFL will result in the emission of much less mercury—only about 2.0 to 2.5 milligrams.

Because CFLs contain mercury, bulbs that fail should be recycled or disposed of through municipal hazardous waste programs. CFLs should not be thrown out in the trash. According to the Energy Star website, if your state does permit homeowners to place used or broken CFLs in the garbage, "seal the bulb in two plastic bags and put it into the outside trash, or other protected outside location, for the next normal trash collection." CFLs should not be disposed of in an incinerator. For more information on proper disposal, log on to Energy Star's website (**www.energystar.gov**). Click on *Lighting*, and then *Light Bulbs*. There's a pdf file you can download to your computer for instructions on proper disposal of CFLs.

LED lights are widely used in automobile, truck, and motorcycle tail lights, and flashlights, but are only beginning to be used in home lighting, so they are not yet as widely available as CFLs.

Go Green!

Outdoor lights provide security but consume a huge amount of energy, especially if left on all day and all night. To save energy, substitute CFLs for incandescent lights and be sure to switch the lights off when they're not needed or consider hooking them up to a timer.

Lightbulb Costs & Savings

	Incandescent Lightbulb (60-watt bulb)	CFL (12 watts)	LED – CC Vivid (2 watts)
Life span (hours)	1,000	10,000	Up to 60,000
Number of bulbs needed to produce 60,000 hours	60	6	1
Bulb cost per 60,000 hours	$40.20 (60 x $0.67)	$12.96 (6 x $2.16)	$34.95 (1 x $34.95)
Electricity used for 60,000 hours (kWh)	3,600 kWh	720 kWh	120 kWh
Total Cost for 60,000 hours (at 10 cents per kWh)	$360.00	$72.00	$12.00
Total Cost (bulbs plus electricity)	$400.20	$84.96	$46.95
Total Savings	none	$315.24	$353.25

What Will It Cost?

Many large home improvement centers and chain stores offer three-, four-, and six-packs of CFLs at a dramatically reduced price. If you purchase a multiple pack, expect to pay around $2 per bulb. If you purchase bulbs singly, you'll pay closer to $5. LEDs cost as much as CFLs did when they first arrived on the scene in the 1980s, but the price of LED fixtures and bulbs is coming down as they become more popular.

What Will You Save?

CFL and LED lights can save a substantial amount of money, not to mention time, since once you install them, you'll rarely, if ever, have to change them. This is a big advantage if you have high ceiling lights. To assess the long-term savings of these bulbs, see the table above.

Cost Estimate: Installation of three energy-efficient light fixtures and bulbs

Includes removal of existing fixtures and installation of junction boxes, wiring, and CFL bulbs for a kitchen light, an outdoor light, and a chandelier

Cost for materials only: **$700**

Contractor's total, including materials, labor, and markup: **$1,050**

Costs are national averages and do not include sales tax.

Project 41

Energy-Efficient Appliances & Electronics

Appliances and electronic devices provide convenience and entertainment, but like everything else these days, come at a cost—they're responsible for about 20% of the typical household energy bill. Fortunately, manufacturers have made enormous improvements in recent years in the energy efficiency of these products. If your appliances or electronics are on their last legs, consider replacing them with new Energy Star models. Not only will you cut your utility bills, you could also reduce your water consumption if you're replacing a dishwasher or clothes washer. Using less energy will help cut back on greenhouse gas emissions, acid rain, urban pollution, and environmentally damaging mining as well.

Purchasing the most energy-efficient of all appliances and electronics—Energy Star-qualified products—may seem like a small measure, but could have an enormously beneficial impact. The EPA estimates that the average home has roughly two TVs, a VCR, a DVD player, and three telephones. If just these items alone were replaced with Energy Star-qualified models in every home in the U.S., it would reduce greenhouse gas emissions by over 25 billion pounds a year, the equivalent to taking over 3 million cars off the road.

What's Available & How Do You Compare Options?

An easy way to identify energy-efficient appliances is to look for the Energy Star logo. Found on over 50 common household products—from dishwashers and refrigerators, to furnaces and air conditioners, to computers, printers, phones, and fax machines—it signifies that the product is one of the most efficient models in its category.

To compare the efficiency of individual appliances, check the yellow energy tags. They indicate how much energy each appliance will use in a year and how each model compares with other similar appliances. For more detailed product information, log on to the EPA's and DOE's Energy Star website (**www.energystar.gov**). Click on *Appliances* or *Home Electronics* in the product listing. Then select the product category—for example, dishwashers. You'll find an extensive list of models by various manufacturers, plus annual energy or water use.

Yellow energy tag

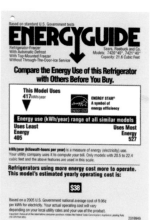

Energy Star logo
Courtesy of EPA

What about Clothes Dryers?

As you look through the Energy Star website, you may notice that it does not include clothes dryers in its list of appliances. That's because most dryers use very similar amounts of energy—and there aren't many ways to make a dryer more efficient. That said, the EPA recommends using the moisture sensor option on your dryer. This automatically shuts off the machine when the clothes are dry and saves energy. Also, if your clothes washer has spin options, choose a high spin speed or extended spin option to reduce the amount of remaining moisture. Less moisture means faster drying time and less energy use.

If some of the data is unfamiliar, the website also offers an explanation of terms and describes key measurements used to compare appliances, such as *water factor* and *energy factor (EF)*. Pay close attention to these ratios. The *modified energy factor (MEF)* rating for clothes washers, for instance, includes *all* of the energy used to clean your clothes, which includes the operation of the motor and the water heated by a water heater. The MEF also includes the amount of energy a clothes dryer consumes to dry the clothes afterwards. (Drying time is affected by how much moisture is left in your clothes after they go through the final spin cycle in the washing machine.) The higher the MEF, the more efficient the clothes washer is.

When Should You Replace Appliances & Electronics?

Installing energy-efficient appliances and electronics makes sense if your old equipment is not working or was manufactured before 1994. Be sure to recycle the old one (instead of just having it hauled away to a landfill) when your new appliance is installed. If the store you're buying from doesn't offer this service, call local appliance recyclers. They're often listed in the Yellow Pages. Appliance retailers may help you find one.

Shopping Tips

When researching the best energy- and water-efficient appliances, check out *Consumer Reports*. Besides comparing models on the basis of energy and water use, the organization evaluates them by other useful criteria, such as customer satisfaction and durability (**www.ConsumerReports.org/energy**). Consider the advantages of U.S. brands. Some foreign-made appliances are considerably more efficient, but can be a bit difficult to locate or service. Buying appliances built overseas also requires energy to ship the appliance to market.

Once you have identified appliances or electronics with the features and performance you want, call local dealers and see if they have the model number you're looking for. This can save a lot of time. The Energy Star website even has a store locator. It won't tell you which stores carry the exact model you want, but it will list the names and addresses of stores nearby to call or visit. The website also provides tips on easy ways to save energy when using appliances.

Many appliances can be installed by inexperienced do-it-yourselfers, which is why this project is rated for beginners. For example, electric dryers and refrigerators (unless they have an automatic ice/water system) just need to be plugged in and maneuvered into place. Plumbing and (especially) gas connections generally need to be handled by a professional installer.

Go Green!

Don't rinse dishes before putting them in the dishwasher. This wastes a lot of water. If you need to remove more than what you can scrape off of plates and pans, fill the sink with water, soak, then wipe dishes off under water, so the tap isn't running the entire time. Select the dishwasher's air-dry option, rather than heat-dry.

Energy Star-qualified clothes washers and dryers save both water and energy.

Courtesy of Frigidaire

Refrigerators

When comparing refrigerator models, remember that even the most efficient side-by-side units use 10% to 25% more energy than standard models with the freezer on the top or bottom, according to the EPA. Also, icemakers and water dispensers typically increase energy use by 14% to 20%. Other drawbacks of these features: higher initial cost and increased likelihood of repair.

Dryers

When shopping for a dryer, look for one with a moisture sensor. They reduce run time and energy use and also minimize wear and tear on your clothes—the longer clothes are in the dryer, the more the fabrics break down. (The lint in the filter consists mostly of fibers from the fabric, and is a sign of wear on your clothes.) It's a good idea to clean the sensor regularly. (See instructions in the owner's manual.)

Microwaves

When comparing microwaves, look for a model with a sensor that helps determine the proper amount of time for cooking foods. It detects heat or moisture given off by food and turns the microwave off at the right time, saving energy and helping to prevent overcooking.

Ranges, Cooktops & Ovens

Gas ranges and cooktops are more efficient than electric models, and cheaper to operate. They use about half as much energy. Choose a model with an electronic ignition, not a pilot light, which wastes energy. If you're replacing an electric stove with a gas model, consider the cost to install a gas line. If there is no gas line in your neighborhood, you'll need to install a propane tank and pay the monthly tank rental fee.

Electric induction stove tops, one of the newest types on the market, are more efficient than conventional electric models, but cost more. If you're purchasing an electric oven, be sure to look into one that comes with a convection option. They use about 20% less energy than traditional ovens by circulating hot air, making food cook faster.

Go Green!

Refrigerator/freezers use more energy than any other appliance, usually one-sixth of your total electric bill. If you keep your refrigerator fairly full, but not stuffed, it will run most efficiently. Keeping a pitcher full of cold water or other liquids in a not-so-full fridge can also help.

How Much Electricity Do Appliances Use?

This chart shows how much energy a typical appliance uses per year and its corresponding cost based on national averages. For example, a refrigerator uses almost five times the electricity the average television uses.

(Electricity costs will fluctuate with power rates.)

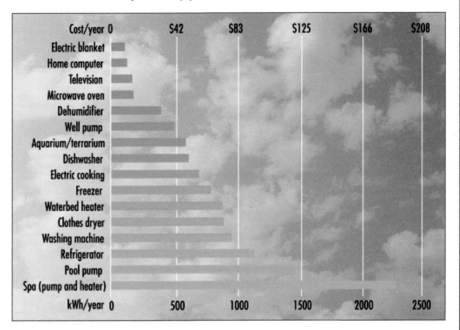

Cost/year 0 $42 $83 $125 $166 $208

Electric blanket
Home computer
Television
Microwave oven
Dehumidifier
Well pump
Aquarium/terrarium
Dishwasher
Electric cooking
Freezer
Waterbed heater
Clothes dryer
Washing machine
Refrigerator
Pool pump
Spa (pump and heater)

kWh/year 0   500   1000   1500   2000   2500

Courtesy of the U.S. Department of Energy—Energy Efficiency and Renewable Energy

What Will It Cost?

Appliance costs range very widely, depending on their capacity, style, colors, and features. While some Energy Star-qualified models can be a little more expensive, many are very competitive in price and features with less-efficient appliances.

Cost Estimate: Installation of a new Energy-Star-rated wall oven, dishwasher, and cooktop

Cost for materials only: **$4,975**

Contractor's total including materials, labor, and markup: **$6,930**

Costs are national averages and do not include sales tax. If you have a professional do several projects in one visit, you'll save money overall.

What Will You Save?

Energy Star-qualified appliances will reduce your utility costs as soon as you install them, and the savings add up over time. An Energy Star clothes washer, for instance, is both water- and energy-efficient and can save up to $110 per year on utility bills, compared to models manufactured before 1994. Energy Star refrigerators use half or even less energy required by pre-1994 models. You could save as much as $140 per year if you replace an old 24 cubic foot refrigerator—without sacrificing any features like automatic ice makers. And since refrigerators last about 13 years, and clothes washers about 9 years, the savings really add up! You'll also be helping to save the Earth by reducing your carbon footprint.

Project 42

Solar Electricity

If you have made your home energy-efficient and are looking for additional ways to reduce your carbon emissions, you may want to consider installing a solar electric system. These systems can be a reliable source of power in many locations, although they're pretty expensive unless your state or local utility offers financial incentives (which many do).

To save money on your system, first implement all the measures you can to make your home or office as energy-efficient as possible. Experts estimate that every dollar invested in energy-efficiency will reduce the cost of a solar electric system (required to meet your demand) by $3 to $5. For example, a $2,000 investment in energy-efficient appliances, compact fluorescent lightbulbs, and other measures, such as insulation and weatherization, will save between $6,000 to $10,000 in the solar system's cost, since a smaller system will meet your reduced energy requirements. Moreover, efficiency measures you implement may entitle you to rebates from your local utility company or tax credits or deductions from your state or the federal government.

Grid-connected solar electric systems may even make sense in areas with moderate electric rates, provided financial incentives are available. Several states currently offer rebates and other incentives that pay up to half the system cost, making solar electricity nearly cost-competitive with conventional power.

In most states, utilities are required to purchase surplus electricity generated by grid-connected customers, although the rates they pay vary. If you're in a state that requires utilities to pay the retail rate (the same rate they charge you for electricity), your system could also help pay for itself.

Further reductions in system cost can be achieved by applying for modest federal incentives. At this writing, the federal government offers a 30% tax credit for a residential solar electric system to a maximum of $2,000. This incentive, although small, helps to lower the cost of a PV (photovoltaic) system a bit further.

More generous incentives are available from the federal government for businesses. Log on to **www.dsireusa.org** to check out current rebates offered by utilities and state governments.

Go Green!

Replace old, inefficient appliances with Energy Star-qualified models (Project 41). Consider whether you really need an extra refrigerator or freezer in your garage or basement. If it's old and inefficient, it may be a huge contributor to your electric bill.

What Is a Solar Electric System What Are Your Options?

Solar electric systems use sunlight energy to produce electricity from one of the most abundant chemical substances on the planet, silicon dioxide. This substance, derived from sand or quartzite rock, is used to produce solar cells. When struck by sunlight, the silicon atoms in solar cells release electrons that form an electrical current. Numerous solar cells are wired together in modules (also called panels), and the modules are linked together in solar arrays.

Solar cells come in four basic types: (1) single-crystalline, (2) multi-crystalline, (3) amorphous thin film, and (4) hybrid. Hybrid solar cells consist of a single-crystal solar cell sandwiched between two layers of amorphous silicon. They vary in efficiency, but are priced fairly similarly. The most efficient solar cells on the market today are the hybrid cells, which tend to cost a little more than the others.

Solar electric systems produce direct current (DC) electricity, which is converted to alternating current (AC) electricity, the type required by most household appliances and electronics. This conversion takes place in a device known as an inverter, a component of solar electric systems. Besides converting DC electricity to AC electricity, the inverter boosts the low-voltage DC electricity produced by the PV array (usually 24 or 48 volts) to 120-volt AC standard household current.

Homeowners have three options in terms of how their solar electric systems are set up: (1) a grid-connected system, (2) a grid-connected system with battery backup, or (3) an off-grid, or stand-alone, system. Grid-connected systems, like the one shown in the drawing on the next page, produce AC electricity that is distributed throughout the house to active circuits via the main service panel—the gray box that contains the circuit breakers. Surplus electricity—electricity produced in excess of the home's demand—is allowed to flow out of the house onto the electrical grid (the electrical wires that supply your neighborhood, town, and city).

At night, when a grid-connected solar system is not collecting energy, household demand is met by electricity supplied by the utility company grid. The electric company keeps track of any surplus electricity your system feeds onto the grid, crediting you each month or at the end of the year.

Grid-connected systems are the simplest and least expensive of all solar electric systems, but they do have one significant disadvantage: if the electrical grid goes down—for example, in an ice storm—the solar system shuts down completely. This protects power company employees who might be working on the lines. Unfortunately, when the system shuts down, it terminates the flow of electricity to household circuits drawing power at the time. Even though the sun may be shining, there is no power in the house!

Grid-connected systems with battery backup are identical to grid-connected systems except that they contain a bank of batteries to store electricity that can be used if the grid goes down. This feature permits a home or business to operate during power failures. In many grid-connected systems with battery backup,

Solar electric arrays like this one consist of numerous modules.

Courtesy of Sharp Electronics Corporation, Solar Energy Solutions Group

1. Sunlight strikes modules, producing DC electricity.
2. Electricity travels to inverter.
3. Inverter converts DC electricity to AC electricity.
4. Electricity travels to home's breaker box and circuits.
5. Surplus electricity is fed to grid.
6. Meter tracks usage to/from grid.

Solar electric system tied to the local grid
Illustration by Anil Rao

however, only critical electrical loads are supplied during an electrical outage. (This saves money by reducing the size of the backup battery bank.) The critical loads typically include the fan in the furnace or pump in the boiler, the refrigerator, and a few strategically placed lights—the same loads you'd supply with a backup generator.

Your third option is an off-grid or stand-alone system, which, as the name implies, is not connected to the electrical grid. Surplus electricity is stored in a battery bank consisting of numerous deep-cycle lead acid batteries. The electricity stored in the batteries meets household demand at night and during cloudy periods—or anytime demand exceeds production.

Off-grid systems are typically installed in rural locations, especially in remote locations that cannot be easily or affordably tied into electrical power lines. They are often equipped with a backup generator to meet power needs should the batteries run low. They may also be coupled with another source of renewable energy, such as a wind turbine, to ensure a steady supply of electricity. (The wind often blows when sunshine is scarce.) My off-grid system, which has provided all of my electrical needs since 1996, contains all three components, a PV array, a small wind turbine, and a backup generator, which I only need to run for about 10 to 15 hours per year to recharge batteries.

When Does Solar Electricity Make Economic Sense?

Solar electric systems are ideal if you're seeking energy independence or are interested in finding ways to cut your use of fossil fuels and help reduce carbon emissions. Unfortunately, solar electricity is one of the most expensive ways to obtain power. That said, there are situations where solar electric systems make good economic sense. Stand-alone systems, for instance, can be quite economical if you're building a new home in a rural area where connection fees (the cost of hooking to the electric grid) are high.

Line extension policies and costs vary by location. Some utilities connect for free, but most charge a hefty fee to run electric wires to your home. In such cases, it may make sense to install an off-grid solar electric system. Even if your home is more than a few tenths of a mile from a power line, avoiding the line extension fee may save enough to pay for a big part of a solar system. If a home is a half mile or more from power lines, grid connection fees of $50,000 are not uncommon. This could easily pay for a good-sized solar electric system. (My system for my super-efficient home only cost $15,000 plus an installation fee of $3,600.)

Grid-connected solar electric systems also make sense in areas with very high electrical costs. If you're paying 20 to 30 cents per kilowatt-hour of electricity, for example, a solar electric system usually makes economic sense—especially if you have made your home efficient, and financial incentives are available to offset your solar investment.

Installing a Solar Electric System

Solar electric systems require a sunny location, typically a south-facing roof with good solar exposure from at least 9:00 a.m. and 3:00 p.m. throughout the year. Most solar electric systems on the market do not tolerate shade. Even a small shadow cast on one module in an array can dramatically reduce the array's output. (There are some exceptions, however. Some solar modules have blocking diodes that ensure that the rest of the array will continue to produce, even if a few modules are shaded. Amorphous silicon applied to standing seam metal roofs tolerates shading a little better than other modules.)

Solar electric arrays can be mounted flush on the roof for aesthetic reasons or may be mounted on racks on the roof or on the ground. (Most solar electric modules perform better when mounted on racks, which keeps the modules cooler, enabling them to produce more electricity.) Some roof racks are adjustable so that homeowners can change the angle of the array with respect to the sun to achieve maximum solar gain as the sun's angle changes throughout the seasons. Arrays

can also be mounted on poles anchored in the ground. Another option is a tracking pole mount. This device allows the solar array to automatically track (follow) the sun on its daily path from sunrise to sunset, thus increasing the system's efficiency. Tracking arrays can boost system output by 20% to 30%, although the additional cost of a tracking mount often offsets this benefit.

PV systems can be installed by homeowners who have experience both in electrical wiring and in installing solar systems—for example, individuals who have received hands-on training in solar workshops. For the most part, however, these installations are best performed by trained professionals. Look for a certified installer who has been in the business at least 5 to 10 years and has installed numerous systems. Log on to **www.findsolar.com** to locate an experienced installer in your area.

Although some solar modules perform better than others, all major PV manufacturers produce high-quality modules backed by an impressive 25-year warranty. Inverters and other equipment used in solar electric systems are also reliable, so it's hard to go wrong when purchasing a system. Some major home improvement centers now sell solar electric systems with installation.

Pole-mounted tracking arrays follow the sun from sunrise to sunset, increasing energy production.

Courtesy of Rochester Solar Technologies

Installation of a solar electric system may require a permit from the local building department. Professional installers typically secure permits for their customers. (Installers can also help with paperwork required to obtain rebates from local utilities or others.)

Installation Tips

If you're thinking of installing a solar electric system, check not only with the building department, but also your local homeowner's association, if any. It may have restrictions on solar systems.

When installing a solar electric system in a region with cold and snowy winters, it's a good idea to place the array in a location that allows for safe, convenient access so you can carefully brush snow from the modules after storms. This also helps if you need to brush dirt, leaves, or other debris off the modules. When installing a system on the ground, be sure it's high enough to avoid being buried in snow. You may also need to fence it off to protect it from animals and children.

If you're thinking of installing an off-grid system, you'll need to purchase batteries designed for renewable energy systems. Car and truck batteries won't work. Most stand-alone systems require deep-cycle flooded lead acid batteries. Learn about the maintenance requirements of batteries and follow the instructions carefully. In grid-connected systems with battery backup, most installers use no-maintenance, sealed batteries designed for renewable energy systems.

For a grid-connected system, contact the utility *before* you make a purchase to iron out details, including payment for surplus electricity you deliver to the grid. Policies for installation and payment of surplus power vary from one state to the next. While all utilities are required by federal law to purchase surplus electricity from solar customers, some companies pay at a discounted rate (the cost of generating electricity) versus customers' retail rates—that is, the same rate they charge their customers (this is known as *net metering*).

Also, be sure the installer carries insurance to protect his or her workers, and never pay for a project until it has been fully installed and tested. At the very least, withhold the last 25% of the payment until the system is up and running to your satisfaction and approved by the building department. Shop around and get several quotes. Be wary of extremely costly systems. Rebates from the federal government, state government, and utilities have led to price inflation in the past. If you suspect price gouging, try another dealer/installer.

Before you begin shopping, it's a good idea to learn more about solar electricity. You may want to read the chapter on solar electric systems in my book, *The Homeowner's Guide to Renewable Energy.* Additional information will help you better understand your options.

What Will It Cost?

The cost of a solar electric system varies widely depending on the size and type of system and the difficulty of the installation—for example, the slope and access of the roof, and the ease of running wires from the array to the inverter. Battery-based systems are usually more costly than grid-connected systems without battery backup.

Costs also vary based on factors including the homeowner's energy usage, the style of the home, and its location and orientation to the sun.

Expect to pay between $8.50 and $12.50 per watt capacity (including installation) for a batteryless, grid-connected solar electric system that meets state rebate efficiency requirements. Rebates or other financial incentives will lower the cost. And, once again, other energy efficiencies in your home will reduce the system size and cost.

What Will You Save?

A properly situated and designed 3.0 Kilowatt system in a sunny Southwestern location might generate $900 of electricity a year, while the same system in the Northeast may only produce $500 worth.

Project
43

Purchasing Green Power

Many people are concerned about their home energy use because of rising fuel costs. Some are also concerned about the way in which is energy is produced, and how it affects the air we breathe, our climate, our national security, and the welfare of future generations all species that share this planet with us.

Fortunately, there are many steps each of us can take to reduce our energy consumption, starting with the energy efficiency measures described in Projects 11–16, 18, 19, and 39. Efficiency measures yield the highest rate of return on our investment. Another great way to reduce our use of conventional energy and its many impacts is to switch to renewable energy resources. (See projects 17, 20, 26, 35, 42, 45, and 57).

While installing a solar hot water or electric system, or a wind turbine may be too costly for many homeowners, there are ways that we can "green" our energy supply. One of the easiest is to purchase green power—electricity generated from renewable energy resources.

What Is Green Power & What Are Your Options?

Many utilities offer customers an option to purchase electricity generated from clean, renewable resources. How companies charge for green power varies. But there are three basic options.

Many companies charge a little extra for green power. You pay the basic rate that's charged to all customers

based on your use, but pay a small additional flat fee for each additional block. For example, my local utility charges an additional $2.50 for every 200-kilowatt-hour block of renewable energy it sells to a customer. If a customer is paying 10 cents per kilowatt-hour for conventional power, say from a coal-fired power plant, and the family consumes 800 kilowatt-hours of electricity in a month (the national average), the utility charges $80 (800 × 0.10) plus $10 ($2.50 for four each of the 200 kilowatt-hour blocks).

Although green power block rates result in a small increase in utility costs to customers, utility companies often "back out" other fees associated with the generation of conventional power, but not green power. In the Denver Metropolitan area, for instance, coal is the main source of electricity. While switching to wind energy results in an additional block fee, the utility reduces their fuel surcharge, associated with electrical

Go Green!

Install motion-sensing light switches in hallways, stairways, or poorly lighted landings in which light is only required temporarily (Project 44).

Commercial wind farm
Photo by Dan Chiras

generation from coal. This helps to offset the green energy fee. (The fuel surcharge covers, in part, the cost of mining and transporting coal to their power plants.) So instead of paying 1.25 cents more per kilowatt-hour (200 kwh blocks at $2.50), homeowners who use green power in this area pay only a little over 0.4 cents more per kilowatt-hour. Not a bad deal for going green.

If you're thinking about buying wind power or some other form of green energy from your local utility on the block plan, be sure to ask if other charges, such as the fuel surcharge, will be reduced as a result. Or check with a friend or neighbor who has switched to help you accurately estimate the cost.

Some utilities offer programs that allow customers to offset a percentage of their monthly electrical consumption, so they receive a blend of renewable and conventional power. For example, a customer may choose to purchase 60% green and 40% conventional electricity. These companies typically charge a little more per kilowatt-hour of electricity consumed to offset the slightly higher premium for green power.

According to the EPA, more than half of all customers who purchase electricity from local utility companies can buy green power *directly* from their local utility. But if your local utility doesn't offer green power, there are other ways to purchase it. For example, if you live in a state that has de-regulated its electrical suppliers, you can purchase green power from one of your local utility's competitors, if they have it available. Many states in the northeast, along with Texas, Oregon, and Arizona, have de-regulated their utility companies, opening opportunities for competitors who sell green power.

Is green power actually delivered to your home? No. Utilities have no way of directing the "green electricity" they generate from a wind farm—or any other source for that matter—to a specific customer. All electricity is delivered to the grid and used by a utility's customer base. When purchasing green power, though, you're enabling the utility to produce and distribute green electricity to the grid. Your payment ensures that green power is being produced and consumed. Without it, the grid would be provided with conventional power.

Green energy can be purchased by anyone who pays a utility bill. You don't have to be a homeowner. You can buy green energy if you rent an apartment and pay your own utility bill, or if you own your own business. To learn more about green energy, log on to the U.S. Department of Energy's Energy Efficiency and Renewable Energy website at **www.eere.energy.gov/ greenpower** and click on *Buying Green Power.* Click on your state to discover your options.

Renewable Energy Certificates (RECs)

If you can't purchase green energy directly from a local utility, there are other options. For instance, you can buy renewable energy certificates (RECs) from one of several dozen national companies, such as NativeEnergy. Renewable energy certificates are also known as *green energy certificates, green tags,* or *tradable renewable certificates.* To understand how an REC works and what you get out of it, consider the following example.

NativeEnergy is one of numerous nonprofit organizations the world over that sells RECs. This company is majority-owned by Native Americans. RECs sold by NativeEnergy help fund construction of wind farms and methane digesters on dairy farms. Methane digesters capture methane gas from cow manure. The methane is burned to produce electricity (as shown in the photo of a methane digester). The purchase of RECs, therefore, has many benefits. It helps make renewable energy projects happen by providing funding required to construct facilities. In addition, purchasing RECs results in the delivery of clean, renewable electricity to the grid, displacing electricity that would otherwise be generated by burning fossil fuels or by nuclear fuels. This helps to build a renewable energy future.

Once again, the green power is not delivered to your home. When you purchase an REC, you're simply making a contribution to the cause. You pay a much smaller premium for an REC than for green power from your local utility. The green power is sold to customers elsewhere. You are helping to offset the price a bit.

Carbon Offsets

Yet another option is the *carbon emissions offset*. Very similar to an REC, the carbon emissions offset is a contribution to nonprofit companies that reduce carbon dioxide emissions. For example, you can purchase a carbon emission offset to cover a plane trip, a car rental, or to offset the carbon dioxide emissions produced by your car or your home's energy use. If you drive a mid-sized car that gets 30 mpg and drive 12,000 miles/year, for example, you will generate about 3.55 tons of carbon dioxide a year. Offsetting these emissions will cost about $19.50 or $1.63/month (according to **www.carbonfund.org**).

Carbon emissions offsets may support renewable energy projects, like RECs. However, they also may support tree-planting efforts and efficiency measures throughout the world. Your carbon emissions offset,

Methane digester
Courtesy of Native Energy

for example, may help reforest a rainforest in South America or pay for the installation of a small solar energy system in a remote tribal village in Africa.

To calculate your carbon dioxide emissions from your home, car, and air travel, you can log on to one of many online carbon footprint calculators. My favorite is **www.carbonfund.org** Their carbon calculator allows you to calculate carbon dioxide emissions from energy use in your home, automobile transportation, and air travel. If you are getting married, this website can even help you calculate the carbon dioxide emissions that result from a wedding, including the air travel of your

Go Green!

If you use outdoor lights for security, be sure to turn them off in the morning—or install photo-sensors that will turn lights on at dusk and off at dawn each day. Compact fluorescent lightbulbs or LEDs will save additional energy. Another option is a motion-sensor light.

friends and relatives, if any. The site also calculates carbon dioxide emissions from other activities in our lives—for example, from producing and transporting food and goods, and from services we use and consume—based on national averages. Like many other sites, the website provides a convenient way to identify and reduce your annual carbon dioxide emissions.

What to Watch Out For

Green energy offers many benefits over conventional power (such as electricity generated from coal or nuclear fuels). But it is not a panacea. One complaint about wind farms is that they kill birds. Like other criticisms, this one is grossly exaggerated. The Audubon Society, a nonprofit organization dedicated to protecting birds, estimates that commercial wind turbines kill approximately 25,000 birds each year. Although a significant number, several scientific studies indicate that it pales compared to the deaths of birds from other causes: pesticides, cats, and collisions with windows, communication towers, and cars and trucks. These activities kill an estimated 800 million birds annually.

Some early wind farms were located in areas that resulted in higher bird kills, new wind farms are sited away from migratory pathways or habitat.

The Audubon Society often consults on placement of wind turbines. When reviewing a wind energy project off the coast of Cape Cod, the Massachusetts Audubon Society wrote, "The consequences of climate warming compel us to increase energy conservation as a first priority. And, to continue to supply our energy needs, wind should be tapped as the most successful and readily available of all renewable energy technologies. The benefits and detriments of Cape Wind must be balanced against the significant threats to Nantucket Sound posed by fossil-fuel use and rapid climate change."

Another complaint about wind is that it costs more. Although the fuel is free, and will remain free forever, promising electrical price stability in years to come, the U.S. Department of Energy notes that "Better energy, just like organic foods, costs a bit more." But why?

According to the U.S. DOE, "there is still a lot of investment to be made in building wind farm capacity. That makes the current price for wind a bit more than continuing to burn fossil fuels in plants that were built and paid for long ago." They point out that "Our investment in wind power ensures a cheap, clean, inexhaustible source of energy now and for the future."

Another concern you'll hear is that there's not enough wind or other renewable energy to meet our needs. Nothing could be further from the truth. Studies show that there is enough wind energy in North and South Dakota alone to satisfy all of America's electrical energy needs! There's also plenty of solar energy and biomass giving us much more energy than we consume.

Other wind farm complaints include noise, visual pollution, and their potential to decrease property values. Studies show that each of these is greatly exaggerated. (For more on the subject, log on to the American Wind Energy Association's website or pick up a copy of my book, *Small Wind Power*.)

So, how can you be sure that your purchase of green energy really ends up doing good? Green-e is a voluntary certification and verification program for green energy producers and renewable energy certificates. They certify about 100 green power marketers in the United States. Their website (**www. green-e.org**) will help you identify certified sources of green power in your state and select among several renewable energy options, including wind, solar, biomass, hydro-electric, and geothermal.

The Environmental Resources Trust certifies renewable energy certificates through its EcoPower certification program, although it does not report on environmental benefits. For that information, you may want to check the Power Scorecard, a web-based tool created by a consortium of environmental groups. It lets consumers compare the environmental impacts of green power and conventional power in select states (**www. powerscorecard.org**)

Project 44 Timers & Motion Sensor Light Switches

As a child, your parents may have continually reminded you to turn off the lights when you left a room—advice that you just couldn't seem to remember. Now, as a parent, the shoe may be on the other foot. You may be the self-designated "light police." Or perhaps you have quietly resigned yourself to making the rounds and switching off lights to save energy.

For those of us who can't seem to remember to shut off a light when leaving a room—there's hope. It comes in the form of timer and motion-sensor switches that turn lights off automatically.

Timer Switches

Timer switches vary in complexity. One of the simplest options is a spring-wound timer. Available in home improvement centers and hardware stores, the timer is installed in place of a conventional light switch. When you enter the room, you simply turn the dial to the desired number of minutes, and the light controlled by the wall switch goes on. When time runs out, the light shuts off.

Spring-wound timers allow you to set the time from one minute to an hour and are great for bathrooms, basements, workshops, garages, sheds, barns . . . you name it. They work well with all kinds of lighting—from compact fluorescent, to ordinary fluorescent, to incandescent. They can also be used to control bathroom fans, hot tubs, whole-house fans, and more.

(I wouldn't use them in bedrooms, offices, or main living areas, however, as they're noisy.)

Another option is an electronic countdown timer. This more sophisticated and quieter device allows you to select one of several options: you can choose "hold" for extended occupancy of a room or select one of four time intervals—10, 20, 30, and 60 minutes—for shorter stays. When entering a room, you press a button to set the time you expect to remain in the room. When your time is up, the lights or fan go out.

Intermatic countdown timer

Courtesy of Intermatic, Inc.

Intermatic spring-wound timer switch

Countdown timers can be used to control all kinds of lights, as well as heaters, motors, and bathroom fans. Read the instructions on the packaging carefully to be sure that the light switch matches your needs and will work with the device or light you have in mind. (See "Shopping Tips" for more on switch compatibility.)

Motion-Sensor Light Switches

Another option is a motion- or heat-sensor light switch. These are fully automated light switches activated by occupancy sensors, devices that detect the presence of a human or a pet in a room.

Two types of occupancy sensors are commonly used. The first and most common one for home use contains a heat sensor and is known as a passive infrared sensor.

The second is an ultrasonic sensor. Like a bat, it sends out high-frequency sound waves, inaudible to the human ear. The sound waves bounce off objects (and people) and return to the sensor. The sensor detects changes in the location of occupants in the room, which indicates movement.

Motion-sensing switches can be set on automatic mode. When on this setting, the light switch activates the light, or lights, that it controls when an individual enters a room. When the lights come on, a timer

is activated. If you remain in the room, the timer is continually reset each time it detects motion. After you leave the room, the lights shut off automatically after a preset interval. (You set the time interval for the shut-off feature.)

Motion-sensing switches can also be operated manually—that is, turned on and off like an ordinary light switch, overriding the automatic timer. In this mode, you can turn the lights on and off as you enter and leave a room.

Some motion-sensing light switches, like those manufactured by Cooper Wiring Devices, contain photosensors that detect natural lighting. If there's plenty of light in a room from windows, the photosensor overrides the motion sensor—keeping the lights from turning on. The photocell is programmable, so you can adjust the light level at which the automatic override occurs.

Sensor light switches can be installed in place of ordinary, manually operated light switches in new or existing homes. If you're installing new lights in a home or a room addition, however, you may want to consider using light fixtures with built-in motion sensors. The LVS company, for instance, makes a fluorescent light fixture with built-in occupancy sensors that can be used in garages, workshops, and basements. If you want to retrofit existing lights, Lamson Home Products manufactures motion-sensing light adapters that can be screwed into conventional light sockets. Also consider installing outdoor security lights containing motion sensors, discussed in Project 58.

Motion-sensing light switch designed for CFLs by RAB

Courtesy of RAB Lighting, Inc.

Go Green!

To save energy when cooking on a stove top, use a lid on your pots and pans to allow lower temperature settings and reduce cooking times.

Why Install Timers or Motion-Sensing Switches?

Motion-sensing light switches are most often used in businesses, because they can save enormous amounts of energy, turning lights on and off in rooms that may be used sporadically, such as conference rooms, bathrooms, copy rooms, storage rooms, and hallways. They're even helpful for private offices, where they can cut electrical consumption by 13% to 50%, according to EPA estimates.

Because nearly 30% of the energy consumed in an office is used for lighting, installing occupancy sensors can result in substantial savings on utility costs—by one estimate, 5 to 20 cents per square foot per year. If you own a business, consider installing motion-sensing light switches in rooms where lights tend to be left on for unnecessarily long periods.

Savings in homes can also be substantial. It all depends on the kind of lighting you're using and how long lights are left on. As a rule, motion sensors save the most when controlling the least-efficient lighting options, notably incandescent lights. They'll save less if you're using energy-efficient lights, such as fluorescent, compact fluorescent, or LED lights.

Installing Timers or Motion Sensors

If you haven't wired an outlet or light switch before, it's a good idea to hire a professional electrician or ask a friend who is experienced in this type of work to help.

If you are skilled in basic wiring—for example, if you've installed light fixtures, light switches, or electrical outlets—installing a timer or a motion-sensor switch should be a snap. Be sure to shut off the power to the switch *before* you begin work, and check with a voltmeter to be sure it's off. Follow the instructions on the package very carefully. If you're skilled in this type of work, you should be able to install a timer or motion-sensing switch in about 20 to 30 minutes.

The first step is to remove the cover plate, then the screws holding the existing light switch in the electrical box. Next, the three wires are disconnected, then reconnected to the timer or motion-sensor switch.

Be sure to rewire correctly and make the connections tight. Pull on them to be sure they won't come loose. (That's how electrical inspectors test wiring.)

When done, carefully insert the wires and the timer or motion-sensing light switch into the electrical box. Screw it in place and then replace the cover plate. Restore power. Adjust the duration of the timer and select the desired light intensity of the photocell override, if needed.

Motion-Sensing Bulb Options

The Motionbulb™ puts motion-sensing technology in easy reach. It's a lightbulb that screws into an ordinary light socket and detects movement up to 25 feet away. The company claims that the Motionbulb lasts 10 times longer than regular incandescent bulbs and uses much less energy. It is recommended for indoor use in garages, basements, closets, laundry rooms, and entryways. The bulb will stay on as long as there is movement in the area, then turn off after a preset time that you control. The company sells a variety of ceiling- and wall-mounted motion sensors, including a bulb that emits an alarm when motion is detected.

Another option is the LED Motion-Sensor Light by Greenlite. It combines the longest-lasting, most energy-efficient type of bulb, LED, with a motion sensor and a photocell. It runs on AAA batteries and doesn't require wiring, so you can use it when and where you need it, or mount it in one location. The light turns off about 30 seconds after motion is no longer detected—or after you turn on another light.

LEDs also come in a sound-activated model. These battery-operated spotlights turn on automatically when they sense a loud or sharp noise and will stay on until ten seconds after the last sound is detected. They can also be turned on and off manually and come with brackets so you can direct them as needed.

What to Watch Out For

When shopping for light switch control devices, be sure that they're compatible with your intended use. Although timers work with all types of light fixtures and can be used to control motors and resistive loads (electric heaters), be sure to check the maximum load ratings—the amp rating or horsepower rating of each timer or motion-sensing switch—and compare it to your intended use. If none of this makes sense, it's probably a good idea to hire an electrician.

Also be sure to check the package or product description for the switch's maximum wattage—the number of watts a switch can handle. Be sure you don't exceed it, or you'll burn out the switch.

Shopping for motion-sensing light switches is a bit more challenging than shopping for timers. The models sold in hardware stores and home improvement centers in my area only work with incandescent lights and/or fluorescent lights, and are not compatible with compact fluorescents. (The electrical surges required to start a CFL can burn out the sensors of motion-sensing switches.)

Manufacturers are pretty good about warning buyers on their packaging about potential incompatibilities. For example, the instructions might indicate that a switch works with incandescent lights. Or they might state that the switch is not suitable for lights containing electronic ballasts (which are found in all compact fluorescent lights). Instructions might read that the switch will only work with lights containing magnetic ballasts or rapid-start magnetic ballasts (which are used in standard fluorescent lighting, but not CFLs).

Although you may not be able to purchase motion-sensing switches for CFLs in local stores, you can buy them on the Internet or through electrical supply outlets. I've found two CFL-compatible motion-sensing light switches online, the WallStopper Occupancy Sensor (through the Environmental Home Center at **www.built-e.com**) and the RAB LOS1000 Wall Sensor (through eBay, **www.elights.com**, and **www.prolighting.com**).

Note that many automatic timers and motion-sensing switches consume a small amount of energy (phantom load) 24 hours a day. (See Project 39.) Some motion sensors come with LED lights so you can find them in the dark—which can be useful if you have switched them to manual operation.

Another factor to consider when shopping for motion-sensing switches is the angle of coverage and the motion-sensing range. The angle of coverage is typically around 150 to 180 degrees, and the motion sensing range between 12 and 40 feet. Choose a switch that is appropriate for your situation.

After installing a motion-sensing switch, expect to spend a little time experimenting with the timer setting to find an optimal shut-off interval. These switches are factory-set with an extremely short setting (often less than a minute). While desirable from an energy standpoint, short settings can be an annoyance. If you're taking a shower behind a curtain, for example, passive infrared sensor switches will very likely shut off before you're done, leaving you in the dark. To avoid such problems, you may want to set the timer for a longer interval—several minutes for a bathroom without a shower and perhaps ten minutes or so for a bathroom with a shower. You can also override the automatic setting when you plan to take a shower,

Go Green!

• To save electricity, replace the most commonly used lightbulbs in your home with compact fluorescents (Project 40).

• To save energy when baking, turn off the oven ten minutes before the baking time is over. There's usually enough heat to finish the process. You don't need to preheat for roasting or broiling. For baking, 5 to 8 minutes should be more than enough time to preheat.

switching the light on and off manually. You may also have to fiddle with the photocell override setting, mentioned earlier, to meet your needs.

Finally, installing a motion-sensing light switch or an electronic timer is slightly different from installing a conventional light switch. You'll need to connect wires from the units to the existing wires in the switch box with wire nuts. But you may also have to shorten the existing wires a bit so you can jam the bulky control unit and the wires back into the electrical box. Motion-sensing light fixtures are installed like any ordinary light fixture.

What Will It Cost?

Timers cost about $17 to $38. Sensor switches for indoor use start at about $15, going up to about $45 or more.

Cost Estimate: Installation of 2 motion-sensing floodlight fixtures and 2 wall switches with built-in timers

Includes junction box and necessary wiring

Cost for materials only: **$300**

Contractor's total, including materials, labor, and markup: **$530**

Costs are national averages and do not include sales tax.

What Will You Save?

The savings accrued from light timers and motion sensors depend on how many of these devices you install, the size of your home, and your family's habits. If you install solar-powered outdoor lighting with sensors, you'll reduce your electric bill even more.

Project 45

Tubular Skylights

Skylights bring natural light into homes and offices, improving visibility and lifting our spirits. If you have a room or hallway you'd like to brighten up during the day without having to install or use electric lights, consider a tubular skylight.

What Is a Tubular Skylight?

Also known as a tubular daylighting device, a tubular skylight fits into small spaces where a conventional skylight would not. It consists of a small, durable plastic lens mounted on the roof and connected to a tubular aluminum shaft (usually 8 to 24 inches in diameter). It is connected to a ceiling-mounted diffuser, a fixture that resembles a modern light fixture. Light enters through the lens or dome, is transmitted down the highly reflective tubular shaft, and is released into the living space via the diffuser.

Tubular skylights work extremely well for a number of reasons. For one thing, the dome-shaped lens brings light in throughout the day, regardless of the sun's angle. Another is the polished aluminum interior of the skylight shaft, which ensures maximum light transmission. Yet another is the diffuser, which disperses natural light over a fairly wide area. Combined, these features enable tubular skylights to transmit a fair amount of light, even on a cloudy day.

Solar tube skylight
Courtesy of Solatube International, Inc.

Go Green!

To save energy, arrange furniture, if possible, to take advantage of natural lighting—so you can read during the day without having to turn on a light.

Why Install a Tubular Skylight?

Besides brightening our homes, skylights provide natural lighting, which can improve our mood, enhance visibility, and make us more productive. Studies have shown that daylighting increases worker productivity and boosts test scores in school children, presumably by creating a more pleasant learning environment.

By reducing the need for electrical lighting during the day, solar tube skylights help cut electrical bills. On a sunny day, for example, the 8-inch DayLite™ skylight provides as much light as seven 100-watt lightbulbs. Their 12-inch model delivers as much light as ten 100-watt lightbulbs. Even on cloudy days, the skylights provide 100 to 180 watts of illumination.

Tubular skylights are widely in use in commercial spaces—for example, big "box" chain stores, factories, and warehouses, where they produce substantial savings on energy costs. In homes, they can also save money, especially when used in areas that require extensive lighting, like kitchens that have numerous high-wattage bulbs in recessed fixtures or track lighting. However, not all installations save tons of money. In fact, it could, in some cases, take many years to pay back the initial investment.

Because they're so much smaller than conventional skylights, tubular skylights provide several key advantages, especially over the older-style skylights found in many homes. One is that they let far less heat in on hot summer days. This reduces the demand for air conditioning and keeps the home more comfortable at a lower cost. During the winter months, tubular skylights lose much less heat than conventional skylights, also saving you money. And of course, any energy savings help reduce our emission of the greenhouse gas carbon dioxide.

Another benefit of these smaller skylights over conventional ones is reduced glare on computers and television screens—resulting in less eye strain and fewer headaches.

Because of their size, tubular skylights are much easier to install than conventional domed or dormer skylights. They can usually be installed without modifications to existing framing and, as mentioned earlier, can fit in spaces like narrow hallways and walk-in closets. Several companies manufacture tubular skylights equipped with supplementary electrical lights for nighttime use.

Installation

Installing a tubular skylight is a job for professionals or knowledgeable and skilled do-it-yourselfers. To determine if you can handle it yourself, check out the installation instructions from the manufacturer *before* you buy the unit (they're often available online) and study them carefully. Hire a professional if you have doubts about taking on the work yourself. There are many companies that sell the units and provide installation.

To install a tubular skylight, you will need the installation kit that comes with the skylight (including flashing); a reciprocating, keyhole, or jig saw; a plumb bob; a utility knife; an extension ladder and step ladder; a screwdriver; nails; and safety glasses. You might also need wire cutters and insulation.

Go Green!

- Install dimmer light switches. They save energy and let you adjust lighting to meet your needs. According to Lutron, manufacturer of dimmers and whole-house lighting systems, you can save 40% on lighting energy by dimming bulbs to 50%—at the same time extending the life of the bulbs up to 10 years. Visit www.lutron.com for an Energy-Saving Calculator. If using compact fluorescents, be sure to buy dimmable bulbs.

- If you have a linear light fixture (for example, over a bathroom sink) that requires a lot of bulbs and provides more light than you need, choose low-wattage bulbs or install a dimmer switch. Use compact fluorescent lightbulbs to save energy.

Before and after photo of bathroom showing the light added by installing a solar tube skylight

Courtesy of Solatube International, Inc.

If you feel confident you can install a tubular skylight successfully, you'll need to cut out two circular holes—one in the ceiling and the other in the roof. To determine where these openings will be situated, first locate the desired position of the skylight in the ceiling. Then climb into the attic and locate the spot. Remove the insulation from this location. Check to be sure that there's a clear path from the roof to the ceiling. Also make sure there are no framing members, electrical wires, or heating or air conditioning ducts in the way. It may be possible to reposition wiring or flexible duct. If not, find a new location for the light tube. Bear in mind that the path does not have to be perfectly straight, as most tubes are flexible and can be bent a bit. Also, be sure that the tube will fit between rafters and ceiling joists.

Once you are sure there are no wires in the way, push a nail through the ceiling in the center of the opening (from below). Climb back into the attic with a plumb

bob. Suspend the plumb bob from the underside of the roof until it lines up with the nail hole in the ceiling. Now, mark this spot on the underside of the roof and drill a hole up through the roof. This marks the center of where the dome will be located. Because tubular skylights are small compared to conventional skylights, you should be able to cut the holes between framing members.

Now, cut a hole in the ceiling using a reciprocating saw. Then go up on the roof and remove the roof shingles where the lens is to be located. Cut a hole in the roof using the template provided by the manufacturer.

After the holes are cut, the roof flashing and lens and the interior diffuser lens are installed. The shaft is then fitted in place. Follow instructions for caulking and installation of flashing very carefully.

Although the installation of a solar tube skylight is a breeze for advanced do-it-yourselfers, at least compared to a conventional skylight, anyone tackling this project should follow safety precautions. Any work that involves climbing up and standing on a roof can be dangerous. Avoid contacting power lines. Wear non-slip shoes. Be careful not to damage the surrounding roof shingles. Stay off the roof (especially metal roofs) if it is snowy or wet, making it very slippery. If a storm is approaching, head indoors. If you tackle this job, choose a comfortably cool day. Roofs and attics can be unbearably hot on sunny summer days.

If you're not skilled or confident working on the roof, or your roof is steep, hire a professional. The job should take a pro a few hours, perhaps a half a day at the most. A trained professional can also flash and caulk the skylight properly to prevent expensive damage caused by roof leaks.

What to Watch Out For

As in many improvement projects, it's always a good idea to check with your building department *before* you purchase a tubular skylight to find out if a permit is required and if there are any restrictions. Some building departments, for instance, only allow installation of skylights with polycarbonate domes. They're stronger than acrylic domes and are reportedly impervious to hail and falling tree branches.

Examine your roof and ceiling very carefully, so you know what you're getting into. Anticipate problems. Measure the attic space to determine the length of the tube you'll need. Measure the roof thickness to determine the type of flashing materials required for installation.

As noted above, before installing a tubular skylight, be sure to check for potential obstructions in the attic or in the roof cavity. You don't want to cut through them by accident. Immovable obstructions may alter the placement of your skylight.

What Will It Cost?

Tubular skylights start at about $300 to $400 for a 10" diameter lens, and cost about $600 for a 14" model. Prices go up if you add features such as a fan or light, and also depend on the length of the light tube needed to connect the ceiling lens to the roof. Factors that can affect professional installation costs include the need to remove electrical fixtures and junction boxes, reroute wiring, or work on a steeply pitched roof—or one made of materials that are more difficult to work with, such as tile or slate.

Cost Estimate: Professional installation of a tubular skylight
Includes cutting and repairing roofing, sheathing, and ceiling wallboard and flashing

Cost for materials only: **$320**
Contractor's total, including materials, labor, and markup: **$750**

Cost comparison to traditional skylights
Includes building a shaft through the attic, and framing modifications

Total cost to install fixed skylight (24" x 48"): **$1,585**
Total cost to install operable skylight (44" x 57"): **$1,915**

What Will You Save?

As mentioned earlier, tubular skylights save energy and money, giving you an endless supply of free daytime light. The savings depend on many factors, including the material and installation costs of the skylight; it's size and how much light it will provide; the type and efficiency of the light fixture it is replacing (compact fluorescent vs. standard incandescent); installation costs of a supplementary electric light fixture, if required; and the cost of electricity in your area. These skylights help save the Earth by reducing greenhouse gas emissions that result from energy consumption.

Project
46

Environmentally Friendly Roofing

Most homeowners have to replace their roof shingles at some point. Exposed to sunlight, heat, cold, rain, wind, and sometimes snow, sleet, and hail, conventional asphalt shingle roofs wear out. If you're lucky, they will last 20 years. If you live in an area with intense heat, high winds, or hail, you may need to replace roofing more frequently.

Re-roofing a home is physically demanding, material- and labor-intensive, and potentially dangerous—a job few homeowners want to undertake themselves. If an old roof has to be stripped off before installing new shingles, it's an even more time-consuming and difficult job. Disposing of old shingles results in tons of solid waste that contains asphalt, a petroleum product, as well as fiberglass. All of this is typically dumped in landfills.

If you'd like a roof that is virtually immune to hail, will outlast a conventional asphalt shingle roof, and is made from environmentally friendly roof materials, consider the products outlined in this project.

What Are Your Options?

Green roofing products are many and varied, ranging from recycled-plastic and rubber shingles to recycled metal roofs, to sustainably harvested or reclaimed wood roofs.

Recycled-Content Shingles

Among the most popular—and perhaps the "greenest"—of all roofing products are shingles made from recycled waste materials, such as plastic, rubber, and wood fiber in various combinations. Some products are made from clean post-consumer waste (waste from homes); others are made from post-industrial waste (factory waste). Using both post-consumer and post-industrial waste helps reduce demand for natural resources.

Recycled-content shingles are amazingly durable and look nice, too. You'd never know they were made from waste materials!

Recycled-content roof shingles not only help divert waste from landfills, but reduce our need to extract and process raw materials. This lowers energy consumption and reduces pollution. Some of these products are recyclable, too, unlike conventional asphalt shingles. Moreover, several green roofing products come with amazing 50-year warranties. A few even carry fire ratings (Class A) that could lower your insurance rates.

Wood Shingles & Shakes

In many parts of the country, wood shingles and shakes have been a popular choice among builders and homeowners. Unfortunately, conventional wood shingles are made from old-growth western cedar.

Recycled-content roof shingles made from recycled PVC plastic and wood fibers

Photo of EcoShake courtesy of Re-New Wood, Incorporated

Although the amount of energy it takes to produce this product is relatively low, the harvest of old-growth trees reduces an imperiled resource and is often carried out in an unsustainable fashion. These shingles are also quite combustible and can no longer be used in areas of the country where there is risk of brush and forest fires.

If you would like to install wood roof shingles, and local building codes permit them, you may want to consider a product made from reclaimed lumber. The Armster Reclaimed Lumber Company (**www.woodwood.com**) in Connecticut, for example, makes roof shingles from wood reclaimed from old water and wine tanks, mills, bridges, and a number of other sources. This company acquires old wood throughout the country and makes an effort to process it locally—close to where you purchase the product—to reduce costs and transportation energy.

Another environmentally friendly wood shingle is produced by Industries Maribec in eastern Canada. They harvest sustainably-grown eastern white pine trees to produce shakes and shingles. These are most commonly used for siding, but can be used for roofs as well, if installed according to the company's recommendations.

Metal Roofing

I'm a big fan of metal roofing, which I installed on my home when it was constructed in 1995. While most metal roofing products are not made from recycled

Go Green!

• Ask your roofing contractor if your old asphalt shingles can be recycled. Some companies grind asphalt shingles to create products for roadway maintenance and repair.

• Consider a light-colored roofing material if you live in a hot, sunny climate. Lighter colors reflect, rather than absorb heat, which could make your home more comfortable and reduce air conditioning costs. Check with your local building department and/or neighborhood association for possible roof color restrictions.

materials, they offer exceptional durability and fire-resistance. They're also ideal for those who want to collect rainwater from their roofs to water their landscapes (Project 61) or even for some household uses, since you don't have to worry about toxic chemicals that might leach from a conventional asphalt roof. Another advantage of metal roofing is that it can be recycled at the end of its life. Since metal roofs are so long-lasting, roofing replacement is less frequent, which means less waste in the long run.

Metal roofs are great in snowy climates, as they allow snow to slide off. This prevents ice dams from forming. (Ice dams can damage roofs of improperly insulated homes.) To protect walkways from snow sliding off the roof, you'll need to install snow bars or some similar device over walkways, garage doors, and entryways.

While most metal roofing products, like standing-seam metal roofs, are made from virgin steel, a number of companies use recycled materials. Rustic Shingles produced by Classic Metal Roofing Systems, for example, are made from recycled aluminum (mostly beverage cans). The shingles resemble wood shakes and come in 11 colors. MetalWorks® Steel Shingles from Tamko Roofing Products, Inc. contain as much as 50% recycled steel and are designed to look like wood or slate. Recycled-Metal Shingles by Zappone Manufacturing are made from either recycled aluminum or copper.

Fiber-Cement Shingles & Slate & Clay Tiles

Another product that scores green points for durability and recycled content is fiber-cement shingles. They are made from cement, sand, clay, and wood fiber. Re-Con Building Products in Oregon, for example, produces FireFree Natural shingles in two styles, one that resembles wood shakes and another that resembles slate. They contain recycled wood fiber, are fire- and hail-resistant, and are backed by a 50-year warranty.

Several companies also offer slate tiles. Slate is a natural material and produces an extremely durable roof tile—one that can last hundreds of years. In fact, one

company offers a 100-year warranty, a deal that will expire long after most of us.

While mining slate and transporting it to market is an energy-intensive process, several slate roof tile manufacturers offer salvaged slate and clay roof tiles. Durable Slate in Ohio sells both. Clay tiles are a highly durable roofing material, although they won't last as long as slate.

Rubber Roofing

Another recycled roof material is reinforced rubber shingles, or shakes, made from the belts of old steel-belted radial tires. The material is coated with ground slate for texture and comes in a choice of colors. A big advantage is a long life and a 50-year warranty, including against hail and other extreme weather. Verify with your local building department that rubber roofs are permitted in your area.

Installing Green Roofing

As mentioned earlier, roofing is not a job for the inexperienced. It involves working at dangerous heights, possibly on steep slopes, and lifting heavy materials. Roofing requires a considerable amount of knowledge and skill, too. So, unless you've done this kind of work before, are skilled in carpentry, and perhaps have guidance from a professional roofer, this is a job best left to the pros. Read up on safety

Go Green!

Install gutter protectors to keep leaves and pine needles from clogging gutters. This will result in longer lasting gutters and will ensure that they don't overflow in rainstorms, causing water to pool around your foundation where it could cause damage. Gutter protectors also reduce potentially dangerous ladder work required to clean gutters.

precautions before you consider any roof work. Be sure not to work alone. If you fall, you'll want someone there to call 911.

Shopping Tips and What To Watch Out For

Green roofing products are many and varied, so compare your options carefully. Be sure to check out the materials' fire ratings, hail ratings, and warranties. Call your insurance agent to see if the product you're considering will qualify you for a discount on your homeowner's insurance.

To re-roof your home, you'll very likely need to obtain a building permit. You'll also need to pass an inspection. Be sure your building department approves the shingle product you've selected *before* you lay your money down!

Although the products discussed in this project offer many benefits, they do have some downsides. One is that some of them are not as widely available as conventional roofing products, so you may have to shop around a bit to find an environmentally friendly roof shingle. Many green building material outlets, like those listed in the Resource Guide at the back of this book, sell green roofing products.

You may also have to shop around to find a roofing contractor who is familiar with—and has worked with—the product you're interested in using. Some of these products are relatively new to the market and, although they've been tested, not many roofers have experience with them. When shopping for an environmentally friendly roof shingle, talk to roofers who have installed it, not just a sales person.

If you're interested in a slate or clay tile roof, either new or recycled, bear in mind that the framing of your roof needs to be strong enough to support the weight of these tiles, which can be substantial. You may need to consult with a structural engineer or with your building department to determine if your framing is up to the task.

What Will It Cost?

Green roofing products typically cost more than mass-produced asphalt shingles, sometimes two to four times more. Bear in mind, however, that you're often getting a product that will outlast two or three conventional roofs, saving you substantially over the long term. You may also qualify for lower insurance rates. These benefits add value to your home whether you stay there for years or sell it. You're also helping promote green building and a healthier and greener world for you, your children, and future generations.

Cost Estimate: Removal of existing asphalt-shingle roofing from a 2,500 square foot, two-story house, and installation of new standing-seam metal roofing

Cost for materials only: **$6,300**

Contractor's total, including materials, labor, and markup: **$11,900**

Alternate Cost, per square foot installed:

Laminated asphalt shingles: **$3.15**

Cedar shingles: **$6.65**

Clay tile: **$9.20**

Costs are national averages and do not include sales tax.

Project

47 Fiber-Cement Siding

I f you're building a new home or a garage, addition, workshop, or barn—or if it's time to replace the ancient, weather-beaten siding on your home—consider one of the newest "old" products on the market today, fiber-cement siding.

What Is Fiber-Cement Siding, and What Are Your Options?

Like conventional siding, fiber-cement siding is applied to the exterior of buildings to protect them—and us—from the elements. This product comes in a multitude of colors and styles that resemble conventional siding materials—notably, stucco, cedar shingles, and wood clapboards. What's different about this product is that it's made primarily from cement, ground sand, and wood fiber—often a recycled wood-fiber waste product—a combination that results in an extremely durable, long-lasting material.

Fiber-cement siding typically costs a bit more than vinyl siding, but less than stucco and traditional wood siding, and much less than redwood siding. It also outlasts its competitors—often by decades—because it resists many common hazards, including fire, wind, insects, and rain. Fiber-cement siding is recommended in all climates, but is ideal for hot, humid regions. No matter how wet it gets, it won't rot.

Because of its durability and long life, fiber-cement siding reduces maintenance and replacement costs as well as resource demand and waste sent to landfills.

Unfortunately, there are currently no recycling programs in place for fiber-cement siding itself. However, it is an inert material that, if sent to a landfill, should not endanger the environment.

Although many builders and homeowners are just discovering the benefits of fiber-cement siding, this material has been around for quite some time—nearly 100 years—so you won't be experimenting with a new product. Fiber-cement siding comes in a variety of colors and styles. One popular choice is planks made with a wood-grained or a smooth finish. These come in widths from 4 to 12 inches—so you can match existing siding if you're building an addition or garage. Fiber-cement siding also comes in wall panels with vertical grooves and soffit panels for the underside of overhangs.

Go Green!

No matter what construction tools or building materials you're buying, always go for quality. This usually means spending more up-front, but you'll save time and money over the long haul and reduce resource use and pollution generated from manufacturing replacement materials.

Here, fiber-cement clapboard siding resembles stained wood.
Photo by Dan Chiras

Fiber-cement siding planks
Photo by Dan Chiras

Fiber-cement siding can be primed and painted at the factory or on the building site. (Some manufacturers prime all of their products.) I recommend factory-primed and painted siding, which often carries a warranty of up to 25 years. For those who want to do the priming and painting themselves, manufacturers typically recommend an alkaline-resistant primer and a 100% acrylic topcoat.

If you want to change the color at a later date, no problem. Water-based acrylic paints adhere very well. What's more, fiber-cement siding does not expand and contract as much as wood siding, so paint stays in place better. It rarely peels or blisters, reducing maintenance time and cost.

Fiber-cement siding is widely available and can be purchased at home improvement centers and lumberyards. Perhaps the best known manufacturer is James Hardie, which offers three products: Hardieplank, Hardieshingle, and Hardiepanel. All have received high praise from builders and homeowners. Other manufacturers include Certainteed, Cemplank, and Maxitile. Certainteed produces ColorMax products in 16 color choices.

Installation

Before installing new siding, you'll probably need to remove all of the old siding—a time-consuming, demanding job. You'll also need to rent a dumpster to haul the waste away. (You may be able to recycle old siding or burn it in a woodstove if it's not painted or treated with chemical preservatives or lead paint.)

Applying new siding is relatively simple as long as you have construction skills, time, and patience. The tools you need include a circular saw or chop saw, cordless drill or hammer, sawhorse, ladder, dust mask, eye protection, level, straight edge, chalk line, and a bevel gauge for marking siding cut for gable ends. If you don't have the necessary skills, hire a professional. A good contractor will do the job right and in a fraction of the time it would take a do-it-yourselfer.

For those who want to take on this project, start by reading the manufacturer's instructions and follow them closely. Manufacturers like James Hardie offer detailed information on their websites. If the siding is installed incorrectly, you may end up creating costly problems and may also void your warranty.

Like conventional wood siding, fiber-cement siding can be applied to both wood and steel studs, but it's normally attached to exterior wall sheathing (OSB or

Weather-Resistant Barrier Materials

A good house wrap underneath siding is an important component in green building since it "breathes," allowing moisture vapor to escape to the outside. This prevents mold, which can cause health problems and damage to your home. In addition to Tyvek®, check out Home Slicker by Benjamin Obdyke, Inc. (www.benjaminobdyke.com), Delta Wrap from Cosella Dorken Products (www.deltams.com), and Construction Film by Gempack in Bloomington, Indiana (800-328-4556).

plywood) on top of an appropriate weather-resistant barrier, such as Tyvek®. Some fiber-cement products can be applied over rigid foam insulation. If you're installing the siding over concrete or concrete block walls, you'll first need to install vertical wood furring strips to which the siding is attached. Check the manufacturer's recommendations for spacing.

Fiber-cement is attached using corrosion-resistant galvanized or stainless steel nails or screws that penetrate into wall studs or exterior sheathing. Many fiber-cement siding planks can be blind-nailed onto exterior sheathing so that no nails show (an advantage over traditional wood clapboards). To do this, each plank is nailed about one inch down from the top edge. The next plank is placed so that it overlaps the nails, hiding them from view. Follow the manufacturer's instructions carefully, as there are some restrictions on blind-nailing wider planks to prevent wind uplift. (Wind can lift wider planks if they're only attached at the top.)

Fiber-cement siding can also be face-nailed, but staples cannot be used due to the hardness of the material. Face-nailing will leave exposed nail heads. Do not under-drive nails or screws.

Whatever system you choose, check the manufacturer's recommendations for placement of fasteners (nails or screws) in relation to the ends and top edge of the plank. Read the instructions for the use of a pneumatic nail gun, which can speed up the process considerably. (You can rent one from a home improvement or rental center. Be sure to get thorough instructions on operating this tool and follow all safety precautions.) Consult wind tables provided by manufacturers for recommendations on fastener spacing, stud spacing, and other important features for your area.

What to Watch Out For

One ingredient in fiber-cement siding is sand, which contains silica. If inhaled during sawing of the siding material, silica can cause respiratory disease (scarring of the lung tissue, called silicosis). Wear appropriate eye protection and a high-quality dust mask. Use a circular saw with a special blade that minimizes dust when cutting fiber-cement siding, such as Hitachi's Hardiblade or Dewalt's PCD Fiber-Cement Blade. You may also be able to cut these products with snapper shears or a guillotine-type cutter.

Dust masks should be worn not only by the installer, but by anyone in the area whenever planks or other fiber-cement materials are being cut or sawn. Do the cutting outdoors, in an area away from other people and pets.

To minimize your exposure to fumes from conventional paints and finishes, choose primed and painted siding from the manufacturer.

Go Green!

When working on any home improvement project, plan what you are going to do, and make a complete and careful list of materials and supplies you'll need. This will save you extra trips to the hardware store or home improvement center to buy or return materials, thereby reducing wasted time, gas, pollution, and wear and tear on your vehicle.

When applying new fiber-cement siding, consider installing additional insulation in the wall cavity or over the exterior sheathing as explained in Project 13. If you add rigid insulation over the exterior sheathing, you'll have to build out the window and door trim as well.

Check local building codes to determine whether you need a permit to install new siding, and to be sure the job, as planned, meets their requirements. Note that even though local building codes may exempt fiber-cement siding from the usual requirement of a water-resistant layer such as building paper or Tyvek over exterior sheathing and under the siding, it's generally a good idea to provide one. See sidebar on the previous page for some environmentally friendly options.

What Will It Cost?

Fiber-cement is more expensive than vinyl, but similar in price to wood, for materials only. Fiber-cement products tend to be more costly to install because they require removal of the existing siding and more preparation. (Vinyl siding can often be placed over existing siding.) Cost is determined by several factors, for example, whether the siding is pre-finished or painted on-site, the style of paint, type of siding, and the size of your house.

Cost Estimate: Cost per square foot to remove existing clapboard siding and install fiber-cement siding

Includes house wrap, insulation board, and painting and priming the new siding

Cost for materials only: **$2.50**

Contractor's total per square foot, including materials, labor, and markup: **$9**

Total cost to repaint/stain conventional siding: **$4,500** (not including prep)

Costs are national averages and do not include sales tax.

Alternate costs per square foot installed:

Fiber-cement clapboards: **$9**

Brick veneer: **$18**

Cedar clapboards: **$8**

White cedar shingles: **$6.25**

Vinyl: **$6.50**

What Will You Save?

Fiber-cement siding typically comes with an impressive (and transferable) up-to-50-year warranty (15 for painted on pre-finished planks). Less-frequent painting (every 15 years, versus every 3 to 5 years for conventional wood plank siding) saves money and also reduces your exposure to toxic fumes from conventional paints, stains, and finishes.

In terms of return on investment, *Remodeling* magazine's 2007 annual "Cost Versus Value" report rated new fiber-cement siding as one of the highest-value projects, with an average return of 88 cents on each dollar invested when homes were sold.

Project 48

Repairing Broken Windows

As energy prices rise, so does the number of newspaper and television ads urging homeowners to replace their leaky old windows with energy-efficient ones. While window replacement is often a good idea and can make a substantial dent in heating and cooling costs, it should be one of the last items on your home energy conservation to-do list. Because the cost of window replacement is substantial, the return on your investment is lower than it is for many other energy-efficiency projects.

If you're on a budget, you'll get more bang for your buck by hiring an energy auditor to perform an energy analysis on your home. Following the simple, often inexpensive, measures he or she recommends can result in huge savings. Included in this list are tasks like caulking leaks in the building envelope to make your home more airtight, adding insulation to your walls and attic, installing insulated shades, tuning your heating and air conditioning systems and sealing ducts, adding a programmable thermostat, and installing a radiant barrier to your attic.

While you are working on these projects, you can address windows that are leaky and in poor condition. You can repair them, apply weather stripping, and even install storm windows. This project focuses on repairs. Refer to Project 49 for storm windows and, if needed, Project 50, for window replacement.

How Leaky Windows Waste Energy

Broken and leaky windows are common in many older homes. Cracked panes and missing putty in old wood windows allow air into a house—cold air in the winter and hot air in the summer. Even broken window locks in double-hung windows permit a considerable amount of air leakage. Besides providing security, window locks force the sashes (the wood that holds the window panes) together, creating a more airtight seal.

The air leakage from these problems can be significant. In many of the older homes I've energy-retrofitted with my students at Colorado College, we've made tremendous strides in reducing air leakage by installing weather stripping around doors and caulking leaks in the building envelope. Our efforts typically cut

Go Green!

To save energy in your home, use shades or consider installing retractable awnings on windows on the south and west sides of your house. They help reduce heat and glare in summer and prevent fading of furniture and carpeting.

air infiltration by about 50%. Because homeowners don't always have the money to install new windows, and because minor repairs can lead to huge savings, we always recommend repairing broken or damaged windows first.

Inspecting Windows: What to Look For

To begin, inspect each and every window in your home from both sides. Look for obvious damage, such as cracked or broken window panes or broken window sash locks. If your home has double-pane windows, inspect each window for moisture condensation or mildew between the panes. (There are window repair companies that treat this problem, but depending on the overall quality and condition of the window and how long you plan to live in your house, it may be better to replace it.)

Also, while inside on a windy day, run your hand around each window to detect possible air leaks. Note each problem and then jot down repair requirements.

Even a small crack in a single window pane can allow air to leak into your home.

Photo by Jessica deMartin

When inspecting older wood windows, also check the condition of the putty that holds the window panes in place. Cracked or missing putty can result in leakage and needs to be repaired.

After your inspection is complete, assess whether you're up to handling the needed repairs. If not, call a handyman to replace cracked glass, missing putty, or broken window locks. These fixes can provide a new lease on life for your windows.

Repairing Putty

To repair cracked putty in an older wood window, first remove all of the old putty. Carefully scrape it off using a sharp chisel. (Warming the putty with a hair dryer or soaking it with linseed oil applied with a brush can make removal easier.) Once you have removed the putty, clean the area with a damp rag. When dry, sand it lightly.

Next, seal the sanded wood with boiled linseed oil. (If you don't, the new putty may not stick. Dry wood draws the moisture out of putty, preventing tight bonding.) Paint the linseed oil on using a trim brush. To apply new putty, form a thin rope and place it around the perimeter of the window pane, using your fingers and a putty knife to create a good weatherproof seal.

Replacing Broken Window Panes

To replace broken panes in windows with metal or vinyl sashes, remove the metal spring or clip, rubber seal, or beveled or plastic molding that holds the glass in place. Wearing a pair of work gloves, carefully remove the glass, then insert a correctly sized piece of glass into the sash. If the glass is shattered, you may want to remove the pieces with a pair of pliers. When the new window pane is installed, replace the spring or clip (or whatever device was used) to hold the glass in place.

To replace a broken window pane in a wood-frame window, you'll need to first remove the putty that holds the glass in place. Scrape it away, as described earlier. Once the putty has been scraped off, remove the glazier's points—tiny metal wedges that hold window panes in place. They're typically spaced four to six inches apart. Use a pair of needle-nose pliers to remove them.

Wearing a pair of gloves, remove the broken or cracked glass, and then scrape out the putty into which the glass was seated. Measure the opening. Deduct an eighth of an inch from the height and width and order the glass to this size. (The eighth-inch deduction allows for expansion of the glass in warm weather.)

Clean and sand the wood, and seal it with boiled linseed oil. Next, apply a thin rope of putty around the opening. (The glass will be seated in this putty.) Replace the glass and insert new glazier points, using a putty knife. (An assistant is helpful when working with larger pieces of glass.) Glazier points should be placed four to six inches apart.

Finally, apply a second bead of putty. To do so, warm it in your hands, and then create a thin rope. Press it in place, and smooth it out with a putty knife. (You may want to dip the tip of the putty knife into the linseed oil to keep it from sticking to the putty.) After the putty has dried, paint it to match the sash.

For more detailed instructions on this and other projects, you may want to check out one of the many home improvement project books, such as *Better Home and Gardens Big Book of Home How-To.* You can also find detailed instructions on the Internet on one of the many do-it-yourself home repair sites, including those hosted by home improvement centers such as Lowe's or Home Depot.

Repairing a Window Lock

If the lock in a double-hung window has come loose, remove the screws that secure it to the sash. Place a drop of wood glue on the ends of a couple wooden matchsticks. Insert the glued ends of the matchsticks into the screw holes. After the glue has dried, saw or break off the ends of the matches. Drill a small hole (slightly smaller than the screws) into the plugged hole. Replace the lock, and screw it in place.

What to Watch Out For

When replacing a window pane, be sure to purchase the same kind (tint) of glass originally installed—so that it matches the remaining panes (in the case of a divided window) or the rest of the windows in the room (in the case of undivided windows). To assist hardware store employees, take a small piece of the old glass in with you when you order the new glass. For safety's sake, wrap the sample in a piece of newspaper. You may want to carry it in a small cardboard box.

When removing glass, be sure to wear heavy work gloves. Safety goggles may also be useful, especially if the glass is shattered. Unfortunately, window glass can't be recycled (it contains lead) with glass bottles and beverage containers. You'll need to dispose of it in your trash.

What Will You Save?

Repairing damaged window glass will immediately help improve the window's energy performance, saving you money on your utility bills and creating a more comfortable home. If the job exceeds your skill levels or requires more time than you have available, it's worth hiring a handyman to take care of it, along with any other small jobs you may need to have done.

Project

49

Storm Windows

Windows are a major source of energy loss and discomfort in many homes. In the winter, they can allow a huge amount of heat to escape, and cold drafts to enter. In the summer, windows allow heat into our homes, creating discomfort and raising cooling costs.

To improve comfort and lower utility bills, many homeowners simply replace poorly insulated, energy-inefficient windows—a project that can easily cost $10,000 to $20,000 on small to medium-sized homes. There are, however, much less expensive options. For a temporary fix, you can install clear plastic over your windows. A more permanent and more effective measure is to install storm windows. We'll explore both in this project.

Heat-Shrink Plastic

Heat-shrink plastic and tape kits are available at home improvement centers, hardware stores, and major discount stores. Installation is easy. First, clean the interior window trim. When dry, attach the two-sided tape around the outside of the interior window trim. Remove the protective paper from the tape at the top of the window.

With a pair of scissors, cut the film about two inches larger than the taped area. Attach the film to the tape at the top of the window, and then stretch it to cover the rest of the window opening. Remove the paper backing on the remainder of the tape, and press the film against it carefully so as to avoid wrinkles and folds. Once in

place, the smaller wrinkles in the plastic can be removed by blowing hot air over the plastic using a hair dryer. The film becomes almost invisible.

Plastic film kits are also available for exterior installation. These kits include tacking strips or removable plastic moldings, which attach to the exterior window trim and allow you to remove the plastic in the summer or replace film that's ripped or torn.

Plastic films are great for renters, including apartment dwellers. They're also ideal for homeowners who don't have the funds available for storm windows or replacement windows. Plastic interior kits typically last one to three years, if left in place, and cost about $3 to $8 per window. Exterior kits cost a little more.

Go Green!

If you replace your old windows or old storm windows with energy-efficient ones, and they're in decent shape, look for a way to recycle them. Check with Habitat for Humanity ReStores or another local housing charity. You'll be helping your community and can receive a charitable tax deduction.

Although plastic film is effective, it may slightly impair views through windows. (It's not as clear as storm windows.) Also, if you want to open your windows in warm weather, you'll also have to remove the plastic and reinstall new plastic before winter sets in.

Storm Windows

A far better option is an interior or exterior storm window. Although there are a number of companies that install high-quality interior storm windows, exterior units are the most common. They've been around the longest and are available in home improvement centers, not just window and glass companies.

High-quality storm windows are a great way to address leaky, inefficient single-pane windows, and are much cheaper and easier to install than brand new windows. Made from glass or plastic, interior and exterior storms seal an existing window opening, reducing drafts. They also provide additional insulation by creating an air space between the existing window glass and the storm window. This air space reduces heat flow from the interior in the winter and reduces heat gain from the outside in the summer.

According to the ToolBase web site, "One field study of interior storm windows at three Florida residences reported heating and cooling energy savings of 29% and noticeably reduced interior window condensation." (Because they raise the interior window temperature, they reduce condensation.) Interior and exterior storm windows also help reduce transmission of noise from outside a home.

What Are Your Options?

Exterior storm windows come in two basic varieties. The first is the removable exterior storm, often found in older homes. These units are typically removed at the end of the heating season and replaced with screens. This obviously takes time and requires a good amount of storage space.

The second, more convenient option is an operable exterior storm window—one that can be left in place, but opened and closed as needed. Most operable storms come with built-in sliding screens.

Existing window

Interior storm window

Interior storm windows are relatively easy to install and can dramatically reduce heat loss.
Courtesy of EnergySavr Window Inserts

Operable exterior storm windows are fairly inexpensive, easy to install, and convenient. They come in either double- or triple-track. Double-trackers contain an outside track that is shared by a pane of glass and a screen. The glass is on the top and the screen is on the bottom. The inside track contains a pane of glass that can be raised and lowered. In the summer, it is raised to allow fresh air in.

Triple-track storm windows have an aluminum frame with three channels that allow you to slide the glass and screens up and down independent of one another. The outside and middle tracks contain panes that can slide up and down. The inner track contains the screen, which can also slide up and down. Because of the extra track, these are the most versatile storm windows.

In recent years, more and more homeowners have been installing interior storm windows. They are ideal for historic homes to improve energy performance without altering the home's exterior appearance. Storm window companies can customize them to fit any size rectangular window. Some firms will produce any geometric shape.

Interior storm windows can be left in place all year or can be removed for ventilation during milder weather. Panes are available in glass, acrylic plastic, or polycarbonate plastic. You can also purchase storm windows with special coatings that resist heat gain (called low-E coatings) or UV-resistant coatings that reduce the amount of UV radiation entering your home. (UV radiation can damage carpets, drapes, and furniture.) Interior storm windows with acrylic or polycarbonate glazing need extra care to prevent scratching or clouding. I clean mine with a special plastic cleaner.

Installing Storm Windows

Although most people have storm windows installed by professionals, it is a relatively simple job. Storm window frames (with windows intact) are simply screwed into the exterior window trim. Screws are driven through screw holes in flanges on the storm assemblies. When installing a storm window, apply a bead of silicone caulk between the mounting flanges and the window trim to create a more airtight seal. Be sure you don't caulk over the small holes (weep holes) at the bottom of the unit. They allow moisture that condenses between the window and storm to escape.

When installing exterior storm windows, be careful to keep them level and do not allow the frame to twist. This could inhibit the raising or lowering of the windows and screen. For more detailed descriptions of installation, check the instructions supplied by the manufacturer. You can also consult one or two of the excellent home improvement books available at home improvement centers and bookstores, or go online for directions.

Interior storm windows are made of glass, polycarbonate, or acrylic plastic, as noted. They are attached to the window opening via vinyl or metal mounting brackets that are permanently fastened to one or more sides of the interior window frame. The pane commonly comes with a magnetic strip for easy attachment to the bracket.

Go Green!

- To clean windows without using harmful chemicals, mix one part vinegar with four parts water, and use a spray bottle to apply. Wipe with newspapers, which won't streak or leave lint behind like paper towels and cloth can.

- To further reduce your energy bills, add a shade or curtain to windows. Even mini-blinds cut down some unwanted heat gain. Studies show that uninsulated draperies can cut window heat loss in winter by one-third, while insulated ones can reduce it by half.

Interior storm window kits are generally easy to install and sell for as little as $55 for a 60" × 30" window. If you hire a professional to install them, expect to pay a lot more. I have even made my own interior storm windows from polycarbonate plastic. I used pieces of trim wood to secure them to the window opening.

Shopping Tips

Most homeowners select aluminum-framed triple-track combination storm/screen windows for convenience. However, there are big differences among products on the market, especially with respect to air-tightness, according to *Consumer Guide to Home Energy Savings*, published by the American Council for an Energy-Efficient Economy. They recommend selecting a storm window with a leakage rate around 0.01, but no higher than 0.03 cubic feet per minute per foot of window edging. Anything higher runs the risk of high air leakage. Check the labels on the windows for this information or ask sales personnel.

What Will It Cost?

In calculating costs for this project, be sure to subtract available energy-savings rebates, if any. Consult your utility company and visit the Energy Star website for more information.

Cost Estimate: Installation of a 2'6" x 5' storm window

Includes caulking window head and jambs

Cost for materials only: **$100**

Contractor's total, including materials, labor, and markup: **$160**

Costs are national averages and do not include sales tax.

What Will You Save?

While storm windows are a lot more expensive than weather-stripping (Project 12) or covering windows with plastic, high-quality units with screens will provide years of convenience, in addition to comfort and energy savings. They could reduce air leakage from leaky windows by 50% to nearly 150%. If you recently installed storm windows, check out available rebates and tax credits.

Project 50

Energy-Efficient Windows

If the windows in your home are letting in uncomfortable drafts, you have several options to improve the situation—and cut your utility bill. The cheapest and often the most cost-effective is to repair them (Project 48) and apply weather stripping to seal the leaks (Project 12). Another approach is to install storm windows (Project 49). Any of these steps will reduce home energy use and can dramatically increase your comfort.

However, if your windows' wood frames are rotted or badly damaged, if there's moisture between the panes of glass, or if your windows won't close properly, you may want to consider replacing them. Don't buy the cheapest windows you can find, though. "If you plan to replace windows—for comfort, appearance, cleaning convenience, modernization, or any other reason, it almost always pays to invest the small added cost in highly efficient windows rather than minimum performance ones," advises the *Consumer Guide to Home Energy Savings.*

Buying new energy-efficient windows can be a challenge in part because windows have become much more complex over the past 20 years, and there are now many options to choose from. To help you make wise choices, let's breeze through a short course on windows.

Window Options

Windows come in many styles, shown in the illustrations (on next page). Their air tightness—and hence energy efficiency—varies considerably. As a rule, non-operable windows (that cannot open) are the most airtight and energy-efficient. Next on the list are casement (crank-out), awning (tilts out at bottom), and hopper (tilts in, usually for basements) windows. The least airtight are single- and double-hung. That said, not all windows are created equal, no matter what their style. A high quality single- or double-hung window may be more airtight than a lower-quality casement window.

When shopping for new windows, select a style that fits with the design of your home, then choose the most airtight and energy-efficient units you can afford. Before buying, be sure to check into incentives from your local utility, your state government, and/or the federal government. Rebates and tax incentives can

To Save Money

If your window frames are in excellent condition, the easiest way to replace a window is to remove the old window and sash and place the new ones into the existing frame. This allows the existing trim to remain in place. If the trim is also worn or damaged, however, you should replace the entire window—the glass, sash, and trim.

Windows come in many configurations to meet a wide range of needs.
Illustrations by Anil Rao

lower the cost of buying a more energy-efficient and better quality window.

How will you know how airtight a window is? Manufacturers list air infiltration rates on prominent labels. Air leakage is measured in cubic feet of air per square foot of glass. (Air doesn't actually leak through the glass, but around the perimeter.) Look for windows with leakage rates of less than 0.3 cubic feet per minute per square foot.

Sash Materials

Another feature to consider is the sash material. The sash is the part of the window that the glass is attached to. There are four basic choices: wood, metal, vinyl, and fiberglass.

By far the most popular—and the greenest—is the wood-frame window. **Wood windows** are attractive, relatively inexpensive, and insulate well. They're also made from a renewable, natural resource. (Some manufacturers make windows from FSC-certified lumber. The Forest Stewardship Council certifies lumber from sustainable forestry operations. Ask the dealer about this greener option.)

The most durable wood windows come with an exterior aluminum cladding that protects the wood sash from sunlight and weather. Wood windows with vinyl cladding are also available, but vinyl production poses risks to workers and residents who live near factories. Vinyl chloride used to make vinyl is a carcinogen. When released from manufacturing plants, it pollutes the air in neighboring communities. Vinyl windows may also contain plasticizers, chemicals than outgas—that is, pollute indoor air in the homes in which they're installed.

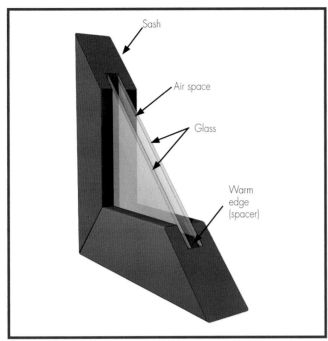

Cross section through a double-pane window
Drawing by Anil Rao

a window's energy efficiency, and, as a general rule, the more panes, the better. Unfortunately, triple-pane windows are very costly, so most people settle for double-panes, which work well in most applications, especially if you also use insulated shades.

Another desirable feature is an edge spacer, or thermal break, located between the panes of glass of all high-quality windows. **Thermal breaks** reduce heat flow (out in the winter, in during the summer) through the sash, improving the window's thermal performance. By reducing heat flow through the sash, edge spacers also reduce moisture and ice buildup along the edge of windows, a problem in cold regions. This, in turn, protects wood frame windows from water damage.

Yet another factor to consider is the window's **U-factor**, the amount of heat that flows into or out of a window. The lower the U-factor, the better the window.

Insulated **vinyl windows** are also becoming popular and may perform better than wood windows. Vinyl is a durable material and never needs painting. However, as noted, it's not environmentally friendly.

Aluminum windows are also popular, but are extremely inefficient if the sashes are not insulated. If you purchase an aluminum-frame window, be sure it's insulated and comes with a high-quality thermal break—an insulated spacer placed between the layers of glass. Thermal breaks reduce heat loss around the edges of windows and dramatically improve their efficiency. Aluminum is also not a green choice because it takes a lot of energy to produce.

Another option is an insulated **fiberglass window**. Fiberglass is a durable material like vinyl, but its manufacture exposes workers to some fairly toxic chemicals. Fiberglass windows probably pose very little hazard to homeowners and families once installed. Again, wood is the greenest window frame option, especially if it is certified as sustainably harvested.

The other green factor is Energy Efficiency, which is determined in part by the **number of panes of glass**. Windows comes in single-, double-, and, much less commonly, triple-pane varieties. Each pane increases

A window's U-factor is determined by:

- The number of panes of glass—the more panes, the lower the U-factor.

- The thermal break.

- The type of gas injected into the space between the layers of glass. Although air is a reasonably good insulator, inert gases (argon or krypton) do a slightly better job. Argon is commonly used in residential windows.

- The application of heat-reflective "low-e" coatings. These thin, transparent layers (silver or tin oxide) are applied to the glass in double- and triple-pane windows. The coatings allow light to pass through, but reduce the flow of heat through the glass. Low-e coatings help retain a home's heat in winter and keep heat from entering in the summer. In cold climates, the low-e coating is on the inner layer of the inner pane of glass in a double-pane window. In warm climates, it's usually applied to the inner layer of the outer pane of glass.

Values below 0.35 are generally recommended. U-factors of 0.22 or lower are the best. Visit the Energy Star website for recommendations for your location: **www.energystar.gov**

Another important factor that's listed on the labels of new windows is **visible transmittance.** This number refers to the amount of light that passes through a window and ranges from 0 to 1. The higher the number, the more light. In some locations, for example, the west side of your home, you may want to install windows with a low visible transmittance to block strong sunlight in the afternoon. These windows will appear tinted. On the north side of your home, you may want to choose a window with a high visible transmittance to let more light in.

Another factor that will help you select an energy-efficient window is the **solar heat gain coefficient**, or SHGC. This is a measure of how much solar energy enters a home through a window. The numbers range from 0 to 1. The higher the number, the more light and heat. A window with a solar heat gain coefficient of 0.7 lets 70% of the sun's energy in.

Glass with a high solar heat gain coefficient is ideal for windows on the south side of your home. This will allow lots of low-angled winter sun into your home to help heat it. For the east or west side of your home, select a glass with a low solar heat gain coefficient—to reduce heat gain in the summer. On the north side of your home, solar heat gain coefficient isn't a concern.

While all this may sound complicated, it's pretty logical. For the south side of a home, the ideal would be windows with a high solar heat gain coefficient *and* a low U-factor—if you want to take advantage of the sun's warming rays in the winter and reduce heat loss at night. Unfortunately, this combination isn't easy to find. Many window manufacturers offer low-e windows with low U-factors, but these products have a rather low solar heat gain coefficient. Two exceptions are Pella and PPG glass. Both companies manufacture windows that are ideal for south-facing glass. If your local window installers don't carry windows that meet these specifications, you can order PPG glass (with high solar heat gain coefficient and low U-factor) through a local

The Most Efficient Windows in the World

One of the most, if not *the* most energy-efficient window on the market today is a fiberglass window from Alpen Energy Group in Boulder, Colorado. These windows are available with a wide range of properties to meet different needs. Their highest-performing windows have a U-factor of 0.10 (R-value of 10), the best performer of any window available as of this book's publication anywhere in the world.

window supplier who is willing to install the glass into the frames they offer. It shouldn't cost much more.

If your mind is reeling with all of this new information, don't be dismayed. Consult with a window retailer/installer for recommendations. Also be sure to specify Energy Star-qualified windows. As mentioned earlier, you can find guidance for your area on the Energy Star website.

Installation

Window installation is a job best handled by professionals. It's easy to make mistakes, especially when sealing a window to reduce air infiltration and moisture penetration. Hire an installer with lots of experience and a reputation for excellent work.

Go Green!

Tubular skylights are a fairly simple and inexpensive way to bring natural light into windowless spaces, such as hallways and interior bathrooms. They can improve the quality of light and reduce your use of energy for electric lighting (Project 45).

Remember that an expensive energy-efficient window is only as good as its installation.

If you are skilled in home construction and want to take on this project yourself, carefully review the manufacturer's instructions. You might also want to hire a professional installer to help or to provide detailed instructions and advice. Be sure to review the steps outlined in home improvement books and on Internet sites hosted by home improvement centers, magazines, and others.

Be especially careful when filling the gaps around the window during installation. When installing windows, you can use a product like DOW Great Stuff™ minimal expanding foam for gaps larger than ¼". More expansive foams can compress window jams and sills, making windows inoperable. Fiberglass insulation will not work as well as spray-in foam insulation.

When installing a window, don't cover the weep holes in the bottom of the window assembly. They allow water to escape. If you cover them, moisture will accumulate and could damage the insulation, the trim, and even your home's structural support.

Consider replacing all the windows on one side of your home—or on one level if yours is a two-story house—to maintain a consistent appearance. If you're replacing the siding on your home, replace the windows first. That way, the new siding can be trimmed and fitted to the new windows to minimize leakage. This will look nicer and provide better overall energy efficiency.

Shopping Tips

When shopping for windows, take your time. Take a list of features you want along with you. Don't let a salesperson talk you into single-pane glass if you live in a warm climate. Double-pane windows improve comfort and reduce air conditioning costs, which can exceed heating costs in colder climates.

When shopping for a professional installer, seek a highly experienced company, and, more important, be sure they send an experienced crew to your home to do the job. Insist on it! Home improvement centers can put you in touch with a professional installer.

Factors to Consider When Buying Windows

1. Style of window—e.g., casement vs. double-hung
2. Window sash/frame material—e.g., wood vs. fiberglass
3. Number of panes—two or more recommended
4. Thermal break or edge spacer
5. U-Factor—0.35 or lower; perferably 0.22 or lower
6. Air leakage—lower than 0.3 cfm/square foot
7. Visible Transmittance—0 to 1
8. Solar Heat Gain Coefficient—Check Energy Star recommendations for your area.

What Will It Cost?

Cost Estimate: Removal and replacement of 8 (26" x 48") windows, casings, and trim

Includes preparation of rough openings and painting of new windows and trim

Cost for materials only: **$2,150**

Contractor's total, including materials, labor, and markup: **$5,400**

Costs are national averages and do not include sales tax.

What Will You Save?

According to the Energy Star program, installing Energy Star-qualified windows can produce utility bill savings of at least $125 to $465 each year if you replace single-pane windows throughout a "typical home" (2,000 square feet, single-story, detached, with 300 square feet of window area, gas heat, and electric air conditioning). Visit **http://www.energystar.gov** to find estimated savings for your area of the country and for different types of windows.

Project 51

Storm Doors

Exterior doors are often a big source of air leakage in our homes. In the winter, they can let tons of cold air in, and in the summer, allow hot air in and cool, air-conditioned air out. One way to reduce these problems is to install a well-made storm door.

A good storm door, properly installed, should form a relatively airtight seal. Like storm windows, storm doors provide an additional air space that serves as an insulating barrier. Storm doors can also protect the main door from weather damage. Lockable storm doors add an extra measure of security.

What Are Your Options?

Storm doors come in many styles and colors with prices ranging from about $80 to $400. They are made from extruded aluminum, insulated aluminum, steel, iron, or wood. Wood doors may be painted or clad with aluminum or vinyl, which protects the wood from the weather. Wood and insulated aluminum provide better protection from heat loss than uninsulated metal storm doors.

Some manufacturers fit their doors with acrylic plastic panes, which are lightweight and resist breakage. Other options include break-resistant tempered glass and energy-efficient low-e glass (which prevents heat from flowing in or out of a home, depending on the season).

Most storm doors come with glass panes that can slide up or down to expose screens, permitting natural ventilation and cooling when needed. Some panes are completely removable, with screen inserts that can be installed in their place.

Most door manufacturers offer prehung storm door kits. The doors are mounted in a frame, which is screwed into the door opening. Kits include all the

Storm doors help reduce heat loss in the winter and heat gain in the summer.
Courtesy of Harvey Industries

hardware needed to install a storm door, including hinges, pneumatic closers, and latches.

Storm doors are available at home improvement centers and building supply outlets. Many of them offer installation as an additional service.

Installation

Storm doors are relatively easy to install if you have some home improvement experience. The job requires attention to detail and some basic tools including a tape measure, drill, hammer, pliers, screwdrivers, chisel, hacksaw, caulk gun, square, and level. Professional installation is a good idea if you're not a skilled do-it-yourselfer.

Pre-framed storm doors are screwed onto existing door jambs, taking care to mount the door level so that it seals the opening and opens and closes properly. Most storm doors can be adjusted so they fit snugly into an existing door frame, but if the opening is slightly too large for a standard door, you may be able to install a device known as a Z-bar extender. It "fills in" the extra space between the door and frame, enabling the storm door to fit more tightly. If this option isn't right for you, you can also have a storm door custom-made for your home. Contact a local handyman or storm door and window installer.

Before installing a new storm door, remove the glass. It accounts for a significant percentage of the door's weight, and removing it makes installation easier. It also helps prevent injury from accidents and breakage. For instructions, check out one of the home improvement project books or online sources, like the do-it-yourself network (**www.diynetwork.com**) or Lowe's and Home Depot's websites.

Shopping Guide

Storm doors vary in price. The more expensive the door, the higher the quality and the more bells and whistles. These include features such as keyed exterior deadbolts, decorative molding, special glazing (e.g., low-e glass), and two door closers rather than one. (A door closer is the device that ensures a storm door closes smoothly and completely.)

Storm doors come in standard door widths—30, 32, 34, and 36 inches—hinged on either side to match your main door's swing. Before you shop, measure the height and width of the door frame (the inside dimensions of the door jamb).

To maximize light and views, or to simply show off a decorative front door, consider installing a full-height glass panel storm door. Most people install mid-view storm doors, which come with a solid panel on the bottom third of the door with two glass panels above. (The glass panels slide in their tracks, allowing access to a screen to allow natural ventilation.) Another option is a high-view door in which the solid section covers about one half the door's height.

If you have pets or small children, a solid bottom panel door (as opposed to a full glass and full screen door) may be a good choice. Dogs and kids may push the screen out at the bottom, eventually tearing it, and may smudge the glass of all-glass storm doors with their noses and fingers.

If security is an issue in your neighborhood, consider a storm door with a heavy-duty metal frame. Security doors are made with either heavy-gauge aluminum bars (designed to withstand a pulling force greater than 250 pounds) or stronger steel bars that are welded in place to protect against intruders. When selecting a

Go Green!

• If your front door doesn't have a door sweep at the bottom to seal out drafts and debris, you can purchase one for as little as $3 at a hardware store or home center.

• On hot summer or cold winter days, keep the outside door closed when family or friends are leaving until they're ready to leave. If someone stops by for a quick visit, invite them in and shut the door. Chatting with the door open wastes a lot of energy and cools down (or heats up, depending on the season) your home unnecessarily.

security storm door, be sure the hinges and deadbolt are tamper-proof.

Also, buy a durable one. Don't buy cheap models. Storm doors take a beating, so you want one that lasts! How will you know if a door is well-made? Durable doors are heavier, close more slowly, and often come with limited lifetime warranties.

Many major storm door manufacturers offer a design-your-own-door program that allows you to mix and match various components. Larson's Designer Door series, for example, lets consumers pick the frame and color they like, then select from one of six styles of glass and six types of hardware.

What To Watch Out For

A storm door may not be appropriate to install over an exterior door that is exposed to direct sunlight. It can increase the temperature of a main entry door (especially one painted or stained a dark color), causing it to expand and warp so that it doesn't open or close properly.

This full-height glass panel storm door maximizes views and daylight.
Courtesy of Harvey Industries

What Will It Cost?

Storm doors (uninstalled) range in price from about $80 to $400, depending on size, features, type of construction and materials, and length of the warranty.

Cost Estimate: Installation of a medium-to-high-quality aluminum storm door

Includes caulking of the door head and jambs

Cost for materials only: **$270**

Contractor's total, including materials, labor, and markup: **$410**

Costs are national averages and do not include sales tax.

What Will You Save?

Since the air leakage from a drafty door can be a major contributor to heat loss or gain, depending on the season, you can definitely save some money on your energy bill by adding a storm door. Savings will vary depending on sun and wind exposure, the type of door you select, and other conditions specific to your home. Also look into possible tax credits and rebates. And if an attractive new storm door also improves your home's appearance, you'll be adding to its resale value in more ways than one.

Project 52 | Door Sweeps

Exterior doors are notoriously leaky, especially older doors in old homes. But even in newer homes, doors allow a lot of cold air in during winter. Why? Winter's dry air can cause a door to shrink, creating larger gaps between it and the frame. One way to prevent air leaks, save energy, and help cut your fuel bills is to install weather stripping along the top and sides of a door (Project 12). Another complementary measure is to install a door sweep.

A door sweep is a type of weather stripping that is mounted directly on the inside bottom of a door. (Conventional weather stripping is mounted on the frame around the door.) Door sweeps are simple devices, often consisting of a strip of aluminum attached to a strip of felt or vinyl. The aluminum portion is screwed into the bottom of the door. The felt or vinyl strip contacts the floor, sealing the opening between the door and the threshold, keeping the cold air out on frigid winter days. Door sweeps also function in the summer, either keeping hot outside air from seeping in, or cool, air-conditioned air from leaking out. They also help keep insects from creeping into our homes.

Installation

Door sweeps can be purchased from hardware stores and home improvement centers and can be installed in a matter of minutes. Just measure the width of the door, then cut the sweep with a hacksaw to fit. Close the door and screw the sweep to the door. (Manufacturers provide screws.) Be sure the felt or vinyl portion contacts the threshold and blocks the flow of air before you screw it in. (The screw holes are slotted so you can adjust the door sweep to close the gap.)

Air leakage at the bottom of an exterior door can also be reduced by adjusting the height of the threshold—and thus the gap between the bottom of the door and the threshold. You can do this by removing the strip of vinyl from the threshold, which will reveal

Go Green!

• Don't forget to clean both the door sweep and weather stripping around the door periodically. Dirt, especially when combined with moisture, can clump on the surface, prevent smooth operation, and cause premature wear.

• If you need to replace your old, worn-out exterior door, consider an insulated door with a foam core sandwiched between fiberglass or steel. You could also add a storm door (Project 51).

several large screw heads. By tightening or loosening the screws, the threshold will rise or fall. If the threshold is too low, raise it a little at a time, checking the gap. To test the height, replace the vinyl strip, close the door, and check for light coming under the door. When the adjustment is correct, you should not be able to see light beneath the door. You should feel a little resistance (but not too much) as the bottom of the door moves over the threshold. If you raise the threshold too much, the resistance will cause the bottom of the door and the vinyl strip to wear out long before their time.

Shopping Tips

When shopping for door sweeps, especially online, you'll find several types. Adhesive-backed PVC door sweeps are made from rigid and pliable vinyl. This product has a self-adhesive strip used to attach it to the base of the door. There's no need to screw it in, although I question how long it will stay in place. Like other door sweeps, they come in 36-inch lengths, designed for the widest exterior doors. You cut it to size using a hacksaw.

If your doors have a large gap, and your floor surface is uneven, you may want to consider the Deluxe Triple Seal Door Sweep (available online at **http://amconservationgroup.com**). This 2-3/8 inch sweep is made from extruded aluminum and vinyl with slotted holes for adjustment. The same company also sells a spring-activated door sweep that lifts automatically when a door opens, and lowers when the door closes. It's ideal for situations where carpet makes it impossible to use a conventional door sweep. (Carpet creates too much friction and will eventually tear the vinyl or felt in a normal door stop.)

What Will It Cost?

Door sweeps are inexpensive, ranging from about $3.50 to $20, depending on the materials they are made of (such as vinyl, aluminum, wood), and features such as drip caps, choice of finishes, soundproofing, and automatic flexing to adjust for uneven floor surfaces. The average cost for a professional service call by a handyman is about $120, so you can save a lot on this simple project by doing it yourself.

What Will You Save?

Installing door sweeps will save a little on your utility bills and improve comfort. The bigger the gap (air leak), the greater your savings. Professional home energy auditors frequently recommend door sweeps, along with weather stripping, to address air leakage that they discover when performing tests on a home. An extra benefit is keeping insects out, which helps reduce the expense and exposure to toxic insecticides inside your home.

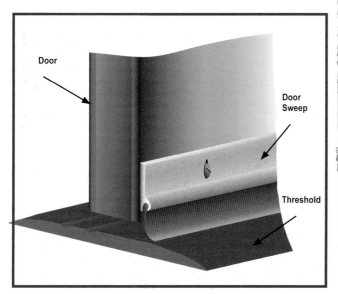

Door sweeps help reduce leakage at the base of exterior doors, a common problem in homes.
Illustration by Jessica deMartin

Project 53 Gutters & Downspouts

Moisture can create significant problems in our homes. Indoor moisture comes from many sources, for example, air condensing on cool surfaces, rain, melting snow, or groundwater seeping into the basement. It can lead to mold and mildew growth, which can make us ill and damage our homes and their contents. Moisture can increase the rate at which potentially toxic chemicals are released from modern building materials. And it can cause a considerable amount of structural damage—such as rotting of wood framing in walls.

Moisture enters through foundations, basement walls, and penetrations in the building envelope (roof and outside walls). One of the main sources is improper flashing around chimneys and vent pipes, and where walls or dormers intersect with roofs.

It's important to address moisture coming in from the outside, since it is also continuously generated inside our homes. Humans, for instance, give off a considerable amount of moisture when we breathe. In fact, each of us loses about one quart of moisture at night as we sleep. (That's why you weigh about 2 pounds less in the morning when you wake up.) Moisture is also released into the air by house plants, running showers and faucets, cooking, dishwashing, and clothes washers and dryers. Even conventional combustion appliances such as gas-, propane-, and oil-fired furnaces, boilers, and water heaters release moisture.

How do you know if you have a moisture problem? The telltale signs are many: damp floors, walls, closets, or cupboards; basement flooding; musty smells; and a clammy, cold feeling. Musty, limp, damp, or wilted books, boxes, and papers are obvious signs of high moisture levels. You may even observe mold growing on surfaces. If you want to be

Flashing at intersection of a roof and wall, if not installed properly, can be a major source of moisture penetration.

Illustration by Anil Rao

more scientific, you can install an inexpensive moisture sensor/thermometer to measure humidity levels. (These devices are sold in hardware stores and home improvement centers.) If moisture levels routinely exceed 60%, you will want to take action to reduce them. But what do you do about it?

This project addresses water entering the basement through the foundation.

The most effective means of drying out your basement actually begin on your roof—specifically with your home's gutters. Surprisingly, many people don't even know if their homes have gutters. If you're one of them, head outdoors right now and take a look.

Nearly all homes require gutters and downspouts to protect the foundation and/or basement from water. If your home was built without gutters, or if your gutters are clogged with leaves or pine needless—or are just old and leaky—water will drip off your roof after rain and during snow melts. It then accumulates in the soil alongside the foundation and may seep into or even flood your basement from time to time.

Properly installed gutters drain thousands of gallons of water away from the foundation of homes every year. They not only help keep basements and crawl spaces dry, but also protect siding and windows from moisture. As a result, gutter installation and maintenance are two of the most important things you can do to protect your home.

What Are Your Options?

Gutters and downspouts are available in home improvement centers and local hardware stores in a wide range of materials, styles, and prices. The most common are made from vinyl, aluminum, and galvanized steel. More expensive are stainless steel, copper, and wood. Wood gutters are typically used only in historic home restoration because of their cost and maintenance requirements.

Vinyl gutters are fairly inexpensive and can be installed by a skilled do-it-yourselfer in a weekend. Unfortunately, vinyl gutters are brittle and can be damaged by falling objects. They are also not desirable

from an environmental standpoint. (They are not currently recyclable, and vinyl production exposes workers and residents who live near factories to cancer-causing vinyl chloride.)

Aluminum gutters are slightly more expensive than vinyl and, because they don't rust, are more durable and save money over the long term because they last longer. Aluminum dents more easily than galvanized steel, but steel rusts. Copper, like wood, is mostly used for historic home restorations. It is expensive, but doesn't rust or require repainting. Stainless steel is perhaps the most expensive, and also a long-lasting option. In purchasing metal gutters, look for a thickness of .032 inches. Thinner materials will not last as long.

Gutters also come in different shapes, or "profiles." The most popular are half-round and "K" profiles. (The front profile resembles the letter K.) Gutters are available in diameters ranging from 4 to 6 inches. The larger the roof, the larger the gutter you'll need. Downspouts, which drain water vertically from gutters, also vary in size and shape (round and rectangular).

Gutters are either seamless or sectional. A seamless gutter is made from a single piece of aluminum fabricated by an installer on-site. The only seams are at corners, where two pieces of gutter meet, and at downspouts. Sectional gutters (like the ones you can

This downspout would be more effective with an extender to divert water away from the house.

buy and install yourself) come in pieces that are joined together during installation. Seamless gutters are less-likely to leak.

Installation

Installing gutters is not a terribly difficult job, but requires two people. You'll also have to work from ladders, which can be dangerous, especially if you live in a two- or three-story home. If ladder work isn't your thing, you may want to consider hiring an installer. A professional will have the equipment and materials needed to do the job correctly and quickly. As mentioned earlier, professionals usually install seamless aluminum gutters.

Seamless gutters last longer than sectional gutters, because seams tend to weaken over time due to expansion and contraction of the joints and cracking of the seam caulk. As a rule, you can expect leak-free service for only 10 to 15 years, at which time you'll need to re-caulk the seams.

Downspouts typically drain at the foundation, usually in the corners of the house. To prevent pooling, it's a good idea to install downspout extenders, additional sections of pipe that transport water away from the house. I recommend at least six-foot-long downspout extenders. You can also install flexible black ABS drain pipe on downspouts to transport water farther away from your home. Downspout extenders can be found at home centers and on the Internet.

Whatever you do, be sure that the water deposited by the drain pipe or downspout extender doesn't drain back toward your home. To prevent this, the soil around the home must be properly graded, so that it slopes away from the house. Also check downspout extenders every month or so to make sure they haven't been accidentally or intentionally disconnected—for example, by children or lawn mowers.

If you don't like the looks of downspout extenders or flexible black drain pipe—or if you don't want to mess with them when mowing your lawn, you can connect the downspout to an underground three-inch PVC pipe, as I've done on my house. For rectangular downspouts, you'll need to buy an adaptor that "marries" the downspout opening to the circular pipe. Adaptors are available at hardware stores, building supply outlets, and home improvement centers.

The PVC pipe attaches to the downspout and runs horizontally along the foundation, then vertically below the frost line to prevent freezing. Be sure the pipe slopes slightly for proper drainage. (A 1% to 2% slope should do—that's a 1- to 2-foot drop in 100 lineal feet.) Drainage pipe can be "daylighted"—drained downhill in an open location—or can be emptied into an artificial or natural pond, if you are lucky enough to have one on your property. The pipe can also be run to an underground storage tank, which can be used to supply water for your garden, trees, shrubs, and flowers. Or runoff can be delivered to a dry well (or "sump"), a hole filled with crushed rock. Locate the hole at least 20 feet away from your home. This is an effective and, therefore, preferred method of ensuring good drainage.

When installing underground drain pipe, be sure to lay it below the frost line to prevent freezing. Note that underground drainage pipes may not be suitable in really cold climates, as the water may freeze in the

Go Green!

• One of the simplest and least costly ways to avoid excess moisture from the basement is to make sure that your clothes dryer and basement-level bathrooms are adequately vented to the outside. A rigid vent should be used for gas dryers, and the duct to the outside should follow the shortest possible route. Sealing the seams of a rigid dryer vent is good practice. Use high-temperature caulk or UL-approved mastic. For electric dryers, the shorter the run and the fewer the number of bends and twists, the more effective the drying will be.

• When replacing damaged old metal gutters and downspouts, be sure you or the installers recycle them. Check with scrap metal or construction materials recyclers.

vertical section of PVC pipe, obstructing flow and causing the water to back up into the gutters or damage the downspout when it freezes.

If you hire a contractor to install gutters, downspouts, and underground drainage, choose carefully. "Gutter installation is an easy start-up business," says Matt Weber on **Extremehowto.com**, "and as a result there may be many new contractors in your area who don't have much experience." It's always a good idea to obtain two or three bids, but, as Weber warns, "Don't necessarily fall for the lowest price. If one bid is significantly lower than another, the gutters used by the low-bid contractor may be made of a thinner, less durable metal." He adds, "When specifying metal gutters, choose the thickest you can afford; 0.032-inch metal is recommended." Also be sure to check out the warranty for the gutters and other components. Look for one that extends at least 20 years with at least one-year coverage on labor.

Maintenance

Maintaining and repairing gutters and downspouts is crucial to their effectiveness and longevity. Well-maintained gutters could last two or three times longer than neglected ones. Inspect your gutters and downspouts at least twice a year and remove leaves or other debris. Look for rust, leaks, and water accumulation in and along gutters. If there is standing water in a cleaned gutter, you may need to adjust its pitch. (Gutters should slope about 1/16 inch for every 1 foot of length.) You can often adjust the slope by

bending the gutter hangers slightly or adding an extra spike or sleeve, depending on your gutter's attachment system.

You can usually remove clogs at the bottom of downspouts by pulling out accumulated debris and by washing them out with a hose from above. Leaf strainers (over the downspout outlet) and leaf guards (covering the entire length of gutter) are a good idea in areas with overhanging trees.

Small leaks can usually be patched with a combination of rust-inhibiting treatment, plastic cement, or roofing cement (depending on the gutter material). Larger holes can be patched with aluminum or plastic strips made for this purpose.

What Will It Cost?

Vinyl gutters run about $3 to $5 per linear foot. Aluminum and galvanized steel gutters cost roughly $5 to $9 per linear foot installed. Wood gutters run from about $12 to $20 per foot, depending on the type of wood. Copper costs about $15, and stainless-steel about $20 per foot, installed.

Cost Estimate: Installation of 106 LF of aluminum gutters and 64 LF of downspouts (enough for an average 2,500 SF, 2-story house)

Cost for materials only: **$460**

Contractor's total, including materials, labor, and markup: **$1,270**

What Will You Save?

Properly installed and maintained gutters could save you thousands of dollars moisture-related damage. By helping prevent mold and mildew, gutters can also protect your health.

Downspout connected to underground pipe
Courtesy of Dan Chiras

Project 54

Grading & Drainage

Moisture entering our homes through basements or crawl spaces causes many problems, among them damage to the structure and the growth of potentially unhealthy mold and mildew. Moisture can also damage stored items and furnishings. Mold can form within 48 hours after a finished basement floods.

Moisture problems can be reduced, sometimes eliminated, by fixing broken or leaky gutters—or installing gutters if there are none. However, if the gutters and downspouts of your home are in good shape, and you've installed downspout extenders or some other means to move water away from the foundation of your home—yet water is still accumulating, you probably have a drainage problem. Rather than flowing away from your home, water pools or is absorbed into the soil around the foundation, seeping into the basement. Pooling can often be fixed by grading—changing the slope of the land so water runs away from a house.

Professional home inspector Ronald W. Gower (Craftsman Home Inspection) finds grading problems on almost every home he inspects. "Most flooding," he notes in an article on **www.homeinspections-usa. com**, "will occur in the spring when the ground begins to thaw and spring rain arrives."

"A grade that pitches towards a home can direct water to the home," says Gower. "This can be critical during the winter when the ground is frozen and snow-covered. A heavy rain can quickly cause flooding next to a foundation wall and then leak into the basement."

Grading Your Property

New-home builders typically slope the soil around a home very slightly away from the foundation. This promotes natural drainage away from the house. If water is puddling around your home, chances are it wasn't graded properly, or someone has altered the slope over time. If so, regrade.

For proper drainage of grassy areas, you'll generally need to establish only a 2% to 5% slope away from the house. (A 2% slope declines 2 feet over 100 feet or 1 foot over 50 feet.) Some experts suggest a 5% slope for the first 10 feet to ensure proper drainage—that's a 6-inch drop over 10 feet. Others suggest a slightly

Go Green!

Plants growing too close to the foundation can cause moisture damage to your home. If you need to transplant young trees or shrubs to a new location, try to move them while they're dormant. Use a garden fork to dig a root ball extending to the plant's "drip line" (the tips of the branches) and get as much as you can of the root system. Replant right away, and water regularly until it's established.

greater slope of 1 inch per foot for the first 8 to 10 feet. Thereafter, the slope can decrease. Slopes of more than 4% or 5% may seem steep in many landscapes.

If only minor grading is required, you may be able to perform the work with a shovel. Identify the areas where water pools, then regrade the soil so that it slopes away from the house. You may want to remove the grass first, regrade, and, replace the sod.

For bigger jobs, you may need to rent a Bobcat or hire a professional with larger equipment. A professional landscaper will often use a transit (like surveyors use) to "shoot" the grade—to determine existing slope. They also use a transit to find the lowest spot on the property to which water can flow.

A professional may also be needed if the surrounding terrain slopes toward a home—for example, if your home is at the bottom of a hill. In such cases, grading alone won't work. Water flowing down the hillside, even underground, can accumulate in the soil around the house. To solve the problem, you may need to install drainage—both at grade level (near the surface) and a below-grade drain to move water away from the house. You can also divert water flowing down a hill away from your home by terracing the land.

One of my clients solved the problem of water accumulating in his backyard (which was at the base of a small hill) in two ways. He installed a larger gutter on his home. (The smaller gutter the builder had installed was overwhelmed by heavy rains and spilled water along the foundation.) He also installed a surface drain at the base of the hill to divert water away from his house.

Installing a French Drain

A French drain is a below-grade drain that consists of a perforated plastic or tile pipe buried at the bottom of the foundation in new construction. (See the illustration to the right.) The pipe is typically wrapped in a fabric that prevents sediment from clogging up the perforations. It is placed in a ditch, covered with crushed rock and then a filter fabric to prevent soil particles from clogging up the pores in the gravel and the holes in the pipe. The pipe around the base of the foundation's perimeter empties into another pipe that drains water away from the house.

While most French drains are installed during new construction, they can also be added to existing homes. In these cases, French drains are usually installed near the home, normally at the lowest point where water accumulates. They don't have to be installed at the base of the foundation as in new construction, nor do they have to be installed around the entire perimeter. In fact, French drains can be installed anywhere water tends to collect on a property—even some distance away from a home. This can help reduce pooling that may interfere with the landscaping or may simply be an annoyance.

French drains do not need to be very deep—only about 10 to 12 inches. Just be sure that you install them deep enough to ensure a downward slope of at least ¼ inch per foot. This may necessitate digging a little deeper.

To begin, observe where water pools. Then map out a strategy—how you'll drain water away from the house. Starting where the water accumulates and will enter the French drain, stake out a ditch, ending where the water will flow out. The ditch should be 10 to 24 inches deep and about 6 to 12 inches wide.

A Word to the Wise

If you're hoping to turn your unfinished basement into living space, be sure the measures you've completed to control moisture are effective *before* you start work. Be patient, too. It may take a full year, or even a few years, to fully test the effectiveness of the measures you've taken since the weather varies from year to year. Wait and see how your drainage system handles wet weather, such as heavy rains, freezes, and thaws.

Don't frame, insulate, and finish exterior basement walls if moisture is penetrating them. Insulation will become wet, fostering mold growth and unhealthy conditions. You'll have to tear the wall down and start over. You don't want to cover up a festering problem or invest time and money in a project that could be ruined.

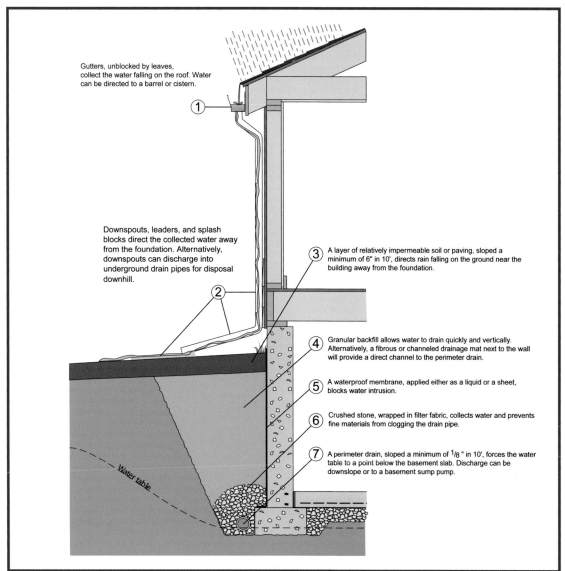

Gutters, unblocked by leaves, collect the water falling on the roof. Water can be directed to a barrel or cistern. ①

Downspouts, leaders, and splash blocks direct the collected water away from the foundation. Alternatively, downspouts can discharge into underground drain pipes for disposal downhill. ②

③ A layer of relatively impermeable soil or paving, sloped a minimum of 6" in 10', directs rain falling on the ground near the building away from the foundation.

④ Granular backfill allows water to drain quickly and vertically. Alternatively, a fibrous or channeled drainage mat next to the wall will provide a direct channel to the perimeter drain.

⑤ A waterproof membrane, applied either as a liquid or a sheet, blocks water intrusion.

⑥ Crushed stone, wrapped in filter fabric, collects water and prevents fine materials from clogging the drain pipe.

⑦ A perimeter drain, sloped a minimum of $1/8$" in 10', forces the water table to a point below the basement slab. Discharge can be downslope or to a basement sump pump.

Water table

A French drain can help prevent water from accumulating around the foundation.

Reprinted with permission from *How Your House Works,* by Charlie Wing

After the ditch is dug, be sure that it slopes properly. Grading is critical, so be sure that you maintain a 1% to 2% slope. You can use long lengths of 2 × 4s and a level to be sure the ditch continuously slopes away toward the drainage area.

Once you are satisfied that the bottom of the ditch slopes properly, place two inches of-inch clean (washed) crushed rock in the trench. Now lay the 4-inch perforated pipe in the ditch. Perforated pipe can be purchased at home improvement centers and hardware stores. When the pipe is in place, shovel in

more crushed rock, covering the pipe with about 2 inches of rock. Now fill the remainder of the ditch with soil, and replant grass.

Some installers line the bottom and sides of the trench with filter fabric before placing the rock in the bottom of the ditch. Once the pipe is installed and covered with crushed rock, the filter fabric is folded over the top of the rock to create a full barrier to silt. The ditch can then be filled with dirt.

Others recommend installing perforated pipe fitted with a filter fabric sock. Filter fabric is designed to stop the movement of the silt. Although this is standard procedure, some experts worry that if the fabric gets clogged with silt, water won't find its way into the pipe, negating your hard work.

While French drains can be fairly effective, installing one for an existing home can be a major project and may require a lot of hard work. If water pools all the way around the home, you will need to excavate around the entire perimeter of the foundation—though you may not need to dig to the bottom of the foundation. Intercepting the water 10 to 18 inches below the surface may suffice. The job will become more difficult, time-consuming, and costly if you encounter large rocks, plumbing lines, electrical lines, or tree roots as you dig—or if you must run the drain under a driveway or walkway.

You'll also need to establish a way to drain the water collected by the pipe away from the home. If you're in doubt about critical details or unable to handle the digging, hire a professional. Also, check with your building department for permits and specific requirements before any major grading or a French drain installation.

Improving Surface Drainage

Another, often more effective, way of preventing moisture from accumulating around a foundation is to intercept it even closer to the surface. One way to do this is to create an impervious surface around your home—for example, a sidewalk around the foundation. This is done around many urban homes with small lots. Be sure it slopes away from the foundation. (A 1% slope is usually advised.)

Another solution, a superficial peripheral drain or surface drain, is shown in the illustration on this page. In this technique, simply excavate a three-to-four-foot wide trench around the foundation, slope it away from the house very steeply, then line it with a couple of layers of 6 mil plastic. The trench only needs to be 12 inches or so deep. When finished, place some bark over the plastic to protect it from being cut by sharp edges of the crushed rock, which will fill the remainder of the trench.

Peripheral drains will capture water that is deposited around your house and divert it away from the foundation.

Why Not Install a Dehumidifier?

Instead of improving the grade or installing French or superficial drains, wouldn't it be easier to use a dehumidifier in your basement to reduce humidity and odor?

Dehumidifiers work and are certainly much simpler than other measures. Unfortunately, they are a stop-gap

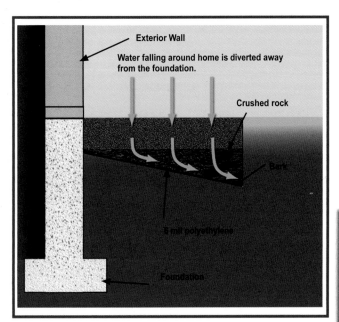

Superficial peripheral drains quickly remove water from rain or melting snow, keeping the foundation and basement drier.

Illustration by Anil Rao

Go Green!

To reduce your use of local water resources, install rain barrels on one or more downspouts of your home. Use the collected water for shrubs, new trees, and other landscaping (Project 61).

measure and, in some cases, their use may lead to other problems. In basements that have serious moisture problems, for example, a dehumidifier draws moisture into the basement from the outdoors more rapidly than would occur naturally, according to University of Minnesota's Extension Service. This can result in two problems—efflorescence and spalling of concrete.

Efflorescence is the buildup of minerals on the surface of the wall. The minerals leach out of a poured concrete or a concrete block foundation. Mineral crystals weaken the concrete and can cause the surface to flake off. This is known as spalling.

Sump Pumps & Interior Drainage Systems

If the measures described in this project don't stop the flow of water into your basement, you may have more serious problems. For example, the water table (the topmost level of the ground water) may be extremely high in your area, or water may be flowing into your basement from uphill sources. In such cases, you may want to consider hiring a professional who specializes in moisture problems. A sump pump may need to be installed, or you may want to look into an interior drainage system. (Check out WaterGuard® and other similar systems on the Internet.)

Always remember that the best way to approach moisture problems is prevention—eliminating, greatly reducing, or redirecting the source of the moisture. Don't let anyone talk you into an expensive basement drainage system if you haven't undertaken the basic preventive measures such as grading and installing gutters, downspouts, and downspout extenders. Start with the easiest and least expensive methods.

What Will It Cost?

There are many possible solutions to wet basements that involve foundation contractors and equipment. The estimate below provides a rough idea of the cost of this kind of work, performed by a professional excavation and grading company.

Cost Estimate: A full day for a crew and heavy equipment, performing a task such as installing a French drain system

Contractor's total, including materials, labor, and markup: **$1,475**

Costs are national averages and do not include sales tax.

Waterproof Membranes

One way to address basement moisture problems is to apply a waterproof membrane or coating on the inside basement walls. This is fairly inexpensive, compared to gutters and drainage systems, and does seem to work—at least for a while. The problem is that in most cases, the water you've prevented from entering your basement doesn't disappear. It is still accumulating in the soil around your house—right up against your foundation. It will most likely find another way in—for instance, through a tiny crack in the basement floor or wall. In addition, waterproofing coatings may deteriorate over time and eventually fail.

What Will You Save?

Any improvements that will keep moisture out of your home can save you untold amounts of money. Mold problems or structural damage caused by water can be unimaginably expensive to correct and can also put your health at risk. If and when you sell your home, moisture problems discovered in home inspections can become a huge obstacle—reducing your home's value and possibly preventing a sale. Evidence of previous moisture damage can even prevent insurance companies from providing coverage.

Project 55
Green Patios, Walkways & Driveways

Groundwater is a source of drinking water for many people worldwide. It also nourishes deep-rooted plants and trees. Replenished by rain and melting snow, groundwater has become an endangered resource, partly because of the impermeable materials used in new developments in and around cities and towns. Roofs, roadways and runways, parking lots, driveways, sidewalks, patios, and tennis courts prevent surface water from seeping into the ground.

What's more, these impervious surfaces often divert water into storm sewers and then into streams. The rush of water may result in costly and sometimes life-threatening floods. Surface runoff also carries toxic pollutants, such as oil and chemicals from paved roadways and parking lots, into rivers, lakes, and reservoirs, where it pollutes drinking water supplies and harms wildlife.

Another problem caused by so much paving is the buildup of heat in and around cities and towns. Asphalt and concrete absorb sunlight and convert it to heat. The buildup of heat around cities and towns is known as the "heat island" effect.

You can do your part in addressing these problems by installing permeable materials if you build a patio, walkway, parking space, or driveway. There are many attractive options that will permit water to drain into the ground. Some even help reduce heat accumulation around buildings.

What Are Your Options?

For patios or walkways, consider installing permeable concrete pavers. The pavers themselves are solid, but if they're spaced correctly, water drains between them. Pavers are placed over a bed of sand or gravel, which filters the water before it percolates into the soil. Permeable pavers come in several attractive styles and are made from concrete or cut stone.

When replacing or creating a new driveway or parking area, consider porous pavers or open-cell concrete blocks. These blocks are designed to support vehicles, but are sufficiently open to allow water to drain through them. The spaces are filled with gravel or sand. You can even grow grass or low ground cover in the open spaces, which helps reduce heat buildup.

Another product that can be used for driveways is pervious concrete. As its name implies, this is a highly

Open cell concrete blocks
Courtesy of the Ideal Concrete Block Company, Inc.

Permeable pavers help restore groundwater and reduce surface runoff, which can lead to flooding in urban and suburban areas.
Courtesy of UNI-GROUP USA

porous form of concrete. It is made from aggregate (small stones) and cement, which binds the aggregate together. However, unlike conventional concrete, pervious concrete contains very little, if any, sand. This results in a substantial void content, basically a lot of holes through which water can flow into the ground.

Pervious concrete is recommended by the U.S. Environmental Protection Agency and geotechnical engineers across the country to help manage stormwater runoff. To learn more, log onto **www.perviouspavement.org** or **www.paversearch.com** (Click on *Permeable Pavers*. Note that these websites use some different terminology.) Both sites contain a wealth of information on the subject and lots of pictures.

Two other intriguing options are Gravelpave[2] and Grasspave[2] made by Invisible Structures, Inc.

Gravelpave[2] is used for driveways, parking areas, and pathways. It is comprised of plastic rings in a grid with a porous geotextile fabric molded to it. The grid and fabric are anchored to a porous base of sand or gravel. The grid is then filled with decorative gravel, forming

Pervious concrete pavement
Courtesy of the Mississippi Concrete Industries Association & the Southeast Cement Assoc.

a driveway or path that allows water to drain easily into the soil beneath. Check the company's website for photos of numerous applications (**http://www.invisiblestructures.com**).

Grasspave^2 is also used for parking areas and driveways. The ring-and-grid structure rests on a sandy gravel base course. The voids are filled with "sharp sand" (sometimes called "builder's sand," it has jagged, not rounded-edges). The other ingredient, supplied by Invisible Structures, consists of a mixture of Hydrogrow polymer and fertilizer. Grass seed or sod is planted on this mixture. Like Gravelpave^2, this product allows for easy drainage, provides stability for driving or parking cars, and adds aesthetic value to a property. (The grass needs to be mowed from time to time.)

Grasspave^2 has a surprisingly high load-bearing capacity (it can even support fire trucks!)—and protects the root systems of grass from compaction, which would normally kill the plants. This product is used for main driveways, but it is not recommended for long-term (for more than a week or so) parking. It works well for rarely used driveways that lead to backyard storage sheds, workshops, or RVs and boats stored in backyards. It has been used successfully in large parking lots for sports arenas, like the Orange Bowl Stadium in Miami, Florida, that are used infrequently.

Installation

Installation of all porous pavers is pretty straightforward and can be carried out by relative novices. Professionals, of course, will often do a better job and complete the work more quickly, since they have experience and the right tools and equipment. Professionally installed driveways, walkways, patios, and other structures may also last longer, making them worth the extra initial investment.

All of the products described in this project require excavation by hand and/or machine. They all start with a 6- to 8-inch-deep bed of sand or gravel, carefully leveled. Before undertaking this project, you may want to read paver patio and sidewalk installation instructions in one of the home improvement books listed in the Resource Guide at the back of the book.

If you install a system of porous or pervious pavers or the Grasspave^2 or Gravelpave^2 yourself, be sure to read and study the manufacturer's specifications, and follow their instructions carefully. When in doubt, call in an expert for consultation or call the manufacturer and talk to their customer installation support staff.

Bear in mind that you may also need to obtain a building permit, so check with the local building department before you purchase materials.

What to Watch Out For

All of these products work well. However, porous or pervious concrete can clog with sediment. If you use this material, take precautions. For example, don't situate the surface down-slope from an erodible hillside—and be especially careful with construction

Gravelpave^2
Courtesy of Invisible Structures, Inc.

Go Green!

• To save water and create a healthier lawn, water longer but less frequently. A deep soaking promotes deep root growth so grass can better withstand dry spells.

• To reduce water consumption, water your lawn early in the morning or in the evening. This dramatically reduces evaporative losses that occur during the daylight hours and can cut your watering time and water bill by half!

vehicles when building a new home or remodeling. They can deposit a lot of mud on the pavement during construction.

*A Grasspave²
driveway*
Courtesy of Invisible Structures, Inc.

What Will It Cost?

Porous and permeable paving products cost more than standard paving materials, such as asphalt and concrete, but they can add value to your home. Permeable paving is a green feature—and pavers can give your home extra curb appeal—both of which contribute to value when you sell it.

Cost Estimate: Installation of a concrete paver walkway 30 feet long by 3 feet wide

Includes a 6-inch gravel base, 4-inch sand base, hand compaction and grading, and concrete patio blocks.

Cost for materials only: **$460**

Contractor's total, including materials, labor, and markup: **$1,050**

Alternate materials, per square foot installed:

Concrete pavers: **$11.50**

Gravel, 6" thick: **$.85**

Asphalt, 2.5" thick: **$1.45**

Concrete, 6" thick: **$5.85**

Crushed stone, 1" thick: **$.70**

Brick, 1-$^1/_2$" thick: **$11**

Paving stones, 2" thick: **$26.50**

Costs are national averages and do not include sales tax.

Project 56

Composite Decks & Porches

Decks and porches continue to be popular home improvements. They increase living space and provide a wonderful location to relax or socialize with family and friends. Conventional wood decks and porches, however, require frequent maintenance and repair. For example, many homeowners power-wash their decks every two to four years, and then treat the wood with chemical preservatives to prevent rotting. Both operations take a lot of time and expose workers and homeowners to potentially toxic chemicals.

If you're thinking about replacing your deck (or porch) or building a new one to improve your home's comfort, curb appeal, and resale value, consider using composite lumber made from recycled plastic and/or wood fiber.

Why Install a Composite Deck?

Composite deck lumber is durable and won't crack, twist, or warp like some wood deck materials. Composite wood is also highly resistant to water, mold, and mildew, and therefore won't swell when wet, or rot over time. Composite decking does not require painting or chemical preservatives. An occasional washing is all that's needed to restore its beauty.

Because it's so durable, composite lumber is also great for use around hot tubs and for porches—even boat docks. Because they resist insects, composites are ideally suited for areas where termites are a problem. Most manufacturers offer a limited 20- or 25-year warranty on their products.

Composite decking also resists staining from a backyard barbeque or environmental stains. Spills clean up easily. Although composite decking materials can be scratched and may experience some wear over time, these problems are minor. And you don't need to worry about burning your feet or getting splinters when walking around barefoot since composite decks are

Composite decks cost more, but outlast wood decks and require very little maintenance.

Courtesy of TimberTech®

Dock made from composite lumber
Courtesy of Trex Company, Inc.

cooler in hot summer sun than wooden decks and the material doesn't splinter.

Composite lumber made from recycled plastic and wood fiber offers many environmental advantages over conventional wood lumber. Its durability, for example, results in a substantial long-term reduction in material and energy use. (More durable deck materials require less frequent replacement.) Durability also leads to a reduction in landfill wastes from disposal of worn-out wood decks. Use of recycled materials in the manufacture of composite deck materials also diverts wood and plastic waste from landfills and helps create jobs in the burgeoning recycling industry. In most cases, making products from recycled materials also requires much less energy than manufacturing them from raw materials. Less energy means less pollution, cleaner air, and a healthier environment for all of

us—including the many species that share this planet with us. Although they cost more up-front, composite decks save money over the long haul by reducing maintenance, repair, and replacement costs.

What Are Your Options?

Composite deck lumber is made from one of four materials or combinations of materials:

- Recycled polyethylene plastic—typically milk jugs and/or recycled plastic bags
- Recycled plastic combined with recycled wood fiber
- Virgin polypropylene with recycled wood fiber
- Virgin wood and virgin plastic

In those products made from plastic and wood, the

plastics encapsulate the wood fibers, protecting them from moisture. The first three represent the best environmental choice because they include recycled materials.

Manufacturers produce 4- and 6-inch-wide planks in three thicknesses: 1-, 1.25-, and 2-inch. Composite boards typically come in 12-, 16-, and 20-foot lengths and are solid, hollow, or ribbed. Manufacturers offer planks with a brushed or simulated wood grain surface. Most products are fairly genuine in appearance, that is, they look like wood, although there are a few exceptions.

Many manufacturers sell all of the matching parts— posts, hand rails, top and bottom rails, and balusters— that you'll need to build a deck. Rails and posts are typically pre-routed to reduce installation time and errors. Some manufacturers also sell matching post caps, fascia, corner molding, risers (for steps), and boards to make benches, storage boxes, and planters. You may want to avoid posts and railings made from vinyl (polyvinyl chloride) for environmental reasons.

Composite decking is available at home improvement centers, lumberyards, and large building materials outlets and through green building material suppliers and local installers. Nearly a dozen manufacturers provide a wide range of products in various colors and textures.

Shop carefully, and read product literature available at building materials outlets or online at manufacturers' websites before purchasing. The variety of products makes it difficult for store personnel to keep track of the features of each product.

Installing a Deck Made from Composite Lumber

Building a deck, porch, or dock with composite lumber is similar to building with conventional wood deck materials because composite lumber can be cut, drilled, routed, and fastened with standard wood-working tools.

To build the substructure of your deck, you will need to purchase galvanized (rust-proof) framing hardware, such as post bases, joist hangers, and rafter connectors. They're used to connect various structural members of the deck.

Design your deck carefully with help from a professional if this is your first project. Many home improvement centers and lumberyards provide free deck plans, some offer mini-courses in deck building, and most sell books with detailed deck plans and sound construction advice. For a complicated deck, you may want to hire a professional to design and build the structure. Also, consult your building department to see if a permit is required—and your neighborhood association, if any, to see if it has any covenants in effect that restrict decks or stipulate their design or location.

Before you start building, it's a good idea to stake out the area where the deck will be, marking boundaries and the location of steps, if any. This will help you decide whether your plans will really work and may lead to minor modifications that improve the design, size, and layout.

Decks are typically built on a substructure supported by 4 x 4 or 6 x 6 wooden posts that rest on concrete piers. The posts, in turn, support horizontal beams. Joists are attached to (or rest on) the beams and to a ledger board on the house. Composite decking is then secured to the joists. The substructure of the deck is typically built from pressure-treated lumber.

Go Green!

If you like the taste of fresh, organic herbs and vegetables, but don't have garden space in your yard, consider a container garden on your deck. Growing your own produce helps reduce trips to the grocery store, and if more of us did it, there would be fewer pesticides used, and less energy required to deliver vegetables to stores. Pick up a book on container gardens or get some advice from your nursery.

When building a deck, care should be taken to ensure that the piers and post locations are spot-on and that the posts are plumb and securely attached to the piers. Joists should be level, straight, and square. Double-check all measurements. Be sure that the deck is firmly attached to the house via a ledger and that moisture will not accumulate at this juncture, as this will cause rotting. Head off this problem by flashing the joint between the ledger and the house or by installing spacers that bring the ledger away from the house—so water can drain away naturally.

Joist spacing for composite materials ranges from 12 to 24 inches, depending on the product and the application—with closer spacing in high-traffic areas. Decking can be laid in various patterns including horizontal, diagonal, or alternating diagonals, also known as herringbone (which requires joists to support it).

Stairs and railings provide access and safety. As a general rule, any deck 18 inches off the ground must have a railing for safety. Balusters provide an additional level of safety for small children and pets and are required by code. Be sure to check your local building code for design and construction requirements and follow them carefully.

Planks can be pre-drilled and screwed into joists. Several manufacturers provide mounting hardware that eliminates the need to pre-drill holes for deck screws, thus greatly reducing labor. It also eliminates screw heads from the deck surface and produces a more aesthetically pleasing and safer deck. Some fasteners also ensure proper spacing of boards so water can more readily drain from the surface.

Decks vary in their level of difficulty from simple to highly complex. If you're a beginner, you may want to hire a professional for all but the simplest decks. Even then, you'll want expert advice when planning and building a deck. If you have some construction experience and want to take this project on, you'll need an assistant or two.

What to Watch Out For

Because composite lumber expands and contracts as a result of changes in temperature, it's important to space the boards correctly. Follow manufacturer's recommendations.

When building stairs, get help if you've never done this type of work. Consistent vertical distance from tread to tread is essential for safety, as is placement of the railing and stringers (supports for risers). Be sure to check with your local building code for stair construction details.

What Will It Cost?

Composite wood products can be two to four times as expensive as pressure-treated decking. However, they are resistant to insects, stains, and moisture, won't crack or split like wood, and some come with long warranties. As a result, you'll save time and money in the long run on maintenance/refinishing and deck replacement.

Cost Estimate: Construction of a 10' x 16' deck using recycled plastic decking and trim

Cost for materials only: **$1,500**

Contractor's total, including materials, labor, and markup: **$3,400**

Alternate square foot cost for pressure-treated lumber: **$2.50**

Costs are national averages and do not include sales tax.

Project 57

Recycled Plastic/Composite Fencing

Fences have a lot of different uses. They define property boundaries; provide privacy and security; add beauty and value to a property; and help to contain children, pets, or livestock. Wood fences have been the top choice of homeowners and builders for many years, but they do have their drawbacks. Wood rots, cracks, and warps over time and requires periodic maintenance (painting, staining, or treatment with a wood preservative every few years) to ensure long life. Most exterior paints, stains, and wood preservatives have toxic ingredients that pose a health risk to whoever is applying them or exposed to them during a short period afterwards. If you're thinking about replacing a worn-out fence or installing a new one, consider installing a maintenance-free recycled plastic material.

Why Choose Plastic Fencing?

Many recycled plastic fence components are made from high-density polyethylene (HDPE), resulting in a durable and weather-resistant product that can withstand extremes of weather. It won't crack or split, even at temperatures well below zero. The material also won't splinter or warp over time and is resistant to insects, such as termites and carpenter ants. It also resists damage from water (and acids from animal waste), and will never rot like wood or rust like metal. Plastic fence posts can also be used with electric fences to contain horses and other livestock. They don't require installation of insulators. (Horses also reportedly don't chew—a problem referred to as cribbing—on plastic fences, like they do on wood fencing.)

Many plastic fence materials are made to look like wood. Moreover, recycled plastic fences don't fade—or fade only very slightly after years of exposure to the elements—

Recycled-content plastic fence is a durable and low maintenance option.

Courtesy of Master Mark Plastics

because the color is embedded in the plastic/composite material. Plastic fencing never needs painting, staining, or treatment with chemical preservatives. Another benefit to urban homeowners and business owners is that many types of paint used by graffiti "artists" won't adhere to the high-density polyethylene in recycled fence materials. Because recycled plastic fence products are so durable, most manufacturers offer a 20-year warranty.

Plastic fence also offers many environmental benefits. For one, it reduces the amount of trash sent to landfills since it has a long life, which reduces fence replacement. Recycled products also require less energy to fabricate than those made from virgin materials, and less energy use means less air pollution. Manufacturing materials from recycled plastics also helps expand a strong market for recycled wastes and creates jobs.

What Are Your Options?

Plastic fencing comes in many varieties, including picket, post and rail, and a standard six-foot privacy fence. Most manufacturers produce all of the components—that is, the posts, rails, and pickets—from recycled post-consumer plastic milk jugs. Some companies manufacture galvanized steel posts and rails coated with recycled plastic to match their recycled plastic pickets. (Steel posts and rails are more rigid than plastic materials. This eliminates the flexing that may occur with hollow plastic components.) Some companies produce preassembled panels (sections) that attach directly to the posts, which make it quicker and easier to install a fence.

One of the newest and greenest fences comes from Heartland BioComposites of Torrington, Wyoming. This fence is made from a combination of wheat straw from local producers and post-consumer high-density polyethylene (HDPE). According to the company, the raw materials include 50% to 60% straw, 35% to 45% recycled plastic, and less than 5% proprietary additives (described by the company as "non-hazardous and organic").

Manufacturers produce panels, posts, pickets, and rails in a variety of colors, including white, gray, brown, and black, and in a simulated wood grain surface. You can also buy individual pickets from some manufacturers and use them to replace worn-out or damaged ones in a fence.

Plastic fencing is available at building materials outlets, home improvement centers, green building material suppliers, and through local installers. You can find a wider selection online if you purchase directly from manufacturers. Be sure to read the product literature and installation instructions (from building materials outlets or on manufacturers' websites) before purchasing. It's a good idea to check the product out up-close before you buy. Ask for samples when buying online.

Installation

Recycled plastic fence can be cut, drilled, routed, and fastened with standard tools. The design, layout, and construction of plastic fences are similar to those for fencing made from conventional wood products.

Fence design is generally pretty straightforward. Posts are typically set anywhere from four to ten feet on center. If you're installing preassembled sections

Go Green!

• Bring your own reusable bags when you shop, but if you ever use plastic shopping bags, be sure to recycle them. Some grocery and discount stores have containers in their entryways for convenient recycling. Who knows, your discards may end up in a fence or deck someday!

• Remember to combine your errands when driving to save fuel, time, energy use, and pollution. Plan your trip in advance so you make a loop and avoid left turns and long lights where your car has to idle. It works. UPS plans all its delivery routes so that, to the extent possible, drivers make only right turns.

Recycled plastic fences are lasting and require little, if any, maintenance.

Courtesy of Heartland BioComposites

(panels), you'll need to set the posts accordingly—usually four or eight feet apart. Eight feet on center is most common.

Corner posts and posts on either side of gates (referred to as main posts) are typically set deeper than the rest of the posts (known as line posts). They're also set in concrete for greater strength. (The line posts can be dug into the soil.) When installing a fence, care should be taken to ensure that the posts are plumb. Temporary braces can be used to keep posts plumb before filling the holes. Use a level when filling a hole with soil or concrete. Be sure that the corners are square.

Once the posts are securely in place, the rails (the horizontal pieces that run from post to post) are attached. In post and rail fences, the rails fit into openings (mortises) in each post. In picket and privacy fences, the rails are screwed or nailed to the posts. Pickets are then screwed or nailed into the top and bottom rails, using a guide board to achieve equal

spacing between pickets. If the rails are metal, the retailer should provide self-tapping screws to attach pickets.

Refer to instructions provided by the manufacturer for details on this and other aspects of fence layout, design, and construction. Like many projects, this one varies in level of difficulty, based on the type of fence and conditions in your yard. If you're a beginner, you may want to hire an installer, especially if your soil is heavy clay, extremely rocky, your property is steep, or if the design is complicated. That said, a simple fence is not out of the reach of novice do-it yourselfers, if they study their options, design their fence based on professional advice, carefully lay out the project in advance, and follow installation guidelines. Intermediate and advanced-level do-it-yourselfers can design and build more complex fences, but will need some help from an assistant during the installation.

Gates are one of the trickiest aspects of fence-building. Check out the designs in home improvement books, or look at gates in your neighborhood and see what style you like. You'll need rails and pickets, but also cross-braces to make the gate sturdy. Or you can purchase one pre-made. If you build it yourself, be sure to install heavy-duty hinges.

What to Watch Out For

Before ordering materials, check with your local building department for zoning restrictions or permit requirements, as well as your neighborhood homeowner's association, if any, for possible covenants that could restrict the type, height, or color of fence you install. Also check your property survey (from documents you received when you bought your house or land) and make sure you're in agreement with your neighbors on where property boundaries are located. You don't want to install a fence only to find that it is on your neighbor's property or too close to it. I've seen it happen!

Before digging holes for fence posts, contact your local utility to find out if they need to flag the locations of buried gas and electric lines. Hitting either one can be dangerous and result in costly damage.

If your yard has a sprinkler system, you'll want to dig very carefully in any areas where piping or wiring may be buried. To correct the problem, the sprinkler service company will have to track it down with detection devices and dig up your landscaping—all of which can be time-consuming and costly.

Be very careful if you use a gas-powered auger for drilling post holes. They do make the job go much faster, but they are rather heavy and challenging to work with, especially in hard or rocky soil. (Be sure to wear work gloves, proper eye and ear protection, and steel-toed shoes, never leave the auger running when not in use—and get some good instruction before you start.)

When building on sloped property, take into account the slope when attaching the rails to the posts. Rails can run either parallel to the slope or can be stepped up by fence sections. You may also need to trim the bottom of pickets to accommodate the slope.

Shop carefully. Not all plastic is recycled. Check the product literature. Many building outlets sell PVC plastic fence that may crack in cold temperatures and is not generally as sturdy as HDPE fencing. I don't recommend PVC fences for this reason, and because of environmental reasons.

What Will It Cost?

Recycled wood/plastic composite fencing is significantly more expensive than basic pressure-treated wood fencing, but somewhat cost-competitive with high-end wood fence materials.

Cost Estimate:
Installation of 320 feet of recycled-plastic stockade fence

Cost for materials only: **$14,450**

Contractor's total, including materials, labor, and markup: **$20,900**

Flooring options, per square foot installed:

Alternate total cost for the same fence, made from pressure-treated wood: **$5,600**

Costs are national averages and do not include sales tax.

What Will You Save?

The savings from plastic composites come through the reduced need for maintenance (no painting or staining every few years as would be needed for wood fencing)—and the fence's longevity (many manufacturers offer lengthy warranties).

Project 58

Outdoor Solar Lighting

Project Rating:

Savings

🍁 🍁 🍁

Environmental Benefit

🍁 🍁 🍁

Level of Difficulty

🍁 🍁 🍁

It used to be that when you wanted to install outdoor path or accent lighting, you had a substantial job on your hands. First you'd have to dig a trench to run electrical wire from the house to the light fixtures. You'd then have to lay wire and connect the lights. When that was done, you'd have to drill a hole in the wall and run the electrical wire to the main service panel (breaker box) or connect to a nearby circuit.

For most people, this meant hiring an electrician at a cost of several hundred dollars, sometimes considerably more (for long driveways or walkways requiring multiple light fixtures). In addition to the cost of the added circuit, you'd need to install a step-down transformer to convert the 120-volt household current to 12-volt current to power the lights. These transformers run day and night, even when lights are off. Conventional path lights also typically require a timer, which uses full power day and night. Together, they add to your electric bill.

Fortunately, there's a cheaper and more environmentally friendly option: solar path lighting. Each light contains a small solar cell that converts sunlight into electricity. This is stored in a small battery that powers the lights at night.

All solar path lights contain a light sensor switch that turns the path lights on and off in response to ambient light levels. When the sun goes down, the lights come on. When the sun comes up the morning, the lights turn off. Some path lights even contain motion sensors that turn the light on when someone drives or walks up, or if a nearby door is opened.

Solar path lights are inexpensive and extremely easy to install. They're often mounted on stakes driven into the ground and require no wiring at all. For this reason, they're also easy to relocate.

Solar path lights provide safety and security while reducing our consumption of energy and lowering our impact on the environment. What's more, they're

Solar path lights installed along walkways are much easier to install than wired path lights and operate free of charge.

Courtesy of Malibu Lights

just one of several outdoor solar light products that homeowners can install without the aid of an electrician.

What Are Your Options?

Solar path lights are used to light walkways, steps, driveway perimeters, patios, and landscape features you'd like to highlight, such as boulders, ponds, trees, and shrubs. Solar path lights usually focus their light downward.

Solar path lights can be mounted in a variety of ways. Some are attached to stakes driven into the ground, as noted earlier. Others come with flange mounts and hanging hooks, which give you more flexibility in positioning them.

Some path lights have on-off switches, which enable you to store up electricity for long run times required for special events, such as an evening pool party or barbeque. Some path lights offer other features as well, for example, high-low power, colored lenses, timers, and photo and motion sensors.

Solar path lights work well in many applications, but have some limitations. For example, they may be difficult to install around a swimming pool bordered by concrete or brick because you can't stake them in the ground. For areas paved with brick or cast stone, you may want to check out solar-powered embedded path lighting such as Solarbricks, which are sold by a handful of companies, including Hotbeam, Solar Brick Light, Inc., and Solar Cynergy. (The company also offers stepping-stone lights.)

Solar path lights have been around for a long time, but have gained in popularity for several reasons. Once dim and not very reliable, solar lights now use bright LEDs instead of conventional filament bulbs.

Solar lights also produce brighter light in low temperatures because of their solid-state construction. In contrast, low-voltage outdoor lights and compact fluorescent lightbulbs operate less efficiently. Yet another advantage of LEDs is that they last a lot longer than standard incandescent lightbulbs and even CFLs. LED bulbs provide dependable service, usually for the life of the fixture.

The Latest in Embedded Path Lights

Solar Cynergy has developed a product that can be used for pools, parking areas, and walkways. Their path lights contain two to eight LEDs (light-emitting diodes) encased in polycarbonate resin and a small photovoltaic cell to produce electricity. The PV cell powers the lights for up to about 15 hours after an 8-hour charge in sunlight. Electricity is stored not in a battery, but rather a capacitor. The company offers a 10-year warranty, but the lights are said to last for more than 25 years, even on driveways or in areas with frequent rain.

Accent Lights

Solar accent lights are typically installed for aesthetic purposes. They produce a subtle glow designed to highlight, but not fully illuminate, objects or pathways. Even though accent lights are not as bright as path lights, they can promote safety, for example, by revealing tripping hazards in your yard.

Because they produce less light, accent lights tend to emit light longer than solar path lights after a full day's charge. They produce electricity even on cloudy days, thanks to their more efficient solar cells. Many accent lights also use amber LEDs, which give off a

Go Green!

If you need more light than solar fixtures can offer, consider using energy-efficient compact fluorescent lightbulbs (CFLs) in outdoor fixtures. They come in many types, including flood lamps and yellow bulbs that don't attract insects. If you leave a porch light on overnight, a CFL can save a lot of money. CFLs also last far longer than conventional bulbs. Purchase CFLs that are rated for outdoor use.

Embedded solar lights around swimming pool
Courtesy of Solar Cynergy

softer light than standard white LEDs and consume less electricity. Some accent lights even "flicker" to simulate candlelight.

Other Outdoor Solar Lighting

You may also want to consider solar post lamps and carriage-style lamps. These can be used in conjunction with path lights and accent lights. Carriage-style lamps can be mounted on the wall beside exterior doors, provided the area has a good solar exposure. Solar floodlights are the brightest of all outdoor solar lights, casting a beam of LED light on driveways, steps, walkways, patios, pools, hot tubs, decks—wherever you need them. They're powered by solar cells, and electricity is stored in an internal battery. Some LED lights are equipped with motion sensors. These are ideal for security lights.

Solar floodlights produce about as much light as a 40-watt incandescent bulb, which is still a fairly impressive beam. Floodlights are often mounted on walls next to entryways on garages, or on posts along driveways, or to light steps. The tiny solar panel may be mounted in a separate nearby location that ensures the best solar gain. The light, solar panel, and battery are connected by a wire.

Solar floodlights tend to be the most durable (well built) of all solar lights. Mounted off the ground, they're also less easily damaged than solar path lights.

Availability

Outdoor solar lights were once difficult to find, but they are now sold at home improvement centers, hardware stores, and even some large discount stores. They can also be purchased online through retailers that specialize in solar lighting or environmentally friendly products like Gaiam Real Goods (**www.realgoods.com**). To take a look at some of the options (including solar-lighted house numbers), log on to **www.solarilluminations.com**

Installation

Solar-powered outdoor lights are fairly inexpensive, especially when you take into account that you're getting the light you need with zero energy cost. They're also very easy to install. Read the directions and go for it!

What to Watch Out For

I've used a number of different solar path lights over the past ten years and have found that, as a rule, the pricier the product, the better. If you skimp, you'll probably be disappointed. The fixtures may work fine for a while, but give out early. I'd recommend lights with nickel metal hydride batteries over nickel cadmium batteries.

Go Green!

Avoid "light pollution"—night-time outdoor light that is too bright, glaring, or directed upward. It can disturb wildlife, such as the nesting and migrating of birds. Too much light can also be a problem for people—not only your neighbors, but any older adults, since their vision takes longer to readjust to changes in light levels.

Solar floodlights like this one are easy to install and won't run up your electric bill. Note the motion sensor at the bottom.

Courtesy of Dan Chiras

They last longer. If you can, buy units that allow you to replace the batteries when they wear out, so you don't have to toss the entire light fixture when the battery fails.

Before purchasing lights, be sure you have decent solar exposure. If your driveway is on the north side of your two-story home and is shaded most of the time, forget it. This is not the place for solar lighting. Solar lights need sunlight to work.

Ground-mounted solar path lights—or any ground-mounted path light, for that matter—are vulnerable. They can be damaged by snow plows or snow blowers. I lost a solar path light mounted along my front walkway after a rare 10-foot March snow storm. Two weeks later, when the snow had melted, the solar light was dead. Water may have shorted it out. If you're concerned about moisture, check out water-resistant solar lights at **www.etsenergy.com/shop** Here you'll even find floating pond lights.

Path lights may also be vulnerable to wind. There have been reports of damage in high-wind areas. Solar path lights are also susceptible to theft, since you need only pull them out of the ground to remove them.

What Will It Cost?

Reasonable-quality individual solar path lights start at about $10 and go up from there, based on design and materials. You can find pole lamps for about $70 and up, staked spotlights starting at about $25, and motion-sensor floodlights for about $100. Because solar path and landscape accent light fixtures are simply staked into the ground, there is no need for a professional for this part of the job.

Cost Estimate: Install solar lighting: 8 landscape and 2 motion-detecting light fixtures

If you hire an electrician, expect a minimal service call charge of about **$100.**

Cost for materials only: **$515**

Professional installation cost for low-voltage lighting (same number and style of fixtures, but conventional, not solar-powered): **$1,400**—including fixtures.

Costs are national averages and do not include sales tax.

What Will You Save?

Solar lights cost nothing to operate or to install, if you do it yourself. You'll save electricity over years and years of use, in addition to the up-front installation cost.

Project 59

Composting

One way you can green your yard—and help the environment—is to compost organic yard waste and fruit and vegetable scraps from the kitchen. Whether your compost operation is a simple pile of leaves and grass clippings in a corner of your yard, or a rotating, aerated plastic bin, the purpose is the same—to turn organic waste into a rich soil amendment.

Composting may not seem like a significant act, but it diverts a surprisingly huge amount of waste each year from landfills—some estimate 30% or more of our trash could be composted. Save your fruit and vegetable scraps—not to mention leaves and landscape trimmings—for a week to see how quickly it adds up! When combined with efforts of others in your community, composting can reduce municipal waste by millions of pounds and cubic feet each year. Composting also reduces the amount of energy required to haul waste to landfills. Less energy means less pollution, cleaner skies, and lower greenhouse gas emissions.

Because compost adds nutrients to soils, it also saves homeowners money by reducing our need to purchase fertilizers. Compost provides food for earthworms and other beneficial organisms that help keep plants healthy, according to the *Guide to Composting*. Strong, healthy plants yield more flowers, fruits, and vegetables.

Compost also improves soil texture, for instance, making clay soil drain more easily. This, in turn, reduces soil saturation that can suffocate roots, literally drowning them. Conversely, compost helps sandy or loamy soils retain moisture, which means less watering and healthier plants.

Growing vegetables and fruits in compost-amended garden soil helps us achieve greater self-sufficiency, reduces the energy needed to produce and transport food, reduces fertilizer and water use, and can become a healthy hobby. Composting may even save you money on trash hauling if your hauler charges based on volume.

What Are Your Options?

As noted earlier, composting can be as simple as piling leaves, grass clippings, twigs, and kitchen waste in an out-of-the-way place on your property. (See the table later in this project for more on what to compost. Keep in mind that grass clippings should usually be left on

Go Green!

If they don't have their own compost pile or bin, ask your neighbors to give you their leaves and grass clippings (provided they don't use pesticides on their lawns) for your compost pile.

your lawn so they decompose and nourish the soil.) You can also bury garden and kitchen waste as you generate it. If you have a large garden, for instance, you can dig a hole in a different spot every few days or once a week, and bury compostable material. In the soil, organic matter decomposes very quickly, releasing nutrients and improving its texture. In the summer, I've found that most organic materials decompose underground in about two weeks—having been consumed by bacteria and worms. Bury waste at least 8 inches deep so that animals can't smell it and won't dig up your garden.

A third option is to compost in a bin. Many homeowners construct bins using leftover building materials, such as concrete blocks, pieces of lumber, or extra wire fence from other projects. Concrete blocks

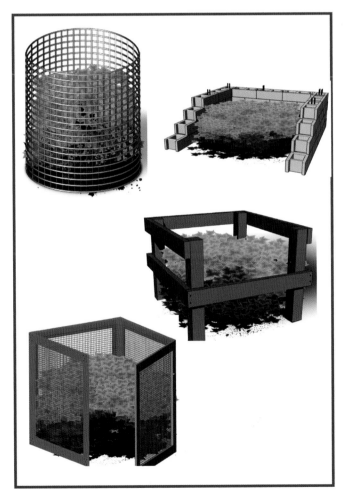

Homemade compost bins

Illustrations by Anil Rao

Make Your Own Mulch

Leaves, grass clippings, and chipped branches make good compost, but also make darn good mulch. So rather than composting these items, you may simply want to spread them around the base of trees or around flowers and vegetables in your garden. (Garden columns recommend shredding leaves and garden debris before spreading. If you use a no-fuel, non-polluting hand-crank shredder, so much the better.)

Mulch reduces water loss on hot summer days, so plants stay healthier, and you spend less time and money watering them. Mulch also controls weeds and, because the soil stays moist longer, it's easier to pull the weeds that do pop up. Mulch also keeps the soil cooler in summer, which is beneficial to plants (like clematis) that require cool root systems. Another benefit of mulch is that it helps keep the soil warmer in winter, which protects the roots of trees, shrubs, and perennials from freezing temperatures. Mulch breaks down over time, adding nutrients to the soil, too.

can be stacked to create a 6 foot × 6 foot or larger bin. Discarded wood pallets, laid on edge, can be used to create compost bins. Fence wire can also be fashioned into a cylinder or strung between posts sunk in the ground. Some people make their compost bins out of snow fence.

Many people build two or more compost bins. They fill one bin at a time and when it's full, start on the next bin. By the time the second bin is full, the compost in the first bin is often ready for use. Some of the finished compost can be mixed with the newer material to help accelerate its decomposition.

Compost bins are available from hardware stores or through online sources, such as **www.composters. com** Some local governments sell compost bins at a discounted rate to promote citywide composting, reduce landfill wastes, save energy, reduce pollution, and save money. Many cities and towns compost leaves, pruned branches, and grass clippings and/or sell or give away compost (and mulch) to residents.

Plastic compost bins are generally the most aesthetically appealing. (Look for recycled plastic ones.) Many have openings at the base that make it easy to remove the fully aged compost, while the newly added materials at the top continue to decompose. When purchasing a compost bin, go for durability. I have found out that thin plastic compost bins don't hold up very well, especially in cold climates where the plastic cracks.

Plastic compost bins like this one are attractive and easy to use.
Courtesy of Sceptor Corporation

Installing or Building a Compost Bin

Building your own compost bin is one of the easiest projects you can undertake. For instructions, check out one of the excellent books on composting at your local library or bookstore. I've found a wealth of information on this topic on the Internet as well. Simply search for "building a compost bin." Lowe's website offers instructions on building a two-bin composting system. The University of Missouri and the University of Wisconsin's Extension services provide instructions and a handy table that will help you select the method of composting that best suits your needs.

Compost bins consist of two basic types, *holding units* and *turning units*. A holding unit is a container or bin where yard and garden materials can be stored

until they have decomposed. Simply fill it up and let nature take its course. Depending on your climate, the material will convert to compost in six months to two years. The warmer and wetter the climate, the more quickly natural microorganisms act, and the faster organic wastes will turn to rich compost. A wire mesh, snow fence, or pallet bin work well as holding units. You'll need two or three bins, so that when one is filled, you can begin filling the next one. Holding bins are very easy to build and require the least amount of work. They are, however, the slowest way to compost.

If space is limited or you'd like to generate compost more quickly, you may want to consider a turning unit. They're basically the same as a holding unit except that you turn the compost with a shovel or potato fork from time to time to speed decomposition. You need to be able to access the compost to mix the materials. Turning compost aerates the pile, providing oxygen to microorganisms. It also mixes wetter ones at the base of the bin with drier materials at the top. Moisture also accelerates the process. It's essential for microbial degradation of compost.

Another type of turning unit is a rotating compost bin, a barrel horizontally mounted on a stand that can be turned with a hand crank. If you mix the materials regularly (every week or two), you can process a larger volume of organic waste in a relatively short time (usually 3 weeks to 6 months, depending on the climate). If you're considering a rotating bin, ask friends or members of a local garden club if they've tried one and what types they recommend.

Go Green!
Instead of toxic chemical weed-killers, try a vinegar-based product—or spray weeds with 10% or 20% regular vinegar.

Based on University of Nebraska Extension Service, Institute of Agricultural & Natural Resources

What to Watch Out For

If you read books or articles on composting, you'll see that some gurus have turned composting into an art. I've always opted for a simpler way—dumping organic material from my kitchen and yard in a pile or a plastic or wooden bin—or burying it directly in my garden. I add material to the pile or bins until they're full. I may turn a pile, but not often. I sprinkle water on my compost from time to time during hot, dry summers to accelerate decomposition. This simple technique has worked for me for many years.

To help promote water penetration into the compost pile, I create a pocket or indentation in the top of the pile. This helps hold the water so it can seep into the compost, rather than run off the sides. When the top material looks dry, I simply sprinkle the pile with a garden hose or a watering can. Don't get carried away with water. While it's important to keep organic matter moist, you don't want it too wet. "Beneficial organisms cannot survive in soggy conditions," according to **www.GardenGuides.com**

I also shovel some soil from my garden into my compost piles, which helps "seed" the pile with microorganisms that break down the organic matter.

The resulting compost is an organic-rich soil, rather than just a rich, organic mix to add to the soil.

Compost piles are used to process plant materials, including fruit and vegetable matter. Don't add bones, dairy products, or fats. They can attract visitors to your pile, including the neighbors' dogs and cats, and hungry coyotes, foxes, rats, and raccoons. That said, there are a few compostable items that few people ever think of adding, such as uncoated cardboard, egg cartons, and cotton clothing (so long as it is not heavily dyed). (I've composted many an old and tattered pair of work jeans.) Coffee grounds compost well, too. Eggshells can be composted, but they break down very slowly. I wouldn't add newspaper or conventionally printed papers, since the inks contain lead and other heavy metals. Bury items like cardboard and old clothes so the pile doesn't look like a trash dump.

Branches, logs, and twigs can also be added to compost piles, but if they're greater than 1/4 inch in diameter, it is a good idea to shred or chip them first. Otherwise, it will take a very long time for them to decompose.

Compost experts advise against the addition of pet feces. I used to bury my dog's and cat's droppings in a flower garden rather than my compost pile. Don't bury it too close to plants, though, as fresh droppings may "burn" plants' roots. You may want to bury small amounts at a time, or bury larger amounts in an out of the way corner, far from this year's plants.

The Fine Art of Composting

There is a great deal of discussion about achieving the ideal carbon to nitrogen ratio for composting. According to the University of Nebraska Extension Service's website, the ideal, for quick composting, is a 30:1 carbon-to-nitrogen ratio. The bottom line is that materials need to be balanced. You can achieve this balance by mixing an equal amount of either brown tree leaves with grass clippings or vegetable and fruit peelings.

Some people add activators, such as alfalfa meal, manure, bone meal, cottonseed meal, or blood meal, to their compost to accelerate decomposition of organic wastes. Another option is to add compost from a finished pile. If you feel the need for speed, sprinkle some activator on the pile or in your bin each time you add a layer of organic material.

Compost piles or bins can be located anywhere, but for best results you should place them in a semi-shaded area so they don't dry out in the summer. I place my bins or piles so they're exposed to sunlight in the fall, winter, and spring to accelerate decomposition. Compost near trees should be turned frequently so tree roots don't grow into them.

Indoor Composting

Some indoor composters are an option for year-round use for apartment and condo dwellers—folks with no yard to hold a conventional compost bin or pile. The compost can be used for house plants, container gardens, or balcony/patio potted plants.

Some indoor systems accept all kinds of food scraps, including meat and dairy products. In the Bokashi kitchen composter, for example, these materials are added to the bin and covered with a special microbial innoculate, a light fluffy sawdust-like mix containing bran, microorganisms, and other ingredients. The microorganisms break down food scraps without producing odor. An airtight lid ensures the proper environment for fermentation to occur. Unfortunately, the innoculate is rather expensive.

Another type of indoor composter is the NatureMill, a fully automatic machine that composts paper and biodegradable food, including meat, fish, and dairy products. In this high-tech device, moisture, airflow, temperature, and mixing are all controlled by a computer. This unit turns waste into compost in a few weeks, according to the manufacturer. An indicator light tells you when the compost is ready to be removed. It's best if you can talk to someone who is using one to see how well it works.

Worm Bins

Some people advocate worm bins for indoor composting. These containers, usually plastic, are kept in closets or other out-of-the-way places and used to grow worms that dine on coffee grounds and organic

kitchen wastes—vegetable matter only. The bins can be useful for true composting enthusiasts who live in cold climates where the outdoor composting season is interrupted by long winters.

Go Green!

Although gas-powered leaf blowers may seem like a fairly easy and convenient way to clean up your yard, these devices require fuel and are noisy and extremely polluting. It's much greener to rake leaves. While manufacturers are improving blower efficiency and emissions, you'll help the environment a lot more by raking your lawn the old-fashioned way. The same applies to mowing. Try a push mower if you have a small lawn.

What Will It Cost?

This project has no cost estimate because building a basic compost pile is an easy, low- or no-cost do-it-yourself job. All you need are some concrete blocks or a bit of lumber or fencing material. Obtain used block or lumber from demolition projects in your area or check with recycled building materials stores or online sources like **freecycle.org** Prefabricated metal, plastic, or wood compost bins start at about $25 and go up to a few hundred dollars, depending on their features.

What Will You Save?

Composting helps the environment by reducing the amount of waste hauled to the landfill—and the fuel needed to carry it there. It also benefits your plants and your budget by providing a free, all-natural fertilizer. Composting might even reduce your trash hauling costs, especially for bulk materials like grass clippings and leaves.

Project 60

Infiltration Basins for Trees & Shrubs

Trees and shrubs add beauty and value to our property, provide wildlife habitat, absorb carbon dioxide to help combat global warming, and provide shade to help cool our homes. To thrive, trees and shrubs need water. You can supply them with well or city water or rainwater captured from your roof (Project 61). However, one of the least expensive and most effective ways to water trees and shrubs is by creating infiltration basins, which naturally collect rainwater falling near trees and shrubs.

Infiltration basins are primarily useful for young trees. If a tree is healthy and mature, with an established root system, it shouldn't need one.

What Are Infiltration Basins?

Infiltration basins are shallow, level-bottomed depressions dug into the earth to collect snowmelt and rainwater that falls near shrubs and trees. The water they collect seeps into the ground, nourishing trees, shrubs, and flowers planted in the basins. Infiltration basins are typically covered with mulch to reduce water loss by evaporation, according to Brad Lancaster, author of *Rainwater Harvesting for Drylands and Beyond.* Leaves that fall from trees and shrubs collect in infiltration basins add more mulch. As any experienced gardener will tell you, mulch not only helps to keep moisture in the soil, it also slowly breaks down, adding nutrients to the soil.

Infiltration basins are highly effective in arid or semi-

arid regions that receive little natural rainfall. The moisture they collect can be supplemented by rainwater harvested from roofs (Project 63) or from "gray water" —water from washing machines, sinks (excluding the kitchen sink), tubs, and showers. Infiltration basins also work well in areas

Infiltration basin
Illustration by Anil Rao

that are blessed with more abundant rainfall. They work so well that there's often no need to provide any additional irrigation water.

Infiltration basins work much better than mounds of mulch applied at the base of newly planted trees, which tend to divert water away from plants. The basins are also more effective than circular berms or earth rings. While circular berms help retain irrigation water and capture some rainfall, they actually deflect water flowing over the ground above the berm away from the tree or shrub, thus reducing the harvested rainwater available to plants.

How to Create an Infiltration Basin

Infiltration basins are easy to make. For relatively young trees and shrubs on your property, dig a shallow circular depression 4 to 6 inches deep around the trunk, at least 1.5 times (and up to three times, depending on the height of the tree) the width of the plant's mature canopy (the distance the branches and foliage extend outward from the trunk). Be careful not

Circular berm around trees
Illustration by Anil Rao

Mulch piled around a tree deflects water.
Illustration by Anil Rao

to dig too deep, or you can expose and damage roots. Some trees have shallow root systems and are quite susceptible to damage.

When digging an infiltration basin, be sure to slope the edges so that water from melting snow or rain storms can flow into the basin from the surrounding landscape. This is especially important on the upslope side, which drains the most water into the basin. For safety, the basin's slopes should be gradual and stable, especially in high foot-traffic areas. You don't want people twisting and spraining their ankles if they step into the infiltration basin.

Also, the bottom of the infiltration basin should be level so that the water is evenly distributed within it. I use the soil removed when excavating a basin to build up the edges on the down-slope side, so I don't have to dig too deep.

For newly planted shrubs or trees, create the basin first, and then plant. If you're incorporating infiltration basins into a newly landscaped home, you may want to position them so that rainwater from gutters and downspouts naturally flows into the basins. You can also connect several basins to a downspout (and one another) so that water flows from the downspout into each basin in sequence. When watering this way, plant the trees and shrubs that need more water closest to the home. The overflow will go onto the next trees.(See Project 62 for advice on planting shade trees.)

What to Watch Out For

When planting trees in infiltration basins around your home, consider the seasonal benefits of shade, but don't plant trees too close to the house or septic system, if you have one, as roots can damage foundations and pipes. Remember, too, the closer a deciduous tree is to your house, the more likely its leaves will clog your gutters in the fall.

When selecting tree species, get advice from a trusted expert at a local nursery. Avoid trees and shrubs with invasive or shallow roots (as they can blow over easily in storms).

Also, bear in mind that mulch decomposes over time, so you'll need to periodically add another layer. You can purchase mulch at home and garden centers and sometimes get it from your town's public works department, if they offer it. Make your own mulch from leaves, grass clippings, and chipped limbs and branches from routine pruning.

You may need to expand infiltration basins as your trees or shrubs grow, if you think they could benefit from additional water—for example, if your region is suffering from drought, or the tree seems to be growing more slowly than normal.

Go Green!

• Work with neighbors to stockpile tree trimmings, and then rent a chipper to create mulch for the entire neighborhood.

• Repair leaks in hoses and turn them off at the faucet when they're not in use—just in case they spring a leak under pressure. Leaky hoses, like dripping faucets, can waste a lot of water. Look for hoses made out of reinforced recycled rubber.

• To clean driveways, walkways, and patios, use a broom. Don't hose them down. It wastes a huge amount of water.

What Will It Cost?

Digging infiltration basins costs nothing unless you buy mulch, provided you already own a shovel—and it requires only a little labor to dig the holes.

Infiltration basins can significantly reduce the need for city water, lowering your water bill, especially if you're planting a lot of new trees and shrubs around your home. Infiltration basins also reduce energy use in homes whose water is supplied by wells, as running water can cause the electric well pump to run for extended periods.

Because infiltration basins help concentrate water and deliver it to the roots of trees and shrubs, they also lead to healthier trees that are less likely to die or become susceptible to insects and disease. This saves money in replacement costs. Faster growth also results in more shade, which keeps your home cooler in the summer and saves on your energy bill.

Project 61

Rainwater Collection Barrels

More and more regions are suffering from devastating drought—even areas once blessed with an abundance of rainfall, such as the Pacific Northwest. When drought strikes, many communities impose water restrictions. To comply, homeowners must cut their water consumption, for example, by installing water-efficient toilets, showerheads, and faucets, and, most commonly, by reducing or eliminating lawn and garden watering.

Unfortunately, water restrictions can be hard on landscaping. While grasses often rebound from periodic drought, many trees and shrubs are not so resilient. They often die or become susceptible to insects and diseases. The damage can be quick and severe in some cases, though other species, like aspen, may not exhibit visible signs of stress for a year or two.

The loss of trees and shrubs can turn a beautiful home landscape into an eyesore, lower property value, reduce shade and raise cooling costs, and result in expensive replacements. Making matters worse, it may take many years—even decades—for replacement trees to reach the height of the older, established trees that once adorned the property.

If you're looking for a way to stave off the effects of drought and protect your landscaping, or you simply want a more economical, environmentally friendly way to water, consider installing a rainwater collection,

or catchment, system. Rain catchment is an ancient practice that dates back at least 2,000 years, when villagers in Thailand captured roof water for drinking, bathing, and other uses and stored it in clay containers.

Rain barrel beneath a downspout collects rainwater for use in watering gardens, trees, and shrubs.

Courtesy of Gardener's Supply

Rainwater collection helps us protect our investment in landscaping and also eases pressure on municipal water supplies, and on groundwater in homes supplied by wells. It leaves more water in streams, rivers, and lakes for fish and other wildlife. It also helps reduce surface runoff in urban and suburban areas. (Runoff from roots can lead to flooding and can pollute nearby water sources with chemicals washed from the urban/suburban landscape and streets.)

Besides helping to protect natural water sources, harvesting rainwater also saves money. How much you save depends on the size of your roof and the amount of rainfall you capture and use.

Plants love rainwater, too, as it is naturally soft (it contains no calcium or potentially harmful minerals). Rainwater is also free of chlorine or fluoride, chemicals added to municipal water supplies to kill potentially harmful microorganisms and to harden teeth, respectively.

Rainwater collected off the roof may not be drinkable without filtration, but it is usually clean enough for plants. Metal roofs generally produce cleaner water than composite shingle roofs, although the latter can still be used for plant watering.

What Are Your Options?

Rainwater can be collected easily from roofs, provided they're equipped with gutters and downspouts—which are a good idea anyway, to prevent moisture from pooling next to your home's foundation. The simplest rainwater catchment systems consist of one or two 50- to 80-gallon rain barrels. A rain diverter that feeds water into the barrels is attached to the downspout.

Rain barrels come in many shapes, sizes, colors, and materials. They can be purchased online or through local garden centers. You can even make your own rain collection system from used barrels—for example, large pickle barrels salvaged from a supplier—or clean steel drums (although plastic won't rust).

How Much Water Can You Collect from Your Roof?

I have two rain collection systems on my house—a very large underground cistern (tank) that holds 5,000 gallons of water and another smaller system, consisting of two 75-gallon plastic barrels that I purchased online from Gardener's Supply. The second system is attached to a section of the roof that's separate from my main collection system. I'm constantly amazed at the amount of rainwater my systems collect—even during drought years! The two 75-gallon barrels, for instance, provide a large portion of my garden's needs each year, and also enough water for a half dozen trees I recently planted—and we only receive about 20 inches of precipitation per year. What's amazing is this water supply comes from a section of roof that is just 12-feet x 20-feet!

As a general rule, every inch of rain that falls on your roof yields about 0.6 gallons of water per square foot of roof. If your roof covers 1,000 square feet, you will collect about 600 gallons of rainwater for each inch of rain. If it rains 20 inches a year in your area, your roof will collect 12,000 gallons a year.

Go Green!

If a tree dies on your property, call around to see if there's anyone who will salvage the lumber and put it to good use—for example, to build furniture or cabinetry or even as firewood. At the very least, be sure the tree is chipped and the wood chips are used as mulch. Consult with a local tree nursery if the tree was infested with carpenter ants, termites, or a fungal disease for advice on the best way to recycle the tree.

Installing Rain Barrels & Diverters

Installing a rain barrel is a pretty simple job. First, locate downspouts that would be suitable for collection (those closest to the garden, for instance). When you have several options, choose the downspout that drains the largest roof area to collect the most water. Find or create a level spot next to a downspout. (You may need to level a spot with a shovel.) Look for an area that's free of shrubbery so you can access the rain barrel without getting scratched. The barrel can be set on the ground or placed on concrete blocks or on a wooden pallet. (Raising the barrel may aid in filling buckets from the spigot near the bottom of the barrel.)

Some rain barrels can be positioned directly below the downspout. To do so, you'll need to cut the downspout and attach an angled segment of pipe so water flows directly into the rain barrel.

You can also connect a rain barrel to a downspout using a downspout diverter. These devices fit into the downspout and deliver water (that would normally flow through the downspout onto your lawn) into the rain barrel. (One of the easiest-to-install diverters, shown on the next page, is produced by the nonprofit group, Sustain Dane in Madison, Wisconsin.) You'll need a hacksaw to cut through the downspout to install the diverter.

When the diverter is installed and secured to the wall (they're often screwed into the siding for stability), connect the hose from the diverter to the rain barrel.

Rain barrels should be equipped with overflow protection, a hose that drains the barrel if it overfills. Be sure to attach this hose and drain the barrel as far away from the foundation as possible.

If you live in an area that gets a lot of rain, or if you would like to collect a lot of water, you may want to install two rain barrels side by side. A second rain barrel is filled by the overflow from the first one. To install two barrels, you'll need a linking kit—a piece of hose that connects the two. Once the first barrel fills, surplus water flows into the second one. Be sure to install an overflow protection hose on the second barrel. You may also want to install a rain barrel or two at each downspout to capture more water.

Rain barrel mounted below downspout with overflow hose

Courtesy of Clean Air Gardening

Go Green!

Eliminate standing water on your property to protect against mosquitoes. Be sure rain barrels are covered with wire mesh or a solid lid, and empty trays beneath flower pots and other containers that may hold water after it rains.

Sustain Dane diverter delivers water from the downspout to the rain barrel.

Courtesy of Sustain Dane

Let's suppose your home measures 30 feet by 40 feet. The overhangs extend out two feet. To determine the square footage, multiply 32 by 42. The result is 1,344 square feet. It doesn't matter whether you live in a one-, two-, or three-story home, the square footage of the roof's rain catchment area is the same. To calculate the amount of water you can collect off a roof, multiply the square footage by annual rainfall in inches by 0.6 gallons of water per inch of rainfall per square foot of roof area. If you live in an area with 20 inches of rain per year, and your roof area covers 1,344 square feet, you could collect 16,128 gallons (1,344 × 20 × 0.6), provided your gutters don't leak and the water falling on the roof does not overflow the gutters during a downpour. To determine the average rainfall in your region, log on to: **http://countrystudies.us/united-states/weather**

Rain falling on a roof picks up dirt and other contaminants, including bird droppings and leaves. Although it won't hurt plants, you don't want to drink this water without filtration and treatment.

While most roofs work well for rain harvesting, some do not. If your roof is old and covered with asbestos shingles or treated cedar shingles, rainwater harvesting is probably not a good idea. Asbestos and chemicals used to treat cedar shingles will contaminate the water. And tar and gravel roofs found on older apartment complexes are not suitable because they leach toxic chemicals into the rainwater.

What to Watch Out For

Many people miscalculate the square footage of their roof by climbing up on the roof and measuring the length and width of the structure. Because roofs are pitched, this gives a false number. The catchment surface is smaller than the actual square footage of the roof.

To calculate the square footage of the roof, start by calculating the total square feet of the footprint of your home by measuring the length and width of the house along the outside walls. Then add the extension of your eaves—that is, how far the roof protrudes beyond the outside walls. This gives the total square footage of rain catchment area.

Go Green!

Mulch shrubs, flowers, vegetables, and trees to reduce water loss through bare topsoil. Mulch reduces the amount of water you need to apply and helps to maintain constant soil moisture levels—which results in healthier plants.

Rainwater harvesting is also not recommended if gutters are soldered with lead or if lead-based paints were used on them. You don't want to put lead into the soil around your plants, especially vegetables and fruit trees. Fortunately, most newer homes have seamless aluminum or plastic gutters, which work fine for rainwater catchment systems. Rainwater harvesting may not be a good idea in highly polluted cities or regions downwind from chemical plants.

Remember, too, that rain barrels may pose a drowning risk to young children and animals, including pets and wildlife. Be sure barrels are covered and inaccessible to them. Spruce Creek's Rainsaver, for example, is a one-piece 54-gallon rain barrel with a solid top designed to prevent access to the barrel. This rain barrel is also fully screened and therefore mosquito-proof. I strongly recommend screened coverings on all rain barrels to keep leaves, needles from coniferous trees, and, more important, insects like mosquitoes out of the water. Mosquitoes are not only annoying, but may carry viruses like the sometimes deadly West Nile Virus and encephalitis.

Don't let water sit in a rain barrel for extended periods. Check with local health authorities (your state health department) for recommendations on water storage.

If you're making your own rain barrel, don't use old oil drums or containers that contained hazardous chemicals. Barrels should be rated as food-grade containers. Plastic trash cans work, provided they're heavy-duty ones.

If it freezes in your area, you may want to drain the barrel before winter sets in to prevent possible damage caused by water in the barrel freezing and thawing. You may also want to store rain barrels in a garage or shed in the winter to reduce exposure to ultraviolet light and to keep them clean.

What Will It Cost?

Most rain barrels are fairly inexpensive. I've found an abundance of manufacturers and models on the Internet. They range in price from about $40 all the way up to $250, depending on size, materials, and special features. If you make your own from a trash or other barrel, you'll need to add the cost for the spigot and hardware, as well as an overflow valve. (Make sure your spigot has appropriate threads on both ends so that you can attach the overflow hose.) You can also check with your local water department. They may offer rain barrels to customers at a very low rate.

What Will You Save?

Use the calculations from this project to project your potential water savings based on the average annual (or growing season) rainfall in your area. Keep in mind the extra savings in plant replacement costs if you're able to keep your landscape alive and well with water from your rain barrel during local watering bans.

Project 62

Energy-Efficient Landscaping

Project Rating:

Savings
🍁 🍁 🍁

Environmental Benefit
🍁 🍁 🍁

Health/Comfort
🍁 🍁 🍁

Level of Difficulty
🍁 🍁 🍁

If you want to reduce the amount of energy needed to heat or cool your home, consider planting a tree or two. Strategically located trees and shrubs provide shade in the summer and protect against wind in the winter—both of which can have a huge impact on your home's energy bills and comfort levels. One study showed that three trees planted near light-colored houses in a residential neighborhood in Phoenix could cut cooling costs by 18%, saving homeowners hundreds of dollars per year. Even greater savings were achieved by planting trees around homes in Sacramento and Los Angeles—where a study showed reductions of 34% and 44%, respectively, in cooling costs.

Besides saving energy, trees help combat global warming. They achieve this important goal two ways:

First, by reducing our demand for energy. This helps reduce the emissions of the greenhouse gas carbon dioxide from power plants. Second, trees absorb carbon dioxide, helping reduce atmospheric concentrations of this gas.

And of course, trees improve the appearance and the value of a home, provide soil nutrients if you compost their leaves, and attract birds and other wildlife—an important benefit to those who are fond of nature's remarkable creatures.

This house has dense trees planted on the north and west sides to help block winter winds and provide some summer shade.

Courtesy of Green Vista Landscaping - Zerkle Residence

Landscaping to Save Energy

Trees and shrubs help us stay cooler in the summer by shading our homes—that is, by reducing the amount of sunlight that strikes the exterior walls and roof. Shading the area *around* our homes, such as sidewalks, driveways, decks, and patios, also helps us stay cooler in the summer by reducing the temperature of the air surrounding our homes. Concrete, stone, or brick materials used for walkways, patios, and driveways collect heat from sunlight during the day—and retain it well into the evening. This makes our homes hotter during the day and the night, and increases our use of mechanical cooling systems. Since shading lowers the air temperature around our homes, homeowners may be able to open windows at night to cool their homes or use more energy-efficient cooling devices like ceiling fans or whole-house fans, rather than energy-intensive air conditioning or evaporative coolers.

Trees and shrubs also cool our homes by a process known as evaporative cooling, which takes place whenever water evaporates from a surface. Perspiration evaporating from our skin, for instance, cools us down on hot summer days. Water evaporating from the leaves of trees and shrubs has the same effect.

As a result of shading and evaporative cooling, a single mature tree can have the cooling effect of five 10,000-Btu air conditioners. And it does this without drawing any energy or creating a single ounce of air pollution!

While it's pretty easy to see how trees and shrubs help us stay cool in the summer, how do they help us stay warm in the winter? Strategically placed trees and shrubs can block cold winter winds, which strip heat from exterior walls and windows that blow across a home. Winter winds also penetrate leaky homes through cracks in the building envelope (Project 12). Cold air blowing through a home robs us of high-priced heat.

How to Get Started

Tree-planting for energy efficiency can vary considerably from one climate zone to the next. Let's explore options by zone.

Cool Northern Climates

In northern climates, summers are fairly cool, so the main challenge is staying warm during the long, cold winters. One way to achieve this goal is to protect your home from winter winds. Wind robs heat from our houses in exposed rural lansdscapes, but also in cities and towns where homes are closer together and winds tend to be milder. In the North, evergreen trees (dense foliage pine and spruce trees) work well as a barrier between your home and cold winter winds.

Before you plant trees, determine which direction the predominant winter winds come from. In most locations, they blow in from the northwest. Call your local weather channel to determine the predominant wind patterns.

If you live in an open area in the country on wind-swept property, you may need to plant several rows of trees to create a thick wind break to the north and west of your home. For advice, contact your County Extension agent.

Walls, fences, or earth berms (mounds of soil) also help block winds and can be used in conjunction with trees or by themselves. If snow drifts across your driveway, walkway, front door, or in other undesirable locations,

The climatic region in which you live affects the landscaping strategies you use.

BA-A124001

U.S. climatic region map

U.S. Department of Energy, www.eere.energy.gov

plant evergreen and deciduous shrubs upwind from them to trap the snow. Even shrubs that lose their leaves in the winter slow the wind and cause much of the snow to deposit immediately downwind of them, preventing drifting.

While evergreens work well on the north and west side of a home, they're not generally recommended on the south side because they can block the low-angled winter sun from entering south-facing windows and warming your home. Even deciduous trees—trees that lose their leaves in the fall—can block 25% to 50% of winter sun. (Their trunks and branches reduce wintertime solar gain.)

Temperate Climates

In temperate climates, heating and cooling are equally important. In those areas, planting evergreen trees to block the prevailing winter winds is advisable. As in cooler northern climates, you shouldn't plant evergreen or deciduous trees on the south side of your home. Doing so will rob you of a good source of winter heat. If your home has a lot of trees on the south side, you may want to trim or even remove the lower branches to allow the low-angled winter sun to enter facing windows.

You can also plant shrubs or bushes near your home—at least a foot away from the house walls, depending on the type of plant and how large it will grow. Shrubs and bushes create "dead air" spaces that can help reduce heat loss. You don't want to plant them too close to the house since moisture (from watering) and their roots can damage your foundation. Shrubs right up against a house can also lead to mold and mildew and hamper repair and maintenance, such as gutter cleaning and painting.

To cool your home in the summer, plant deciduous shade trees on the north, east, and west sides of your home, again, not too close. Trees will shade the house and help cool backyard decks, patios, and driveways. Shade trees also provide evaporative cooling. (Arborists recommend planting trees far enough away so that branches and limbs will not contact the house, as they can damage roofing or scrape paint off in a high wind or an ice or snowstorm, not to mention clogging gutters and providing a path for destructive insects to enter.)

If you want trees on the south side of your home, plant only deciduous trees and then only high-crowned species—that is, trees with tall trunks and high foliage—to maximize heat gain in the winter. If you're considering installing a solar hot water or solar electric system on your roof (Projects 35 and 42), be sure your trees will not shade it.

When selecting new trees, ask local arborists or knowledgeable employees at tree nurseries for their recommendations for high-crowned trees. Also ask about their mature height and find out which species have the least invasive root systems—so you can protect your foundation and sewer and water pipes. Check out species that are native to your area, which generally require the least water and fertilizer and are the most resistant to insect damage and disease.

Hot, Humid Climates

In these climates, cooling is the main challenge—and a huge one at that! In these regions, deciduous trees can be planted on all four sides of a home to provide shade and evaporative cooling. It's a good idea to trim trees as they grow, removing lower branches, to help ensure adequate air flow around and through your home. The moving air will make your home feel cooler.

Go Green!

• When planting trees and shrubs, select species that are native to your local area. Trees help cool homes in the summer and reduce heat loss in the winter, and they also help to lower atmospheric carbon dioxide levels.

• Help make your community healthier, cooler, and more beautiful by supporting groups like the Arbor Day Foundation that plant and provide free trees. Encourage schools, local organizations, and local government to plant trees, too!

It's also a good idea to plant shrubs and trees to shade patios, decks, and driveways. Because the late-day and, to a lesser extent, the early morning sun can result in substantial overheating, you want to plant trees on all sides of your home.

Hot, Arid Climates

In hot, arid climates, like the desert southwest, where daytime temperatures often soar into the low 100s for several months in a row, staying cool can be a big challenge. Shading helps enormously. As in temperate climates and hot, humid climates, plant trees and shrubs to shade roofs, walls, and windows. Select species that tolerate hot, dry air and sun and require the least amount of water. Also, shade your central air conditioner's condenser (the part that sits outside). Don't block the air flow, but be sure it is shaded. According to a study conducted by the Florida Solar Energy Center (FSEC), shading can increase air conditioner efficiency by 10%.

Plant trees and shrubs that will not block cooling breezes. Bear in mind that trellises and vegetation planted close to the house walls can trap heat, so they are not advised. Allowing room for breezes to blow into and around your home is especially important for nighttime cooling in arid climates, where the evening air is considerably cooler than daytime temperatures (thanks to low atmospheric humidity).

What to Watch Out For

When planting trees, be sure to follow directions from the nursery carefully. To benefit more quickly from their cooling effect, plant fast-growing species. Ask your nursery for recommendations. In my experience, I've also found that larger (and more expensive) trees from nurseries have a better chance of surviving the first few years.

Larger trees are also more costly to plant because heavy equipment will probably need to be brought in to dig the hole and lift the tree into it.

The first few months and years of a tree's life in its new location are also the most precarious. Be sure to water newly planted trees as instructed by the nursery and continue watering for a couple of years, especially during dry, hot summer weather. To supply water, you can collect rainwater from the roof of your home, garage, and shed and store it in rain barrels (Project 61). Be sure to mulch around trees, too. Apply it evenly, though, not in mounds that slope away from the tree and drain water away. Mulch holds moisture in the ground, ensuring a steady supply to roots. Ask your nursery for instructions on the correct amount of mulch. This is crucial, as too thick a layer can be very damaging to the tree's health. Also consider infiltration basins (Project 60).

One experienced arborist I talked with suggested when planting trees and shrubs that you "roughen" the edge of the hole. Don't leave a smooth vertical surface. This, he said, would allow the roots that grow out laterally from the plant just beneath the surface to penetrate the soil more easily.

When you plant a tree or shrub, you may also want to use a growth supplement containing beneficial mycorrhizal fungi (pronounced my-core-rise-el). (The word "mycorrhiza" means "fungus root.") According to the Iowa State University Extension service, these beneficial fungi attach to plant roots and help the roots

Go Green!

- To help control mosquitoes and other insects, install a bat house on your garage, shed, or a nearby structure. Bats love mosquitoes, and one bat can devour as many as 1,000 of these troublesome pests in a single evening!

- If you live in the desert, before you invest in an air conditioner, be sure to make your home as energy-efficient as possible. Try cooling your home using cool nighttime air (by opening the windows or running a whole-house fan and ceiling fans). If that's not enough, consider an evaporative cooler rather than an air conditioner (Project 25). These coolers are very effective and use much less energy.

absorb minerals (most notably, phosphorus) from the soil. The Extension Service notes that, according to scientists' estimates, 95% of plants have mycorrhizal fungi of some sort associated with their roots. By helping plants take up nutrients, the fungi improve the plants' ability to survive environmental stresses.

If you're thinking of planting a tree in the strip along the street, you may need a permit from your town or city. They may want to know the type of tree and give you instructions for planting, such as distance from the street, utility lines, and light posts. Some types of trees are prohibited in some cities because of characteristics like aggressive roots or brittle wood that easily breaks in high wind. Check with your utility company about buried water, electric, gas, or sewer lines before you dig!

Select a smaller-scale tree if you must plant it underneath a power line. Also consider the life span of a tree. Some smaller trees may live only 15 to 20 years. And think about the effects of shading and leaf-dropping on your neighbors' property.

Depending on conditions in your yard and the size and type of your new tree, staking may be helpful to offer support until the roots become established. At that point, support wires must be removed so they won't cut into the trunk and kill the tree.

Deciduous trees on the south side of your house help keep it cooler in summer and, when the leaves fall, warmer in winter.

Photo by Jessica deMartin

What Will It Cost?

The cost of energy-efficient landscaping could be nothing at all—if you obtain free trees from your town government or an organization like the Arbor Day Foundation and plant them yourself—and if you have a supply of mulch available. Free trees are likely to be small seedlings though, so if you want to see an effect on your home's interior temperature and energy bills in the near future, you might want to invest in larger trees. Prices range widely, depending on the species, local availability, and individual nurseries' labor costs for planting. In a few towns and cities, the local public works department will plant trees at no cost in front of or alongside your house in the strip between the sidewalk and the street.

Cost Estimate: Delivery and installation of trees and shrubs

Includes excavation of holes for planting, mixing and backfilling soil by hand, planting the trees and shrubs, and applying bark mulch, 3 inches deep. Plants include a bagged and burlapped 4'–5' Norway Spruce and an American Arborvitae, a 5-gallon container rhododendron, a common lilac, and a 2½"–3" caliper (trunk) Norway Maple.

Cost for materials only: **$390**

Contractor's total, including materials, labor, and markup: **$520**

Costs are national averages and do not include sales tax.

What Will You Save?

Depending on how effectively you choose your trees and their locations, you could achieve savings of 10% to 45% on your heating and cooling bills. It all depends on where you live, how intense the sun is, and the effect of wind in your area.

Project 63

Drip Irrigation System

Watering gardens, shrubs, and trees can take a lot of time out of your busy schedule if you do it by hand with a hose. But it also consumes a huge amount of water. About 30% of a typical (family of four) household's total water use is devoted to outdoor activities, and at least half of that goes toward watering. (The rest is used for swimming pools, washing cars, "sweeping" driveways, etc.) Some water use experts indicate that half of the water applied to lawns is wasted as a result of evaporation, over-watering, or run-off. To save time, money, and water, an increasingly precious resource, consider installing a drip irrigation system.

Drip irrigation systems deliver water directly to plants, with minimal waste from evaporation and over-spray. They use a fraction of the water of sprinklers or hoses to do the same job. Reducing water use can save a substantial amount of money on water and sewer bills and helps reduce our demand on local water sources. Using less water also reduces the use of energy and toxic chemicals (notably chlorine) required to deliver "potable" or clean, drinkable water to our homes—water that is then used outdoors to irrigate our yards.

Properly installed drip irrigation systems ensure the right amount of water reaches the roots of plants. This helps reduce fungal diseases, such as powdery mildew and black spot, in humid climates by minimizing water accumulation on a plant's leaves. Drip irrigation systems also save a considerable amount of time for those of us who hand-water or water with conventional sprinklers that have to be moved around the yard.

What Are Your Options?

Drip irrigation systems range in complexity. The simplest is a garden hose that runs from an outdoor spigot to a garden or shrub bed. The hose is attached to a porous rubber soaker hose. The soaker hose runs along rows of garden plants. Water oozes out of holes in the hose, seeping into the ground, supplying the roots of plants.

Soaker hoses can be purchased at home improvement centers, hardware stores, garden centers, and large discount stores. They're usually made from recycled rubber. They are installed at the faucet and connected

Go Green!

To save water, mulch flower beds, vegetable gardens, shrubs, and trees. Water early in the morning or in the evening to reduce evaporation. Less frequent, deep watering is better than more frequent, shallow watering. It promotes deeper root growth that helps plants withstand dry conditions.

to two or more garden hoses (with Y or multiple connectors) to water different zones simultaneously.

To automate a drip irrigation system, consider installing a battery-powered timer. Timers are installed at the spigot and can be set to water at a set time and for a certain number of minutes every two or three days—or however often you need to ensure an adequate supply of water. (Be sure that you comply with local watering restrictions, if any, in your area.) Timers are convenient and enable us to leave for vacation confident that our plants will be watered in our absence.

Slightly more sophisticated irrigation systems consist of a garden hose that runs to a main feeder line, smaller-diameter black plastic tubing. It delivers water to even smaller solid plastic tubes. They are connected, in turn, to small porous rubber tubes that run down rows in gardens, delivering water to plants. Plastic couplers and T-fittings allow you to customize the system to ensure that water is delivered only to the plants, not the unplanted areas around them. (Soaker hoses don't provide as precise a control.)

This is the type of system I installed in my vegetable garden. It was inexpensive, easy to install, and has provided years of reliable service. Components can be purchased at local discount stores, home improvement centers, hardware stores, nurseries, and garden supply stores. Drip irrigation kits are also available online through suppliers such as the Drip Depot. They also sell kits for gravity-fed systems (for use with rain barrels, for instance).

To water individual plants such as shrubs or trees, as opposed to flowers or vegetables planted in rows or beds, you have three options. You can run solid plastic tubing to each plant, then connect it to a section of soaker hose that encircles the plant. Or, you can connect the solid plastic tubing to tiny spray jets that deliver water to the ground near the base of the shrub or tree. Or you can install drip tubes or "button drippers" that release a small stream of water at the base of each plant. For advice on watering trees and shrubs, check your local extension service, water department, or nursery.

While it is usually pretty easy to design an unobtrusive drip irrigation system to supply water to a garden or two on your property, multiple gardens—for example, several flower beds, shrubs, and a vegetable garden that require watering—may require installation of a

Soaker hoses slowly water plants, allowing moisture to penetrate to the roots without waste.

Photos by Jessica deMartin

Go Green!

more sophisticated and less visible subsurface delivery system. In these systems, water is delivered to various "targets" by PVC pipe that runs underground to each flower bed or garden. The pipe is typically buried four to six inches below the surface. The PVC pipe feeds soaker hoses or spray nozzles, or drips on or near the surface.

Installing a Soaker Hose

Installing drip irrigation systems is usually pretty straightforward, a job even most novice do-it-yourselfers can tackle—unless your landscaping is complicated, or you're installing an underground system. In such cases, the services of a professional landscaper or sprinkler/irrigation system contractor are well worth it.

If you're planning to use a soaker hose, you may first need to install a backflow prevention valve. This device screws into the spigot and is required by law in some areas of the country to prevent dirty water from contaminating your drinking water. (Modern outdoor faucets come with backflow prevention valves built into them, so you shouldn't need to install one if your home was built within the past 10 to 15 years.)

Next, install the timer, if required. You may also want to install a pressure regulator if your household water pressure is 50 pounds per square inch (psi) or higher. Pressure regulators reduce water pressure to about 10 to 12 psi. They lessen the chances of a hose bursting and water spraying, instead of seeping, through the pores in the soaker hose. I control the rate of flow at the spigot, rather than installing a pressure regulator.

For best results, limit soaker hose runs to 100 feet. Longer runs may not provide enough water to plants near the end of the hose. Also be sure the hose is as level as possible. Because water pressure within the soaker hose is low, it won't perform well on uphill slopes. Soaker hoses also don't work on downhill slopes. Water flows through too fast.

When laying out a soaker hose, be sure that both the connecting garden hose and soaker hose are free of kinks that block the flow of water. Also, be sure to flush the soaker hose a couple of times a year to remove

sediment and other matter that can clog the small holes that allow water to seep out of it. To do so, remove the end cap on the soaker hose and run water through it for a few minutes.

To save water, cover the hose with two to three inches of mulch. This protects the hose from sun damage and also reduces evaporative losses. Be sure the faucet doesn't leak. If it does, fix or replace it. For more advice on soaker hose installation, check out these websites: **www.savingwater.org** and **www.soakerhose.com**

Installing an Above-Ground Drip Irrigation System

To install a drip irrigation system with micro-soaker hose, first read the manufacturer's instructions. If you haven't planted the garden yet, lay out your rows, so you know where you'll be planting your flowers or vegetables. Then draw a diagram of the irrigation system that indicates where the solid tubing and a micro-soaker hose should go. You can stake out the system and run string along the course the hoses will take.

To install a system, first lay out the main section of tubing (the manifold) to which all of the smaller solid feeder tubes will be connected. Cut the main section of tubing with a hacksaw and attach a fitting to connect to a garden hose. Attach a plug on the other end. (The main section of tubing can be connected directly to an outdoor spigot or to a garden hose.)

Now attach the smaller feeder tubes by pushing the barbed connector into the plastic. It's sharp enough to penetrate the tubing, but works best on warm days when the plastic tubing is softer. Attach one end of the solid tubing and run it to the row, then cut it with a sharp pocket knife. Install a connector and attach the micro-soaker hose. Run it down the row, cut it to the correct length, and then insert a plastic cap in the end to prevent water from spilling out. (You can also connect the micro soaker hose directly to the main section of solid tubing.) Now install the next line. Plastic tees can be used to branch a soaker hose or a solid hose to deliver water precisely where it is needed.

After you have installed your system, "walk the line" to ensure that all emitters (drip lines) are working properly. Newly installed systems will sometimes weep around newly punched holes. This is normal and should decrease over time as the tubing seals itself. Check for proper placement of emitters to ensure that each plant is getting its fair share of water, and that sprayers or drip buttons are not obstructed.

Installing a Sub-Surface Irrigation System

Sub-surface systems require excavation of trenches and installation of PVC pipe. Before installing a system, draw a diagram, and then stake it out. Carefully measure all pipe runs and add them up so you can order the right amount of ¾-inch PVC pipe. Then determine the number of couplings; 23-, 45-, and 90-degree elbows; and tees you'll need. Make a list of supplies as you go. (Be sure to add a few extra elbows and couplings and an extra length of pipe. You can always return uncut surplus.)

You may also want to install a backflow prevention valve, an automatic a timer, and a filter to keep water lines and drip tubes from becoming clogged. (A cleanable 200-mesh filter is highly recommended.) Remote timers can be installed to control water flow to individual zones.

In colder climates, you may need to install drain valves to drain the PVC pipe before winter sets in. This prevents water inside the pipes from freezing, causing severe damage. If required by your town or city government, you may also need to install rain and freeze sensors. Rain sensors (Project 64) prevent automatic watering systems from turning on during or after rain storms to prevent over-watering. Freeze sensors detect freezing temperatures and prevent systems from turning on, which could damage plants and the system itself.

Once you have secured all supplies, dig the trench for the water lines. Because the trench is only 4 to 6 inches deep, you can usually dig it with a shovel. If the soil is dense (for example, with a high clay content) or rocky, you can rent a ditcher from a local rental store. (You'll need a pickup truck or a trailer hitch and a trailer on your vehicle to haul it to your home.)

Once the ditch is completed, pipe can be laid out and joined. Plastic couplings are used to connect sections of pipe. Elbows are used to create turns. (Minimize turns if you can to help ensure adequate line pressure.) When connecting pipe to fittings, wipe the end surface of the pipe and the inside of the fitting with a clean rag. Apply pipe primer and then glue on both surfaces. Insert the pipe in the coupling or elbow. PVC pipe can be cut with a hacksaw.

Run pipe horizontally through the trench, then attach vertical sections using branch tees. These feed water into drip tubes on the surface for flowers and vegetables. Drip tubes can be covered with mulch to protect against sun damage, reduce evaporative losses, and create a more aesthetically appealing landscape. Drip tubes should be about 2 inches apart in flower beds and around bushes. Drip tubes for watering mature trees should be about 12 inches below the surface.

Go Green!

• If your lawn is irrigated by an automatic sprinkler system, inspect for damaged or missing sprinkler heads when it's running. If your system is set to go off in the middle of the night or very early in the morning, problems like water gushing from a broken sprinkler head could go unattended for a long time, wasting huge amounts of water.

• To save water, consider low-water and/or native plants. Many nurseries sell a variety of attractive native grasses, flowers, shrubs and trees that will reduce watering needs. You don't have to surround yourself by desert vegetation (unless you live in a desert) to have a beautiful, water-conserving yard. Ask a local nursery for advice on hardy plants that are appropriate for your yard.

Supply pipes should be staked with metal stakes at least every three feet to prevent them from moving in the ground. This movement is caused by changes in air temperature inside the small tubing, which creates a lifting effect.

For advice on installation and proper spacing, check online or contact a local landscaper. Or hire a landscaper or lawn irrigation specialist to be sure the system is properly designed and installed. Ask friends and neighbors if they know a reliable contractor. Not only is a quality installation important, but you will also need someone to provide trustworthy maintenance and repair in the future. Remember, too, that different plants require different amounts of water, so try to group plants that have the same water requirements together.

Subsurface irrigation systems can be operated manually or by timers, which apply water on a pre-set schedule. Some sophisticated timers, like those used for sprinkler systems, can be controlled by rain or soil moisture sensors. Project 64 discusses both of these options.

What Will It Cost?

The cost of a drip irrigation system varies with its complexity. If all you need is a section of garden hose and two or three soaker hoses, your costs will be minimal—around $30 to $50. If you add a timer, costs go up, but timers are pretty inexpensive. When buying a new hose, be sure to purchase a high-quality one—reinforced rubber is usually a good bet; cheaper ones don't last long, and you don't want to add more garbage to the landfill. Look for recycled-rubber hoses.

Components or a basic kit for irrigating a garden cost around $30 to $50. Costs will go up with a more complex system and more connectors and tubing. The deluxe kit from the Drip Depot costs a little over $80.

Underground systems are more costly and time-consuming to install. They might cost you $2,000 to $4,000 or more, depending on the length, number, and complexity of pipe runs, and the size of your yard.

Cost Estimate: Installation of a drip irrigation system for a 20' x 40' area (800 square feet)

Includes excavation; installation of supply lines, fittings, and adapters; and backfilling and cleanup.

Cost for materials only: **$185**

Contractor's total, including materials, labor, and markup: **$1,850**

Costs are national averages and do not include sales tax.

What Will You Save?

Drip irrigation systems are 90% efficient, versus sprinkler systems, which are only 50% to 75% efficient, according to Colorado State University Extension Service. As a result, you'll be able to significantly reduce the amount of water you use, save a precious natural resource, and cut your water bill.

Project 64

Rain & Soil Moisture Sensors

Studies show that most Americans significantly over-water their lawns—wasting time and energy (if they do it by hand), money, and an increasingly depleted natural resource. Although many people think that more water leads to healthier lawns, the truth is that the root zone can only hold so much water. Excess moisture simply drains into the subsoil and is of no use to the grass. Too much watering can even damage plants by leeching valuable nutrients from the topsoil and by causing root rot and disease.

How Can You Reduce Outside Water Use?

First, experts recommend setting an automatic sprinkler system so it runs either early or late in the day to reduce the amount of evaporation. They also suggest watering less frequently, but more deeply, to promote deeper root growth and healthier grass.

Watering should also be adjusted by season and may not be necessary at all during the wetter, cooler months. Even in the hottest, sunniest climates, for example, in Florida, studies suggest as much as a 30% reduction can be achieved by seasonally adjusting watering rates.

Yet another way to reduce watering is to install a rain sensor, a device that shuts off an automatic sprinkler system if it's raining or has recently rained. They are used in conjunction with automatic sprinklers as well as irrigation systems. Rain sensors, also called rain switches, are simple electronic devices that override the automatic timer on irrigation or sprinkler systems, shutting them off to prevent watering when the soil is already wet.

Why Install a Rain or Soil Moisture Sensor?

Automatic sprinkler and irrigation systems are controlled by programmable timers that turn them on and off on pre-set days and times. Unfortunately, these controllers don't monitor weather, so they sometimes water a lawn or irrigate a garden even if it is raining "cats and dogs."

It's the Law!

Rain sensors are required by law on sprinkler systems for new homes in several states, including Florida, New Jersey, Minnesota, and Connecticut, and in many communities within other states, especially those with dry, hot summer climates. For example, Florida has required installation of rain sensor devices on all automatic irrigation systems since 1991.

Another even more effective option is to install a soil moisture sensor. These devices monitor the water content of soil at the root zone and turn sprinkler systems on when the grass really needs water. This saves substantially more water than a rain sensor connected to a sprinkler system and results in a healthier lawn.

By preventing the system from turning on when it's raining, sensors not only reduce your water bills, but can also lower your sewer bill, because many municipalities charge for water and sewer separately and base sewer costs on total water use. (Some cities provide a separate meter for sprinkler or drip irrigation systems to avoid this problem.) Rain sensors also help reduce energy costs in homes supplied by wells since the less often the well pump runs, the less you'll pay for electricity.

Besides saving water, rain sensors help conserve vital resources—groundwater and surface waters. They also reduce excess surface water run-off (from lawns and paved areas that receive excess spray). Run-off is a problem not only because it wastes water, but because it transports chemical fertilizers and pesticides into rivers, streams, and lakes. Finally, rain sensors help prevent root rot and fungus from excess watering that can lead to an unhealthy lawn and landscape.

How Does a Rain Sensor Work?

Rain sensors for irrigation systems are available in two basic types, wireless and hard-wired. Wireless sensors are connected to the controls of an automatic watering system remotely through a transmitter; hard-wired systems are connected by wires.

Rain sensors help prevent overwatering, saving water and money.

Courtesy of Hunter Industries

Most rain sensors use a small hygroscopic disk that swells when moistened by rain. Expansion of the wet disk depresses an electrical switch. When the disk dries, it shrinks, and the switch is released. When activated, rain sensors send a signal to the main control of an automatic lawn sprinkling system or to the valve that controls the flow of water to the system, suspending all watering.

To prevent sensors from turning off the system in the event of a brief, inconsequential rain storm, sensors can be adjusted in increments of ¼ inch rainfall to achieve the desired setting. They're usually set to turn the sprinkler system off after ¼ to ½ inch of rain has fallen.

Some irrigation rain sensors also contain freeze sensors. Required in some jurisdictions, freeze sensors prevent the sprinkler system from operating when air temperatures drop to the freezing point. These sensors are typically installed in climates that experience occasional freezing weather where irrigation systems

Go Green!

• If you have an automatic sprinkler, check it for leaks every year in the spring. Small leaks waste a huge amount of water over the long term. To see if the system is leaking, shut down all water use inside your home. (Make sure that there are no leaks indoors, for example, at faucets and in toilets.) Once you're sure no water is running and there are no leaks inside, check your water meter to see if water is flowing through your system. If it is, the irrigation system may be leaking. You may want to hire a professional to locate and repair the leak.

• To reduce pollution, use a manual reel or push mower for small yards, or an electric model for larger lawns. (Electric mowers consume much less energy than gas-powered mowers and dramatically decrease noise and air pollution. Newer models come with long-lasting rechargeable batteries.)

Soil moisture sensors can help you dramatically cut back on outdoor water use, while still allowing for a beautiful lawn and garden.

Photo by Jessica deMartin

have become very popular in recent years. Although pricier, they're much easier to install. You can also place these sensors farther from the sprinkler control than wired units.

How Do Soil Moisture Sensors Work, and What Are Your Options?

Soil moisture sensors are used on farms, golf courses, and around commercial buildings with extensive lawns. These devices turn the water on according to moisture levels in the soil and control automatic irrigation systems more accurately than rain sensors.

Several types of soil moisture sensor systems are available in a range of prices. They include a sensor and a controller, wired into the irrigation or sprinkler system controls. You can set the soil moisture at the level you want the irrigation system to turn on.

Soil Moisture Sensor Installation

Soil moisture sensors are more technically sophisticated than rainwater sensors. For best results, two or more soil sensors should be installed at mid-root level in a representative portion—that is, a section that's pretty typical of the entire lawn with respect to soil quality, exposure to rain and sun, slope, and so on.

are not emptied—"blown-out"—before the winter. Freeze sensors protect the irrigation system, but also prevent water from icing walkways, streets, and plants.

Rain Sensor Installation

Installing a rain sensor is pretty easy, although you need to understand electrical wiring and have experience with it. Be sure to read the directions and follow them carefully. Shut off the appropriate circuit before beginning work. If in doubt, hire a professional landscape company or sprinkler system installer.

When installing a rain sensor, pay special attention to placement of the unit. Sensors are typically mounted in open areas that are not obstructed by trees, roof overhangs, or other obstacles that could prevent rain from reaching the sensor. Check the manufacturer's instructions for ideas on placement of the sensor. Privacy fences are often a good location. If you're installing a hard-wired sensor, you'll need to place it near the timer to reduce wire runs. Wireless sensors

Go Green!

- If you water your lawn with a sprinkler, never water on a windy day or during the heat of the day. Both practices can waste a lot of water.

- Use natural fertilizers and pest control agents on your lawn to protect your family, pets, and wildlife. If you use conventional products, apply them sparingly. According to the EPA, most homeowners apply two to three times more than is needed.

(Avoid unusually wet areas—for example, those that receive a lot of water from gutter downspouts.)

Wires are run underground from the sensors to the sensor controller, which is typically mounted next to the sprinkler/irrigation controller. The wiring is similar to that involved in wiring a rain sensor.

Soil moisture sensors are a little more difficult to install than rain sensors; the key difference is that wires must be run underground from the sensors back to the controller. Be sure to read instructions carefully when installing a unit. A competent do-it-yourselfer who has experience with electrical wiring should have minimal trouble. When in doubt, call in a pro.

Soil moisture sensors require a little tuning after installation. You can't simply install a system, then forget about it. You may, for instance, need to monitor the condition of your lawn for a month or two and make adjustments to the controller until it's working correctly. Once the system is "tuned," however, you'll be able to sit back and enjoy the free time and savings.

Shopping Tips

Although soil moisture sensors are often installed in golf courses and commercial landscapes, they're beginning to be used for homes. You may have to buy a unit through a lawn irrigation company or a landscaper. You may not find them in local hardware stores or home improvement centers.

Go Green!

- Adjust sprinkler heads and the water flow of automatic sprinkler systems to avoid overshoot—watering hard surfaces such as nearby streets, sidewalks, and driveways. For a small, hard-to-irrigate area, either water by hand or remove the sod and replace it with shrubs, which require less watering, or stones or bark mulch, which require no watering at all.

- To reduce lawn watering and create a healthier lawn, set the height of your lawn mower (by adjusting the wheel height) to around 2.5 to 3 inches. Cutting grass to this height puts less stress on the plants and reduces water use, though you will need to mow more often.

What Will It Cost?

Rain sensors cost around $60. A professional installation will cost roughly $120 to $150. Freeze sensors cost about $25 to $50. Soil moisture sensors are priced at about $100. Add another $100 or more for a professional installation.

What Will You Save?

Whether you pay for city water or for electricity to run a well pump, a rain sensor will pay for itself, usually within a year. Sensors may also extend the life of your irrigation system's moving parts, since they will be used less frequently.

How much water and money will a rain sensor save? This depends on the cost of water in your area and the amount of rain that falls on your property. A recent study in Florida found that rain sensors cut water use for homes by 45% on average, it would save nearly $160 in one year, easily paying for the cost to install it.

Soil moisture sensors can reduce water use even more. Florida researchers found that these devices reduced water use, on average, 69% to 92%. The lawns that were tested remained healthy and green.

Project
65

Solar Pool Heater & Cover

Swimming pools offer many benefits, including family fun on hot summer days, exercise, and even physical therapy. Unfortunately, many pool owners find that they enjoy their pools less frequently than expected. Early- and late-season swimming is just too chilly. Pool heaters combat this problem, and some homeowners use them year-round. While effective, pool heaters use a lot of energy. It is expensive to heat tens of thousands of gallons of water. If you're looking for an affordable, renewable-energy solution, consider a solar pool heater.

What Is a Solar Pool Heater?

After solar-powered attic fans and solar outdoor lights, solar pool heaters are probably one of the simplest, least expensive, most cost-effective renewable energy technologies around. A solar pool heater consists of collectors that are typically mounted on the roof of a home or on a nearby structure, like a garage or pool house. Water from the pool circulates through pipes to the solar collector, where it is warmed by the sun. The heated water is then returned to the swimming pool, raising its temperature.

Solar pool heating systems use the existing pool pump to circulate water through the collectors. These systems are typically equipped with sensors that regulate their operation, for example, turning on when the sun is shining, and off at night. Solar pool heaters can be used to heat both above- and in-ground pools.

Solar pool heaters are typically used to maintain the pool temperature in the mid 70s to the high 80s. They can be installed to extend the swimming season by a few months or to heat a pool year-round in warmer climates.

Solar collectors for swimming pools come in two basic varieties: glazed and unglazed. Glazed collectors, like those used to generate domestic hot water (Project 35), consist of a glass-covered insulated metal box. Inside the box are copper tubes through which pool water circulates. Unglazed collectors are much simpler and considerably less expensive. They generally consist of heavy-duty rubber or plastic tubes installed directly on the roof. They are treated with an ultraviolet (UV) light inhibitor to extend the life of the collector. A local installer can help you determine which system is right for you.

In warm, sunny parts of the country like Southern California and Florida, unglazed solar pool collectors can provide comfortable temperatures even during the winter. (During the hottest days of summer in these climate zones, solar pool heating systems are typically switched off to prevent the pool from overheating.) Solar pool heaters can even be used to *cool* a swimming pool in warm climates. How? By circulating water through the collector at night. This releases excess heat from the pool into the nighttime air, cooling the pool down.

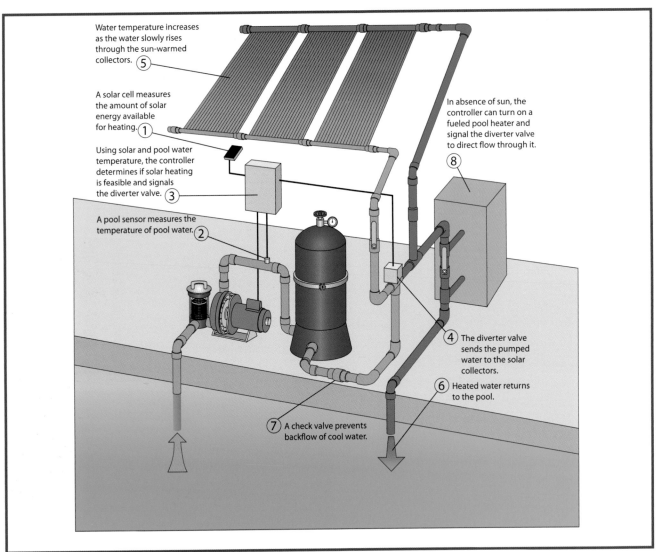

Water temperature increases as the water slowly rises through the sun-warmed collectors. (5)

A solar cell measures the amount of solar energy available for heating. (1)

Using solar and pool water temperature, the controller determines if solar heating is feasible and signals the diverter valve. (3)

A pool sensor measures the temperature of pool water. (2)

In absence of sun, the controller can turn on a fueled pool heater and signal the diverter valve to direct flow through it. (8)

(4) The diverter valve sends the pumped water to the solar collectors.

(6) Heated water returns to the pool.

(7) A check valve prevents backflow of cool water.

Solar pool heaters are a natural way of heating a swimming pool.

Reprinted with permission from *How Your House Works*, by Charlie Wing

Which System Is Right for You?

The type of system you choose depends on your climate and your desires. If you live in a cooler northern climate, you may need a glazed collector system. Since they're more efficient than unglazed collectors, they'll provide heat earlier in the season. Glazed heaters may even permit year-round heating in some areas. To prevent water from freezing in the pipes, make sure the system is designed to drain completely back to the pool when it's not running. Otherwise, water in the pipes and collectors can freeze, expanding and cracking the pipes.

If you live in a warmer area like Florida, you'll probably want to install an unglazed collector because they're less expensive and don't need to produce as much heat. Although you may have to shut the system down during the coolest part of the winter, unglazed collectors may be more cost-effective than a more expensive glazed system that may not really be needed, according to the online resource, *A Consumer's Guide to Energy Efficiency and Renewable Energy*.

Installing a Solar Pool Heater

Although solar pool heaters are a fairly simple renewable energy technology, they're generally installed by professionals. An installer will start by evaluating the solar potential of your home. If there is sufficient sun exposure, he or she will recommend a system sized to meet your needs and will provide a bid that includes the cost of equipment and installation. The installer may also compare the up-front and long-term operating costs of the solar system to several other common options, such as a conventional gas or electric pool heater or an air-source heat pump. Comparisons will allow you to make an informed decision.

What to Watch Out For

When selecting a contractor to install and maintain your system, find an experienced and reliable company. It's worth paying a bit more if necessary. When interviewing potential installers, ask for references and be sure to follow up and visit some installations, if possible, so you can see for yourself what these systems look like, how they work, and whether your contractor's clients are happy with the company. Be sure the firm is licensed and insured, too. Some states require a plumber's and/or solar contractor's license. To find out, contact your local building department. Your state's contractor licensing board should have a record of any complaints lodged against state-licensed contractors. You can also contact your local Better Business Bureau to check up on local installers.

Go Green!

- Use nontoxic natural pool cleaners like Natural Chemistry's Pool Perfect to clean your pool. Ordinary pool cleaning and maintenance requires the use of toxic chemicals like sulfuric acid and sodium hypochlorite. Pool Perfect is a natural-enzyme product that breaks down organic waste to carbon dioxide and water.

- Check out the solar lighting options for your pool area. LED lights are another energy-saving choice. They come in blues and greens that can enhance the pool atmosphere in the evening.

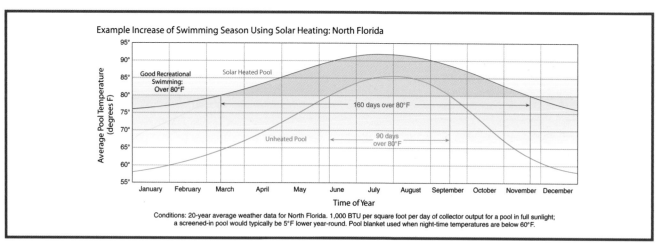

Water temperature with and without a solar pool heater. Solar pool heaters extend the swimming season and save tremendously on energy bills.

Reproduced from *Home Power* magazine, Courtesy of Tom Lane, Reprinted with permission. © 2003, Home Power, Inc. www.homepower.com

Unglazed solar pool collector
Courtesy of Hot Sun Industries, Inc.

By covering your pool, you can also reduce evaporation by 90% to 95%, according to the Department of Energy, and save a tremendous amount of water. An uncovered outdoor pool that is 18' × 36' can lose 7,000 gallons a year!

Pool covers are fairly inexpensive, starting at roughly $85 to $150. Bubble covers and solar blankets work well at retaining heat, but they're not anchored, so offer no protection to children who are able to access the pool.

Before buying a system, make sure that there are no restrictions on solar installations imposed by your local building department or homeowner's association if there is one for your neighborhood.

Bear in mind that maintaining a solar heating system after it's installed is just as important as a good installation. Proper maintenance will keep a system running smoothly for ten to twenty years. You can perform maintenance yourself, but be sure to ask the installer for advice and read the section on inspection and maintenance in the owner's manual. The system should require very little maintenance if the pool's chemical balance and filtering system are checked and adjusted regularly. The glass of glazed solar collectors may need to be cleaned periodically in dry climates where rainwater doesn't provide a natural rinse.

Conserving Heat & Water with a Pool Cover

The simplest, most cost-effective way to keep your pool warm is to cover it at night and on cloudy days with a pool cover. Covers reduce surface evaporation (which cools pool water the same way evaporation of perspiration cools us). Covers alone can add a month or two to your swim season.

What Will It Cost

A solar pool heating system usually costs between $3,000 and $5,000 installed, according to *A Consumer's Guide to Energy Efficiency and Renewable Energy*. The cost depends on the type of heater, whether it is roof- or ground-mounted, and the pool size. For example, a 16' × 32' pool might need half the number of solar collectors required for a 20' × 40' pool.

What Will You Save?

Solar pool heating systems typically pay for themselves in energy savings (compared to a conventional gas or electric pool heater) in a year or two. They also tend to last longer than gas and heat pump pool heaters, which means lower replacement costs. Remember, solar heaters have **zero operating cost**, unlike gas and electric heaters for which you will incur both the installation cost and high operating expenses for fuel every year.

Part

2 Building a New Green Home

Building a New Green Home

Most of the projects in this book are for people who want to make the homes they live in healthier, more comfortable, energy-efficient, and economical. The materials and systems described in the projects can also be incorporated into new homes. If you're planning to build a new home, however, there's a lot more you can do. Here are some ideas, many of which apply to green remodeling projects, too. (You may also want to consider buying an existing home and turning it into your green dream home. This uses fewer resources.)

Select a Green Building Site

If possible and desirable, build on a lot within town limits. Being close to work, school, shopping, and other necessities reduces the pollution and fuel use of commutes, enhances community, and prevents the destruction of undeveloped natural landscapes.

Select a site that offers good year-round sun exposure for solar electricity, passive solar heating and cooling, and solar hot water—and, depending on your location, wind for pumping water and generating electricity. Another good feature is a slope that allows "earth sheltering" of the home, which reduces fuel bills and helps protect homes from the wind. Also important are good drainage and healthy soil for growing vegetables, fruit, and wildlife-attracting flowers and trees. Nearby recycling facilities, bike paths, parks, and recreation are a plus—and you'll want your home to be a safe distance from high-voltage power lines and substations.

Site the Home Optimally on the Lot

Orient the home so that the long axis runs east to west for maximum wintertime solar gain. Preserve as many trees as possible, and make sure the home complements the site's natural vegetation, geology, and topography.

Protect the Site During & After Construction

Minimize land disturbance when building. Put felled trees to good use—for example, as building timber, firewood, or mulch. Plant new trees to replace those you've removed. Meet with the contractor and subcontractors to create a plan to protect trees and other vegetation during construction. Cordon off shrubs and vegetation you want to protect and mark them with a brightly colored ribbon. Limit excavation and trenching around trees and protect them from damage by heavy equipment by wrapping cardboard around their trunks. Fertilize trees before building begins, and water them. Place plywood around the base of trees to protect roots and soil from being compacted by equipment during construction.

Be sure that soil erosion measures are taken before and during construction. Design driveways to minimize soil erosion and use permeable paving to reduce runoff. Stockpile removed topsoil for later use. And be sure workers don't dispose of hazardous materials on the site.

Build a Healthy House

Select low- or no-VOC (including urea-formaldehyde) engineered lumber for use in living spaces. If engineered lumber is used, air it out for at least two weeks in a dry location before installation. You may also want to seal engineered lumber with water-soluble polyurethane to prevent outgassing of hazardous fumes. Select environmentally friendly and healthy flooring products, including wool carpeting, recycled-content tile, bamboo, cork flooring, and natural linoleum. And specify low- or no-VOC paints, stains, finishes, and adhesives. Use environmentally friendly and healthy insulation.

Pay special attention to roof flashing, sealing air gaps, and other ways to prevent penetration of water through walls, including the foundation. Keep building materials dry prior to installation. Hire a builder who is knowledgeable about the materials and techniques needed to prevent mold formation inside your home.

To reduce interior moisture levels, prevent mold, and thus protect your home's air quality, be sure exhaust fans with timers are installed in bathrooms, the kitchen, and the laundry room. All fans should be vented to the outside. Install metal-shielded wires in the home to protect against magnetic radiation. Test for radon *before* you build and *after* construction is complete. If pre-construction tests indicate problematic levels of radon, install a radon protection system.

Design & Landscape for Energy Efficiency

Insulate the foundation and building envelope (walls and roof) above and beyond local building code minimums and be sure insulation is installed correctly. Seal all cracks in the building envelope to prevent infiltration and exfiltration. You may also want to test the home for airtightness during and after construction (after insulation is installed).

High-quality energy-efficient doors, windows, and heating, cooling, and ventilation equipment are a must. Select Energy-Star qualified products and install programmable thermostats. Energy-efficient lighting (CFLs and/or LEDs), motion sensors, and timers for light switches will save energy, along with ceiling fans, attic fans, and whole-house fans, which cool more efficiently.

You can plant trees and other types of vegetation that will provide shade from the summer sun, but won't block the low-angled winter sun. Plants can also provide windbreaks to protect against winter winds.

Capture Sunlight for Passive Solar Heating

To heat your home naturally, concentrate the windows on the south side of the home. Insulate and weatherize really well, and install the proper amount of thermal mass (building materials that absorb solar energy during the day and release it at night or on cloudy days). Design so that all rooms are heated directly by the sun, if possible, and, in sunny climates, create sun-free zones where you can live, work, and play without being drenched in sunlight and heat.

Design for Passive Cooling

To cool your home naturally, minimize both internal and external heat gain. To control heat sources inside the house (internal heat gain), use CFL and LED lightbulbs and task lighting, place (super energy-efficient) windows where they'll maximize daylighting, use energy-efficient appliances and electronics that give off less heat, and isolate heat-generating appliances, such as water heaters, from the main living area.

To reduce heat gain from the outside (external heat gain), orient the long axis of the home toward true south, site the home to take advantage of breezes to ventilate the house naturally, and install solar tube skylights rather than conventional skylights. Overhangs over windows protect them from the summer sun. Plant shade trees (especially on the north, south, and west sides of the home), and install window shades. Light-colored paint and roofing materials will help reflect the heat.

Other ways to keep heat out include a radiant barrier in the attic, energy-efficient, low-E windows that are positioned well for breezes, and wall and roof insulation. An open floor plan helps circulate breezes.

Generate Electricity from Renewable Energy

Consider installing a solar electric system and/or a wind generator or purchasing green power, if available from your local utility.

Choose Green Building Materials

For foundations, use fly ash in concrete. It's a waste product from coal-fired power plants that reduces the use of cement (which requires a lot of energy to produce). You can also build with insulating concrete forms, such as Tech Block™, or build on a rubble trench foundation.

For walls, use energy-efficient products, such as Tech Blocks or structural insulated panels. If you can, use natural products such as straw bales. For roofs, use structural insulated panels or pre-engineered trusses, roofing felt made from recycled materials, and environmentally friendly roofing materials, such as metal roofing or recycled-content shingles.

For insulation, install environmentally friendly products such as damp-blown cellulose, liquid foam insulation (such as Bio-Based Foam and Icynene), cotton or wool insulation, or formaldehyde-free, recycled-content fiberglass.

For exterior siding, use environmentally friendly products such as natural plasters, siding or shingles made from recycled wood fiber and cement, or metal siding made from recycled aluminum. Be sure the builder includes a drainage plane to convey water from the siding to the ground. For trim, choose salvaged lumber (including wood from an on-site teardown). Use FSC-certified lumber for framing and finger-jointed lumber and trim.

For subfloors, use low- or no-formaldehyde oriented strand board. Avoid formaldehyde-containing products like particleboard, furniture and furnishings, cabinetry, and window treatments in conditioned space to protect indoor air quality. For finish flooring, select environmentally friendly, healthy materials such as tile, cork, bamboo, and wool or recycled-content carpeting. Choose low- or no-VOC paints, stains, and finishes. For decks, porches, and docks, choose composite lumber, made from recycled materials. Composite lumber can also be used for fascia and trim.

Reduce Wood Use

The best way to conserve wood is to build smaller. You can also design the home in two-foot increments to minimize waste. Advanced framing techniques minimize lumber use without sacrificing quality, durability, or strength. Considering the lifetime of the home, you'll use less wood if you build a durable structure. This means protecting the roof, exterior walls, windows and doors, and foundation from water, the main source of damage.

Use salvaged wood and FSC-certified lumber, engineered lumber, prefabricated trusses, and composite (recycled wood and plastic). Be sure the contractor uses waste wood and recycles unusable scrap materials.

Conserve Water

Specify water-efficient fixtures and appliances throughout the house. You could also install a rooftop rainwater catchment system. Rainwater can be used indoors to flush toilets and do laundry (and even shower, if the water from your roof is clean)—and outdoors for watering gardens, trees, and shrubs. A gray water system is another option. Water from showers, washing machines, and sinks (not the kitchen sink) can be piped to water your landscape, provided you don't use toxic cleaning agents. Consider installing a composting toilet that turns human solid waste into a soil nutrient that can be buried on your property around trees or in flower gardens, enriching the soil.

When preparing a lawn for seed or sod, apply compost and other organic material to create a thick, rich layer of topsoil *before* planting. Organic matter adds nutrients to the soil, retains moisture, and promotes beneficial microorganisms, all of which result in a healthier lawn that uses less water. When selecting plants for your yard, choose native vegetation, which require less water than exotics. In arid or semiarid regions, plant xeric vegetation, that is, grasses, flowers, shrubs, and trees that require very little water.

Mulch gardens, trees, and shrubs to reduce water demand, control weeds, and ensure robust plant growth. Mulch can be made from tree limbs that are pruned on the site—and even waste lumber from the construction—so long as it doesn't contain toxic chemicals such as formaldehyde.

Plant vegetation that requires the most water near driveways, sidewalks, and downspouts. Water from these structures will supply plants naturally. Dig infiltration bases around all new trees and shrubs to help ensure an adequate supply of water. You can also install rain or moisture sensors to prevent overwatering if you have a sprinkler or drip irrigation system, and position sprinkler heads so they minimize wasted water sprayed on sidewalks, driveways, and streets. Wherever possible, install root-zone and drip irrigation systems (instead of sprinklers) to reduce water use.

Landscape for Food & Wildlife

Devote part of your yard to edible landscape—growing vegetables, fruit, and/or herbs. Allocate part of your yard to wildlife. Small ponds and flower gardens support birds and butterflies, giving back to nature. Contact the National Wildlife Federation's Backyard Habitat program for advice.

See the Resource Guide at the back of this book for more information.

Part

3 Appendix

Safety Tips 287

Glossary 289

Resource Guide 294

Index 299

Safety Tips

Safety is an essential component of a successful home improvement project. Knowing the risks and doing your best to eliminate them will lead not only to a job well done, but also to a safe new space in your home—built correctly. Be sure to comply with the requirements of your local building codes. As a word of caution, tackle only the projects you can handle. If you are unsure of how to do something, consult or hire a professional. If you are undertaking a project yourself, follow the safety guidelines listed below.

Protect yourself: Wear the proper clothing and gear to protect yourself from possible hazards. Avoid loose or torn clothes, especially when working with power tools. Wear heavy shoes or boots, safety glasses when working with power tools, a hardhat if materials or tools could fall on your head or if you could hit your head on overhead obstructions, and work gloves when possible. Use hearing protection when operating loud machinery or when hammering in a small,

enclosed space. Wear a dust mask to keep from inhaling sawdust, insulation fibers, or other airborne particles.

Organize the work area: Make a point of keeping your work space neat and organized. Eliminate tripping hazards and clutter, especially in areas used for access. Take the time to clean up and reorganize as you go. This means not only keeping materials neat, but also remembering not to leave nails sticking out; pull them or bend them over.

Do not strain yourself: When lifting equipment or materials, always try to let your leg muscles do the work, not your back. Seek assistance when moving heavy or awkward objects, and remember, if an object is on wheels, it is easier to push than to pull it.

Check equipment for safety: When working from a ladder, scaffold, or temporary platform, make sure it is stable and well braced. When walking on joists, trusses, or rafters, always watch each step to see that what you are stepping on is secure. Do not use gasoline-fueled

equipment inside a building or enclosed area.

Follow product manufacturers' recommendations: When working with adhesives, protective coatings, or other volatile products, be sure to follow the manufacturers' installation and ventilation guidelines. Pay particular attention to drying times and fire hazards associated with the product. If possible, obtain from the supplier a Material Safety Data Sheet, which will clearly describe any associated hazards.

Shut off affected utilities: When working with electricity or gas, be sure you know how to shut off the supply when needed. It may be wise to invest in a simple current-testing device to determine when electric current is present. If you don't already have one, purchase a fire extinguisher, learn how to use it, and keep it handy.

Use tools correctly: Keep in mind that you'll need special tools for some jobs. Study how to use them, and practice with them before undertaking final moves on your project. When using power tools, never pin back safety guards. Choose the correct cutting blade for the material you are using. Keep children or bystanders away from the work area, and never interrupt someone using a power tool or actively performing an operation. Keep drill bits, blades, and cutters sharp; dull tools require extra force and can be dangerous. Always unplug tools when leaving them unattended or when servicing or changing blades.

A few tips on hand tools:

- Do not use any tool for a purpose other than the one for which it was designed. In other words, do not use a screwdriver as a pry bar, pliers as a hammer, etc.

- Do not use any striking tool (such as a hammer or sledgehammer) that has dents or cracks, shows excessive wear, or has a damaged or loose handle. Also, do not strike a hammer with another hammer in an attempt to remove a stubborn nail, get at an awkward spot, etc. Do not strike hard objects (such as concrete or steel), which could chip the tool, causing personal injury.

- If you rent or borrow tools and equipment, take time to read the instructions or have an experienced person demonstrate proper usage.

Green home remodeling can be a satisfying and rewarding experience. Proper planning, common sense, and good safety practices go a long way to ensure a successful project. Take your time, know your limitations, get some good advice, and have fun!

Glossary

absorber plate A black metal plate in a solar hot-air collector that absorbs sunlight and turns it into heat.

AFUE (Annual Fuel Utilization Efficiency) An efficiency standard for heating, ventilating, and air conditioning equipment.

air barrier Material installed to reduce air movement through the roof and exterior walls of a building.

allergen Any substance, including mold, pollen, dust, and chemicals, that causes an allergic reaction.

anode rod A metal rod, typically made of aluminum or magnesium, placed inside a water heater to protect the tank from corrosion.

asbestosis A debilitating lung disease caused by inhaling asbestos fibers. Asbestos is sometimes present in old homes in pipe and furnace insulation.

attic fan A fan (wired to a circuit or solar-powered) installed in a roof or gable end of a home to vent the attic. It draws cool outside air in through the eaves, cooling the attic and reducing summer heat gain to living spaces below.

back-drafting Potentially dangerous introduction of polluted air caused when replacement air is drawn into a building through vent pipes, such as the water heater flue pipe. Home energy auditors should test for carbon monoxide and check for back-drafting before sealing the cracks in the building envelope.

baffle A device used in a wood stove that directs exhaust gases back over the fire, where they ignite, extracting more Btus from the wood.

biodegradable Able to break down or decompose when subjected to elements of nature (water, bacteria, etc.)

blower door device A tool used by energy auditors to discover air leaks throughout a home.

boric acid A nontoxic natural substance, sometimes incorporated into natural insulation products and used as an insect repellant.

building envelope The barrier between a building's inside space and the outdoors: the walls, foundation, and roof.

carbon dioxide The main greenhouse gas released into the atmosphere when fossil fuels are burned.

carbon emissions offset Premiums that consumers can pay to nonprofit companies that support carbon-dioxide-reducing measures (such as tree planting or renewable energy production), indirectly offsetting the consumer's own emissions. Similar to RECs.

carbon footprint The amount of carbon dioxide released into the atmosphere from the energy used by a particular individual or group.

carcinogen A substance shown to cause cancer.

casein paint A natural, water-based paint containing casein, the protein in milk.

catalytic burner A ceramic honeycomb-like device that improves efficiency in wood stoves by burning hydrocarbons from exhaust gas.

cellular shades Also known as honeycomb shades, window shades that provide insulation from heat and cold.

cellulose insulation A widely used type of insulation made from recycled paper and blown into walls and attics.

certified forest product, or certified wood A product from forests that are well-managed to protect and replenish trees.

CFLs (compact fluorescent lights) Lightbulbs that use far less energy and last much longer than standard incandescent bulbs. CFLs are, however, not as long-lasting or efficient as LED lights.

chimney liner A flexible or rigid (sometimes a combination of the two) pipe that runs the length of a masonry chimney flue. The liner exhausts combustion gases to the outside and protects the flue. It also prevents the accumulation of creosote in the flue, protecting against house fires.

chimney pillow A device that inflates and seals off the chimney when the fireplace is not in use.

composite lumber Wood-like building material, usually made from recycled plastic and wood fiber, that is known for its durability and ease of maintenance. See also **engineered wood**.

compost Organic soil amendment created by the decomposition of plants and other biodegradable materials.

composting toilet A toilet that requires little or no water and converts human waste into fertilizer.

cotton batt insulation All-natural insulation made from waste from blue-jean factories.

creosote A mixture of organic compounds that deposit on the inner surface of chimneys and flue pipes. If ignited, it creates an intensely hot fire that can ignite nearby combustibles, such as wood framing in an attic.

daylighting Admitting and controlling natural light in a space to achieve energy and cost savings.

deconstruction A systematic dismantling of a building, often accompanied by recycling of the materials.

dioxin A toxic substance released by some industrial processes.

door sweep Weather stripping, often consisting of a strip of aluminum attached to a narrow piece of felt or vinyl, that is used to seal the opening between the bottom of a door and the threshold.

downspout diverter A device that fits into a downspout and diverts rainwater into a rain barrel or away from a house.

drip irrigation A landscape watering system that relies on flexible tubing placed on the ground. It releases small amounts of water at the base of plants, which minimizes evaporation.

dual-flush toilet A toilet that conserves water by allowing different settings for liquid and solid waste.

duct blast test A procedure performed by home energy auditors to measure leakage in the home's heating and air conditioning ducts.

earth berm A mound of soil that can help block a structure or plantings from wind. Berms can reduce heat loss in the winter and heat gain in the summer.

EER (Energy Efficiency Ratio) A standard of measure indicating an air conditioner's efficiency when operating in higher temperatures.

efflorescence The buildup of minerals on the surface of a concrete wall.

energy-recovery ventilator (ERV) A mechanical device that removes stale, polluted air from a building and replaces it with fresh outdoor air, while capturing most of the heat and some of the moisture from the outgoing air.

Energy Star® The U.S. Environmental Protection Agency and Department of Energy standard for rating the energy efficiency of appliances, electronics, lighting, and more.

engineered flooring A flooring product composed of a wood veneer glued to a core material. Engineered flooring is intended to provide greater stability, especially where moisture or heat are factors.

engineered wood A composite wood product made from pieces of recycled/reconstituted/scrap wood and fibers bonded together with adhesive to create a durable and resource-friendly substitute for raw-sawn lumber.

evaporative cooler A less expensive, less energy-consuming alternative to central air conditioning for dry, hot climates. Also known as a "swamp cooler" or a "desert cooler."

evaporative cooling The cooling effect that occurs when water evaporates from a surface.

exhaust fan A fan (ventilated to the outside) used in kitchens and bathrooms to remove moist or contaminated air from a home.

faucet aerator Small screen-type device that reduces water flow from a faucet by adding air into the stream.

fiber-cement siding A siding product that contains cement and cellulose (wood) fiber. It is durable, low-maintenance, and considered a greener option that conventional wood siding.

fiberglass blanket and batt insulation A commonly used form of insulation, sold in rolls or pre-cut batts, and installed in walls or placed on attic floors.

fireplace insert A steel or cast-iron shell that fits into a wood-burning fireplace. Fireplace inserts improve efficiency and reduce emissions.

fly ash A waste product from coal-fired power plants that can be used as an ingredient in concrete to reduce energy consumption and increase resistance and strength.

French drain A below-grade drain that consists of a perforated plastic or tile pipe buried at the bottom of the foundation in new construction. The pipe empties into another that drains water away from the house.

furr To install wood or metal to a wall (for example, a concrete basement wall) to provide a means of installing insulation, drywall, or paneling.

geothermal heat A heating system that captures heat from the ground through pipes (installed either horizontally or vertically), reducing the amount of energy needed by the home's conventional heating system.

grading Changing the slope of the land so water travels away from a house.

gray water Wastewater from bathtubs, showers, and washing machines that can be used for flushing toilets or watering landscape.

Green Seal A nonprofit organization that certifies a variety of products as environmentally preferable.

grid-connected solar electric system A solar collection system that is connected to the local power company grid. The homeowner is credited for energy the system generates in excess of what is used in the home.

ground-source heat pump A geothermal heating and cooling system that uses the moderating temperature of the earth to heat or cool a home.

heat island A term used to describe a town or city, typically with concrete structures and paved areas, that collects heat during the day and is several degrees hotter than undeveloped or rural locations.

heat pump Device that uses refrigeration technology to extract heat from the outside air (air-source heat pump) or from the ground (ground-source heat pump, or geothermal).

HEPA (high-efficiency particulate air) filter An air filter used in heating, cooling, and ventilation systems and vacuum cleaners. True HEPA filters (as opposed to "HEPA-type") reduce the circulation of allergens such as mold, pollen, and dust.

home energy audit A process in which energy experts locate a home's air leaks and identify inefficient energy uses.

hypo-allergenic Containing reduced or minimal substances that could cause an allergic response.

IAQ (indoor air quality) The health of a home's indoor air. IAQ is affected by humidity, allergens (pollen, mold, dust, etc.), and chemical fumes released by building materials such as vinyl flooring, formaldehyde-containing laminates, or paints with VOCs (volatile organic compounds).

incandescent lights Conventional, inefficient lightbulbs that heat tungsten filaments, which give off light and a considerable amount of heat.

infiltration basins Shallow, level-bottomed depressions dug into the earth around newly planted trees and shrubs to collect snowmelt and rainwater for hydrating the plants.

infrared (heat) camera A device used to detect uninsulated or under-insulated areas in a home and gaps in the building envelope where heat is escaping in the winter and entering in the summer.

isocyanate A glue used in making some building materials, such as bamboo flooring. Once dry, it produces no toxic pollutants.

jute A natural fiber used for carpet and carpet pad.

laminate floors A layered type of flooring with a structural core covered with a plastic laminate wear layer.

LED (light-emitting diodes) lights Extremely efficient lightbulbs/fixtures that last much longer and use far less energy than incandescent and CFL lights. They also contain no mercury, as CFLs do.

life cycle analysis An evaluation of the cost and/or environmental impacts of a material—including the energy cost, resource use, and pollution from extracting raw materials, producing finished products, transporting products to market, using the product during its life, and disposal impacts.

light pollution Nighttime outdoor light that may disturb natural systems, such as the nesting and migration of birds.

light tube See **tubular skylight**

linoleum A natural flooring product made from pine tree resin, linseed oil (from flax seed), powdered limestone, pigment, and small amounts of zinc-based drying agents.

liquid foam insulation High R-value insulation that is applied from a spray can or, in larger quantities, pressure-sprayed. The product expands and hardens as it cures.

low-emissivity (low-E) coating A coating applied to window glass that allows the transmission of visible light, but only low levels of heat, resulting in a reduction in heating and cooling requirements.

low-voltage lights Lights, often used for landscape lighting, that operate on 12 to 50 volts rather than the standard 120 volts.

lumen Unit of measure for light intensity.

mastic A paste that is painted over the seams between sections to seal metal ductwork. It outlasts duct tape and metallic tape. (Floor mastic, a different material altogether, is used to glue tile and other flooring.)

Material Safety Data Sheet (MSDS) Information sheet prepared by a manufacturer. Includes a product's ingredients, health effects, toxicity, and instructions for storage, disposal, protective equipment, and spill or leak procedures.

MDI (methylene diphenyl isocyanate) A resin considered safe for homeowners since it does not outgas hazardous chemicals in finished products. However, it can cause dermatitis (skin rash) and respiratory problems among factory workers.

melamine A plastic material that is glued to particleboard.

mildewcide A substance added to paint to resist mold and mildew. It can cause allergic reactions in some individuals.

milk paint An all-natural paint containing milk proteins. It emits no harmful gasses.

mold A naturally occurring biological organism that grows in moist conditions. Mold can cause mild to severe health effects in a home's occupants.

multiple chemical sensitivity (MCS) A rare, but debilitating autoimmune disease marked by allergy-like and other physical reactions to several types of air pollutants, such as outgassed chemicals from plastics, paints, carpeting, and cabinetry. Once exposed, people with MCS become highly sensitive to numerous other chemicals, including those found in deodorants, perfumes, and cleaning products.

mycorrhizal fungi Beneficial soil fungi that attach to plant roots and help them absorb minerals from the soil.

native landscape Use of indigenous plants in environmentally conscious landscaping because they have adapted to thrive in the local environment and require little, if any, irrigation, fertilizer, or pesticides once established.

net metering An arrangement between a utility company and a consumer in which the utility will buy back excess power created by the consumer's grid-tied solar or wind electric system at a rate equal to retail utility charges.

Norbord A low-VOC, high-recycled-content cabinetry, made from MDF.

outgassing, or off-gassing The release of airborne particulates, often from installed construction materials, such as cabinetry and paint, that can cause allergic reactions and other health problems in the home's occupants.

passive solar heating Design strategy that allows homes and other buildings to be heated by the low-angled winter sun without mechanical systems like solar collectors.

pellet stove A steel or cast-iron stove resembling a wood stove and used to burn dry, compressed pellets made from sawdust and wood chips.

permeable pavers Concrete paving stones that allow water to drain through or around them into the soil below, thereby reducing often-polluted stormwater runoff into natural waterways.

PET plastic A type of polyester made from oil, which is used to make soda bottles. PET plastics are a healthier alternative to PVC.

phantom loads Electrical devices, such as televisions, cordless phones, and battery chargers, that draw power even when switched off.

photovoltaics (PV) Devices that convert sunlight directly into electricity. They generate power without noise, pollution, or fuel consumption.

post-consumer recycled waste Materials that have completed their life cycle as a consumer product and are used to make new products. Examples include paper, cardboard, plastics, metals, aluminum cans, and glass.

post-industrial waste (PIW) Waste material from manufacturing processes. Recovery and recycling of PIW reduces the need for landfills, the use of virgin resources, and pollution and energy use.

potable water Clean, drinkable water.

PrimeBoard An MDF substitute made from wheat straw and a non-formaldehyde-resin.

programmable thermostat A device that allows homeowners to program settings for heat and air conditioning to save energy.

radiant barrier A reflective sheet or spray-on material applied to attic floors, rafters, or roof decking to reduce the flow of heat in and out of a home.

radon A naturally occurring radioactive gas that can enter a home through the soil beneath it, putting occupants at risk of cancer.

rain catchment system Connected gutters, downspouts, and barrels or cisterns that capture and store rainwater for irrigation and indoor use (if properly filtered).

rain sensor An electronic device that shuts off an automatic sprinkler system when it rains, conserving water when irrigation isn't needed.

reclaimed (salvaged) wood Wood reclaimed from old buildings, barns, mills, bridges, and trees removed from urban and suburban neighborhoods. Reclaimed wood is often tighter-grained, harder, and more dimensionally stable than new-growth wood.

Renewable Energy Certificates (RECs) One REC, or "green tag," represents one megawatt hour of renewable energy. RECs may be sold by those that produced it to offset the cost of generating the renewable energy.

rope caulk A putty-like cord that comes in a roll and is used to insulate windows. It can be applied in winter and removed in the spring so windows can be opened.

R-value A standard of measure for a material's resistance to heat flow. A higher R-value provides more insulation.

SEER (Seasonal Energy Efficiency Ratio) The cooling capacity of an air conditioner. By law, all new air conditioners must have a SEER of at least 13. The higher the number, the more efficient the unit.

soaker hose A hose (often made of recycled rubber) with tiny holes or pores that allow water to slowly seep out, irrigating plants while conserving water.

soil moisture sensor A device that measures moisture levels in soil, which, in turn, regulates the controller of automatic sprinkler systems, ensuring that water is applied only when needed.

solar attic fan A solar-powered fan that exhausts hot air from an attic, thereby reducing the heat entering a home and helping lower energy use for air conditioning.

solar electric systems Systems consisting of solar collectors mounted in sunny locations, often on roofs, that use the sun to produce electricity. Can be grid-tied (connected to the local utility grid) or stand-alone (completely independent of the utility grid).

solar heat gain coefficient (SHGC) The amount of solar energy that a window allows to pass through it, expressed as a number between 0 and 1. The higher the number, the more solar energy can be gained.

solar hot-water system A system that consists of a solar collector, typically mounted on a roof, that absorbs heat from sunlight, which is used to heat water for domestic uses and for heating homes.

solar path lighting Exterior landscape lights that come on at night, powered by batteries that are charged by the sun.

spalling A condition in concrete walls in which the surface flakes off, usually as a result of moisture damage.

styrene butadiene, also known as SB latex A substance used for carpet backing in conventional carpeting. SB latex contains several potentially toxic chemicals.

surface drain Also called a superficial peripheral drain, a surface drain that eliminates water that pools around the foundation of a home. It consists of a trench sloped away from the foundation, lined with 6 mil plastic, and filled with crushed rock.

switch-and-receptacle An electrical outlet controlled by its own switch. When the switch is turned off, the flow of electricity to the plug is terminated.

tankless water heater (TWH) Small water heater that heats water as it is needed, rather than storing it continuously in a large tank. TWHs conserve energy by eliminating standby loss.

tracking solar collector A solar collector typically pole-mounted to the ground. They often track the east-west movement of the sun for maximum energy collection.

tubular skylight A compact skylight that consists of a durable plastic lens mounted on the roof and connected to a tubular aluminum shaft. Light enters through the lens, is transmitted down the highly reflective tubular shaft, and is released into the living space through a ceiling fixture known as a diffuser.

virgin-fiber carpeting Carpet made from materials (not natural ones) in their first use, that have not been recycled.

VOC (volatile organic compound) A chemical found in many building products, such as paints, that evaporates, emitting toxic fumes in a home.

voltmeter A device used to measure the voltage drop between two points in an electric circuit. Voltmeters are used to ensure that power has been disconnected to a particular circuit before work is done.

whole-house fan A high-capacity fan mounted in a central hallway ceiling in the top story of a home. The fan draws cool outside air into the home through open windows. The air flows through the house and is vented out through the attic.

worm bin An indoor composting container that uses worms to process fruit and vegetable kitchen wastes.

xeriscaping Landscaping that uses drought-tolerant plants.

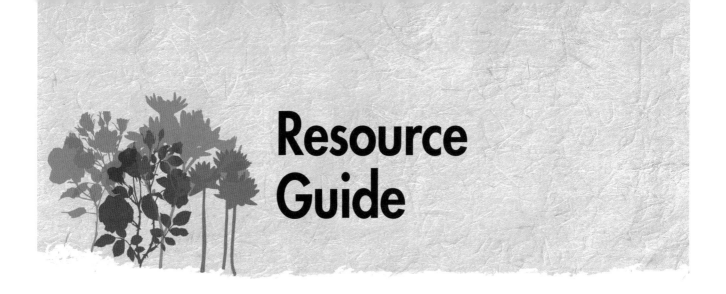

Resource Guide

Following are books and pamphlets, newsletters and magazines, organizations, and green building material suppliers that may be useful to you in your quest to create a green home. The bold text in the annotations indicates the main focus of each resource.

Books & Pamphlets

Indoor Air Pollution: An Introduction for Health Professionals. American Lung Association, Environmental Protection Agency, Consumer Product Safety Commission, and American Medical Association. Online publication. Detailed information on the **health effects of the most common indoor air pollutants**.

A Citizen's Guide to Radon. The Guide to Protecting Yourself and Your Family from Radon. 2nd ed. U.S. Environmental Protection Agency. A very basic online **introduction to radon. www.epa.gov/iaq/radon/pubs/citguide.html**

Consumer Guide to Home Energy Savings, 7th ed. American Council for an Energy-Efficient Economy. **Energy-efficiency, including energy-saving appliances**.

Creating The Not So Big House. Taunton Press. Introduction to the **art of building small houses** with floor plans and many beautiful photos.

EEBA Builder's Guide–Cold Climate. Energy Efficient Building Association. **Building efficient homes in cold climates**.

EEBA Builder's Guide–Hot-Arid Climate. Energy Efficient Building Association. **Advice on building in hot arid climates**.

EEBA Builder's Guide–Mixed Humid Climate. Energy Efficient Building Association. **Building efficient homes in humid climates**.

Energy-Efficient and Environmental Landscaping. Moffat. Appropriate Solutions Press. **Landscaping strategies for saving energy and water, including plant varieties suitable for your climate**.

Green Building Guidelines: Meeting the Demand for Low-Energy, Resource-Efficient Homes. Sustainable Buildings Industry Council. **General guide to green building**.

Green Remodeling. Changing the World One Room at a Time. New Society Publishers. **Green remodeling.**

GreenSpec: The Environmental Building News Product Directory and Guideline Specifications. BuildingGreen, Inc. Comprehensive list of **green building materials**.

Home Heating Basics. Chelsea Green Publishers.

Prescriptions for a Healthy House: A Practical Guide for Architects, Builders, and Homeowners. 2nd ed. New Society Publishers. **Healthy home building and remodeling**.

Rainwater Collection for the Mechanically Challenged. Tank Town Publishing. Humorous, informative guide to aboveground **rainwater catchment systems**.

Solar Living Source Book. New Society Publishers. **Wind and solar energy and energy-efficiency**.

The Best of Fine Homebuilding: Energy-Efficient Building. Fine Homebuilding. Taunton Press. Detailed, somewhat technical **articles on residential energy efficiency,** including insulation, windows, house wraps, skylights, and heating systems.

The Complete Book of Underground Houses: How to Build a Low-Cost Home. Sterling Publishing. **Earth-sheltered housing**.

The Healthy House Answer Book: Answers to the 133 Most Commonly Asked Questions. The Healthy House Institute. Basics of **healthy home building**.

The Healthy House: How to Buy One, How to Build One, How to Cure a Sick One, 3rd ed. The Healthy House Institute. Detailed guide to all aspects of **healthy home construction**.

The Home Energy Diet. New Society Publishers. **Detailed ways to save energy in homes**.

The Homeowner's Guide to Renewable Energy. Dan Chiras. New Society Publishers.

The Inside Story: A Guide to Indoor Air Quality. U.S. Environmental Protection Agency. Online publication for those interested in learning more about **indoor air quality issues and solutions**. www.epa.gov/iaq/insidest.html

The Natural Home: A Complete Guide to Healthy, Energy-Efficient, Environmental Homes. Chelsea Green. **Natural building, site selection, energy efficiency, renewable energy, and alternative waste water systems**.

The New Ecological Home: A Complete Guide to Green Building Options. Dan Chiras. White River Junction, VT.

The Solar House: Passive Heating and Cooling. Dan Chiras. White River Junction, VT.

What You Should Know About Combustion Appliances and Indoor Air Quality. U.S. Environmental Protection Agency. A great introduction to the **effects of indoor air pollutants from combustion sources**. www.epa/iaq/pubs/combust.html

Your Green Home: A Guide to Planning a Healthy, Enviornmentally Friendly New Home. New Society Publishers. **Primer on green building**.

Magazines & Newsletters

Ecological Home Ideas
Green building/remodeling topics.
www.ecologicalhomeideas.com

Mother Earth News
Articles on green building—from natural building to solar and wind energy—to natural swimming pools—to green building materials.
www.motherearthnews.com

Environmental Building News
The nation's leading source of **objective information on green building**, including alternative energy and back-up heating systems. Archives of issues published from 1992 to 2001 available on a CD.
www.BuildingGreen.com

Home Power **Practical articles on solar electricity, wind energy, solar hot water, energy efficiency, and passive solar heating and cooling.**
www.homepower.com

Natural Home
Articles on green building, especially **natural building and healthy building products.**
www.naturalhomemagazine.com

Organizations

Building America program Leaders in promoting ene**rgy-efficiency and renewable energy** to achieve zero-energy buildings. (202) 586-9472
www.eere.energy.gov/buildings/building_america

City of Austin Green Builder Program. *Sustainable Building Sourcebook* Excellent resource listing **green building materials**.
www.greenbuilder.com/sourcebook

Database of State Incentives for Renewables & Efficiency
Gives details, state by state, on rebates for investing in energy efficiency.
www.dsireusa.org

Energy-Efficient Building Association Offers conferences, workshops, publications on **energy efficiency**.
(651) 268-7585
www.eeba.org

The Healthy House Institute
Offers books and videos on **healthy building**.
(812) 332-5073
http://hhinst.com/index.html

Indoor Air Quality Information Clearinghouse
Distributes EPA publications and answers questions on **indoor air quality**, and makes referrals to other nonprofit and government organizations.
(800) 438-4318
www.epa.gov/iaq/iaqxline.html

Midwest Renewable Energy Association
Offers valuable workshops on **solar energy, wind energy, and other topics**.
(715) 824-5166
www.the-mrea.org

National Arbor Day Foundation, Building with Trees Program
Information on planting trees, including ways to protect them during construction.
www.arborday.org/Programs/BuildWTrees.html

National Association of Home Builders Research Center
A leader in green building, including energy efficiency. Sponsors conferences, research, and publications. Publishes Green Building Guidelines for builders and homeowners.
(301) 249-4000
www.nahbrc.org

National Radon Hotline
Access to local contacts who can answer radon questions.
(800) SOS-RADON
www.epa.gov/iaq/contacts.html

National Wildlife Federation, Backyard Wildlife Habitat Program
Information on creating **wildlife habitat in your backyard**.
800-822-9919
www.nwf.org/backyard

Real Goods Solar Living Institute
Nonprofit organization offers **workshops on solar and wind energy, natural building, organic gardening, and many other topics**.
(707) 744-2017
www.solarliving.org

Solar Energy International
Offers a wide range of **workshops on solar energy, wind energy, and natural building**.
(970) 963-8855
www.solarenergy.org

U.S. Green Building Council
Nonprofit organization that has done more than any other group to promote green building. They recently released a green building certification program for residential structures.
(800) 795-1747
www.usgbc.org

U.S. Consumer Product Safety Commission
Contact them for **information on potentially hazardous products or to report one**.
(800) 638-CPSC
www.cpsc.gov

U.S. Department of Energy and Environmental Protection Agency's ENERGY STAR program
Offers a wealth of **information on energy-efficient appliances, lighting, and electronics**.
(888) 782-7937
www.energystar.gov

Recycling

Earth Works' Recycle My Cell Phone
www.recyclemycellphone.org

Eco-Cell
www.eco-cell.org

FreeCycle
www.freecycle.org

Habitat for Humanity
http://www.habitat.org/env/restores.aspx

MyGreenElectronics
www.mygreenelectronics.org

MyBoneYard Recycle
www.myboneyard.com

Reuse It Network
www.reuseitnetwork.org

The following list includes, as a starting point, manufacturers mentioned throughout the projects as sources of equipment and supplies. This is not intended to be a complete list of all available sources, nor is it an endorsement of any particular products.

Building Materials Retailers

Amicus Green Building Center
www.amicusgreen.com

Bettencourt Green Building Supplies
www.bettencourtwood.com

Building for Health Materials Center
www.buildingforhealth.com

Eco of NY
www.environmentaldepot.com

EcoBuild
www.eco-build.com

EcoHome Improvement
www.ecohomeimprovement.com

Eco Home Center
www.ecohomecenter.com

Eco Design Resources
www.ecodesignresources.com

Eco-Products, Inc
www.ecoproducts.com

Eco-wise
www.ecowise.com

Environmental Building Supplies
www.ecohaus.com

Environmental Home Center
www.environmentalhomecenter.com

Green Home
www.greenhome.com

Green Building Supply
www.greenbuildingsupply.com

Maine Green Building Supply
www.mainegreenbuilding.com

Natural Home Products
www.naturalhomeproducts.com

Planetary Solutions
www.planetearth.com

Real Goods
www.realgoods.com

Refuge Sustainable Building Center
www.refugebuilding.com

SolSource
www.solsourceinc.com

Green Product Manufacturers & Websites

Flooring Materials & Adhesives

Aged Woods, Inc.
www.agedwoods.com

Amorim Flooring, Inc.
www.amorim.com

Appleseed Wool Corporation
www.appleseedwoolcorp.com

Armster Reclaimed Wood Company
www.reclaimedlumberco.com

Armstrong
www.armstrong.com

Aurora Glass
www.auroraglass.org

Bamboo Adavantage Flooring
www.bambooadvantage.com

Bamboo Flooring Directory
www.bamboo-flooring.com

Bedrock Industries
www.bedrockindustries.com

Bostik
www.bostik.com

Carpet America Recovery Effort (CARE)
www.carpetrecovery.org

Carpets Inter
www.carpetsinter.com

Crossville, Inc
www.crossvilleinc.com

Earth Weave
www.earthweave.com

EcoBuild
www.eco-build.com

EcoTimber
www.ecotimber.com

Evirotec
www.enviro-tec.com

Fireclay Tile
www.fireclaytile.com

Forbo
www.forbo.com

Goodwin Heart Pine Company
www.heartpine.com

Interface
www.interfaceinc.com

Mohawk
www.mohawk-flooring.com

Nature's Carpet company
www.naturescarpet.com

Oceanside Glasstile Co.
www.glasstile.com

Quarry Tile
www.quarrytile.com

Sandhill Industries
www.sandhillind.com

Sealflex
www.sealflex.com

Shaw Industries
www.shawfloors.com

Stardust Glass
www.stardustglasstile.com

Teragren
www.teragren.com

Terra Green Ceramics
www.terragreenceramics.com

UltraGlas, Inc.
www.ultraglas.com

WE Cork, Inc
www.wecork.com

Paints, Stains, Finishes, & Wallcoverings

AFM Safecoat
www.afmsafecoat.com

Aglaia
www.aglaiapaint.com

American Clay Earth Plaster
www.americanclay.com

American Pride Paints
www.americanpridepaint.com

Benjamin Moore (Eco-Spec)
www.benjaminmoore.com

Bioshield
www.bioshieldpaint.com

Duron (Genesis Odor-Free)
www.duron.com

Glidden (Glidden Spread 2000)
www.glidden.com

ICI Paints (Lifemaster 2000)
www.iciduluxpaints.com

Kelley-Moore (Eviron-Cote)
www.kelleymoore.com

Livos
www.livos.com

Olympic Paint
www.olympic.com

Pittsburgh Paints (Pure Performance)
www.pittsburghpaints.com

Sherwin-Williams (Duration Home® and Harmony®)
www.sherwin-williams.com

Cabinetry

Green Leaf Cabinetry
www.greenleafcabinetry.com

Neil Kelly Cabinets
www.neilkelly.com

Norbord
www.norbord.com

PrimeBoard
www.primeboard.com

Assessing Energy Usage

The Energy Detective
www.theenergydetective.com

Home Energy Saver
www.hes.lbl.gov

Weather Stripping & Insulation

Efficient Attic Solutions
http://efficientattic.com

Johns Manville
www.jm.com

M-D Building Products
www.mdteam.com

Q-Lon, by Schlegel
www.schlegel.com

Insulating Paint

Hy-Tech Thermal Solutions
www.hytechthermalsolutions.com

Insuladd
www.insuladd.com

Insulating Window Shades

Gordon's Window Décor
www.gordonswindowdecor.com

Plow and Hearth
www.plowhearth.com

Smith+Noble, LLC
www.smithandnoble.com

Symphony Shade
www.symphonyshades.com

The Warm Company
www.warmcompany.com

Window Quilts company
www.windowquilts.com

Heating & Cooling

AdobeAir, Inc.
www.adobeair.com

AirScape
www.airscapefans.com

Carrier
www.carrier.com

Coolerado Cooler
www.coolerado.com

Fantech
www.fantech.net

Fujitsu
www.fujitsu.com

Harman Wood Stoves
www.harmanstoves.com

Honeywell International, Inc.
www.honeywell.com

Mitsubishi
www.mrslim.com

Quadra-Fire
www.quadrafire.com

Regency Wood Stoves
www.regency-fire.com

SunRise Solar Inc.
www.sunrisesolar.net

Radon Testing

Alpha Track
www.accustarlabs.com

Pro Lab
www.reliablelab.com

Water-Efficient Plumbing Fixtures

Caroma
www.caromausa.com

Danco
www.danco.com

Europa Elite
www.alsons.com

Sloan FLUSHMATE®
www.flushmate.com

Water Heaters

Heliodyne
www.heliodyne.com

Hills Solar
www.hillssolar.com

Paloma
www.palomatankless.com

Rheem
www.rheem.com

Solar Direct
www.solardirect.com

Takagi
www.takagi.com

Trendsetter
www.trendsetterindustries.com

Pool Heaters

ECS Solar Energy System, Inc.
www.ecs-solar.com

Hot Sun Industries, Inc
www.h2otsun.com

Natural Chemistry's Pool Perfect
www.naturalchemistry.com

Solar Panels Plus
www.solarpanelsplus.com

Storm Doors

Harvey Industries
www.harveyind.com

Paving

Gravelpave[2]
www.invisiblestructures.com

Ideal Concrete Block Company, Inc
www.idealconcreteblock.com

National Ready Mixed Concrete Association
www.perviouspavement.org

PaverSearch
www.paversearch.com

UNI-GROUP USA
www.uni-groupusa.org

Decks & Fences

Heartland BioComposites
www.heartlandbio.com

TimberTech°
www.timbertech.com

Trex Company, Inc.
www.trex.com

Outdoor Lighting

Malibu Lights
www.malibulights.com

Solar Cynergy
www.solarcynergy.com

Composting

Bokashi Kitchen Composter
www.bokashi.com.au

Garden Gourmet
www.gardengourmet.com

NatureMill
www.naturemill.com

Outdoor Water Efficiency (rain cisterns and irrigation devices)

Clean Air Gardening
www.cleanairgardening.com

Gardener's Supply
www.gardeners.com

Green Vista Landscaping
www.greenvistalandscaping.com

Hunter Industries, Rain Clik rain sensor
www.hunterindustries.com

Index

A

absorber plate, 71
air conditioners, 109–111, 264
air-flow ratings, 121
air quality, 24
air-source heat pump, 85–87
annual fuel utilization efficiency (AFUE), 77, 84
anode rod, 142–145
appliances, 42, 108, 119, 148
    energy efficient, 176–179
asbestos, 44, 55, 78, 83
attic fans, 114–118
attics, insulating, 54–55, 56, 61, 101
    sealing, 50–51
    ventilation, 104
auditor, home-energy, 40–43, 45, 54, 55, 78
awnings, retractable, 206

B

back-drafting, 120
bamboo flooring, 7–10, 23
baseboard heat, 65, 81, 82, 88
basements, insulating, 53, 54, 55, 61
batch solar water heater, 151
batteries, 65
blower door test, 43
boilers, 89, 93
    energy-efficient, 81–84
boric acid, 7
building codes, 13

C

cabinetry, 36–39, 129
carbon dioxide, 89, 128
carbon monoxide, 129, 138, 145
    detectors, 84
carbon offsets, purchasing, 187–188
carpeting, 10, 13, 19, 24–26, 129
    pad, 25–26
    wool, 27–29
caulking, 46–52
ceiling fans, 68, 85, 92, 108, 112–114, 118, 119
cellular shades, 66–67, 68–69
cellulose insulation, 53, 56
chimney pillow, 49
cleaning
    counters, 22
    floors, 12
climate, zones in the U.S., 262–264
clinkers, 97
collectors, solar, 71–75
compact fluorescent lightbulbs (CFLs), 109, 119, 171–175, 182, 282
composite lumber, 236–243
composting, 96, 248–252
computers, power-saving mode, 167
Consumer Reports, 6, 27
cooling systems, high-efficiency, 106–111
cork flooring, 3–6

cork flour, 14
crawl spaces, 57
    insulating, 53, 54, 55
    radon in, 124
creosote, 92, 99
curtains, insulating, 66–70

D

Database of State Incentives for Renewables and Efficiency, 79, 84, 88, 150, 180
decks, 236–239
DEHP, 160
dioxin, 15
dishwasher, 147, 148, 177
diverters, for rain barrels, 258, 259
doors, sealing, 49–50
doors, storm, 209–212
door sweeps, 48, 221–222
downspouts, 223–226
    extenders, 58
drainage, 227–231
drip irrigation, 266–270
driveways, 232–235, 281
drought, 256
dryers, 178

E

Earth Plaster, 33, 34
EER, 109
electrical boxes, fan-rated, 117
electricity, solar, 180–184, 283
energy audit, 40–45
energy-recovery ventilator, 127–130
engineered wood, 8, 282
evaporative cooler, 106–109, 264

F

fans
 attic, 114–118
 ceiling, 68, 85, 92, 108, 112–114, 118, 119
 solar attic, 119
 whole-house, 51, 119–121
faucets, 156–158
 aerators for, 156–158
 leaks in, 144
 water-efficient, 139
fencing, recycled plastic, 240–243
fertilizers, natural, 273
fiber cement
 shingles, 200
 siding, 202–205
finishes, 30–35
fire codes, 104
fireplaces, 129
 inserts, 98–100
 sealing, 49
flashing, of roof, 155, 223
floodlights, 246, 247
flooring, 282
 bamboo, 7–10
 carpet, 24–29
 cork, 3–6
 laminate, 6, 17–19
 reclaimed wood, 11–13
 tile, 20–23
floors, insulating, 57–58
foam gaskets, 50

foam insulation spray, 56–57
forests, 9, 18
Forest Stewardship Council (FSC), 18, 22, 37, 283
formaldehyde, 7, 10, 19, 25, 36, 39, 129
fossil fuels, 76, 81, 101
French drain, 228–230
freon, 110
furnaces, 89, 93, 129
 energy-efficient, 76–80
 gas, 76–78
 oil, 78

G

geothermal, see ground-source heat pump
glazing, 71, 74
grading, 227–231
green home, building a, 281–284
green power, 185–187
Green Seal, 35
ground-source heat pump, 85–87, 88, 111
grout, 22
gutters, 223–226
 protectors for, 200

H

hardness rating, of bamboo, 8
heat exchanger, 107, 128
heat output, 95–96
heat pumps, 85–88, 111
heat-recovery ventilator (HRV), 127
heat-shrink plastic, 209–210
HEPA filter, 127
high-density polyethylene (HDPE), 240
house wrap, 204
hydronic heating systems, 81

I

indoor air quality, 45, 51, 128, 129
indoor composting, 252

infiltration basins, 253–255
insulating, 53–59
 paint, 60–62
 shades & curtains, 66–70, 93
insulation, 43, 93, 101, 129, 282
 for floors, 57–58
 foam, 47
 for pipes, 135–138, 145
 for roofs, 54, 61
 for walls, 54, 55, 56–57
irrigation, 266–170
isocyanate, 7, 37

J

jute, 25, 26, 28

L

laminate flooring, 6, 17–19
landscape lighting, 244–247
landscaping, energy-efficient, 261–265, 282
lawnmower, 272
leaf blowers, 252
leaks, 41–42, 46–41, 129
 faucet, 144
 sealing, 93, 101
lightbulbs, 171–175
light emitting diodes (LEDs), 58, 167, 168, 172, 245, 246, 277, 282
lighting
 accent, 245–246
 energy-efficient, 171–175
 floodlights, 246, 247
 landscape, 244–247
 solar, 244–247
light pollution, 246
linoleum, 6, 14–16
locks, window, 206

M

mastic, 48, 78
material safety data sheets (MSDS), 19, 31
metal roofing, 199–200
methylene diphenyl isocyanate (MDI), 19, 37
microwaves, 178
milk paints, 32
mold, 58, 59, 61, 75, 104, 129
motion sensors, 189–193
motor-driven window shades, 70
mulch, 249, 254, 266
multiple chemical sensitivity (MCS), 27, 31, 39

N

North American Board of Certified Energy Practitioners, 154

O

outgassing, 16, 25
outlets, 50
ovens, 178, 179

P

paints, 30–35
    insulating, 60–62
passive cooling, 102–103, 282–283
passive solar heating, 282
path lighting, 244–247
patios, 232–235
pavers, permeable, 232–235
pellet stoves, 94–97
PERC, 128
permeable pavers, 232–235
PET plastic, 24, 26, 127
PEVA, 160
phantom loads, 167–170
pipe insulation, 140
pool cover, 275–278

pool heater, 275–278
porches, 236–239
porous pavers, 232–235
post-consumer waste, 21
power meter, 168
PrimeBoard, 36
programmable thermostat, 55, 63–65, 80, 81
putty, window, 207, 208
PVC, 160

R

radiant barrier, 101–105, 283
radiant floor heating, 81, 82, 83, 88
radon, 129–130, 282
    testing and mitigation, 122–126
rain barrels, 256–260
rain sensors, 271–274
rainwater collection, 256–260
ranges, 178, 179
rebates
    for solar water heaters, 155
    for water-efficient toilets, 166
reclaimed wood flooring, 11–13
recycling, 42, 96
    of appliances, 110
    of cabinetry, 36
    of carpet, 28
    of electronics, 170
    of water heaters, 144
reflective insulation, 136–137
refrigerator, 177, 178
renewable energy certificates (RECs), 186–187
roofing, 198–201
roofs, insulating, 54, 61
R-value, 48, 50, 54, 56, 59, 75, 80, 104, 135

S

salvaged wood, 11–13
sawmills, 94
SB latex, 25

sealants, 62
sealing leaks, 42, 46–51
SEER, 86, 109
shade, 112, 153, 261–265
shades, insulating, 66–70, 93
shingles
    fiber-cement, 200
    recycled-content, 198
    wood, 198–199
shower curtains, 129, 160
showerheads, water-efficient, 125, 131, 136, 139, 145, 147, 148, 159–161
siding, environmentally friendly, 202–205
sinker logs, 12
site selection, for new green home, 281
skylights, tubular, 194–197
soaker hoses, 266–267
soffit vents, 58–59
soil moisture sensors, 271–274
soil suction, radon mitigation, 125
solar attic fans, 116–118, 119
solar electricity, 180–184, 281
solar heat gain coefficient, 216
solar hot air collector, 71–75
solar hot water systems, 85–88, 151–155
solar pool heater, 275–278
Solar Rating and Certification Corporation (SRCC), 155
sprinklers, 271–274
standby loss, of hot water, 146
storm doors, 218–220
storm windows, 209–212
sump pump, 231
switches, 50
    light and motion sensor, 189–193

T

tankless water heater, 146–150
The Energy Policy Act of 2005, 155
thermal breaks, 215

thermal expansion device (TXV), 111

thermal mass, 71

thermostat, programmable, 55, 63–65, 80, 81

tile, recycled, 20–23

timers, 189–193

toilets, water-efficient, 162–166

trees
  infiltration basins for, 253–255
  protecting during construction, 281
  for shade, 112

tubular skylights, 194–197

U

U.S. Department of Energy, 44, 48, 59, 79, 80, 96, 97, 101, 104, 118, 128, 139, 141, 147, 148, 154, 186, 278
  Consumer's Guide to Renewable Energy, 76, 82
  safety recommendations, 103
  Zip Code Insulation Project, 56

U.S. Environmental Protection Agency (EPA), 78, 89, 92–93, 110, 122, 157, 161, 166, 168, 172, 176, 177
  radon information from, 124, 125

U-factor, of windows, 215-216, 217

V

ventilation, attic, 104, 114, 117

vermiculite, 44, 55

vinyl flooring, 15, 16, 129

visible transmittance, 216

volatile organic chemicals (VOCs), 6, 16, 18, 22, 30, 31, 32, 33, 34, 35, 36, 37, 45, 51, 61, 282

W

walkways, 232–235

walls, insulating, 54, 55, 56–57

warranty, of anode rod, 142

washing machine, 147, 148, 177

water heater, 129, 142–150
  adjusting temperature of, 139–141
  blanket for, 135–138, 140, 145
  flushing, 131–134, 145
  instantaneous, 146
  on demand, 146
  point-of-use, 146
  replacing anode rod of, 142–145
  tankless, 146–150

under-the-sink, 146

waterproof membrane, for basements, 231

WaterSense, 157, 161, 166

weather stripping, 46–52

whole-house fans, 51, 119–121, 264

wildlife, 18, 281, 284

windows
  coverings for, 61, 66–70
  energy-efficient, 213–217
  repair, 42, 206–208
  sealing leaks in, 49–50
  storm, 209–212
  types of, 215

wind turbines, 185, 188

wood flour, 14

wood stoves, 89–93, 94, 96, 129

wool carpeting, 27–29

worm bins, 252